FastTrac® NewVenture™

ENTREPRENEUR MANUAL

MAKING YOUR

ENTREPRENEURIAL

DREAM A REALITY

Ewing Marion
KAUFFMAN
Foundation

TAKE CHARGE OF YOUR BUSINESS®

A program of the Kauffman Foundation

TAKE CHARGE OF YOUR BUSINESS®

A program of the Kauffman Foundation

NOTICE OF NONDISCRIMINATORY POLICY AS TO PARTICIPANTS

Acknowledgements

Program Design Team

Ewing Marion Kauffman Foundation
    Judith Cone
    Stefanie Weaver
J. Diane Awbrey, PhD
Mary Beth Izard, Achêve Consulting Inc.
Kathryn Nadlman
Leslee Anne Terpay, Terpay Knowledge Resources, Inc.
Jodie Trana, Advant•Edge Business Services

Content Development Team

David J. André, Attorney & Counselor at Law
Beth Hagan, PhD, Associates in Entrepreneurship Education
Cathi Ryckman Hight, Hight Performance Group, Inc.
Todd Pitman, CPA
Will Thalheimer, PhD, Work-Learning Research
Jean T. Zimmerman, JZ Company, Inc.

Production Team

Cathleen Bethay
Amy Carter
David Carter
Jennifer Jantz Estes, Muthos LLC
Darla J. Knoth

Contributors, Reviewers, Advisers

Mary Abrahams
Karen Anderson
T.J. Becker
Chris Bouchard
Herbert Brown
Barbara Cunningham
Marylou Dewald
Robert Donato
Monica Doss
Joe Edwards
Carol Frank
Liz Allen Fey
Debra Filtzer
Rob Fuller
Tim Fulton
Laswanda Green

Patrick Gregg
Fran Gretz
David Hensley
Cathy Herlihy
Sue Hesse
James J. Hill Reference Library
  Lori Happel-Jarratt
  Patricia Hoskins
  Nikki Marchand
Jeffrey S. Horvath
Timothy W. Knox
Bill Lohrey, CPA, JD
Wallace W. Meyer, Jr.
Barry J. Moltz
Daniel Nathanson
Scott Pemberton

Gordon Platt
Tim Putnam
Joanne W. Randolph
Peter Rassel
Janice Schonwetter
Kay A. Saunders
Barbara Schneider
Todd Smart
Adam Smith
Sally E. Smith
Tina Sterling
Clinton Tymes
Sharon Tillman
Denise Upah
Don Wilson
Virginia Wilson
Remound Wright

On a bitterly cold day in January 1993, Ewing Marion Kauffman scheduled to launch a new program for entrepreneurs called FastTrac®. Kauffman was legendary in Kansas City because his company, Marion Merrell Dow, provided more than 3,000 high-paying jobs, he was the owner of the Kansas City Royals baseball team, and through his foundation, he helped families in disadvantaged areas get an education—even paying for college for many.

On that same morning, however, nature decided to dump on Kansas City one of the worst snowstorms in its history. Kauffman's staff debated whether to cancel the event, since people were being asked to stay off the roads, and Kauffman was extremely ill. He wanted to hold the event just in case someone did go to the trouble to get there. That day, 900 people showed up. Yes, some came because it was sponsored by "Mr. K" as he was affectionately called; but most came because they had a hunger to learn how to start and grow a business. They wanted to invest in themselves even if that meant braving the storm.

That Kansas City FastTrac® kickoff was one of the last public appearances for Kauffman, who passed away later that year at the age of 76. He was grateful for the opportunity to build a company and to share his abundance with others. He loved entrepreneurs and all they stood for—self-reliance, innovation, hard work, and providing good paying jobs and benefits. He was proud that his foundation was championing entrepreneurship.

It was my privilege to be hired in 1994 to oversee the development of FastTrac®. Today, all over the world people are participating in the various FastTrac® programs. Some are just thinking of going into business, some want to learn how to grow their business, some want to build networks, find coaches, and learn about additional resources for themselves.

The Ewing Marion Kauffman Foundation is proud to have played some small part in the decision-making process, skill development, and network building of hundreds of thousands of people engaged in the entrepreneurial process.

Judith Cone, Vice President
Entrepreneurship
Ewing Marion Kauffman Foundation

Ewing Marion Kauffman

The late entrepreneur and philanthropist Ewing Kauffman established the Ewing Marion Kauffman Foundation as the first foundation to focus on entrepreneurship as one of its primary areas of interest.

There is more to Ewing Kauffman's beneficence than his fortune. He had an instinct for the future. He understood how to bring organizations to life to be productive and vital. Above all, he had a zest for life and a social awareness that was grounded in his belief in people. The Kauffman Foundation of Kansas City develops and advances innovative ideas that set the groundwork for institutional change, advance entrepreneurship in America, and improve the academic achievement of children and youth.

From modest beginnings, Kauffman grew Marion Laboratories into a billion dollar pharmaceutical giant and established the Kansas City Royals, bringing major league baseball back to Kansas City. With his business succeeding beyond his wildest dreams, Kauffman turned his vigor, intellect, and wealth to a new style of philanthropy. He lost patience with charity work that never seemed to attack the core problem it sought to remedy. He wanted to dig deep and get at the roots of issues rather than talk about addressing the symptoms. Undaunted by the size of the challenge or the lack of resources, Kauffman encouraged his staff to become immersed in research, consult with the best minds, and devise bold approaches to address complex social problems. He told friends he was having more fun giving money away than he had earning it. He told associates he expected his foundation to be exemplary.

An epitome of American entrepreneurship, Kauffman saw business enterprise as one of the most effective ways to unleash human potential and stir the economy to life. He viewed entrepreneurship as the most powerful strategy to help individuals gain economic independence and serve as a catalyst for creating jobs and wealth in society. Today the Kauffman Foundation is devoted to advancing entrepreneurship as one of the fundamental aspects of life in the United States. Focusing on research, education, technical assistance, and policy, we work to increase the number and success rate of individuals engaged in the process of starting or growing their own business or idea. We work with partners to design programs based on the proven principles, techniques, and leadership tactics that make starting and growing a business a more common choice for Americans of all walks of life.

The Kauffman Foundation's FastTrac® programs are part of a wide range of resources developed in collaboration with hundreds of successful entrepreneurs who have shared their knowledge, insights, and stories so that others might learn from them. We hope that all entrepreneurs will find them useful as they work to write their own entrepreneurial success stories.

For more information on FastTrac®, the nation's leading, award-winning business training program for entrepreneurs, go to www.fasttrac.org or call (800) 689-1740. To order FastTrac® materials, call the FastTrac® fulfillment center at (877) 450-9800. For more information about the Kauffman Foundation and entrepreneurship, go to www.kauffman.org, or call (800) 489-4900.

Table of Contents

Introduction

The road to successful entrepreneurship begins with passion for an idea, a business plan based on research and analysis, and the persistence to pursue the vision. Whether you have always dreamed of being an entrepreneur or recent circumstances triggered thoughts about starting a business, FastTrac® NewVenture™ is designed to introduce you to the key elements of successful entrepreneurship.

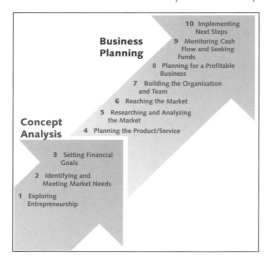

Written by entrepreneurs for aspiring entrepreneurs, FastTrac® NewVenture™ offers essential business information to help you develop your entrepreneurial skills and build your business on a strong foundation. FastTrac® offers non-traditional, experiential learning with hands-on coaching sessions. Opportunities to network and learn from your peers as well as seasoned entrepreneurs and professionals who work with start-up businesses are a key part of the experience.

In this program, you will develop a business concept and take it through each step of the business planning process. Through readings and research, activities and action steps, you will plan and analyze your entrepreneurial vision by creating a thoroughly researched and tested Business Plan.

FastTrac® NewVenture™ is divided into two parts: concept analysis and the business planning process.

Concept Analysis

The first three modules focus on developing a business concept that will help you achieve your goals. In these modules you will establish a personal vision, write your business concept statement, and research and analyze the concept for feasibility.

Each of these three modules explores a key element of successful entrepreneurship:
The Entrepreneur – How do you develop the skills needed to be an entrepreneur? What are your personal and professional goals? What is your business concept?

The Market – How do you research whether a market exists for your product or service? Who are your most likely customers?

The Money – What are your financial goals? Will you have enough money to start? Will your business concept help you achieve your goals?

The first step in your entrepreneurial journey is to define your **personal vision**. Your personal vision is a statement about your goals for yourself and the business. Your personal vision includes an analysis of your personal, professional, and financial goals. It is critical in assessing concepts to find a business that is right for you.

A **business concept statement** communicates the specifics of your proposed venture. It includes a set of cohesive ideas about how your product or service will be created and delivered to a market. The business concept statement answers many questions about your business. It includes a description of the products or services, the customers, and how you will reach them. A clear business concept statement will be helpful in communicating your idea to others and serves as the basis for the planning process.

An important part of developing your business concept is conducting **market research**. You will learn how to identify the information you need and how to research it. The results of your research will provide critical information as you make decisions about your business concept.

You will screen your business concept for a different aspect of feasibility in each of the three modules. This **feasibility analysis** is a self-assessment which provides an opportunity to rate your business concept against key criteria. Does it match your personal vision? Is there a market for your product or service? Does it meet your financial goals? You can use this information to improve the feasibility of your business concept and to compare one business idea against another.

Business Planning

The last seven modules will guide you through each step of the business planning process. A key outcome of this program is a researched, developed, and written **Business Plan** that articulates your business concept. After your plan is complete, you will use the **Feasibility Checklist** to test for product/service, market, and financial feasibility.

This process will help you determine whether the business has a market, can make a profit, and can provide the money you need. A Business Plan will also help you reduce the normal risks of start-up and increase your chances of success by replacing guesses with facts.

You will build your Business Plan one section at a time by conducting the necessary research and answering relevant questions for each action step. Observing due dates for action steps provides you with a workable timeframe for completing the plan during the program.

Your Business Plan will contain several sections, including management and organization, the product/service, marketing, and financial. These sections will be completed progressively throughout the program. After collecting and analyzing information for your specific business concept, you will complete the action steps in each module to compile the section's plan. The electronic templates streamline this process by providing questions to answer in a pre-formatted Word or Excel® template.

After completing this program, your Business Plan may have the following uses:

Personal Uses for a Business Plan	Internal Uses for a Business Plan	External Uses for a Business Plan
• Analyze the business concept and test its feasibility • Broaden your understanding of the business • Convince yourself and others that you know what you are doing	• Address specific concept challenges • Ensure alignment of all aspects of the business • Clarify goals of the business • Develop an effective marketing strategy • Identify back-up suppliers • Forecast profits accurately • Determine the amount of money needed to start the business • Guide decision making • Communicate with the management team	• Communicate goals to external parties • Negotiate deals with suppliers • Recruit employees • Raise funds necessary to start the business • Solicit suggestions from mentors and advisers

Program Components

FastTrac® NewVenture™ provides a wealth of resources and materials to aid you in the planning process. The FastTrac® sessions, the Entrepreneur Manual, and the online FastTrac® Toolkit work together to help you develop your entrepreneurial skills and plan your business.

FastTrac® Sessions

At each FastTrac® session, you will discuss key concepts and apply them to your business. You will learn from your peers as well as your facilitator and business coach. Guest speakers, including experienced entrepreneurs and professionals such as attorneys, bankers, and accountants, will share tips and helpful information with you.

Networking is a valuable component of this program. Most successful entrepreneurs had a group of supporters who helped them throughout the business planning, start-up, and growth stages. Few entrepreneurs achieve success without building a support network. You will have many opportunities during this program to meet and talk with entrepreneurs from your community.

During the session, group activities will reinforce the concepts you are learning. At each session, hands-on coaching will get you started on the actions steps needed to develop your concept, plan your business, and test it for feasibility.

Entrepreneur Manual

The Entrepreneur Manual includes ten modules that guide you through the concept analysis and business planning process. You will complete the Reality Checks as you work through the content of the manual. They are designed to help you turn your entrepreneurial dreams into reality. Occasionally, you will be invited to Check Your Knowledge using additional activities and resources to support learning.

Activities in the Entrepreneur Manual should be saved to complete during sessions. Action Steps also appear in the Entrepreneur Manual, but are introduced in facilitation or coaching sessions, and will be completed between sessions.

Financial Facts Worksheets are introduced in Module 3 and used in subsequent modules to capture researched costs and assumptions that you will use to complete the Financial Plan in the electronic toolkit.

FastTrac® Toolkit

To access the FastTrac® Toolkit, go to www.fasttrac.org/toolkits and click on Fast Trac® NewVenture™. The Toolkit houses the business planning templates, actions steps, activities, videos, and More Info Resources.

The Toolkit has folders for the ten modules plus one that contains all the Templates, Sample Plans, and Glossary. This folder includes a Word-based Business Plan Template to record planning information and completed action steps and to create a written Business Plan. The Financial Template is an easy-to-use Excel-based template that will streamline your financial projections.

In each module folder, you will find additional resources as well as action steps and activities that appear in the Entrepreneur Manual. The More Info Resources lists of Web sites, books, and other sources of information are just one more way to develop your entrepreneurial skills.

Your Role

You will gain the most from the FastTrac® NewVenture™ program when you take an active role in the planning process. Read the module before and complete the action steps after each session. To be successful, conduct the recommended research and analysis as you develop your concept and plan your business. Participate in group discussions, coaching sessions, and networking opportunities with one another, staff, and guest speakers. Get the most you can out of this program to make the most of your new venture.

Exploring Entrepreneurship

Are you ready to turn your entrepreneurial dream into a reality? Before you buy your first piece of inventory, rent your facility, or print business cards with a great name and logo on them, you need to lay the groundwork for success. Do you have what it takes to be an entrepreneur? What is your goal for this business? How does that goal match your plans for your life, your family, retirement? If you answer these questions before you begin, your business has a greater chance of survival, success, and satisfaction.

This module will not only help you answer some of these questions, it will also help you hone your business idea into a well-designed concept. The clearer your business concept, its market, and financial potential, the better base you have to begin the planning process. As you screen your business concept for feasibility in these first three modules, you will be able to decide whether to continue the business planning process, modify the concept, or pursue a different concept before you spend a lot of money, time, and energy on the business itself.

Key Questions
- What is entrepreneurship?
- What are the characteristics of a successful entrepreneur?
- What are my own entrepreneurial traits?
- What is my personal vision?
- What is a business concept statement?
- How do I turn my idea into a business concept?
- Does my business concept match my personal vision?

Action Steps
Due Date

❑ 1.1 Create My Personal Vision _____

❑ 1.2 Develop a Business Concept Statement _____

❑ 1.3 Evaluate a Business Concept Against My Personal Vision _____

❑ Read Module 2 Identifying and Meeting Market Needs _____

❑ _____ _____

❑ _____ _____

❑ _____ _____

Defining Entrepreneurship

Becoming an entrepreneur means more than just starting a business. Entrepreneurship is a process through which people pursue opportunity, use resources, and initiate change to create value. Throughout the FastTrac® NewVenture™ program, you will develop entrepreneurial skills and apply them to your own business.

Entrepreneurs are people who see problems as opportunities, take action in response to needs, and accept calculated risk in the hope of creating value. They look for problems that customers will pay to solve. They are driven by a need to control their own destinies and bring their dreams to the marketplace.

Your entrepreneurial success is directly related to your ability to see opportunities resulting from needs in the marketplace, rapid change, and new trends. Successful entrepreneurs know what is happening in an industry, look for expanding markets, and predict how change and trends will impact the marketplace. They see opportunity in the midst of chaos and act while others procrastinate.

In his book, *Daring Visionaries*, Ray Smilor tells this story about one entrepreneur's uncanny ability to identify opportunities: A venture capitalist, an entrepreneur, and a Hell's Angel biker sat next to one another during a plane trip. A fly landed on the venture capitalist, who brushed it off. It landed on the entrepreneur, who brushed it off, and then it landed on the biker, who grabbed it and ate it. Moments later another fly landed on the venture capitalist who brushed it off so that it landed on the entrepreneur. The entrepreneur grabbed the fly, turned to the biker, and said, "Do you want to buy a fly?"

Entrepreneurs:

- **Recognize an opportunity** – Identify an unmet need or want, and develop a product or service that meets it.
- **Put together a sales and marketing plan** – Pinpoint prospects and ways to reach them.
- **Convert prospects to customers** – Verify that others are willing to pay for the product or service.
- **Manage risk** – Educate themselves about potential risks, and take action to minimize or eliminate those risks.
- **Find financial capital** – Determine needed resources and where to find them.
- **Build a management team** – Assemble a network of people to serve as advisers, employees, consultants, and mentors who have the information and skills to help them succeed.

"An entrepreneur's job is all about feeling lost and finding a way back," says Harry Vardis, president of Creative Focus, Inc., an Atlanta, Georgia, qualitative research firm he launched in 1997. "Think like a pilot," Vardis advises, "It's about maintaining altitude. It's about correcting for the inevitable ups and downs in order to stay airborne."

TiP You do not need a fantastic idea to start a business, you need a feasible one.

What do you need to become an entrepreneur: A great idea? Lots of experience? Let's explore these questions.

Successful entrepreneurs develop feasible ideas into profitable businesses. Most people start companies based on existing products and services with well-established markets. Few new enterprises can thrive solely on new discoveries or inventions.

You can gain valuable knowledge and experience from mentors, reading, research, work experience, college coursework, and seminars. One of the most common entry strategies is to use knowledge and skill you've acquired in an earlier job, according to entrepreneurship researcher Amar V. Bhide in his book *The Origin and Evolution of New Businesses*. Bhide's research says knowledge is a key factor in success. In Bhide's study, 12 percent of the founders thought their success came from an unusual or extraordinary idea," and 88 percent reported their success as mainly due to the "exceptional execution of an ordinary idea." Many of the latter start-ups were people already knowledgeable in their industry.

Experience within an industry or business can give you a distinct advantage towards building a successful business. Experience, however, is not required. You can apply your energy and enthusiasm to learn about a new field, its trade practices, and techniques.

Entrepreneurs find creative ways to overcome obstacles. Finding the funds to get started or reaching that first customer may require nontraditional approaches. Unlock your creativity as you explore your potential to become an entrepreneur.

You can start a business at any age if you have the drive, enthusiasm, and physical stamina. It requires balancing commitments, it costs money, and it involves taking risks. Use the Reality Check *Am I an Entrepreneur?* to determine which aspects of successful entrepreneurship you already exhibit.

Launching a business is similar to having a child, says John Friess, co-founder of wired. MD®, which provides streaming-video patient education to doctors. Entrepreneurs must "commit, prepare, establish a date against which to plan and work—and finally, deliver," explains Friess. "Just as the expectant parent's due date acts as the benchmark against which all progress is measured, a firmly established launch date holds business people accountable."

Ideas vs. Execution

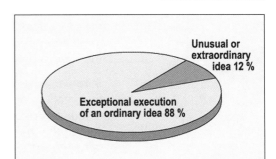

Reality Check ✔

Am I an Entrepreneur?

How much control do I want over my future?

Am I counting on a fantastic idea or a feasible one?

Am I building on my experience in an industry or stepping out on a journey into new territory?

How do I describe my desire, drive, and enthusiasm for my new business idea?

Managing Entrepreneurial Risks

Entrepreneurial success is far from guaranteed. You will take personal and financial risks to get what you want. But this does not mean you need to be a reckless spendthrift to be an entrepreneur. As you think about your new business, you can plan and prepare in order to balance the risks with the rewards.

Some analysts estimate that up to 70 percent of all new businesses close after two to five years of operation. Astute entrepreneurs survey the entrepreneurial landscape, take calculated risks, and reduce the risk factor through research and planning. Studies have shown that most entrepreneurs are only moderate risk takers when asked to choose between risks and payoffs.

In evaluating personal risk, Dale Coyner and David Paul, founders of Communicast®, felt it was riskier *not* to launch their company, when balancing the potential to increase sales and profit and create security for their growing families against the risks of working for someone else. From a purely financial perspective, they argued that turning their futures over to an employer would have been less preferable than placing a bet on—as a noted business writer once said—the "CEO of You, Inc."

Reality Check ✔

How Do I Feel About Taking Risks?

Check *yes* or *no* to answer the questions below. The more *yes* answers you give, the more comfortable you are with risk.

	Check One	
	Yes	**No**
I often seek out new and different things to try.	❏	❏
I enjoy the challenge of finding a solution when I run into a problem.	❏	❏
The discomfort of doing something new or different is just part of the learning process.	❏	❏
It is not hard for me to ask for help or guidance from others.	❏	❏

What are some ways you can minimize risk?

One way to reduce the risk of starting a new business is to take time to design a product, test it, market it, and develop and grow the market. A business often takes several years or more to break even. Some entrepreneurs have became millionaires or even billionaires in a few years, like Jerry Yang of Yahoo!®, but such instant success is rare.

TiP No universal law dictates that risks equal rewards. Many low-risk businesses may reap significant rewards and high-risk ventures may reap minimal rewards.

Seasoned entrepreneurs are quick to emphasize the importance of building a strong team to balance the risks of entrepreneurship. They know the value of involving the right people in their business from the start. Seeking assistance from trusted advisers, mentors, and outside professionals can save you from making expensive mistakes as a defense against risks.

Another way you can control risk is to start small, perhaps with a home-based business, and test the business concept. Experiment with the marketplace on a small scale and obtain customer feedback. This approach doesn't mean your business must stay small. You may dream of building an international billion-dollar business, but testing the business concept on a limited basis at the beginning just makes good sense.

Another way entrepreneurs manage risk is to carefully plan their business and write the plan down. The process of writing a business plan helps you to determine whether your business has a market, can make a profit, and can provide you with what you need. With proper planning, you will reduce risks by replacing guesses and suppositions with facts and research.

Developing Entrepreneurial Traits

To further understand entrepreneurship, let's examine what it takes to be a successful entrepreneur. Although many people possess characteristics similar to successful entrepreneurs, the level and intensity of these qualities often set entrepreneurs apart. What are these distinctive entrepreneurial qualities?

One common characteristic of entrepreneurs is a strong **desire to succeed**. Connected to this desire is a **passion** for what they are doing. Randy Komisar, former CEO of Lucas Arts Entertainment®, sustains himself through passion. He integrates his life and his work with a powerful core belief: Time is short. Don't squander any of it. "Passion pulls you forward," he says. "There is no way to avoid it. You have to go there."

Other entrepreneurial characteristics include the **determination**, **physical energy**, and **resiliency** to tirelessly pursue a vision and overcome the setbacks and disappointments often experienced in launching and growing a successful business.

Persuasiveness can also be key to starting a business. Entrepreneurs need to convince others—bankers, accountants, lawyers, and customers—to join their team. But good entrepreneurs are also **accountable**. They take responsibility for their successes and failures.

Entrepreneurs typically have **confidence** in their ability to create their own destiny, relying primarily on themselves to do it. They have the confidence and **self-discipline** to take action in the often ambiguous, confusing environment of the start-up venture, frequently identifying opportunity in the chaos. They are willing to learn from success and failure.

Many entrepreneurs operate successfully from strong **ethics**. They treat people fairly and behave honestly. They are motivated by **social responsibility** to share their time and wealth to support their community. Many entrepreneurs give back by mentoring new entrepreneurs.

TIP *Nothing in the world can take the place of persistence. Talent will not; nothing is more common than unsuccessful men with talent. Genius will not; unrewarded genius is almost a proverb. Education will not; the world is full of educated derelicts. Persistence and determination alone are omnipotent. The slogan 'Press on' has solved and always will solve the problems of the human race. — Calvin Coolidge*

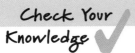

What Entrepreneurial Traits Have I Seen?

What entrepreneurial characteristics and skills have I observed in successful entrepreneurs?

Some people claim that perhaps the most significant trait of entrepreneurs is their ability to **recognize market opportunities**. How engaged are you in scanning the marketplace and assessing potential opportunities? Others see **monitoring and controlling resources** as the most critical. Are you able to develop, monitor, and control the operations of a business? How much do you value the control systems required by your business or industry?

Studying the traits of entrepreneurs can benefit you in two ways. First, after learning what it takes to be successful in the entrepreneurial world, you can see whether you have the traits you need to be an entrepreneur. Second, if you decide that you have the desire to start a business, you can develop and strengthen the most important traits.

When you evaluate yourself against entrepreneurial characteristics, be honest with yourself. Do you have these characteristics? If not, what must you do to obtain them? In the Reality Check *Entrepreneurial Traits* evaluate yourself for common entrepreneurial characteristics. Then prepare an action plan to strengthen those characteristics you wish to develop further.

 Reality Check **Entrepreneurial Traits**

Step 1 Review characteristics, skills, knowledge, and abilities. Evaluate the strength of your entrepreneurial traits by circling the number that best represents how well each trait applies to you. A 3 indicates strength and a 1 indicates weakness.

Entrepreneurial Characteristics	Strong	Average	Needs Improvement
a. Desire and Passion *I have a fervent drive to succeed and zeal for the tasks required.*	3	2	1
b. Energy *I have stamina to tackle problems.*	3	2	1
c. Ability to Thrive on Uncertainty *I can prosper in an environment with many questions and few answers.*	3	2	1
d. Determination and Resiliency *I can hang on in hard times and recover quickly.*	3	2	1
e. Accountability *I take responsibility for my own success.*	3	2	1
f. Persuasiveness *I convincingly communicate with others—bankers, vendors, employees.*	3	2	1
g. Self-Discipline *I can do the tasks necessary to succeed, whether pleasant or unpleasant.*	3	2	1
h. Self-Confidence *I believe that somehow I can solve whatever problems arise.*	3	2	1
i. Social Responsibility *I am passionately motivated to share success and wealth by giving back.*	3	2	1
j. Ethics *I deal with others with honesty and integrity.*	3	2	1
k. Ability to Value Appropriate Control Systems *I value the management and control systems necessary to run a business.*	3	2	1

Entrepreneurial Traits continued

Entrepreneurial Skills, Knowledge, and Abilities	Strong	Average	Needs Improvement
l. Problem Solving	3	2	1
m. Networking	3	2	1
n. Market Awareness	3	2	1
o. Low Support Needs	3	2	1
p. Business Knowledge	3	2	1
q. Good People Judgment	3	2	1

l. Problem Solving
I have an ability to anticipate and troubleshoot problems. Problems present opportunities.

m. Networking
I connect with others and build strategic relationships.

n. Market Awareness
I can scan the marketplace and assess potential needs and gaps.

o. Low Support Needs
I provide for my own needs with little support from others.

p. Business Knowledge
I have a basis for making effective, profitable business decisions.

q. Good People Judgment
I can pick the right people to help execute my vision.

Step 2 Prepare an action plan. Select three areas to improve that will most benefit your future business. Beside each item, identify two steps you will take to improve or strengthen it. A sample has been given for you.

Characteristic

Sample: *I don't value the control systems that keep track of where money is going.*

1

2

3

Action Plan

Sample a: *I need to find an accountant who could help me understand the budget process.*

Sample b: *I will take a course in basic accounting.*

1a

1b

2a

2b

3a

3b

Discovering My Personal Vision

TIP *If you don't know where you're going, you might wind up somewhere else.*
— Yogi Berra

The decision to start a business is similar to embarking on a challenging journey. A successful trip is one that meets the traveler's objectives. In order to get the most out of a journey, travelers generally plan ahead. In the table below, notice how the steps of preparing for a trip parallel the steps of planning a new business.

Planning a Journey	Planning a Business
Make a decision on the destination considering all the places you would like to go.	Prepare a personal vision, including your personal and professional goals.
Outline the activities you would like to do while on the journey.	Write a business concept.
Decide who will go with you on this trip.	Build a team and/or a network.
Consider the services (fuel, food, and lodging) needed along the way.	Plan uses of resources.
Make a list of things to pack for the trip.	Write a business plan.
Identify the amount of money needed for the trip and how to pay for it.	Identify sources and uses of funds.
Decide how long you want the trip to last.	Plan an exit strategy.

TIP *If you fail to plan, you plan to fail.*

Travelers who plan well take into consideration personal goals for the trip, opportunities presented by the destination, financial considerations, and time limitations. The better you plan before you begin, the better the chance your journey will be a success. The same applies to the entrepreneur starting a business venture.

You may be thinking, "I don't like to do all that planning when I travel. I just like to head out on the open road and see where it takes me." Many ex-entrepreneurs have had this same attitude about business.

The first step in business planning is to analyze your personal vision. By doing so, you will be better prepared to select a business that is right for you. Your personal vision also helps keep in focus that your business is a part of a bigger life plan, rather than an end in itself.

Making Personal Choices

When defining a personal vision, you will have some personal choices to make. Do you want opportunities to travel? Do you prefer physical labor to a desk job? Do you like to work with people or behind the scenes? Pursue a business that can support the lifestyle you envision.

Consider these personal choices when planning your business:

Work hours – Think about the days of the week, times of day, and number of weeks a year that you plan to devote to the business. For example, if one of your primary goals for starting a business is to spend more time with your family, you should seriously reconsider the thought of opening a business that requires long hours of operation, such as a retail store or restaurant.

Flexibility – How much flexibility is important to you? Do you need to be available to assist family members or friends throughout the day/week? Do you like setting your own schedule? Although flexibility seems attractive, some people feel they work best in a more structured environment.

Location – Where do you want to live and work? Some entrepreneurs select a location before choosing a business. Then they evaluate business concepts based on compatibility with the location.

Travel – Are you looking for travel opportunities or trying to avoid them? Craft your business to match your attitude toward travel.

Morals, beliefs, and standards – To achieve ultimate satisfaction, you may want to seek a business that supports and cultivates your morals, beliefs, and standards.

Physical requirements – Consider your age and health when evaluating business ideas. You must weigh the mental and physical requirements of the business against your current physical condition.

Family involvement – Starting a business will have a significant impact on the whole family. You need to recognize this impact, evaluate it, and discuss it with family members before launching a new venture.

Future personal income – What income do you need to support the lifestyle you have or want? Most aspiring entrepreneurs have a future lifestyle in mind. The profitability of the business and its corresponding personal income will have a significant impact on your lifestyle.

Making Professional Choices

Entrepreneurship can bring you limitless professional growth opportunities. The first step is to define what is important to you in your professional life. Consider these professional choices:

TiP Develop humility to counteract ego.

Power or status – Some people have a desire for control and recognition. If these are important to you, you will be interested in pursuing business opportunities that provide it. Beware that the quest for power is often driven by ego, which many entrepreneurs say is their most negative trait. Ego can drive you to stop listening to advisers and employees and start thinking you are always right.

Social interaction – Your personal preference for working alone or with others is an important consideration. Will you have frequent contact with colleagues and peers, or will most of your interactions be among people with whom you share little in common?

Involvement in daily operations – Some entrepreneurs strongly feel that as founders they want to be involved with everything. If you feel this way, you should take care to be the majority owner (owning more than 50 percent of the business) to control all of the business decisions and limit your organization to a manageable size.

Expertise, skills, and preferences – Many entrepreneurs play to their strong suit and buy the services of others in areas where they are weak. You must know your strengths and weaknesses in order to hire the appropriate outside help.

Job security – Examples abound of owners whose basic goal for being in business is to provide for their own security and make a stable income.

Future professional goals – Successful entrepreneurs take time to envision themselves five or ten years into the future. Starting a business now that takes away from where you want to be in five years is like taking a long, unnecessary detour.

Growth business or lifestyle business – A growth business is one in which fast growth is the goal. Growth businesses, however, may not always meet the personal objectives of the founder. Jana Matthews, founder and CEO of Boulder Quantum Ventures, cautions that the demands of a growing company may be so complex and intense that they can overshadow everything else, making it easy for entrepreneurs to neglect their personal life. The goal of a lifestyle business is to meet your personal objectives. This goal may limit growth. Learn to balance and integrate your personal and professional lives based on your vision of the future.

Reality Check ✓

Personal and Professional Choices

Check the issues that are most important to you in your personal and professional lives:

Personal
- ❏ Work hours
- ❏ Flexibility
- ❏ Location
- ❏ Travel
- ❏ Morals, beliefs, and standards
- ❏ Physical requirements
- ❏ Family involvement
- ❏ Future personal income

Professional
- ❏ Power or status
- ❏ Social interaction
- ❏ Involvement in daily operations
- ❏ Expertise, skills, and preferences
- ❏ Job security
- ❏ Future professional goals
- ❏ Growth or lifestyle business

Identify whether any choices from one list conflict with choices on the other. List them here.

Which choice takes priority?

Establishing a Personal Vision

In your first action step for this program, Action Step 1.1 Create My Personal Vision, pp. 27 – 30, you will have the opportunity to examine what is important to you and to create the type of life that will bring you satisfaction. This step is critical in finding the right business for you.

Your personal vision captures the lifestyle you desire, including the time you have for the business, the place you want to work, your family's involvement, and your financial goals. It will also reflect your professional aspirations, including the type of work you enjoy, future professional goals, and the role you wish to play in the business.

By identifying your personal vision, you will be able to determine whether a business concept is a good match. You may discover that some of your goals conflict with one another. In that case, try to determine priorities or compromise between the conflicting goals. Ultimately, the outcome should reflect what you want your business to be. There are no wrong answers. The only mistake you can make is not to take the time to establish what is truly important to you. If you don't identify your goals, the rest of the business planning process will be of little value.

Align Growth and Vision

For Art Stinson, growing his business according to his personal vision has become important. But that wasn't always the case. For years Stinson was trapped in the idea that his own worth was measured by his paycheck. Then the large real estate development company he worked for went bankrupt. Stinson was devastated: "I thought it was the worst thing in the world."

In the stagnant economy of the late 1980s and early 1990s, he couldn't find another job in the area and didn't want to force his family to relocate. So in 1991 he founded Trace Ventures, a residential construction and remodeling firm in Nashville, Tennessee.

Stinson started Trace Ventures with "no resources, no seed money, nothing." Initially the sole employee, Stinson didn't have a plan or schedule for growth. But as business picked up, he realized he had to hire more people. He took FastTrac® in 2000 to help him manage the company's growth, but the program also reinforced his dedication to helping others and sharing his company's rewards with his employees.

"I wanted to set up a company that treated its employees with dignity and respect," Stinson says. In the beginning, he told his new staff he couldn't afford to provide benefits right away, but if they stuck with him, he promised to get benefits for them as soon as he could. He kept his word, and his employees now have paid holidays and vacation, health insurance, and a new retirement plan. He recently added a company-match employee reward program for outstanding work called "performance incentive plan," and he is working on adding more benefits.

Stinson also uses his construction skills to reconnect with his community. Instead of giving his clients fruit baskets or gifts, Stinson often performs charity work at Christmas. He sends customers a card explaining that the work is done in their names. People go out of their way to call and thank him. "They feel proud and honored," Stinson says.

On one holiday project, Trace Ventures joined with another contractor to help convert an old church into a day-care facility for Bethlehem Centers®, a local nonprofit organization working with inner-city families. Stinson also fixed up properties for the Magdalene House, which provides group homes and job training for prostitutes trying to leave the streets and turn their lives around.

Stinson's employees stay with him because they buy into his vision. "They feel like they have a stake in this company," Stinson says. Turnover at Trace Ventures is low. "Losing that job was the best thing that ever happened to me," he adds.

Developing My Business Concept

Entrepreneurs are idea people. They see opportunities everywhere. But it takes more than an idea to make a business. A business concept is a bridge between a business idea and a business plan. It focuses your thinking so that you can identify the specifics of your proposed venture.

Sample Concept Statement

Hernandez, Brown, and Santos Legal Services specializes in guiding management through the often complex array of patent and trademark issues. Hernandez, Brown, and Santos is differentiated by having all clients receive the focused patent and trademark law expertise of the firm's founders, saving clients both the time and expense that occurs in larger firms when the actual work is handed off to junior associates. Years of relevant legal experience coupled with the firm's network systems ensure clients receive the most effective representation. Marketing plans to acquire new clients—small and mid-sized companies looking to outsource their patent and trademark needs—include an interactive Web site which provides immediate answers to more routine legal issues and direct-mail personalized letters with personal phone call follow-ups by the firm's three principals.

Converting an idea into a concept requires you to think about how the product or service will be sold and who will buy it, the benefits of the product or service, how it is differentiated from similar ones, and methods of delivery.

Preparing a written concept statement helps you unearth critical components of your venture and begin researching key factors that will be more thoroughly addressed in your business plan. As your business idea takes form as a concept statement, you can evaluate the business more effectively for potential problems and pitfalls.

A clear business concept also enables you to succinctly describe the precise nature of your business to suppliers, customers, lenders, and resource team members, an important skill of successful entrepreneurs. For example, it is not sufficient to say "I want to start a management consulting company." This tells the listener little. Instead, you might say, "I plan to start a management consulting company providing strategic planning services to mid-sized businesses in the Southeast. Each consulting team, tailored to meet the unique needs of the client, provides assessment and planning services to help clients improve efficiency and institute processes for innovation and change, resulting in cost reductions and sales increases." This version tells the listener a lot more than the first version.

In this module, you will learn the elements of a business concept and the mistakes to avoid in writing one.

Defining Products and Services

Your business concept identifies the exact product or service you plan to offer. It includes the purpose (reason for being) of the product or service and its unique features and distinct characteristics.

When discussing the unique features of your products or services, you may be tempted to use buzz words, such as *best, most advanced, latest.* Instead, define exactly how your product or service is the best or the most advanced. Is the "best" chocolate chip cookie made with imported chocolate, or is it three inches wide and one inch thick and made with real butter? Does the "most advanced" electronic gadget have more buttons for the buyer to play with or fewer buttons for simplicity?

When writing your business concept, be as specific as possible to provide a comprehensive picture of your product or service. Consider these examples of vague terminology reworded to show how they can present a more complete picture of a business idea:

Vague	**Descriptive**
The best Italian restaurant	An Italian restaurant located in a renovated nineteenth-century home featuring cuisine from Northern Italy
Supervision for commercial construction projects	Value engineering, project management, and cost control management to the construction industry
Quality event planner	Corporate event planner helping businesses design and execute successful conferences, meetings, and business retreats

Your business concept statement should answer the following questions:
- What do you want the product or service to be known for? (What is the desired reputation?)
- What in particular sets the product or service apart from competitors?
- What is your niche in the marketplace?
- How was the need for the product or service determined?

Your business concept statement shows how your business solves a problem or fulfills a need, is unique, and works as planned.

Solve a Problem or Fulfill a Need

Like most entrepreneurs, you are probably very aware of the physical or technical features of the product or service you wish to market. You may, however, encounter difficulty stating the purpose of your product or service. If so, think about these questions:
- What are the physical or technical features of the product or service?
- What is the purpose of the product or service? What problem does the product or service solve, or what need does it fill?
- What makes this product or service unique—better than the competition?
- Is the product or service workable? Does it do what it is intended to do?

Tip Customers don't buy products or services, they buy solutions.

To explain the purpose of the product or service, answer the question, "What problem or need does the product or service fill?" For example, 7-Eleven, Inc.®, stores appear to sell food, but they are really about convenience. The stores are easy to slip into when a customer only needs a few items and is in a hurry. For additional convenience, the stores are centrally located. By identifying the problem solved or need fulfilled, you can clarify the major benefits of your product or service to the customer.

Businesses fail when they are not able to find enough customers who perceive a need for their products or services.

Identify the Uniqueness of a Product or Service

Successful concepts have products or services that differ significantly in meaningful ways from competitors. Just copying the competitors' products or services typically will not lead to a successful product or service. You need to set your product or service apart from its competition. What is the point of difference? Is it faster or slower, larger or smaller, less expensive or higher priced with higher quality? Does it provide added features resulting in new benefits to the customer?

The uniqueness of your product or service may be defined by how it meets the needs of a market niche. Just be sure that the market niche stems from customer needs, warns Valorie Seyfert, co-founder of CUSO Financial Services in San Diego. "It's easy to get carried away and assume that customers want to buy what you have to sell," she says. "Don't. Instead, talk to them and find out."

Start-up businesses can make money by serving a small segment of a larger market with a unique product or service. The key is to position such endeavors in a way that they really are not competing directly with large, established companies. For example, specialty soap could be positioned as a luxury product designed to pamper the user and bring the spa experience into the home, thus not competing directly with such giants as Procter & Gamble® and Kimberly-Clark®.

Uniqueness in the business concept may also provide an opportunity for you to legally protect your concept from being easily copied by a competitor. By protecting your products or services with patents, copyrights, trade secrets, trademarks, and/or service marks, you may be able to secure a more lucrative market position as well as build wealth in the business.

Prove that the Product or Service Works

Some products and services just don't work. All sorts of great-sounding inventions are used as a basis for a concept. Many never get to market; the inventor cannot make the invention work satisfactorily outside the laboratory. A new product or service must work well and fit into accepted practice to be accepted in the marketplace.

If a product or service fits nicely into the existing market, resistance to it will be much less. Products that require consumers to change the way they act or think are much slower to be adopted. Big-screen TVs originally encountered acceptance problems because they did not fit into many homes. Since they were big and awkward, they took up too much space. Today's mega-screen TVs are less than six inches deep and fit more easily into a home. Consider how your product or service might fit in to existing markets.

Reality Check ✓

How Do I Define My Product/Service?

	Yes	No	How?
Does my product solve a problem?	❏	❏	_____
Does my business fulfill a need?	❏	❏	_____
Is my product/service unique?	❏	❏	_____
Can my product/service be copyrighted, patented, or trademarked?	❏	❏	_____
Does my product/service fit into an existing market?	❏	❏	_____

You will further define your product or service as you write your business concept statement and proceed with other modules in this program.

Writing a Business Concept Statement

Potential investors, customers, and clients usually will not spend much time trying to understand the nature of a business being presented to them. Entrepreneurs who cannot clearly and succinctly define their business concept, may cause others— potential suppliers, customers, investors, lenders, and resource team members— to question their capability to successfully launch and grow a business. Here's how one residential rental property management company answered the questions others had about its new business:

Questions	Answers
a. What is your service and what does it do?	Our business is property management. We advertise properties, screen tenants, collect rents, and maintain properties.
b. How is it different from other services?	We specialize in properties in the Culver City area.
c. Who will buy the service?	New landlords, absentee landlords, and landlords tired of the headaches of property management will buy our services.
d. Why will they buy the service?	Our knowledge of tenant/landlord law, convenience, and efficiency are good reasons to hire us.
e. How will the service be promoted and sold/offered?	We will place signage on the property of rental homes, advertise in the Yellow Pages®, a Web site, and network through landlord associations.

This company can use these answers to develop a business concept statement that easily and succinctly summarizes its activities. Use the Reality Check *What is My Business Concept?* to start answering these questions for your business concept.

Reality Check ✓

What Is My Business Concept?

Answer the following questions as completely as you can with what you currently know about your business idea. Your responses will help you prepare for Action Step 1.2 Develop a Business Concept Statement, pp. 31 – 33.

a. What is my product/service and what does it do?

b. How is it different from other products/services?

c. Who will buy the product/service?

d. Why will they buy the product/service?

e. How will the product/service be promoted and sold/offered?

TiP The acid test for a well-defined concept statement is to tell it to strangers and have them relate it back precisely.

You will find that your business concept statement will change during feasibility testing and business planning as you learn more about the market and the profitability of the business in upcoming modules. Your business concept will eventually appear in the Executive Summary of your Business Plan. If it is not clearly and concisely stated, then the reader may immediately lose interest and not read any more of the plan.

Eventually, you should be able to accurately and clearly describe the essence of your business to others in two or three sentences. In some cases, a single sentence may do. You can consider this your one-minute marketing speech.

To create a one-minute marketing speech:
1. Answer the question – What does the business do?
2. Use the words *work with*, *want*, or *offer*.
3. State how your business solves a problem or offers a solution.
4. Describe what makes your business unique.
5. Tell a quick story.
6. Keep it to sixty seconds or less.

Following is how a one-minute marketing speech might begin:
- We work with Atlanta entrepreneurs who want to start their own business and small business owners looking to grow their revenue streams. We have helped over 1,000 business owners achieve their revenue goals the first year of business….
- Jackie's Treasures offers one-of-a-kind, hand-painted furniture for the discerning art or antique collector. We offer exquisite art from around the world hand-selected by our experts….
- Soho Software works with companies that want low-cost software support 24 hours a day….

Many entrepreneurs refer to this one-minute marketing speech as their elevator pitch. The idea is that you can describe your business concept clearly and concisely on a brief elevator ride. In this short time, you need to explain both the unique aspects of your business as well as exactly what the business does.

Reality Check ✔

One-Minute Marketing Speech

List some ideas for your one-minute marketing speech or elevator pitch.

Even when your concept is clear, it will change over time as you learn more about the market and the economics of your new business. In fact, if your business concept does not change as you compile the Business Plan, you may not be "listening" to the market and financial facts. For example, COLECO®, famous for Cabbage Patch® dolls and hand-held video games, started out as the Connecticut Leather Company. Additionally, the Ball brothers originally built the successful Ball® Mason Jar business. Today the Ball Corporation mainly works in the aerospace industry as well as metal and plastic packaging.

Finding a Market Niche

Patience and perseverance helped Sara Blakely, founder of Spanx®, Inc., find her market niche. "It took me two years to design and perfect my product and get Spanx Original Footless pantyhose manufactured," said Blakely. "But that time enabled me to make the calculated decisions that determined my success as a niche product in the massive industry of retailing. In an effort to compete against 'the big boys,' I carefully considered how I would name my company, position the brand, and design the packaging so that it would get noticed and purchased. I knew nothing about the retail business outside of the fact that I was a consumer who loved to shop, and I wanted Spanx footless pantyhose to be in the stores I loved. I cold-called and landed all of the top high-end retailers in the country—Neiman Marcus®, Nordstrom®, Saks Fifth Avenue®, and Bloomingdale's®." A clearly defined market is one attribute of a successful business concept.

Attributes of a Successful Business Concept

Certain attributes help a product or service succeed in the marketplace. Businesses that offer a product or service with the following attributes have a better chance of success:

Solves a serious problem – Concepts that deal with serious problems like diseases or safety issues are given full consideration by the market.

Involves significant savings – A concept that saves either the customer or the seller a lot of money will have a strong demand and a higher price.

Fits into the existing scheme of things – A product or service that fits nicely into an existing system, will experience much less resistance than if new systems or changes in consumer behavior are necessary. If the customer has to change current assumptions, thinking, or actions, the selling cycle will be much longer.

Attracts media attention – If your product or service is special, it may attract the attention of the news media and its promotion will be greatly facilitated. Without unique features, it is just another product or service fighting for a place in the market.

TiP Just because your concept solves a serious problem does not guarantee its success. Standards of consumer demand and profitability must still be met. Many investors lose money when faulty concepts are given the go-ahead just because they deal with serious matters.

Reality Check ✔

Positive Attributes

Check each positive attribute of your business concept.

❑ Solves a serious problem   ❑ Attracts media attention

❑ Involves significant savings   ❑ Identifies a market

❑ Fits into the existing scheme of things   ❑ Joins a rapidly expanding market

Summarize the strengths of your concept:

Identifies a market – Successful products and services have a clearly defined customer. Can you identify yours? Who is your first customer? Who is the next?

Joins a rapidly expanding market – An expanding market, such as children's educational products, is more attractive to entrepreneurs and investors than stagnant markets.

Fatal Flaws of Business Concepts

Many new enterprises are doomed from the start because the concepts upon which they are based are somehow fatally flawed. Perhaps the concept sounds good, but it will not work in the real world. Perhaps the concept solves a problem that only exists in the entrepreneur's mind, and the intended customer perceives no need for it. Or perhaps the market is just not large enough for it to make the enterprise successful.

These fatal flaws signal the need to significantly modify or change your business concept:

No real need – Businesses fail when they do not fill a need perceived by enough people to make operations profitable or when they do not solve a problem people are willing to pay money to fix.

Does not work – All sorts of great-sounding inventions never get to market because the inventor cannot make the invention work satisfactorily outside the laboratory.

Potential marketing traps – A marketing barrier may lie hidden in the marketplace. For instance, a product may threaten the career of the person who is supposed to buy it. For example, an entrepreneur who has developed a software product that corporations can use to efficiently collect and organize account data may have a difficult time convincing a manager to purchase it if would affect the need for his job or other jobs in his department. Any product or service that requires a person to change could create a marketing trap. It is important to assess the intended customer's reaction to the concept.

Unfortunate economics – Although your concept may work and people may perceive a need for it, if costs are too high, customers will not be willing to pay enough for your business to be profitable.

No protection – Some concepts can be easily copied by other organizations capable of quickly exploiting the market, perhaps driving you out. Investors are leery of new enterprises that have no sustainable competitive advantage—no patents, copyrights, trade secrets, organizational or distributive advantages, location monopoly, or cost advantage.

Obsolescence – How long is the life of your concept? Many concepts are so faddish that an enterprise based on them has only a few months to make its profits. One large firm had to write off millions of dollars in research on a new type of microprocessor when a technical competitor surpassed it with another approach to the same problem.

Potential installation problems – Many concepts sound great until the realities of placing them into use sink in. Products that work well in the laboratory may not work at all in the field. Consider the installation issues surrounding your product.

Requires education – If the new product will be successful only after the customer has been trained to use it, watch out. Education is a slow, costly process. Few people welcome reading an instruction manual and having to learn how to use a new product. Instead, they are much more comfortable using familiar products.

TiP Many customers say they will buy but don't buy when the product is available.

TiP You don't have to start from scratch. Entrepreneurs can take products to market faster and more economically if they buy the rights to existing products rather than develop their own.

of positive attributes
and flaws online at
www.fasttrac.org/toolkits.

Requires change in consumer behavior – Consumer behavior is learned over time through numerous experiences in the marketplace. Consequently, consumer behavior is stable and regular. If your concept requires a change in consumer behavior, consumers may resist unless the rewards are obviously sufficient to motivate them.

Inaccurate assumptions – People frequently get into trouble with assumptions. One important procedure in developing your business plan is to identify all of the assumptions on which it is based and then severely question them. For example, the assumption that the market will love the product (since you do) needs to be examined closely. So does the assumption that the target market will continue its present state of prosperity. What facts support your assumptions?

Inconvenience – Many new products and services fail because they are inconvenient. Products that people must assemble or that must be returned to the factory for repair may be rejected in favor of those offering more convenience. How convenient is your product or service?

Reality Check ✓ Fatal Flaws

Check each potential flaw or problem of your business concept.

❏ No real need
❏ Does not work
❏ Potential marketing traps
❏ Unfortunate economics
❏ No protection
❏ Obsolescence

❏ Potential installation problems
❏ Requires education
❏ Requires change in consumer behavior
❏ Inaccurate assumptions
❏ Inconvenience
❏ Service requirements

How can I address or overcome identified flaws or problems?

Service requirements – Does your concept require service? If so, by whom? A service aspect to a concept greatly complicates it. Be prepared to explain how you propose to handle whatever service requirements are connected with your concept.

Invest in the necessary research to understand how your proposed product or service differs from what's currently available, advises John Friess, co-founder and vice president of marketing at wired.MD. Determine what quantity you can produce at an acceptable quality, whether you can offer it at a price the market can bear, and what legal entanglements might exist. "At wired.MD, for example, we found that we couldn't protect the delivery mechanism for our videos," says Friess, "but we could protect the content by trademarking the name 'streaMed,' which stands for 'streaming video medical information.' "

Action Step 1.2 Develop a Business Concept Statement on pp. 31 – 33 will help you take a business idea that sounds fantastic in your head and turn it into a clearly described business concept. Articulating the business concept in a written statement is an important step toward developing a plan and becoming an entrepreneur.

Testing a Business Concept Against My Personal Vision

No guaranteed, statistically accurate process exists to calculate the probability that a business opportunity will match your personal vision. Much of this evaluation must be done subjectively. Still, it helps to have a tool to guide you through the process of determining how well your business idea matches your personal vision.

Action Step 1.3 Evaluate a Business Concept Against My Personal Vision on pp. 31 – 33 will help you identify the personal vision criteria that are most important to you. It gives you a mechanism to judge how well your business concept meets your personal vision. You may also use this tool to compare the ability of one business concept against another to meet your vision.

If a business concept does not match your vision, you will need to revise the concept or seek a new one. Resist the urge to hang onto a business concept that does not meet your personal vision. In the long run, you will be happier identifying another opportunity which is a better fit.

TIP Logistical difficulties ruin many concepts. A business that sells a product but does not offer service to maintain it has a flawed concept.

Summary

Module 1 focuses on you and your proposed venture. By examining entrepreneurship and common entrepreneurial traits, you can assess yourself as a potential entrepreneur. The action steps guide you in the process, defining your personal vision and evaluating your business concept against it. You can review and modify your initial business concept statement as you gather and analyze additional information throughout this program.

Key Things to Remember

- Entrepreneurs are people who recognize opportunities, take action, manage risk, use resources, utilize a network, and ask for help when necessary.

- You can reduce both the personal and financial risks inherent in starting a business by careful planning.

- Successful entrepreneurs share a number of similar traits that are likely to lead to business success.

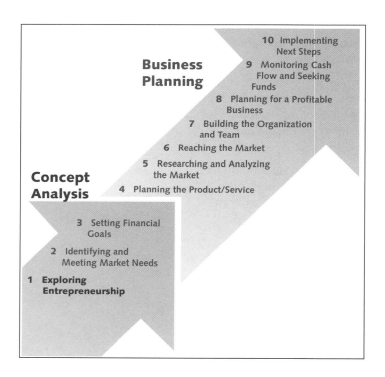

- Evaluating a business concept against your personal vision should be one of your first activities.

- Personal and professional choices help form the foundation of your vision and business.

- You must define your product or service based on consumer need, uniqueness, and function.

- You should be able to clearly describe the precise nature of your business concept.

- Your concept statement will be modified as additional information comes available during the planning process and over time as a result of learning about the market and the profitability of the business.

Congratulations on completing the first module in this entrepreneurial adventure. In Module 2 you will continue to refine your business concept by comparing your idea to the marketplace, learning to recognize and evaluate opportunities and discovering how to research your concept in relation to the market, its industry, and its competition.

Activity 1a   Business Concept Statement

Identify the key components in a business concept statement and evaluate the statement's overall effectiveness.

Directions

Having a clear, concise, and complete concept statement is critical in clarifying your business concept and communicating that concept to others. An effective concept statement includes answers to these key components:

- WHAT does the product or service do?
- HOW is it different from other products or services?
- WHO will buy it?
- WHY will they buy it? Is the product or service different from other products or services?
- WHERE will it be sold?
- WHEN will it be ready to be sold?
- HOW will it be promoted and sold?

Follow the steps below to evaluate a business concept statement for its overall effectiveness.

Step 1   Read the concept statement. Review the concept statement for Donovan's Detail or Pro-Specialty Advertising below.

Sample Business Concept Statement – Donovan's Detail

In a world where more people are seeking prestige, luxury, and comfort, there is an ever-increasing demand for quality automotive detailing. Donovan's Detail will meet that demand by providing professional external and internal detailing of cars, SUVs, and limousines at the customer's site.

What makes Donovan's Detail unique? We concentrate on the customer…not just the car! We will meet with customers to find out what type of detailing they want. Several packages will be offered to them. The services available include environmentally-safe car wash, wax, velour and carpet cleaning, leather and vinyl dressing, and window polishing.

After considerable research and development, Donovan's Detail will be established in a garage located near several office parks. This location will attract the professionals needed to support the business. Donovan's Detail grand opening, planned for April, will be promoted to these professionals through targeted mailings and advertising in the newsletters of surrounding businesses.

Sample Business Concept Statement – Pro-Specialty Advertising

Pro-Specialty Advertising assists its customers in giving memorable, unique corporate wearables and promotional items. Pro-Specialty provides a broad array of merchandise, including golf shirts, hats, mugs, and trophies, as well as hard-to-find items such as imported cut glass and brass office accessories. Merchandise can be customized with corporate logos or personal monograms. Express service is available.

Currently Pro-Specialty Advertising sells to small and medium-sized companies in the tri-state area. In the future sales will be expanded to include larger sized companies and an online catalog will allow sales nationwide. Clients will be reached through a direct sales force, Yellow Pages advertising, a Web site, and participation in trade shows.

Activity 1a **Business Concept Statement** continued

Step 2 Identify key components. Using one of the sample concept statements, answer the following questions related to key components of an effective concept statement.

WHAT does the product or service do?

HOW is it different from other products or services?

WHO will buy it?

WHY will they buy it? Is the product or service different from other products or services?

WHERE will it be sold?

WHEN will it be ready to be sold?

HOW will it be promoted and sold?

Activity 1a **Business Concept Statement** continued

Step 3 Evaluate the concept statement for overall effectiveness. Identify ways in which it might be improved.

How effective is the concept statement for Donovan's Detail or Pro-Specialty Advertising?

What suggestions (if any) do you have for its improvement?

Activity 1b   Building My Network

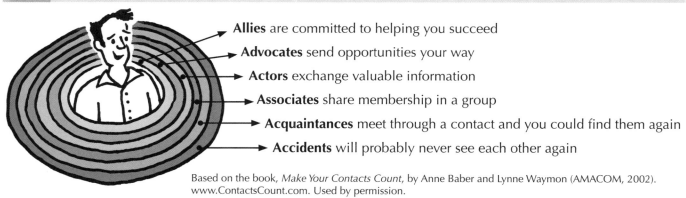

Allies are committed to helping you succeed

Advocates send opportunities your way

Actors exchange valuable information

Associates share membership in a group

Acquaintances meet through a contact and you could find them again

Accidents will probably never see each other again

Based on the book, *Make Your Contacts Count*, by Anne Baber and Lynne Waymon (AMACOM, 2002). www.ContactsCount.com. Used by permission.

Step 1 Introduction Activity. Introduce yourself to nine members of the FastTrac® NewVenture™ class. Since they are members of the class, they are Associates. Your challenge is to teach them as much about you in the time allowed as you can and to develop trust in each other's character and competence.

Name	**E-mail and/or phone**
1.	
2.	
3.	
4.	
5.	
6.	
7.	
8.	
9.	

Step 2 Networking meeting. To develop a more meaningful relationship with Associates, you need to share information, find things in common, and, if possible, identify future areas of mutual benefit.

To that end, during each of the following nine FastTrac® NewVenture™ sessions (prior to session, at break, after session, between sessions) engage a different person listed above in a one-on-one conversation and do the following:
• Share information about yourself, business concept, work experiences, and skills.
• Tell stories that illustrate your character and competence.
• Share resources you know of or have found helpful (i.e. accountants, attorneys, bankers).
• Identify potential areas of mutual benefit.

Action Step 1.1 **Create My Personal Vision**

Establish a personal vision to help me decide what type of business is best for me.

Directions
A. Establish personal criteria. Consider the questions and comments below and write your answers in the space provided to establish your personal criteria.

1. How many hours do you want to work per week during the start-up phase? During the maturity phase? *Most entrepreneurs work well over forty hours each week. Be realistic about your number. The number of hours you want to work and the needs of the customer must mesh.*

2. Do you need flexible work hours? What will take precedence, family or business? *Is flexibility a necessity for you or an added bonus? In most businesses, customers need prompt responses. How much flexibility is necessary for you and your family?*

3. Where is the desired location for the business? *Are you interested in a certain business idea and want to find a location that will support it? Or have you already selected a location and are trying to find a business that will be successful there?*

4. How much would you like to travel for your business? How often and for what duration? *Do you seek travel as part of the business or a perk of the business? Or do you wish to avoid travel altogether? Travel can add both excitement and stress to your life.*

***Action Step* 1.1** **Create My Personal Vision** continued

5. What morals, beliefs, or standards do you hold? *Do you have strong beliefs that will affect the way you do business? Identifying these now will help you build a company that can reflect these beliefs.*

6. What specific physical requirements or restrictions do you have? *Are you looking for physical activity in a business or are you avoiding it? Do you have specific physical or health requirements that need to be considered?*

7. Will your family be involved? Supportive? *Family support can make or break a new business. What support do you expect to receive from family—for example, emotional, financial, time commitment?*

8. What level of income do you need for the lifestyle you desire? *A good starting point is to prepare a personal budget to see what your current lifestyle costs. Consider your dreams, but be realistic about future goals.*

B. Establish professional criteria.

1. What level of power or status is important to you? *How important is it to you to have a sense of power and control? Will your business provide you the recognition and visibility that you desire?*

Action Step 1.1 **Create My Personal Vision** continued

2. How involved do you plan to be in the daily operations of the business? *Do you want to run everything, or do you like to delegate and manage? If you want to be a hands-on entrepreneur, you may be limiting the company's growth potential. How will your involvement change over the course of the business's life?*

3. What type of work do you enjoy? What expertise and skills do you already possess? *Hopefully you will be working in this business for some time to come. It is critical to concentrate on a business that you enjoy and that builds on your expertise.*

4. How important is security? No one plans to fail when starting a business. *Still, you need to think about how important job security is to you. Are you looking for a steady income? Wanting steady work? Build your business with this in mind.*

5. What do you see yourself doing in five years? Ten years? *You are in control of your future. Knowing what you want in the future can help you build a business that will make those dreams come true.*

6. Do you plan to create a growing business or a lifestyle business? To what size do you want your business to grow? *A lifestyle business is limited in size, but can be very emotionally rewarding because it is built to achieve the personal goals of the entrepreneur. A growth business will often put more demands on the entrepreneur, but also creates greater financial rewards when the entrepreneur is ready to exit.*

Action Step 1.1 **Create My Personal Vision** continued

C. Write a vision statement. Keeping in mind the goals you've set for your personal and professional criteria, write a short statement about your personal vision.

Personal Vision

Action Step 1.2 **Develop a Business Concept Statement**

Prepare my business concept statement.

Directions

A. Identify the key components of your business concept. Answer the questions on the Business Concept Development Worksheet to identify the key components of your business concept. In the first column, make notes or general points that you want to include. If you completed the Reality Check *What is My Business Concept?* on p. 16, insert that information. In the second column, write a brief summary of your answers in sentence format. These sentences will be combined to form the final business concept statement. Place a ✔ in the third column if your answer needs additional research.

> **EXAMPLE**

ABC Company provides (1. product/service). ABC product/service is (2. different from competitors). Customers (3. who will buy it) purchase ABC product/service because of (4. benefits). ABC markets it product/service to customers by (5. promotion and sales).

Business Concept Development Worksheet

Answer each question or insert answers from the Reality Check on p. 16.	Summarize your answers in sentence format.	Needs research (✔)
1. WHAT is your product/service and what does it do?		
2. HOW is it different from other products/services available?		
3. WHO will buy it?		
4. WHY will they buy it? • Price • Convenience • Provide sense of safety/security/well-being • Better • Pleasurable experience		
5. HOW will it be promoted and sold?		

Action Step 1.2   Develop a **Business Concept Statement** continued

B. **Determine if the information provided is factual or needs to be researched.** Formulate questions in the box below for each item you checked on p. 31 that needs research. Some items may have more than one question to research. This box will help guide your market research in Module 2 Identifying and Meeting Market Needs.

Items requiring further research

List the questions you identified as needing additional research.

1. Product/Service

2. Uniqueness

3. Customers

4. Benefits

5. Promotions/Sales

Action Step 1.2 **Develop a Business Concept Statement** continued

C. Write the business concept statement. Blend the sentences from the second column on the Business Concept Development Worksheet to form one statement in the Business Concept Statement box below.

Reminders
- Add words or phrases to make the "cut and paste" version and then edit it so it reads clearly and smoothly.
- Keep the statement fewer than 150 words.
- Focus on content at this point more than spelling or grammar. It's the information that's important.

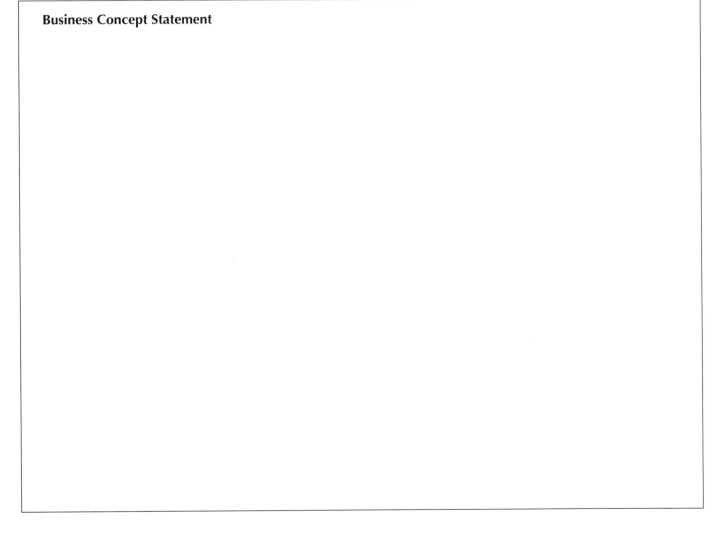

Business Concept Statement

D. Get feedback about your concept statement. The acid test for a well-defined concept statement is to hand it to other people and have them relate it back precisely. Give your concept statement to two people. Ask them to relate back to you the concept as they understand it. After receiving their feedback, make any adjustments to clarify your business concept statement.

33

Action Step 1.3   Evaluate a Business Concept Against My Personal Vision

Decide if this business concept has the potential to fulfill my personal vision.

Directions

A. **Review your personal vision.** Take a minute to review the personal vision you created in Action Step 1.1. Make any changes you feel are necessary to adequately define what success means to you.

B. **Identify non-negotiable criteria.** Read the criteria in the first column of the charts on pp. 35 – 36. If a criterion is non-negotiable for you, check the small box in the corner of the criterion statement. For example, maybe the number of hours you are willing to work per week is critical. A   in the box indicates that this criterion cannot be compromised.

C. **Rate how well the business concept matches your personal vision.** Look closely at the five options across the chart that describe potential responses to each criterion. Circle the number, 1 to 5, that most closely represents your response to that criterion. Be honest!

Action Step 1.3   Evaluate a Business Concept Against My Personal Vision
continued

Personal Criteria	1. Does not meet my personal goal.	2. Somewhat meets my personal goal.	3. Might meet my personal goal.	4. Meets my personal goal very well.	5. Meets my personal goal perfectly.
a. Aspects of owning and operating my own business appeal to me. ☐	1. I am unsure about whether this is a good idea for me. It might not be.	2. I've considered this and believe it might be right for me.	3. The good aspects of owning a business clearly outweigh the negative ones.	4. I'm fairly sure that owning a business is what I would like.	5. I've wanted to own my own business since I was a child.
b. The number of hours per week I will need to work in the business is acceptable. ☐	1. I don't know how I will find the time for this business, given my other commitments.	2. I will need to manage my time better if this is going to be successful.	3. I'm not sure how many hours I will need to work, but I think this will work out.	4. I am fairly confident that the number of hours I will need to work will be acceptable.	5. I will work the number of hours that are needed to succeed.
c. The degree of flexibility of my work hours suits me. ☐	1. I see potential conflicts with the daily routine of this business.	2. I am concerned this schedule may not be right for me.	3. I think the work schedule will be okay.	4. The schedule required for this business will be good for me.	5. I have always dreamed of this type of schedule.
d. I will be able to operate in a location that works well for me. ☐	1. This is a terrible location.	2. The location is not the best.	3. I think this location will work for me.	4. This location should work well.	5. I couldn't ask for a better location.
e. The amount of business travel required matches my desired level of travel. ☐	1. This is way too much/little travel for me.	2. This is probably not the best level of travel for me.	3. The amount of travel is okay.	4. I think I'm looking forward to traveling this much/little.	5. This is my travel dream. Just the right amount.
f. This type of business is in keeping with my morals, beliefs, and standards. ☐	1. I will be embarrassed for people to know I'm doing this.	2. I may have to change my standards for this business to work.	3. I'm not certain how in line with my beliefs this business is.	4. This business is pretty much in line with my morals, beliefs, and standards.	5. This business is in perfect sync with my morals, beliefs, and standards.
g. The physical requirements of the business are within my capability. ☐	1. I don't believe I have the physical strength or stamina for this work.	2. I can probably handle the physical requirements for a little while.	3. I think I have the physical capability this business requires.	4. I am very sure I can handle the physical requirements.	5. The physical requirements of the business appeal to me. I can't wait to start.
h. The level of support I will receive from my family is satisfactory. ☐	1. My family thinks I've lost my mind.	2. My family may come around eventually.	3. My family will probably support me after I get going.	4. My family is always supportive so they will be now also.	5. My family is super supportive and can't wait to help me out.

Action Step 1.3 Evaluate a Business Concept Against My Personal Vision
continued

Professional Criteria	1. Does not meet my professional goal.	2. Somewhat meets my professional goal.	3. Might meet my professional goal.	4. Meets my professional goal very well.	5. Meets my professional goal perfectly.
i. The business will provide me with a level of status and power that I will value. ☐	1. I will probably keep this business a secret. The fewer who know the better.	2. I will probably become accustomed to the step down in status and power.	3. I'm not sure if this provides me any status and/or power.	4. I think I will appreciate the status and power my new business will give me.	5. I have dreamed about this level of status and power. Now I will have it.
j. The amount of time I will need to be involved in daily operations suits me. ☐	1. I never dreamed I'd have to do anything in daily operations.	2. I'm not going to like spending the time needed in daily operations, but I can stand it.	3. I'm not sure how much time I'm going to spend. It might be OK.	4. My time in daily operations will suit me to some extent.	5. The amount of time I will need to be involved in daily operations suits me perfectly.
k. My skills and abilities match those needed to make the business successful. ☐	1. I don't have any skills or ability for this business.	2. I can probably improve my skills to make this business work.	3. My skills and abilities are largely untested.	4. This business is a pretty good match for what I do well.	5. My skills and abilities perfectly match those needed to make the business successful.
l. I will have a sense of job security in my business. ☐	1. I will worry about the lack of job security in my business.	2. I will have minor concerns about job security in my business.	3. I'm not certain how secure I will feel about job security.	4. I will have no worries about job security in my business.	5. I will have a strong sense of job security in my business.
m. I believe that the business will help me reach my long-term goals. ☐	1. I see little connection between this business and my long-term goals.	2. This business may be a little useful in helping me reach my long-term goals.	3. I'm not certain if this business will help me reach my long-term goals.	4. I believe that the business will be somewhat helpful in reaching my long-term goals.	5. I believe that the business will help me tremendously in reaching my long-term goals.
n. The business matches my desire to own a certain type of business, for example, lifestyle or growth. ☐	1. This type of business does not suit me at all.	2. This business is marginally close to the type I would like to have.	3. I don't really know what type of business I would like.	4. This business is very close to the type I would like.	5. The business perfectly matches my desire to own a certain type of business.

Action Step 1.3 **Evaluate a Business Concept Against My Personal Vision**
continued

D. Evaluate how well the business concept matches your personal vision. Pay close attention to whether or not those items you marked with a check as non-negotiable received high scores. If not, is there any way the business concept can be altered to improve its ability to meet your criteria? If such adjustments cannot be made, should you continue to pursue this business concept or search for another? Summarize your results below:

Identifying and Meeting Market Needs

Will your business concept attract enough customers to be a profitable business? How will you know? To provide the best possible basis for success, you will want to become sensitive to the needs, wants, and habits of the market in which you will do business. You can learn to spot trends, observe people, ask questions, and listen to what industries, customers, and competitors are saying and doing. You will research and analyze the market to understand industry characteristics, to determine the typical customer who will purchase your products and services, and to gain insight into the competitive climate of your industry.

This module explores strategies for identifying and evaluating opportunities for business start-up and growth. You will learn how to research industry characteristics, develop a customer profile, and identify your potential competitors. Throughout this program you will analyze and refine the information you collect to confirm or modify your business concept. You will use market research as a basis for many business decisions—from product promotion and distribution to pricing and projecting sales.

Key Questions
- How do I identify potential business opportunities?
- Does my business concept represent an opportunity in the marketplace?
- What is market research and why is it important for my business concept?
- What information do I collect for my market research?

Action Steps   **Due Date**
❏ 2.1 Conduct Market Research   _____
❏ 2.2 Evaluate and Refine My Business Concept   _____
❏ Read Module 3 Setting Financial Goals   _____
❏ _____   _____
❏ _____   _____
❏ _____   _____

Recognizing Opportunities

TIP Make a list of daily nuisances that you and others experience. Then, brainstorm creative solutions to these irritations and inefficiencies to uncover hidden opportunities.

Where others see problems and chaos, entrepreneurs see opportunities. Entrepreneurs are quick to identify an unmet need or want in the marketplace and provide a product or service that meets it. This skill in scanning the marketplace and identifying needs and gaps is a discriminating characteristic of successful entrepreneurs. You need to develop it.

Innovative businesses are springing up all around. Do you ever ask yourself, "I wonder how they came up with that idea?" Successful businesses are continually changing their product or service lines and moving into new markets. Opportunity recognition is a continual process throughout the life of a business.

For More Information about common entry and exit strategies, go to www.fasttrac.org/toolkits.

While you are identifying and evaluating opportunities for your business, you may want to consider common entry and exit strategies used by many entrepreneurs. In addition to the various ways to start a new business, you may also want to consider buying an existing business or a franchise. Smart entrepreneurs not only plan their entry into the market, but also their exit. Some choose to build wealth in a company to sell it. Others may plan to pass it on to their children. By considering how and when you would like to exit your business, you force yourself to analyze what you really want from a business. Your exit will make a difference in the choices you make, from the type of business you start to how you grow it.

Identifying Problems and Needs

Some of the best entrepreneurial opportunities come by identifying a market need or solving a problem for customers. You may be able to identify problems or needs based on your personal experiences and observations of those around you. Jenny Craig, founder of Jenny Craig, Inc.®, weight management centers, stated, "What really started me off in this business was my own research into what kinds of food I should be eating." Likewise, Joseph and Judy Roetheli discovered a market need when trying to treat their dog's halitosis. The product they created, Greenies®, a breath-freshening pet treat, is now sold in more than forty-four countries. You may uncover needs by listening to customers in your business or industry.

TIP *Keep on the lookout for novel and interesting ideas that others have used successfully. Your idea must be original only in its adaptation to the problem you are working on.* — Thomas Edison

Lifestyle or business problems present entrepreneurial opportunities. Can you provide a product or service better, more quickly, or less costly? People are perpetually looking for cost-effective solutions to their problems. Entrepreneurs are solution-oriented and good listeners. They are troubleshooters and uncover ideas that will make people's lives easier, more economical, or more pleasurable.

Stay-at-home mom Tamara Monosoff had a toddler with a knack for unwinding toilet paper. A former business consultant, Monosoff turned the problem into an opportunity by inventing a special latch to keep the paper rolled up. The TP Saver® may not sound glamorous, but it's profitable. Monosoff projects more than $1 million in annual sales for Mom Inventors, Inc.®, her Walnut Creek, California, company.

What is important to people today? What are their priorities? Current and potential customers can provide a wealth of information. Ask open-ended questions to discover consumer dissatisfaction with current products and services. Use their answers to create a product or service that meets their needs.

Studying Industries, Markets, and Competition

The more you know about the marketplace and industry in which you operate, the better able you are to identify gaps, needs, and unfulfilled wants. You will gain an edge over the competition by developing many of these habits:

Look for growth industries – Growth industries experience rapidly expanding customer demand. One advantage in a growth industry is that in many cases not enough time has elapsed for a lot of competition to develop. Position yourself in an industry that is going to grow rapidly in the next decade or so.

> **TiP** You cannot be creative in a vacuum. Understanding your industry releases creativity.

Peter Click was among the first U.S. importers of Australian boutique wines. Click fell in love with Australian wines while working at a wine shop in Australia. He later took a six-month "walkabout" to explore Australian vineyards and launched the Click Wine Group in 1987. Although business was difficult at first, his Seattle, Washington, company has grown quickly. The Click Wine Group now generates more than $25 million in sales.

Examine new knowledge – Scan trade journals, browse in the library, and talk to people in your industry to discover what is new and exciting. Ask questions about other organizations, markets, products or services, and challenges. New knowledge often results in rethinking old ways and inventing different ways of packaging, delivering, or marketing products or services.

Study the competition – Find out what the competition is doing. Careful gathering and analyzing of competitive data is known as *market intelligence*. What are competitors doing right? What are their weaknesses? Before launching a new business, scour the marketplace to see who is already there and ask industry experts, customers, and suppliers about present and possible rivals.

Read constantly – Plan to spend a significant amount of time reading and scanning publications. Entrepreneurs read intuitively, looking for what is different, new, and exciting. They read publications outside of their own industry as well as major metropolitan newspapers and local business journals, which cover community developments and trends in local markets.

> **TiP** One study revealed that innovators often spend as much as a third of their business day just reading.

Use commercial research – Leading sources include Dun & Bradstreet® and the Risk Management Association® (RMA). Business reference librarians, such as those at the James J. Hill Reference Library in Minneapolis, Minnesota, or your local library can provide assistance in finding these and additional research sources. Many commercial research companies charge a fee for research services. The second half of this module is designed to help you get comfortable with conducting market research.

Many first-time entrepreneurs mistakenly believe that if they build a better mousetrap, customers will flock to their door. Battle-scarred veterans have learned the hard way that building a business is all about listening to the marketplace and giving the market what it wants.

Researching Demographics, Lifestyles, and Habits

Changes in tastes, lifestyles, and habits are constant and volatile. By anticipating and responding quickly to such changes, you greatly increase your chances of having a successful business. Demographic and lifestyle changes are constantly evolving, but often their consequences are not readily apparent. You will be able to anticipate many potential opportunities years in advance by studying changes, such as the aging baby boom population, ethnic shifts, and movements of populations to different geographic areas.

Consider these ways to find market information:

𝖳𝗂𝗉 *You can observe a lot just by watching.* — Yogi Berra

Monitor demographic changes – Population statistics change more rapidly today than in the past. For example, Peter Francese of American Demographics, Inc.®, points out that the fastest-growing age group in America is people eighty-five years or older. For this market, assisted-living centers, recreational activities, and delivery services are fertile ground for new opportunities.

Engage in people watching – Watching people's behavior and listening to conversations provide ideas on needs and desires in the marketplace. Successful entrepreneurs are excellent people watchers. For example, at social functions entrepreneurs do more than make small talk. They use the occasion as an informal focus group, asking questions and listening to others. These questions help identify opportunities.

Reverse Marketing

Sally Smith and a business partner in Iowa used a research process called *reverse marketing* to identify their business opportunity. Instead of developing a product or service and then determining its distribution and audience, Smith scrutinized the marketplace first. "The idea was to identify what people wanted to buy and work backward from the delivery point," Smith explains. "I started with the consumer group I knew best—baby boomers—because I was one of them."

She began reading voraciously—everything from newspapers and trade publications to trend books like *The Popcorn Report*. She interviewed successful CEOs of large companies and talked to members of trade associations, economic development agencies, and chambers of commerce.

As she researched, certain facts grabbed Smith's attention. For example, the mail-order industry was experiencing significantly higher growth than traditional bricks-and-mortar retailing. Drilling down deeper, Smith discovered that food was the best-selling category for catalogers. Then she looked at large, privately held companies selling through direct mail, which included Omaha Steaks®, Harry and David®, and The Honey Baked Ham Co.® "The dots began to connect," Smith says. "They were shipping meat, and here I was, sitting in a state known for its pork."

Next, Smith visited the National Pork Producers' Association to find out why no one was selling pork through catalogs. "They gave me a long list of reasons why it couldn't be done, but they also told me something else," Smith says. "The industry was about to kick off a $10 million advertising campaign, 'The Other White Meat,' to boost the image of pork." More dots connected as Smith saw how she could benefit from those marketing dollars.

The Iowa Pork Producers Association® had trademarked a specific cut of pork known as the "Iowa Chop," which gave Smith the signature product she needed for an exclusive mail-order meat business. It also sparked the company's name, Chops of Iowa.

Launched in 1989 in Des Moines, Chops of Iowa was so successful that it acquired its own USDA plant at the end of its second year. Four years after starting the business, Smith and her partner were ready to deploy their exit strategy and sold Chops of Iowa to a regional corporation—one that Smith had identified during her initial research process.

"Quantify and qualify everything you can through research," Smith says. You may have a gut instinct about something, but validate that hunch through research. And conversely, validate research findings through your feelings. When you are looking for opportunities, "Head and heart go hand in hand," Smith stresses. "They complement and support each other."

Travel the information superhighway – Online information provides a great source for the latest information in various industries. Spot new trends on the Internet, exchange information on electronic bulletin boards, and shop various e-commerce sites. Helpful online resources include the James J. Hill Reference Library at www.jjhill.org and the Ewing Marion Kauffman Foundation's eVenturing site at www.eventuring.org.

Keeping an eye on lifestyles and consumer habits can lead you to a good idea or help you refine one you already have. The activities and action steps in this module are designed to show you how to monitor the market for opportunities.

Watching Trends

Success as an entrepreneur is related to your ability to spot trends. The long-term staying power of trends distinguishes them from fads, which are of much shorter duration. The secret of this technique is watching the media, the Internet, and professional journals for recurring themes and emerging behaviors. Attending trade shows is another way to keep abreast of trends in an industry. Simple activities such as scanning junk mail for clues about new products and noting the best-selling nonfiction books may provide information on trends you can develop into opportunities.

Look for trends through these resources:

- **Trade and industry associations** – Review trade and industry information and join associations and conventions that serve your industry.
- **Other entrepreneurs** – Having already taken the entrepreneurial leap themselves, these individuals have proven their ability to identify business opportunities and are typically very alert to industry changes and marketplace needs.
- **Vendors and suppliers** – Through their close work with customers, vendors and suppliers become a valuable resource for information about new products and services as well as customers' unmet needs.
- **Entrepreneur's infrastructure** (accountants, lawyers, bankers) – These professionals can provide valuable information about changes or the latest trends affecting their industries and the marketplace.
- **Various governmental agencies** – The government has a host of agencies whose mission is to collect and report information on the economy and society. Others provide valuable assistance to entrepreneurs launching and growing businesses.
- **Professors and business librarians** – These professionals stay current in their specific fields and often have in-depth knowledge of trends and problems in their area of study.

Some recent market trends that affect businesses include emerging technology, outsourcing, working at home, time scarcity, shifting interest in sports, and obesity.

Your personal network can be another vital source of industry information. If you maintain good relationships with people throughout the business community, they may lead you to market opportunities you might not find on your own.

For More Information

on trends that impact your life and business go to www.fasttrac.org/toolkits.

Reality Check ✓   **Recognizing Opportunity**

Does my business concept come from one or more of the following opportunities?

- ❏ Solving a problem
- ❏ Identifying a need
- ❏ Studying the market
- ❏ Learning industry characteristics
- ❏ Responding to competition

- ❏ Researching demographic trends
- ❏ Being sensitive to lifestyle changes
- ❏ Supporting emerging consumer habits
- ❏ Watching emerging trends

If not, how do I describe the source of my business concept and how do I know it is a sound business opportunity?

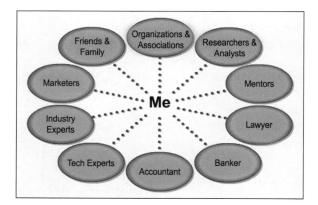

Mining Personal Contacts. Building a network of people to provide information and feedback is a great way to identify trends. Understand that it takes persistence to build this network. It may take several meetings to fully acquaint advisers with your situation.

Establishing a Personal Network

Successful entrepreneurs build a network or team of people to serve as mentors and advisers throughout the life of their business. This network provides insights and information concerning the business's market or industry. You can build such a network through industry and trade associations, professional and business organizations, interactions with service providers (accountants, attorneys, and bankers), and suppliers.

Mentors and advisers – Sometimes you work so intently on the intricacies of your business that you may lack a broader perspective of the business environment in which you operate. A network of mentors and advisers is key in providing you a more general and objective point of view.

When you need a mentor, search professional associations and civic groups for people whose skills and expertise you respect. A mentor can provide objective business advice, open doors to new opportunities, introduce you to people and necessary resources, and critique your performance.

It will probably take six to eight meetings to become thoroughly acquainted with potential mentors or advisers. Once they are familiar with you, the challenge will be to get them to relate your abilities to new opportunities in the marketplace. The best way to encourage people to help you is to help them first.

Other professionals – Establishing a network of professionals who provide you state-of-the-art information is also an excellent way to spot trends and opportunities. Such a network helps you scan the environment for opportunities and provides helpful feedback concerning them.

As you can imagine, staying engaged in your community, industry, and market to spot opportunities requires a great deal of energy. So that you do not waste time and effort, learn how to evaluate the opportunities you see to determine their fit with your personal vision and current business concept. Module 7 discusses how you can transition some members of your personal network into valuable management team members or infrastructure for your business.

Reality Check ✓

Personal Network

Who in your personal network would be helpful in identifying potential opportunities? List their names below.

Evaluating Opportunities

Since many ideas are not business opportunities, take time to determine which ideas fit you and your goals and whether you can develop them into a feasible business.

Sometimes this process is somewhat random and informal. Other times, it may be very analytical. Perhaps you have already discarded one or more of your original ideas because you questioned their personal fit and market viability.

The careful pursuit and evaluation of business opportunities takes patience. Evaluating business opportunities is like panning for gold. The prospector starts with a shallow pan full of mud, pebbles, and river water. The gold is heavier so it sinks to the bottom. He carefully watches for gold while he swirls the pan in circles allowing mud and worthless rocks to spill out over the side. If he is careless, the gold will spill out with the mud. If he is observant, he will be awarded with gold flakes in the bottom of his pan.

Spend some time evaluating each idea on your shortlist—those ideas you are most passionate about and you feel have the greatest potential to succeed. By doing so, you will develop a better idea of the overall suitability of each as a potential business venture. Some tough decisions arise throughout the evaluation process, but the process itself is not hard.

TIP Don't eliminate opportunities too early in the process. You may pass up a really promising idea without giving it adequate consideration.

Harry Vardis, founder and president of Creative Focus, Inc.®, advises entrepreneurs to set aside a specific time to brainstorm—and a different time to evaluate those ideas. Don't mix the two or you may be discarding valuable seeds before you know what they might grow to be.

Your evaluation process should include these factors:

Match with current concept – You already have a specific concept in mind. In evaluating additional ideas, consider their match with your original idea. If they don't match, you might still find some value in the new idea, but you must decide whether to abandon the old and go with the new or stick with the plan and shelve the new idea for later.

Fit with personal vision – Each potential business opportunity must be assessed against your personal vision. For a business to provide long-term satisfaction, it needs to meet your personal goals.

You evaluated your business concept against your personal vision in Action Step 1.3. This evaluation provides the first litmus test of whether or not your business idea is right for you. When you consider additional ideas, repeat this process with each.

TIP Be willing to let go of opportunities that don't meet your personal vision. A great opportunity for someone else may not bring you success as you have measured it.

Talents and skills – A look at the match between your talent and skills and those required in the proposed business venture will help you determine how easy it will be for you to start your business. If the new venture requires a significant amount of learning, the timeline for starting it will be longer and the possibility of mistakes greater. You can overcome personal gaps in skills or knowledge by putting together a team to help you launch the business.

Risks and rewards – A certain amount of risk is involved in all entrepreneurial ventures. The risks vary greatly depending on the type of business you wish to start. Are the risks acceptable to you? Do the rewards compensate for the risks? Astute entrepreneurs take calculated risks and reduce the risk factor by researching and planning their business concepts, industries, and markets. As we discussed in Module 1, you can reduce risk by starting small, perhaps in your home, to test your concept.

As an entrepreneur, you will invest a great deal of time, energy, talent, and money into a business. As with other investors, you need to evaluate the potential return on your investment.

Competitive advantage – To stand out from the crowd, businesses need a competitive advantage. Competitive advantage is achieved when a business has an edge over the competition through price, quality, or superior products or services. Having a competitive advantage means that your customers will choose to buy from you rather than from competitors. Achieving a sustainable competitive advantage is what every business strives for because without it your business has limited opportunities for growth.

Does your business concept have the potential to create a competitive advantage in the marketplace based on price, quality, or superiority? If not, you should be wary of such an endeavor. Your market research, discussed later in this module, will provide additional information about your competitive environment and enable to you determine your competitive advantage more specifically. We will discuss competitive advantage as it relates to your business concept and Marketing Plan in more detail in Module 5.

Durability – Will the opportunity last long enough for you to seize it and reap its rewards? How quickly will the window of opportunity remain open? These factors make a significant difference in determining the attractiveness of a venture. For example, a business based on a long-term trend, such as a changing demographic, has an enduring window of opportunity.

When you compare the history of the industry to its current size and future growth potential, you will learn a great deal about its stability. Comparisons are particularly helpful in established industries such as finance and retail. Be wary of making assumptions about industries with relatively short and volatile histories, such as information technology.

Growth potential – Does your long-term strategy include growing your business in revenue, size, and/or locations? Although many entrepreneurs start out with a small business in mind, this vision often grows with the business. Assessing growth potential at the onset makes the possibility of growth more likely when you are ready to pursue it.

You may now be asking yourself, "How will I know?" How do other entrepreneurs find out about the risks and rewards involved in their business? How do they learn about the industry and its potential for growth? How do they establish their competitive advantage, compile a customer profile, or identify and analyze their competition? For all these questions, the answer is the same: *Research*.

If you are not already an industry expert or marketing professional, you can catch up by conducting market research on your business idea, its industry, customers, and competition.

TIP Looking for a new, rapidly growing industry to succeed as an entrepreneur? So is everyone else. Consider industries with steady, long-term growth prospects and a clear market need.

Reality Check ✓   Business Idea Evaluation

Answer the following questions for each business opportunity you have identified that successfully matches your personal vision. Although you may not be able to answer these questions with 100 percent certainty, answer to the best of your ability. As you gain additional information through market research, you will be able to answer with greater confidence. You may wish to revisit this evaluation later.

Business Idea: _____

	Circle One	
a. Does this idea match or complement my original business concept?	Yes	No
b. Does this idea fit my personal vision?	Yes	No
c. Do I have the talents and skills to implement this idea (or the ability to put together a team to do so)?	Yes	No
d. Are the risks associated with this type of venture acceptable to me?	Yes	No
e. Are the rewards (intrinsic: personal growth, satisfaction, self expression, and extrinsic: financial, recognition) adequate to offset the risks associated with the venture?	Yes	No
f. Will I be able to obtain a competitive advantage in the marketplace?	Yes	No
g. Is the window of opportunity for starting and growing the venture sufficient in length?	Yes	No
h. Does the idea allow for possible future growth?	Yes	No

Based on your responses to questions a – h, determine whether this business idea should be pursued further. Circle *Go*, indicating you plan to continue with this idea, or *No Go*, indicating that this idea should not be pursued further.

                                                 Go   No Go

Understanding Market Research

Simply stated, *market research* is defined as the process of gathering data on goods and services to determine whether the product or service will satisfy customers' needs. Market research can identify market trends, demographics, economic shifts, customer's buying habits, and important information on competition. You will utilize this information to define your target markets and establish a competitive advantage in the marketplace. For market research to be useful, the information must be timely and relevant to your business.

TIP Applying for business loans, designing marketing campaigns, or building your customer base will be easier with market research than without it.

A successful new venture sells customers goods and services they want or need and continually grows a base of satisfied customers. Hundreds of thousands of people consider starting new businesses each year, and each of them will ask themselves the same questions: Does my product or service fill a need? Who will buy my product or service? What will my price point be? What are the trends in my industry? Who are my competitors?

This information isn't just interesting or "nice to know." Rather, it is essential information to guide you in making strategic business decisions. By gathering research about your business concept, industry, potential customers, and competitors, you can uncover or verify unmet customer needs in the marketplace, and, many times, discover new ideas for products or services. Market research can provide you with value that should exceed the time and cost of the research itself. It can help you minimize your financial risks by determining if your product or service will succeed or fail in the marketplace, and perhaps save you from making costly mistakes.

Market research helps you to:
- **Communicate effectively** to your target markets through advertising and promotions. By researching your customers and their spending and buying habits, you can create marketing campaigns to meet their specific interests and needs.
- **Identify and understand opportunities** that exist in the marketplace. For example, through preliminary market research, you might find an opportunity to start your business in a geographic location you had not considered before, where little or no competition exists for your product or service.
- **Pinpoint potential obstacles or problems** with your business concept. Through research, you may uncover direct or indirect competitors you had not considered before who may inhibit your ability to gain a competitive advantage in the market. You might also discover future development plans that could include big-box retailers in your target market location. This information is important to discover because it can help to **minimize your short-term and long-term financial risks**.
- **Benchmark and evaluate your success.** By knowing the size of your market, how your competitors are doing and who their customers are, you can set goals to reach your market, grow your customer base, and track how you are doing in relation to the competition.

TIP Start early to conduct your research. It frequently takes more time than you anticipated.

Consider this example of how research can lead you to a market opportunity: The idea for PROTEC® came to founder Michael Matthews while he was a police officer attending law school. Researching a paper in employment law, he learned about the high cost to employers of employee liability lawsuits and rapid changes in employment law. Thinking there might be a demand for employee screening services, he spent seven months interviewing employers, studying competitors, and researching public record and law databases. Today, his firm keeps clients abreast of their employee obligations and verifies prospective employees' Social Security number, criminal history, motor vehicle records, civil record, and much more. Because he took the time to research the market, competitors, and relevant legal issues, Matthews was able to develop a feasible idea into a successful business.

You may have already started doing market research when you came up with your business concept. You recognized some need or opportunity in the market that prompted you to develop and move forward with a business idea. Keep in mind that you will continue to analyze the market as you plan, start, and grow your business. Success depends on a lot of things, but when you have collected information on your industry, customers, and competitors, you will be better prepared to make strategic decisions and drive your business forward.

Whether you are buying an existing business and looking to expand into new markets or introducing a new product or service, primary and secondary market research will provide you with valuable information to help you develop a strong Marketing Plan.

Primary Research

Primary research is data collected specifically for your business. It is obtained by observing or communicating with customers or competitors. Primary research data could be collected through **surveys**, **interviews**, **focus groups**, or direct **observation** of potential and existing customers, and similar businesses in the industry. The information can provide insights into customers' needs or perceptions, the benefits of a product or service, packaging or delivery options, or other information you need.

Some entrepreneurs hire market research firms to conduct this research. Since primary research involves watching or talking with a number of people, tabulating results, and then determining insights, outsourcing the task might be costly. You might prefer firsthand knowledge of the data as it is collected. You can conduct primary research yourself. Instead of paying someone else for the time and know-how, you can develop your own research tools, initiate contact with potential participants, and perform research tasks.

You will begin gathering data in this module, and you will learn to analyze that data in Module 5. Here are some primary research techniques you may want to use:

Surveys – A common, inexpensive, and effective way to collect primary research data is by using customer surveys. They give feedback about a product or service through questions people answer in person, over the telephone, by mail, by fax, or via the Internet. You can survey customers to learn about their needs, problems, and opinions regarding your proposed product or service. The information you gather using this technique is current and helpful for determining whether a market for a new product or service exists. Also, surveys can result in future sales by giving potential customers a preview of the product or service.

TiP Test your survey with a small group first. Testing often reveals unclear questions that do not gather the type of information you are seeking.

Interviews – Conducting interviews is similar to using customer surveys and is usually done over the phone or in person. Individual interviews are usually no longer than thirty minutes, although they may be longer if participants are willing. Because interviews involve more dialogue between the researcher and participants, this research technique will provide you with in-depth responses and the most relevant information.

TIP When conducting a survey or an interview, avoid leading questions or biased presentations that may result in skewed answers and unreliable data.

Here are some steps for using a customer survey or interviews:

Step 1 Determine your goals by asking what you want to find out and deciding how you will use this information.

Step 2 Select key questions that will give you valuable information for your research. Questions should focus on customers' needs, their preferences on product or service features and benefits, pricing, location, marketing sources, or buying behaviors. Consider these examples of survey or interview questions:

- If two restaurants are located close together, what makes you choose one over the other?
- What is your favorite grocery, retail store, or bookstore? Why do you enjoy shopping there?
- Which companies do you refuse to do business with? Why?
- Who do you buy this product from? What do you like best about buying from that company?

Step 3 Decide which method is best for collecting the data you need. If you have a small number of people to reach, perhaps twenty or fewer, you might choose to conduct surveys or interviews by phone or in person. If you want to reach more people, you might consider conducting a survey by Internet or fax. The complexity of the questions will determine the best method for gathering information from your target market.

If the sequence of later questions can be determined by how customers respond to previous ones, then surveys conducted over the Internet work well. For example, if you want feedback on customers' preferences, an Internet survey site allows customers to post comments about products or respond to an online questionnaire. Depending on how they respond to specific questions, the software pulls up subsequent questions. If you need to see their reactions to a product or service, then you need in-person contact. For example a live taste-test booth could be set up in a shopping area where customers could sample products and provide feedback to a researcher.

For More Information
about surveys and interviews go to www.fasttrac.org/toolkits.

Step 4 Summarize and evaluate the information gathered. Determine if similar responses indicate a trend within your market. Take into account respondents' motives for taking the survey, the time allotted, incentives offered, and other factors that may affect the validity of the answers.

Focus groups – Focus groups can provide marketing insights while identifying the hidden needs of potential customers. This popular research technique is used to collect information from a group of people instead of using a one-to-one approach. Focus groups allow you to collect more information in the same amount of time at a fairly reasonable cost. You also get different data due to the interaction among participants than through individual approaches.

You can benefit from using this research technique, especially when identifying niche markets and learning more about a specific group of customers. You can also gain valuable insights to forecast future markets. Keep in mind, however, that the viewpoints of a small number of people in a focus group may not always reflect attitudes of the market as a whole. Be sure you include a large enough cross section of your market in the focus group.

Use these steps to conduct a focus group:

Step 1 Determine your goals for the focus group by deciding how you will use the information you are seeking.

Step 2 Develop questions to ask participants and an agenda for the focus group(s).

Step 3 Invite focus group participants who have demographics similar to your customer profile.

Step 4 Plan the logistics for conducting the session.
- Schedule the focus group meeting at a convenient time for participants. A typical focus group takes about one to two hours.
- Find a meeting room or relaxed atmosphere to ensure an informal discussion of participants' opinions and feelings.
- Find an unbiased, skilled moderator to lead the group. The moderator asks broad questions at the beginning and then focuses the group discussion on the specific information you want to obtain. Moderators can skillfully probe the group, stressing the importance of sharing different points of view and emphasizing that there is no right or wrong answer.

Step 5 Use a data collection source that doesn't interfere with the discussion. It is best to record or videotape the focus group discussion. You can then analyze and interpret feedback from participants and compare it to your business concept and other market research.

Reality Check ✓ | **Finding Focus Group Members**

Who are five to ten people currently in my network (for example, family, friends, business colleagues, church members, club members) who are similar to potential customers?

List them here:

_____   _____   _____

_____   _____   _____

_____   _____   _____

_____   _____   _____

The people on this list could become your first focus group!

Observation – The observation research technique is used to collect customers' reactions and behaviors without actually talking with them. This technique is most valuable when you want to learn how customers approach products or services without the potential bias of a researcher. Customers react normally because they think no one else is watching. For example, if customers in a restaurant were given a complimentary slice of cheesecake to try out a new brand, research observers could record initial reactions when customers taste the cheesecake that indicate whether or not they seem to enjoy it. Observation was the basis for the popular television show, *Candid Camera*, in which customers were exposed to a pre-determined scenario or situation while being videotaped.

TIP Get in the habit of continually researching customers' needs and opinions. You will gain clarity and purpose to guide your business through intense competition in an ever-changing marketplace.

Secondary Research

Secondary research is information already gathered for another business or purpose. This research is the easiest and least expensive to use since it is gathered and shared by other people. Examples of secondary research include information from magazine articles, books, publications, trade journals, libraries, or data collected by the Census Bureau or chambers of commerce. This information may be available in print or online. Information collected usually focuses on industry trends, customer demographics, and spending habits. If you expand your business into different markets or offer new services as part of a current business, secondary research can be very valuable.

Tip If you are not comfortable using technology for research, rely on advice from other entrepreneurs, business librarians, and researchers who have experience researching in this manner.

Secondary research sources are not usually available in real-time. Sometimes information is not available for months or even a year after it is collected. Depending on when the information was collected and your purpose for the research, it may not be relevant for your business. If you have a new product or service or a niche market, secondary research information may not be available. Working with a research professional, such as a reference librarian, you can determine which sources have the most bearing on your research needs. In some rare cases, you may find that conducting primary research is the only means to collect relevant information for your business concept.

Some timely secondary research is available electronically on Web sites or in electronic databases. Looking for information on the Web, however, can require a huge time commitment. Do not waste time "surfing" for information without a plan for what you are looking for. If you don't know where to look, how to access information, or what information would be helpful, ask a librarian, a colleague in your industry, or a resource person at the Small Business Development Center. You can save time by preparing your research approach before sitting down at the computer.

Types of Research	Advantages	Disadvantages
Primary Data	• Deliver specific results that can be very important when you launch a new product/service. • Are usually the most timely and relevant to your business.	• May be difficult to gather since your competitors might not want to share information or customers are hard to reach. • Can be time-consuming and costly to send out surveys, conduct interviews, or host focus groups.
Secondary Data	• Can be relatively inexpensive. • May be easy to access via the Internet or trade associations.	• Might not be the most up-to-date or exactly relevant to your business. • May not always be specific enough.

It's Not All in Their Heads

It took nine months for two former Microsoft® employees to create the hottest new board game since   . Their business idea developed due to market research in a few key areas.

First, the founders recognized that a lot of intellectual capital was going into online, PC, or PlayStation®-style games instead of the board game market. Second, board games go back centuries and have endured many different competitive threats. This history gave the brainiacs confidence that board games are here to stay. Finally, when researching start-up costs, they found the level of capital required to launch a board game was significantly less than the investment required to get into the high-tech video-game industry.

When beginning primary and secondary research to flush out the concept of their "whole brain" game, the two soaked up as much knowledge as they could about the history of social games, comparing their findings against the criteria for their game. Their conclusion was to develop a left brain/right brain game, but neither knew much about the hypothesis, so they began researching the field of intellectual psychology. They discovered a Harvard researcher named Howard Gardner whose *Theory of Multiple Intelligences* explores eight core competencies in which people demonstrate intelligence, such as linguistic, mathematical, and spatial. This research became the design framework for the game *Cranium*.

The inventors identified a number of occupations that people might pursue if they are gifted in one of Gardner's intelligences. They then broke down the findings into subject matters or areas of interest that those same people would be exceptionally strong in, ensuring each player a moment to shine. In total, they came up with fourteen different activities, each one innovative in its own right.

Cranium's target audience is made up of individuals between the ages of twenty-five and thirty-five, with an attractive disposable income. Research shows that this demographic group seems to have a natural social tendency to play games such as *Cranium* and *Pictionary*. The company has spent zero dollars on marketing efforts and indicates the most effective selling tool is sitting down and playing the game. The time and energy they spent on market research in the beginning resulted in a product that nearly sells itself.

Market research can provide you with information about your industry—its current size, growth potential, and general operational patterns. Market research can also tell you about customer characteristics in a particular market segment and about how your target market spends money. It can reveal motivational patterns and other psychological aspects of your target market, including customer perceptions, values, and opinions. Market research also provides you with information about your competitors and how economic, political, or environmental trends in the marketplace could affect your business.

TiP Market research provides the basis for many decisions that affect a company's financial outcomes.

Whichever style of market research you opt for—and you should consider a blend of several approaches—you need to focus on the value of the information, its accuracy, and relevance to your business concept. Many key business decisions will be based on the information you gather.

Collecting the Right Data

Knowing how to conduct market research and what information to collect will save you time. Gathering the right market data will be integral to building a successful Business Plan and helping you identify your competitive advantage, which we will discuss in later modules. You will collect data based on variables that will help you understand your industry, your customers, and your competition. By following the steps outlined in this program, you can feel confident that you have gathered valuable data about your business concept to determine if it has a high probability of success before you commit time and financial resources.

These market research steps should help you with this process:

1. **Brainstorm your business concept or opportunity.** You've already started this step in Module 1.
2. **Set research goals.** What do you wish to prove? It's helpful to frame your research goal as a question you are seeking to answer. For example, ask: "Is my business concept feasible from a market perspective?
3. **Identify the information** you need to answer your research question by generating a list of additional questions that should be answered. For example, "Does my business concept solve a problem or fulfill a need in the market?" or "How does my concept compare with others like it in the market?"
4. **Research primary and secondary sources.** Check the information you gather against your original research question.
5. **Analyze and interpret the data collected.** This step will help you identify trends, similarities, and contradictions in the data. Check the research question against analyzed data. You will use this analysis to create your Marketing Plan.

The first step of the research process is to brainstorm your business concept or opportunity. You have already done some of that in Module 1. Step 2, setting research goals, is often overlooked; yet it is essential to the success of your research endeavor. Research goals typically relate to solving a problem, evaluating an opportunity, or planning for the future. Time spent at this step can save hours down the road as you gather and analyze data. What do you need to know? What information do you need for accurate decision-making?

In setting research goals, consider the information you will use to determine if your business concept is feasible. The next three sections identify the kind of information you may be looking for about your industry, competition, and customer. You will analyze this market information in Module 5 and use it to complete your Marketing Plan in Module 6. The remainder of this module gives you some practical suggestions for finding the information you need.

Industry Profile

To conduct business in your industry successfully, you should know the industry's size, potential for growth and profitability, notable trends unique to your industry, typical distribution channels, and other information that will help you stay competitive.

Current size – Knowing the current size of your industry can help you place your new business in its larger context. It can help you determine whether this industry is growing, stabilizing, or declining. You can compare its current size with historical information to find this out. You may not find answers to all of these questions on your specific industry, but they are worth asking:

- How many similar companies exist nationally, regionally, and locally?
- How does the current size of the industry compare to historical figures from five or ten years ago?
- How many companies do business primarily or exclusively on the Internet?
- How many companies do business internationally?
- What are the total dollars spent, or the total units consumed, by buyers nationally, regionally, and locally?

Growth potential – A study of the history and current size of your industry may reveal a great deal about the opportunities as well. Historical comparisons are helpful in established industries such as finance and retail, because they reflect how the industry has grown over time.

Beth Marcus started researching different industries that might benefit from a glow-in-the-dark fabric called IllumiNite®. When her research indicated the opportunity in the four-legged market, Marcus started Glow Dog, Inc.® Glow Dog entered the growing pet supplies and services industry and now has a hundred wholesale customers, including PETsMART®, the largest pet superstore in the country.

Don't miss the double-edged issues of industries with relatively short and volatile histories: potentially hidden risks and rewards lurk in a market without sufficient industry information. In some rapidly changing industries, such as technology, the double-edged issues may be unavoidable. You should conduct careful research and analysis to offset the higher risks.

Consider these questions to research industry growth:
- What is the growth pattern for the industry? Is it growing, declining, or remaining stable?
- What factors attribute to this growth potential?

Profitability – You can evaluate your business's potential to succeed financially by reviewing your industry's profit characteristics. It's important to know an industry's historical and expected gross margins and net profits. You will learn in Module 3 that *gross margin* is a measurement of the profit you retain after you deduct direct costs of your products or services from sales. *Net profit* is the amount of money available from sales after all costs and expenses have been paid.

Asking these questions can help you find out about your industry's profit expectations:
- What factors contribute to profit in this industry?
- What are the industry's standards for gross margin and net profit percentages?
- What factors affect gross margin and net profit?

Industry trends – Understanding trends specific to your industry helps you identify opportunities for starting and expanding your business within it. These trends may be based on seasonality, economic fluctuations, or customer demographics, such as aging populations or baby booms. For example, retailers tend to see an increase in sales during specific holidays such as Valentine's, Mother's Day, and Christmas. Movie theatres experience their busiest seasons during summer months and the holiday break between Christmas and New Year's. Most new movie releases occur during these busy seasons. These purchasing trends will affect how you plan for cash flow and marketing campaigns, so you need to learn what to expect from your industry.

TiP Weather can affect some industries. Popular resorts in the hospitality industry depend on the weather to attract vacationers to ski lodges or sandy beaches.

Industries may also have a direct or indirect impact upon one another. For instance, bank interest rate increases or decreases affect investment and real estate industries. Consider which other industries play an important role in your industry and how they might affect trends.

Consider these questions about trends as you research your industry:
- What are the primary trends in the industry?
- What trends in outside forces such as seasonality, economic fluctuations, demographics, or changes in other industries might affect this industry?
- What opportunities and threats do these trends create?

Do not merely collect information about your industry as if you were completing an assignment. Draw conclusions about what the information means to you and your business. Remember, your analysis may identify the point of difference between your product or service and the rest of your industry that directly shows you how to leapfrog your competition.

Distribution channels – A major challenge for a new business is to select the appropriate distribution channel to market what it offers. A *distribution channel* is the method you use to get your products or services to your target markets. You will choose from a variety of distribution channels in Module 5 as you begin to compile your Marketing Plan. Before you get to that point, however, you should educate yourself about the ways businesses in your industry have traditionally reached their markets.

Consider these questions about distribution:
- What are the common ways that businesses in this industry get their products or services to their target customers?
- Are these distribution channels exclusive to this industry?

Now take the Reality Check *Industry Profile* to see which industry characteristics you already know and which you need to research.

In addition to industry information, you will need to do research on customers who purchase from that industry and competitors within it.

Reality Check ✔ — Industry Profile

What do you already know about your industry, and what do you still need to know?
Check the following items to determine what you still need to research about your industry.

Industry Characteristic	Already Know	Need to Research
Current size	❏	❏
Growth potential	❏	❏
Profitability	❏	❏
Trends	❏	❏
Distribution channels	❏	❏

Customer Profile

It's important to decide who your customer really is. Do Aunt Molly and Cousin Fred really represent the customer who will make your product or service successful?

By identifying and knowing your customers, you can assess their needs and consider if your business concept will meet those needs. Research will assist you to determine the customer group most likely to purchase and use your product or service. This group will become your *target market*. Your target market may be businesses or consumers. By identifying your target market, its demographics, and its buying and spending habits, you will be able to focus your marketing and advertising efforts more effectively.

In the preliminary stages of your market research, you may have multiple potential markets for your product or service. You will want to use a variety of methods to pinpoint the markets that are most likely to receive your business concept well. Creating a customer profile is one method of describing the individuals who make up your target market. A customer profile can provide a clear picture of the type of person or business you are planning to serve. This information helps to drive your marketing strategy, promotional design, and sales process. You will look at a customer profile in this module and concentrate on other aspects of your target market in Module 5.

TiP The *target market* is a customer group that can be reached through marketing. The *customer profile* is a picture of a typical member of that group.

Check Your Knowledge of customer roles online at www.fasttrac.org/toolkits.

The Chooser vs. the User

Sometimes the customer who chooses your product or service is not the end-user—the person who uses it. For example, you might create a great board game for children. But children are not the ones who actually buy your game. The child is the User, but the Decision Maker is probably the child's parents. The Buyer may be the mother or the adult who picks the game up at the store. The Influencer is anyone who provides the Decision Maker and Buyer with information. In this example, the Influencer may be the child's teacher, another parent, a neighbor, or family friend. In this case, the child might also play the role of the Influencer as well. When you describe your customer, consider whom you will be marketing the product or service to and who will buy it.

When another business is the customer, you typically have multiple persons in these roles. In the chart, you can see the purchasing steps and different roles in selecting a proposal from a new marketing consultant.

LEVEL OF INVOLVEMENT		User	Decision Maker	Buyer	Influencer
■ Very involved					
▦ Somewhat involved					
□ Not involved					
PURCHASING STEPS					
1.	Need defined	■	▦	□	▦
2.	Budget establishment	□	■	▦	■
3.	Proposals requested	▦	■	■	▦
4.	Proposals reviewed	■	▦	■	▦
5.	Contract completed	□	■	■	□

Purchasing Process. When a business is the customer, multiple individuals may be involved at each step in the process. One common arrangement is shown here. Understanding the purchasing process and identifying business customers is part of the market analysis.

B2B vs. B2C Markets

Businesses can target other businesses or consumers. Your customer profile will vary depending on whether your customers are businesses or consumers. Entrepreneurs often refer to this distinction as B2B (business-to-business) or B2C (business-to-consumer) markets. While some products or services may only be marketable to other businesses or only to individuals, some may fit both categories. In that case, careful analysis can help you determine which market has the greatest potential.

Whether your business is B2B or B2C, you will want to look for *demographic* and *psychographic* information.

For More Information about identifying customers go to www.fasttrac.org/toolkits.

Demographics – Customers may be grouped by similar variables such as age, gender, occupation, education, or income levels, geographic location, industry, number of employees, number of years in business, products or services offered, or other defined criteria. Generally, the Census Bureau, government, or industry sources provide demographic information. Studies and trends are usually reported using predetermined variables from these sources.

Psychographics – Customers may also be grouped by similar psychographic variables such as values, beliefs, buying patterns, perceptions, and lifestyle choices such as recycling, fitness, travel, and hobby interests. Psychographic variables provide insights into how and why customers buy. Although this information is valuable to know, it is harder to collect and find because customers' preferences change over time and this type of information often must be collected directly from the source.

As part of your Marketing Plan, you will create an expanded profile of the potential customers who make up your target market. For example, a golf ball manufacturer who is trying to identify the type of golfer most likely to purchase its product will want to look at the characteristics of customers in the golf market. The golf ball manufacturer needs to know demographics on customers: where customers purchase their golf balls, how often they buy them, how much they pay, and their psychographic factors for buying golf balls, such as perceived value, desire for prestige, and price range.

You can collect demographic information about your intended customer from the Census Bureau and other secondary research sources that track consumer information. Psychographic information may require using surveys, interviews, and other forms of primary research to collect information specific to your intended customer.

Reality Check ✓   **Who Is My Customer?**

Who is the primary User of my product/service?

Are the User, the Decision Maker, and the Buyer the same person for my product/service?   ❏ Yes   ❏ No
Explain.

Who influences the buying decision?

Is my business primarily ❏ B2B or ❏ B2C?

When businesses are your customers (B2B), you will want to collect general market information about them. This type of demographic information can usually be obtained from the Department of Commerce, Small Business Administration (SBA), or industry experts. Psychographic information for businesses may be harder to locate as secondary research. B2B data may be collected from conducting informational interviews or reading about businesses you are interested in, contacting trade associations, industry experts, and others who are familiar with the industry or business group. You may find yourself doing industry profiles not only on your industry but also on your customer's industry if the two are not the same.

Marketing a product or service to a business has some major differences from marketing to individuals. In sales to businesses, you may have fewer, larger customers, which can increase your efficiency and profits as well as your risk. Energy Sentry products help conserve energy used by home appliances. Selling these products to individual consumers would be prohibitively expensive, so they developed a marketing strategy to work closely with local power companies. The devices were then sold in large batches; one rural power company bought 9,000 units for its customers.

Before deciding which customers are the best fit for your product or service, you will want to consider their distinctive aspects. For example, when marketing to businesses, does a proposal need to be submitted for each sale? Do these customers expect to negotiate prices and terms? Such considerations can affect the profitability of your business.

You will answer demographic and psychographic questions about your primary customer in Activity 2a.

Competitive Profile

As part of your market research, you will find out as much as possible about your competitors. You may have more competitors than you think. Generally, you should identify two types of competition for your business and research them. They are known as *direct* and *indirect* competitors. For example, if you make burritos and sell them frozen to grocery stores, your most likely direct competitors are probably other burrito makers in the market. But what about competitors who market frozen hamburgers, corndogs, and Philly steak sandwiches to the same grocery stores? And, what about the ones who offer pizza, microwave dinners, or other ready-made food in the frozen department that give customers choices other than your burritos? These are all indirect competitors who also compete with your burrito business.

> **TiP** Ideally, your company is the only one providing a particular set of benefits to your target market.

Your customers have a choice among all these options for a quick lunch or dinner. They could also choose to eat in a restaurant or make dinner at home using fresh ingredients purchased from other grocery departments. With a limited budget, you'll have to consider competitive threats to your business and decide how you will position your product or service effectively.

Learning as much as possible about the competition will help you define your position in the marketplace. The sources you will use to research competitors will depend on your type of business. The Yellow Pages, Internet, and the Thomas Register of American Manufacturers® can be helpful resources. Information about competitors may also be available through the local chamber of commerce or trade association chapter. Your industry's trade association can also provide contact information for industry leaders or comparable businesses in other parts of the country.

> **TiP** If you can prove that your product or service has no competition, it likely has no market.

Direct Competitors

Direct competition for any business includes entities that sell similar products or services in the same market. Burger King® and Wendy's® restaurants are direct competitors in the fast food market. Osco® and Walgreen's are direct competitors in the drugstore market. Direct competition also includes dissimilar businesses that sell similar products or services in the same market. Bookstores and grocery stores both carry best-selling paperback books. Customer service businesses, such as hair salons, carpet cleaning, dry cleaners, and professional service businesses commonly have many direct competitors. With mega-stores dominating most suburban areas, these big-box retailers now offer many services once provided by small entrepreneurial businesses.

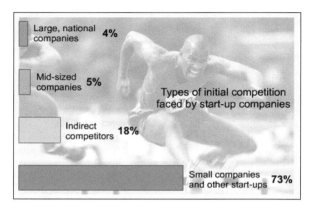

Sources of Competition. Business start-ups should expect as much as 73 percent of their direct competition to come from small companies. They may also have to face up to 18 percent of their competition from those competing indirectly. (Source: *The Origin and Evolution of New Businesses* by Amar Bhide. Used by permission.)

More so now than ever before, direct competitors are not always located in the same geographic area. Many businesses are using mail order, telephone sales, or Web sites to sell their products or services. To identify direct competitors, you can use the Yellow Pages®, Internet, and surveys to learn where people currently purchase similar products or services.

To gain a competitive advantage in the marketplace, you will need to differentiate your product or service from your direct competitors' product or service. To do this, you must first understand the needs of your customer and identify the strengths and weaknesses of your direct competitors. Then, you can ensure that your product or service meets the needs of the customer while incorporating your strengths and improving on competitors' weaknesses. Market research can help you do all this.

Some entrepreneurs have conducted research by working for the competition before starting a similar business. They may also contact their competitors' employees and ask questions about products or services, pricing discounts, and areas for improvement. Interviewing competitors' customers or visiting the competition may also yield this information.

One of the best strategies you can use is to interview a competitor who competes outside of your target location. By talking with a competitor outside your trade area, you may obtain a significant amount of information about the industry, the marketplace, and the operations of the business that local competitors will not share.

TiP If you can't think of any direct competitors, look in the Yellow Pages or local chamber of commerce's membership directory. Suppliers, consultants, bankers, accountants, and attorneys can also provide information about competitors.

Look deeper if at first you don't see direct competitors in your community. Potential customers may be buying similar products or services from a competitor who offers a different mix than you plan to carry or from a competitor over the Internet. Are potential customers currently buying your product or service from a superstore or a cut-rate competitor and, if so, why would they choose you instead? For example, one entrepreneur thought his auto parts store would have no competition since his community had no other similar stores. Then he learned his potential customers were happily buying automotive supplies at the nearby Sears® and Wal-Mart®. When he realized he did not want to compete with these stores, he chose to pursue another type of business.

Indirect Competitors

Indirect competitors can be more difficult to identify. The indirect competitor sells different products or services that fulfill the same need or provide the same benefits as yours. For example, someone buying a Valentine's Day gift may consider roses, a box of chocolates, or perfume to fill the same need. McDonald's® and Burger King are direct competitors because they both sell hamburgers. Their indirect competitors might be Subway® and Taco Bell®. They do not sell hamburgers, but offer other alternatives for people to spend their fast-food dollars. Be sure to consider indirect competitors as you analyze the feasibility of your business concept.

Targeted customers can also be indirect competition when they provide the product or service themselves or eliminate it entirely when times are tough financially in industries such as house cleaning, lawn care, fitness, or food preparation. Even B2B service businesses have indirect competitors. For instance, a training consultant must compete with companies that sell Web-based training courses or training videos.

Reality Check ✓ **Competitive Profile**

Here are three *direct* competitors for my product/service:

a.

b.

c.

Here are three *indirect* competitors for my product/service:

a.

b.

c.

What other products/services could be substituted for my product/service?

How could I find out what customers are substituting for my product/service?

Whether your competitors are direct or indirect, you must have a superior or differentiated product or service to successfully compete in the market. It might be necessary to create a marketing program that educates potential customers about the advantages of buying the product or service from you rather than the competition. You will work on this competitive advantage in Module 5.

In Activity 2b during the session you will identify your direct and indirect competitors.

Future Competition

TIP Review emerging trends to determine possible future competitors for your business.

You should always consider how much time you have before another company begins competing for your existing customers and locations. You may have an advantage in the market today, but others will note this and counteract with a competitive strategy.

You need to continue reading about the industry in order to identify trends that may motivate potential competitors to enter your market. You can anticipate the moves of these competitors and be ready to deploy your competitive strategies to maintain and grow your market share. Also, you will benefit from anticipating customers' future needs. As time goes by, your customers' needs may change. If your competition is more in tune than you are with the changing needs of the customer, then it can steal your market share. All the competition will need to do is to take the product or service, make minor changes to reflect your customers' new preferences, and offer it to them. It can be difficult for a successful business to recognize the need to change and stay ahead of the competition. Successful entrepreneurs plan for change.

Action Step 2.1 Conduct Market Research includes worksheets to help you collect the information you need. Depending on the amount of research you conduct or information you collect, you may consider using a binder or folders to keep your notes and information organized.

Gathering and Analyzing Data

As part of your action steps, you will be conducting market research and analyzing your findings throughout this program. You will want to gather information from both primary and secondary research sources to identify industry trends, customer characteristics, and competition. The data you collect can also provide information on the buying habits of your customers and help you determine if your product or service has a high likelihood of selling.

TIP Start by deciding the questions you want answered. Then look for the information that will answer them.

Once your data has been collected, you will want to organize and review them to determine if you need to refine your business concept or if you feel confident to move forward based on your preliminary research findings. Action Step 2.2 can help you make this determination. If you proceed, you will complete a detailed analysis of your market research in Module 5 and use it to develop your Business Plan. You may decide that additional research may be required before you can complete your analysis.

In spite of its importance to developing a Business Plan, research is frequently the weakest part of the planning process. It requires the most action, such as talking to potential customers, conducting research at libraries and on the Internet, and visiting competitors. You cannot obtain this kind of information sitting at a desk. As a result, you may be tempted to neglect the research and make decisions based on gut instinct rather than hard facts. Don't. Now that you know the questions you need to answer concerning your industry, customers, and competition, you can plan the time and resources you will need to do thorough and effective research.

Reality Check ✓ — What Information Should I Collect?

Check the box that indicates the information you will research for your business concept.

Industry Profile

❏ Size of industry
❏ Growth potential
❏ Expected gross margin percentage
❏ Expected profit
❏ Seasonal trends that impact the industry
❏ Economic trends that impact the industry
❏ Other industries whose trends impact the industry
❏ Distribution channels
❏ Other_____

Customer Profile

❏ Size of group
❏ Gender differences
❏ Age
❏ Race
❏ Education levels
❏ Income levels
❏ Marital status
❏ Number of children
❏ Number, type of pets
❏ Occupation
❏ Media or publications frequently read
❏ Industry or market segments
❏ Number of employees
❏ Length of time in business
❏ Products/services outsourced
❏ Geographic location
❏ Other_____

Customer Spending Habits/Patterns

❏ Average dollars spent per month or per year on specific products/services
❏ How often they buy/use similar products/services
❏ Number of cars or homes owned
❏ Home owner or renter
❏ How disposable income is spent
❏ Purchases made in person, by catalog, by phone, or over the Internet
❏ Payment type for goods or services (cash/credit)?

❏ Average amount of debt
❏ Bulk or seasonal buying
❏ Proposal or bidding process to buy products/services
❏ Outsource functions and production to suppliers/vendors
❏ Local, national, or overseas buying
❏ Other_____

Customer Motivational Patterns

❏ Perceptions of similar products or services
❏ Product or service qualities/characteristics valued
❏ Preference for superior service, convenience, or low price
❏ Typical decision maker (position, gender, or user)
❏ Purchases dependent on others' perceptions (peers, friends, family)
❏ Other_____

Competitive Profile

❏ Direct and indirect competitors in the market
❏ Possible future competitors in the market
❏ Strengths and weaknesses (pricing, service, convenience)
❏ Niche in the market
❏ Opportunities for differentiation
❏ Advertising methods and results
❏ Annual sales and revenue
❏ Location(s)
❏ Distribution channels
❏ Sources for production, inventory, or services
❏ Other_____

Market Trends

❏ Political, social, environmental
❏ Governmental policies that may impact my business, target market, or industry now or later
❏ Economic factors that may influence the market now or later
❏ Other_____

The specific primary and secondary market research sources you will use depend on your type of business and the target markets you are trying to reach. Demographics, customer buying and spending habits, information on competitors, and developing industry trends can be obtained from a variety of sources. Resources exist specific to every type of business and market. Many resources can be found on the Internet. A list of resources by the type of information you may be seeking is listed below.

Industry Research

You will want to start researching your industry using the NAICS or SIC code. To find an SIC or NAICS code, go to the U. S. Census NAICS Web site at www.census.gov/naics. Enter a key word that describes your industry into the search box on the left-hand side of the page, or browse codes by clicking the NAICS to SIC/SIC to NAICS button. Once you've located the relevant industry code(s), you can use the U.S. Economic Census and related reports to assist you in gathering industry statistics. This resource is available online at www.census.gov. Additionally, you can use these codes to access other industry information, some of which is grouped by industry type:

T i P Some entrepreneurs become members of private research libraries, such as James J. Hill Reference Library, to keep abreast of industry research. Members of the Hill Library can conduct research through www.HillSearch.org.

HillSearch Members

In HillSearch, simply click on "Research An Industry," then "Search industry trade journals" to search in EBSCO® or ABI/Inform®, databases with access to thousands of industry journals. In those databases, simply enter in key terms for your industry and "growth" or "trends" to find topical information.

Manufacturing – *Manufacturing & Distribution USA* provides statistical information and leading companies in all manufacturing and wholesale industries. The Annual Survey of Manufactures, available online at www.census.gov/mcd/asm-as1.html, gives more detailed statistics.

Restaurants – The National Restaurant Association publishes a number of resources that provide relevant industry data, including a *Restaurant Industry Forecast* and *Quickservice Restaurant Trends*. Get started online at www.restaurant.org.

Service businesses – The Census Bureau produces the Service Annual Survey online at www.census.gov. Many trade magazines cover specific service industry sectors, such as *ABA Banking Journal, Best's Review of Life & Health (Insurance)*, and *Spa Management*.

Retail – Many trade magazines focus on the retail industry, including *Chain Store Age* and *Stores*. Additionally, the National Retail Federation provides some timely information online at www.nrf.com.

Technology businesses – Use information services such as the *American Bulletin of International Technology, Selected Business Ventures* (published by General Electric), *Technology Mart, Patent Licensing Gazette*, and the *National Technical Information Service* to find technology information.

Gale Business & Company Resource Center is an online database that includes data from publications such as *Market Share Reporter, Encyclopedia of American Industries, Encyclopedia of Global Industries*, and other industry publications and company directories. Search for specific company information or find market share, industry overviews, company rankings, and articles on just about every industry.

Franchises – You can find lists of franchises for sale, franchising tips, and more at the *Start-Up Journal* from the *Wall Street Journal*. Another useful resource is Franchise Opportunities, an online directory of franchise business opportunities and information, at www.franchiseopportunities.com.

Licensing resources – One licensing information resource is the International Licensing Industry Merchandisers' Association (LIMA), which sponsors an annual show in New York City; see their Web site at www.licensing.org. *The Licensing Resource Directory*, published annually by Expocon Management Associates, lists alphabetically more than 3,000 owners and categories of products and services as well as tips, support organizations, consultants, designers, and other professionals specializing in licensing. Other resources include *The Licensing Letter* and *The Licensing Letter Resource Sourcebook* from EPM Communications, which lists the top 4,000 executives involved in the licensing industry. Two other publications relating to licensing are *The Licensing Report*, a weekly newsletter, and *The Licensing Book*, a monthly magazine, from Adventure Publishing®.

Governmental Resources

The government provides excellent resources for learning about industries in the United States.

Department of Commerce – The Department of Commerce provides extensive information about products and services across the United States at www.commerce.gov.

Patent and invention resources – Find patent information online through the U. S. Patent & Trademark Office at www.uspto.gov.

Libraries

In addition to newspapers and commercial magazines, many libraries contain the following sources of secondary research material:

Dun & Bradstreet and **Standard & Poor's** – Dun & Bradstreet provides a number of databases, such as the Dun & Bradstreet Million Dollar Database, which lists public and private companies and their annual sales. Standard & Poor's also has a number of resources, such as NetAdvantage®, which has more in-depth financial information on larger public companies.

The Statistical Abstract of the United States – This abstract provides basic information such as income levels, employment figures, industry outputs, and useful market information, and is available online at www.census.gov/statab/www/. Many of the charts are summaries of more detailed data; check the source listed on the chart you consult for more information.

Encyclopedia of Associations – Trade associations often collect valuable statistics and provide networking information on the industries they represent. Use this encyclopedia to find information on more than 25,000 United States trade associations, including lists of publications available and association contact information, including Web sites.

Encyclopedia of Business Information Sources – This encyclopedia lists resources such as trade magazines, databases, handbooks, trade associations, statistics, and more for over 1,100 business and financial topics. Use this guide to get started finding relevant sources for your industry and market research.

Standard & Poor's *Industry Surveys* – Standard & Poor's provides in-depth surveys on over fifty major industries, such as apparel and footwear, biotechnology, healthcare, and retailing. The industry surveys are updated four times per year and include information on industry trends, consumers, market share, leading companies, and leading company financials.

ReferenceUSA – You can search this database of more than 12 million private and public companies nationwide by NAICS or SIC code, geography, size of company and more.

Your librarian can assist you in locating other relevant resources.

Trade and Professional Organizations

Use the *Encyclopedia of Associations*, which is published annually and available in most libraries, to identify associations in your industry. Once you have identified some associations in your industry, call about services they offer.

Get started online by searching the **American Society of Association Executives Gateway to Associations**, online at www.asaenet.org, for more than 6,000 local and national association Web sites.

Trade publications provide timely information about activities in your industry and are a great way to recognize and capitalize on emerging trends. When you find the appropriate trade association for the industry you are researching, check to see what publications it sponsors.

Customer Research

Use zip codes as the standard tool to search for customer demographic data. If your customers are businesses you will continue to use NAICS and SIC codes. Most of your research sources for other B2B customers will be found in the Industry Research section above. Some secondary research for your B2C customer profile may be available from the following sources:

Governmental Resources

The government not only provides information about industries in the United States, but also about its population and their spending habits.

Census Bureau – The Census Bureau tracks demographics including age, race, population, median income, geographical information, and other useful information. Obtain information from the Census Bureau online at www.census.gov or via telephone at 301-763-INFO (4636).

Bureau of Labor Statistics Consumer Expenditures Survey – This survey provides information on the spending habits of consumers. Find them online at www.bls.gov/cex/home.htm or via telephone at (202) 691-6900.

Trade and Professional Organizations

Visit or become a member of a trade organization that relates to your product, service, or target market. Associations can often provide valuable "insider information" from those who are in a similar industry, which can help you identify customers' buying patterns. Most members are more than willing to answer your questions or share their stories, which can be very valuable when starting your business.

Become a member of a national organization that can provide you with information such as white papers, consumer surveys, and market surveys. This source can be an inexpensive way to obtain very reliable research data.

Competition Research

General secondary information on your competition is readily available through the following resources. You may need to conduct primary research on local competitors by visiting their locations, interviewing customers or employees, or reading local media and watching for trends in your area. Remember, for national information on competitors in your industry, use the sources listed in the Industry Research section above.

Governmental Resources

In some of the same places you found industry information, you will probably find helpful research about your competition.

Department of Commerce – Industry, products, or services information may help you identify competition and/or niche opportunities. Contact the Department of Commerce to find out how to access its publications on industry, products, and services at www.commerce.gov.

National Association of Secretaries of State – This association, online at www.nass.org, provides contact information for each state's office of business registrations. Visit individual state Web sites for contact information, searchable directories of state businesses, and filing information.

Libraries

Many libraries contain the following sources of secondary research material:

Trade journals – Industry and trade journals often report on industries, products, services, companies, competitors, and proposed products. Look for a journal that focuses on your industry, such as *Nation's Restaurant News, Chain Store Age*, or *Chemical Market Reporter*. Some general publications that focus more exclusively on entrepreneurship include *Entrepreneur, Success, Inc.*, and *Home Office Computing*.

Small Business Sourcebook – This excellent guide for sorting through business references and data profiles 224 types of business resources (such as articles, books, and trade associations) for everything from accounting services to beauty shops.

Your librarian can assist you in locating other relevant resources.

HillSearch Members

Create a competitor list by clicking on "Create Company Lists," then select "D & B" (Dun & Bradstreet) for larger competitors and "ReferenceUSA" for smaller competitors.

Trade and Professional Organizations

Trade organizations and professional gathering offer some of the best resources for finding out about your competition.

Chamber of commerce – Join your local chamber of commerce to meet and network with competitors in your area.

Online trade organizations – Local online discussion groups relating to your product or service and electronic newsletters can keep you up to date on what your competitors are up to and help you gather relevant information about your industry or target markets.

Local newspaper – This valuable local resource will give you information about upcoming community events sponsored by local organizations.

After you have conducted preliminary market research, go back and compare what you've learned to your original business concept and personal goals. Action Step 2.2 will help you make this comparison.

Summary

In this module, you were able to analyze your business concept from a marketing perspective. Understanding how your product or service fits into the market and whether it fulfills a need is vital to its success. To identify market needs you can learn to spot trends, observe the environment, ask questions, and listen. The smart entrepreneur uses creative sources to help identify new business opportunities.

Key Things to Remember

- Studying markets, industries, competitors, demographics, lifestyles, and habits helps you stay abreast of the current business climate and research business opportunities.

- The process of evaluating opportunities is vital to starting a successful business.

- You can conduct primary market research (data specific to your business) and secondary market research (existing and available data relevant to your business) to determine if your product/service meets a need in the market.

- By knowing what type of information you need on your industry, customers, and competition, you can save time when conducting market research for your business.

Market research may seem daunting now, but you will soon find that it energizes your attitude toward doing business. As you learn about your industry, your customers, and your competition, you can create a dynamic plan to enter your industry, reach your customers, and stay ahead of the competition. All of these aspects have an impact on the financial feasibility of your business, which you will discover in Module 3.

Activity 2a   Customer Profile Worksheet

Identify major customer groups and their distinguishing characteristics.

Directions
In this activity you will clearly describe your customers and identify the type of market research you need.

Step 1 Identify major customer groups. Identify in the chart below which of the distinguishing demographic variables, psychographic variables, and buying behaviors best describe your customers. Not all variables and factors will apply to your situation. If something doesn't apply, skip it.

Demographics (age, gender, geographic location)

B2C Customers	*B2B Customers*
❑ Age	❑ Number of employees
❑ Gender	❑ Organizational structure
❑ Profession	❑ Location of headquarters
❑ Education level	❑ Types of products and services they provide
❑ Household income level	❑ Annual revenue
❑ Marital status	❑ Number, size, and location of branches
❑ Number of children	❑ Year founded
❑ Geographic location	❑ Other
❑ Other	

Psychographics (why they buy)

B2C Customers	*B2B Customers*
❑ Conservative	❑ Market leader
❑ Liberal	❑ Innovative or cutting-edge
❑ Conformist	❑ Liberal
❑ Experimental	❑ Conservative
❑ Environment-friendly	❑ Environment-friendly
❑ Socially conscious	❑ Employee/family-friendly
❑ Growth-oriented	❑ Fast growing/adopting new ideas
❑ Fun-loving	❑ Stable/set in their ways
❑ Cutting-edge	❑ Other
❑ Trend follower	
❑ Fashion-forward	
❑ Family-oriented	
❑ Other	

Activity 2a **Customer Profile Worksheet** continued

B2C Customers	B2B Customers
How many family members are typically in your customers' households?	What growth stage is the company in? (start-up, growth, stable, or decline)
What hobbies and/or sports do your customers enjoy?	What is the type of workforce they employ? (for example, younger, education level, part-time)
	Who is the decision maker in the business you are selling to?
What types of entertainment do they enjoy? (for example, movies, theater, opera)	
	Do identifiable common characteristics of managers or executives exist?
What publications do they subscribe to?	What is the company's culture?
	What is the management style?
What do they do in their free time?	What trade associations do they belong to?
	What publications do they subscribe to?

Activity 2a **Customer Profile Worksheet** continued

Buying Behaviors (where, when, what, and how they buy)

B2C Customers	*B2B Customers*
What benefit is the customer looking for?	What benefit is the customer looking for?
How often will they purchase?	How often will they purchase?
What is the customer's decision-making process?	What is the customer's decision-making process?
What factors are most important to your customers:	What factors are most important to your customers:
❏ Price	❏ Price
❏ Quality	❏ Quality
❏ Brand name recognition	❏ Brand name recognition
❏ Customer service	❏ Customer service
❏ Variety of services	❏ Variety of services
❏ Discounts and sales	❏ Discounts and sales
❏ Attractiveness of packaging	❏ Attractiveness of packaging
❏ Convenience of store location	❏ Convenience of store location
❏ Store appearance	❏ Store appearance
❏ Convenience of product/service use	❏ Convenience of product/service use
❏ Guarantees/Warranties	❏ Guarantees/Warranties
❏ Technical support	❏ Technical support
❏ Flexible payment terms	❏ Flexible payment terms
❏ Financing	❏ Financing
❏ Other	❏ Other

Step 2 Complete the Customer Profile Worksheet. Using the information from the checklist, write a customer profile in the Customer Profile Worksheet on p. 72 for each customer group identified.

Step 3 Identify research needed on major customer groups. Additional research regarding your customers will help you later when you determine the size of your target market, how to reach potential customers, and how to best sell your products or services. What market research on your major customer groups would be helpful? Note this information in the right-hand column of the Customer Profile Worksheet.

Step 4 Complete the research. Verify the draft customer profile by actually conducting primary and secondary market research.

Activity 2a **Customer Profile Worksheet** continued

Customer Profile Worksheet

Step 1 Identify major customer groups	B2B or B2C?	Step 2 Complete the Customer Profile	Step 3 Identify research needed
EXAMPLE *For a shuttle service to and from the airport, the main customer group is businesses whose sales force and other employees make regular business trips.*	*B2B*	*Medium to large businesses (over $1,000,000 in annual revenue) within forty miles of the airport who maintain a traveling national and/or international sales force or development team.* *Key motives for choosing a shuttle service include reliability and efficiency.* *They purchase frequently, one or more times a month, typically by telephone.*	*Need to know the number of businesses in the designated area who fit the customer profile.* *Library or Internet research of census data for SIC and NAICS codes within a forty-mile radius of the airport would reveal how many businesses meet the criteria.*
Customer Group A	B2B or B2C?	**Customer Profile A**	**Research Needed A**
Customer Group B	B2B or B2C?	**Customer Profile B**	**Research Needed B**
Customer Group C	B2B or B2C?	**Customer Profile C**	**Research Needed C**

Activity 2b   Competitors – Direct and Indirect

Consider all the alternatives my customers have to buy a product or service similar to mine.

Directions
Follow the steps below to discover your direct and indirect competitors.

Step 1 Identify direct competitors. Direct competitors are businesses that sell similar products or services in the same market. Consider companies located in the same geographic region as well as companies, such as mail order or Internet-based, who can reach your potential customers. Also consider direct competitors that may sell similar products or services to your business as a sideline to their normal business. You may want to review your answers to the Reality Check *Competitive Profile* on p. 61. List your direct competitors. You may want to look in directories and on the Internet to find other competitors when time allows.

Possible direct competitors	Information I will collect on my direct competitors	Research sources I will use

Step 2 Discover indirect competitors. Indirect competitors are businesses who sell products or services that fill the same need as your business. List businesses that are your indirect competitors. This list may be much longer than the direct competitors list. It may be necessary to discuss categories of competitors rather than to list specific company names. You may want to review your answers to the Reality Check *Competitive Profile* on p. 61.

Possible indirect competitors	Information I will collect on my indirect competitors	Research sources I will use

Activity 2b **Competitors – Direct and Indirect** continued

Step 3 Recognize other forms of indirect competition. Sometimes customers will create the product or perform the service themselves. Other times, customers eliminate the purchase entirely when times are tough financially. This action is also a form of indirect competition.

Could customers be competitors to your product/service?   ❑ Yes   ❑ No
Explain:

Examples of other direct competition:

Examples of other indirect competition:

Step 4 Verify direct and indirect competition. Verify your information by actually conducting primary and secondary market research.

Action Step 2.1 **Conduct Market Research**

Identify resources for questions that I need to answer through market research.

Directions
This worksheet lists all the categories in which you may collect information for your market research. You may also want to review Reality Checks in this module to decide if there is additional information you want to know.

Category – Information Needed	Possible Sources	Comments
INDUSTRY/OPPORTUNITY		
What is the history of this industry?		
What is the current state of the industry?		
What are the trends?		
What are the long-term prospects?		
Do seasonal factors exist?		
What are the existing distribution networks?		
How does the industry treat new enterprises or the introduction of new products?		
What are the industry's pricing policies?		

Action Step 2.1 **Conduct Market Research** continued

Category – Information Needed	Possible Sources	Comments
MARKET		
What are the customer-perceived benefits of what you are selling?		
How do your products/services differ from competitive products/services?		
If your product/service were not special, why would people buy from you?		
What is the present size and growth potential of the market as a whole?		
What percent of the market will you have now and in the future?		
What is the present size and growth potential of your target market?		
What are the characteristics of your target customers? (Use demographic and psychographic variables.)		
What are customer reactions to your product/service?		

Action Step 2.1 **Conduct Market Research** continued

Category – Information Needed	Possible Sources	Comments
COMPETITION		
Who are your direct and indirect competitors?		
Are competitors' sales steady? Decreasing? Increasing?		
How are competitors' operations similar and dissimilar to yours?		
What products do competitors offer? What price? How do they promote?		
What is your competitive advantage?		

Action Step 2.1 Conduct Market Research continued

Category – Information Needed	Possible Sources	Comments
ADDITIONAL INFORMATION TO COLLECT		

Action Step 2.2 **Evaluate and Refine My Business Concept**

Compare market research results of my business concept to market feasibility criteria for an ideal business.

Directions

As you collect information about your industry, customers, and competition, you will want to reflect on how well your business concept fits into a given industry, where you will get customers to buy your product or service, and how well you will be able to compete in the marketplace with this concept. The following steps should help you understand more about your business concept and its feasibility in the larger market.

A. **Review your market research information.** Take a few minutes to review your market research results. Write down any insights you gained after collecting data about the industry, potential customers, and competitors.

B. **Evaluate your business concept against the Market Feasibility Checklist.** Read the criteria in the first column of the chart on pp. 80 – 81. Look closely at the five options across the chart that describe potential responses to each criterion. Circle the number, 1 to 5, that most closely represents your response to that criterion. Be honest!

C. **Determine if your business concept needs refinement.** Answer the questions below to consider what changes you would make to your business concept to better meet the needs of the market or to gain a competitive advantage. List additional research you want to conduct.

What refinement, if any, do I need to make to my business concept to make it more feasible in the market?

What additional research will I need to collect?

Action Step 2.2 Evaluate and Refine My Business Concept continued

Market Feasibility Checklist

Market Criteria	1. Does not meet market criteria.	2. Somewhat meets market criteria.	3. Might meet market criteria.	4. Meets market criteria very well.	5. Meets market criteria perfectly.
a. Customers perceive a need for product/service.	1. Customers are totally clueless about my type of product/service.	2. Customers must be educated about my products/services before they see a need for them.	3. Customers must be convinced to buy from me instead of my competitors.	4. Customers need my products/services and will often select them over competitors'.	5. Slam dunk! My customers need my products/services and want to buy from me.
b. Market can be recognized and measured.	1. My customers could be just about anyone, so targeting a certain group may not be easy.	2. I have many potential customers, so I need to do more research to find my target market.	3. I have identified my potential customers, but they will be somewhat difficult to reach because of their demographics/buying patterns.	4. With some effort, I can use my customers' demographics/buying patterns to find them.	5. My potential customers are easy to find because of their demographics/buying patterns.
c. Existing competition has identifiable weaknesses.	1. I have lots of competition who have been in this business longer than I.	2. I have no competition! Hmmm, I wonder why?	3. I have identified my competition, but I do not know its weaknesses.	4. I know my competition and its weaknesses, but I need more research.	5. I have limited competition, and I know its weaknesses.
d. Distribution system is established and receptive.	1. I must develop a brand new distribution system.	2. My current distribution system offers only limited options.	3. I've found a distribution system already established with several options.	4. Several distributors seem receptive to carrying my products/services.	5. Unbelievable! Distributors are calling me wanting to carry my products/services.
e. There is an identifiable competitive advantage in the marketplace.	1. A competitive advantage would be hard to find.	2. There is a small competitive advantage in the marketplace.	3. I'm not sure a competitive advantage exists.	4. There is a small identifiable competitive advantage in the marketplace and I am in a somewhat unique position to use it.	5. There is an identifiable competitive advantage in the marketplace and I am in a unique position to use it.

Action Step 2.2   **Evaluate and Refine My Business Concept** continued

Market Feasibility Checklist

Market Criteria	1. Does not meet market criteria.	2. Somewhat meets market criteria.	3. Might meet market criteria.	4. Meets market criteria very well.	5. Meets market criteria perfectly.
f. There are few competitors to serve the needs of the market.	1. There are many competitors to serve the needs of the market.	2. There are quite a few competitors to serve the needs of the market.	3. The competition is not clear.	4. There are a few competitors to serve the needs of the market.	5. There are almost no competitors to serve the needs of the market.
g. The business concept can be modified to serve the needs of a specific, underserved market niche.	1. The business concept cannot be modified to serve the needs of a specific, underserved market niche.	2. The business concept can be modified with some difficulty to serve the needs of a specific, underserved market niche.	3. The business concept might be modifiable to serve the needs of a specific, underserved market niche.	4. The business concept can be modified to serve the needs of a specific, underserved market niche.	5. The business concept can easily be modified to serve the needs of a specific, underserved market niche.
h. The customer profiled would respond favorably to the current business concept.	1. I don't think the customer profiled would respond at all to the current business concept.	2. The customer profiled would respond somewhat unfavorably to the current business concept.	3. How the customer would respond to the current business concept is unclear.	4. The customer profiled would respond somewhat favorably to the current business concept.	5. The customer profiled would respond very favorably to the current business concept.
i. There is a sufficient market for the business.	1. There is an insufficient market for the business.	2. There is a relatively small market for the business.	3. The size of the market is not clear.	4. The size of the market seems sufficient enough.	5. There is a perfectly sufficient market for the business.
j. Customers purchase frequently.	1. Customers will only buy once from me, so I must find new customers all the time.	2. Most customers will only buy once from me.	3. Customers will buy more than once, but not frequently.	4. Some customers will purchase products/services frequently.	5. Wow! Customers currently purchase similar products/services very frequently.

Setting Financial Goals

What are your financial reasons for starting a business? What does financial success mean to you? Is it worth trying to attain? This module will help you answer these questions and determine whether your business concept will help you reach these goals. As you navigate the financial aspects of planning a new venture, this module will introduce you to the major financial concepts you will encounter.

You will also start thinking about the three major aspects of financial feasibility—start-up costs, profitability, and cash flow. You can begin estimating start-up costs now and continue to refine your estimates throughout the program. In Modules 8 and 9 you will look more carefully at profitability and cash flow based on the numbers you begin estimating now. Module 3 will not provide absolute proof that your concept is profitable. It will, however, give you some indication whether the concept warrants additional study.

Key Questions
- How does financial planning affect the success of my business?
- How do I set financial goals for my business?
- Where do I find accurate, relevant financial information for my business?
- What types of costs do I need to identify and plan for?
- What sources of funding are realistically available for my start-up and ongoing operations?
- Does my business concept pass the screening test and what modifications are necessary?

Action Steps   Due Date
- ❏ 3.1 Estimate Start-Up Costs   _____
- ❏ 3.2 Evaluate My Business Concept Against My Financial Goals   _____
- ❏ 3.3 Consider Potential Funding Sources   _____
- ❏ 3.4 Complete My Business Concept Analysis   _____
- ❏ Read Module 4 Defining the Product/Service   _____
- ❏ _____   _____
- ❏ _____   _____
- ❏ _____   _____

Using Financial Information as a Roadmap for Success

When you travel, what are the many tools you use to have a successful trip? A car, sunglasses, a compass, a map? One of the many tools you use on your business journey is your financial savvy. It can be your roadmap to success. Throughout this module, keep in mind the value of financial information in navigating your new business venture.

As you screen your business concept for financial feasibility in this module, you will concentrate primarily on personal financial goals, start-up costs, and financing options. You will also get a short course in the language of business. In each subsequent module, you will continue assessing financial feasibility by identifying the potential costs associated with individual areas of your Business Plan. Your test of financial feasibility will be complete after a thorough analysis of profitability and cash flow in Modules 8 and 9.

Matching a Business Concept with Your Income Goals

If you have done a good job of collecting and analyzing information so far in the business planning process, you may find that you need to change your business concept according to new information you have gathered. It may even seem that you must make an adjustment to your personal goals. Whenever possible, revise your business concept, not your personal goals. If you compromise your personal goals for the business concept, you may not find long-term satisfaction in your venture.

Why Financial Feasibility?

TIP Feasibility testing can help you determine the financial potential of your business concept.

Why should you be concerned about financial feasibility? By now you have worked to establish whether your business concept fits your personal vision and how it meets a need in the market. The third basic question of concept feasibility, however, asks about the ability of the business concept to 1) be profitable and 2) fulfill your personal financial goals.

At the end of this module you will ask these three questions of your business concept to test its feasibility:
- Does my business match my personal vision?
- Does my business meet a perceived need in the market?
- Will my business be profitable?

Many entrepreneurs start businesses that only pass two of the three feasibility questions. Then they wonder why they were unsuccessful or dissatisfied in their venture. If you want to start a barbecue restaurant, for example, you may be able to prove a market exists and that the restaurant will be profitable. If the proposed business, however, does not match your personal vision because of the time demands of a restaurant, it will not be successful for you.

Similarly, if you establish a business that matches your personal vision and meets a particular market need, but does not pass the financial test, it will not be successful. Just as Danny O'Neill of The Roasterie® adjusted his original business concept prior to starting his business, this feasibility testing can help you to adapt your business concept to what you want, what the market needs, and what the business is able to provide.

Smell the Coffee

When Danny O'Neill wrote his first business plan in 1993, it was a little lofty, admits the founder of The Roasterie, a specialty coffee company in Kansas City, Missouri, which generates nearly $5 million in sales. "I had this grandiose idea to combine a coffee shop and roastery," O'Neill explains. "There would be a glass wall down the middle separating the two and people in the café could sit and drink coffee while they watched roasting operations on the other side."

O'Neill was passionate about coffee. As a high school foreign exchange student, he had spent time in Costa Rica, where he helped pick coffee beans in the fields. Over the years, O'Neill had become a coffee connoisseur and when he decided to leave his sales and marketing job at a large paper company, coffee seemed to be the perfect venue for his entrepreneurial ambitions.

As O'Neill searched for the right location, a friend suggested he meet with Dick Banner at the small business counseling organization SCORE. "Unlike most people, Dick didn't give me a hundred reasons why I shouldn't be doing this—which was good because that approach just makes me frustrated and even more determined," O'Neill recalls. Instead, Banner asked O'Neill some simple questions: Who will run the café? Who will roast the coffee? Who will sell it? "It soon became obvious that there was no way I could handle everything I wanted to do," says O'Neill.

So O'Neill decided to scale back and focus on a wholesale coffee-roasting business with the goal of winning two new accounts each month. The revised plan may have been less exciting, he admits, "but it was manageable, lowered my risks, and reduced the collateral I would need."

In another cost-cutting measure, O'Neill decided to start his business in his basement, rather than renting or buying commercial space. "A building codes administrator suggested the idea, and looking back, it was probably the second most important piece of advice anyone gave me," O'Neill says. Instead of the $300,000 he had originally projected, O'Neill was able to launch The Roasterie with $20,000 in personal savings.

Twelve years later, however, O'Neill decided to revisit his original vision and open a retail store. Located in Kansas City's Brookside neighborhood, The Roasterie Café sells pastries, soups, salads, and sandwiches in addition to the company's hallmark espresso and espresso-based beverages.

The catalyst for the café is twofold: to continue building The Roasterie brand and to serve as a training ground and "living laboratory" for both the company's staff and its wholesale customers. "For ten years, we had compelling reasons against opening a retail location," O'Neill says. "We didn't want to be distracted, and we didn't want customers to feel we were competing with them. But recently, potential customers have expressed disappointment that The Roasterie didn't have a retail setting. They felt we could offer them better service and training if we had our own store."

Although a retail location is a significant investment, O'Neill now has the financial wherewithal—and experience—to support it. "We've already established our brand as a wholesaler, so the retail location is not as great a risk, and we can be more discriminating in what we do," he says. "We're in a position to do this right from day one and should hit the ground running."

By changing his concept at start-up, not his personal goals, O'Neill was able to start his business with manageable risks. With patience and smart decision-making, he eventually achieved a version of his original concept.

Too often, entrepreneurs discontinue their feasibility analysis when information is hard to find. Determining financial feasibility can also be difficult. Sometimes finding the information requires effort. Other times, the process of establishing financial feasibility seems daunting. Perseverance at this stage in the process will help you build a successful business and help you meet your own personal financial goals. How much is success worth to you? How much do you want to avoid failure?

Setting Personal Financial Goals

This module provides easy-to-follow steps that will help you evaluate your personal financial goals for success. These goals are the foundation you will use to test the business concept for financial feasibility throughout the program. Testing for adequate profitability prior to starting the business helps ensure that the business is generating enough money to meet your personal financial goals.

Starting a business that merely pays you a salary is not sound business practice. Your business must be profitable enough to cover its own expenses and still pay you a salary. Achieving your personal financial goals will require you to focus on the financial health of your business. The Reality Check *Personal Goals Worksheet* helps you establish personal financial goals and business profit needs that must be met.

Your business must generate profits in order to cover your personal financial goals. You will need to determine the specific amount of money you want and need personally and compare that to the amount of money the business will be able to produce. The next step is to prepare financial projections. To make financial projections, you need to be familiar with some basic financial language.

Introduction to Financial Concepts

Just as you compared your own entrepreneurial characteristics with that of successful entrepreneurs in Module 1, you will want to compare your business's financial projections with other successful businesses. Establishing business goals based on the reported success of another business is called *benchmarking*. In addition to *financial projections* and *benchmarking*, the language of business contains many terms that you need to be comfortable using. Then you can collect information, project financials, and align and compare financial information with confidence.

Have you ever traveled to another country and didn't fluently speak the language? Travelers who have know that they can get by on a few words or they can find interpreters along the way; however, the experience is not as rewarding as if they could speak directly with the people they meet. As a business owner, you may find that not understanding accounting and financial concepts can be a similar experience. These concepts are not difficult, but they still may be foreign to you. To succeed at business, you need to learn the language of business, which will enable you to understand the financial reports and information generated from your business and to communicate with others regarding this information.

TIP You don't have to be a Certified Public Accountant to know how to read and use basic financial statements to make decisions based on the financial position of your company.

Check Your Knowledge

of financial concepts online at www.fasttrac.org/toolkits.

Reality Check ✔ **Personal Goals Worksheet**

What aspects of owning and operating your own business especially appeal to you?

How much money are you willing to invest in your business?

What portion of this investment will come from your own savings and what portion will be borrowed?

What salary do you require?

What salary do you want? Be realistic with this figure. Consider your dreams, but be reasonable as well.

Are you prepared to lower your standard of living until the business is established? For how long?

In addition to your salary, what additional business profit is needed? Place a check beside the items below that you plan to do.

	Amount needed
❏ Grow the business	$ _____
❏ Buy a house	$ _____
❏ Buy a car	$ _____
❏ Plan vacations	$ _____
❏ Pursue a hobby/passion	$ _____
❏ Improve my overall lifestyle	$ _____
❏ Go back to school	$ _____
❏ Save for college	$ _____
❏ Invest in retirement	$ _____
❏ Pay off debts	$ _____
❏ _____	$ _____
❏ _____	$ _____
❏ _____	$ _____
❏ _____	$ _____
Total	$ _____

How much could you earn investing your money instead of starting a business?

What salary could you earn working for someone else?

If the total amount is greater than what you expect to earn through this business concept, you should reconsider the concept.

The Accounting Equation

| Assets | | Liabilities | | Equity |

Backyard Solutions
Year-End Balance Sheet (Projected)

	2005
Assets	
Current Assets	
Cash & Equivalents	$110,320
Net Accounts Receivable	15,291
Inventory	5,352
Security Deposits	-
Other Current Assets	-
Total Current Assets	**130,963**
Fixed Assets	
Property, Plant, & Equipment	$72,000
Less: Accumulated Depreciation	(14,095)
Other Non-Current Assets	-
Total Non-Current Assets	**57,905**
Total Assets	**$188,868**
Liabilities	
Current Liabilities	
Accounts Payable	$ -
Line of Credit	-
Other Current Liabilities	8,428
Total Current Liabilities	**8,428**
Long-Term Liabilities	
Loans	37,735
Mortgages	-
Other Non-Current Liabilities	-
Total Non-Current Liabilities	**37,735**
Total Liabilities	**$46,163**
Equity	
Equity Investments	$85,000
Retained Earnings	57,705
Less: Owner's & Investor's Draws	-
Total Equity	**$142,705**
Total Liabilities and Equity	**$188,868**

Balancing Act. When done correctly, the Balance Sheet balances the Total Assets with the Total Liabilities plus Equity.

Balance Sheet

A Balance Sheet reports what the company owns, what it owes, and the net worth that remains for the owners of the business. These classifications are broken into the following categories: assets, liabilities, and owner's equity. The formula in which these categories are used is assets = liabilities + equity.

This Balance Sheet formula is also called the accounting equation. The Balance Sheet, or accounting equation, balances the value of the assets with the rights that creditors and business owners have to those assets.

Assets – Assets can be described as things in your business with value, such as cash, equipment, inventory, and investments. In the same way you might own your car or house, these items are owned by the business. The business may not have the sole rights to these assets, however, just as you may share the rights to your car or house with the bank that lent you money.

On the Balance Sheet, assets are divided into *current assets* and *non-current assets*. Current assets include cash or assets that can or will be turned into cash within one year. Examples of current assets include cash, accounts receivable, and inventory. All assets not expected to be converted into cash within one year are considered non-current assets. These include fixed assets, such as land, facilities, equipment, and vehicles—physical assets being held by the business for the purpose of producing revenues. Other non-current assets include long-term notes receivable and intangible assets such as goodwill, patents, and copyrights.

Liabilities – Liabilities describe others' rights to the value in the business, such as banks that have loaned the business money and vendors who have allowed the business extended payments. This amount can be compared to the amount of money you still owe on your house or car, which are personal liabilities. Your business may need to borrow money to fund start-up costs or to cover cash shortages from operations as your business is growing. You may also receive credit terms from your vendors (individuals or businesses that you purchase products or services from)—these are called *accounts payable*. By allowing you to pay for your purchases in the future, they have, in essence, given you a short-term loan.

You will see liabilities divided into *current liabilities* and non-current or *long-term liabilities*. Current liabilities include those liabilities you expect to pay within the next year. These include accounts payable and other payables you plan to pay within the year. Since lines of credit typically have a renewal provision included in the loan agreement, they are also usually classified as current. Long-term liabilities include notes payable, such as loans from banks or other financial institutions that have payment terms over several years. These loans might be for the purchase of a company vehicle, building, inventory, or equipment.

Equity – Owner's equity is the difference between assets and liabilities. It shows the owner's rights to the value of the company. Depending on the structure of the company, this number could reflect what you as the sole proprietor own in the company or what you and the other stockholders own if your company has multiple owners.

One account in equity that seems to stump many business owners is called *retained earnings*. This account represents the amount of cumulative earnings or net income that has not been paid out to owners in dividends or owner's draw. The amount in retained earnings, however, may not always be equal to the amount of cash the business has on hand. This discrepancy occurs because you may re-invest the earnings of the business in new equipment or even a new building. You may also make a strategic decision to increase the operations of the business and, therefore, need to purchase more inventory. The retained earnings account may also show a negative number if the business has not been profitable or the business owners have taken out more money than the business has generated in income.

In spite of all of the information it reports, the Balance Sheet does not provide details about the financial performance of your business—its profitability. This information is reported in the Income Statement.

Income Statement

The Income Statement shows the net income or loss your business has experienced over a period of time. It is your company's financial grade card. The time period could be a day, week, month, quarter, or year. This report helps you determine if your business is making or losing money. The Income Statement displays the revenue (sales) earned by your company and the expenses it incurred to generate those revenues. Then it records Net Income based on those revenues and expenses for the intended period of time.

Revenue – Revenue can be described as money earned from conducting the business's activities. It is sometimes called Net Sales on the Income Statement.

Expenses – Expenses are costs associated with supporting the business's activities. The expenses that appear on the Income Statement are generally the same expenses that the Internal Revenue Service allows as deductions for income tax purposes.

Net Income – The ultimate goal of any business is to produce a positive net income or profit over the long haul. Many early-stage businesses expect to lose money for a period of time while they are getting their operations up-and-running and entering their products or services into new markets. In testing the feasibility of your business concept, you should determine how much you expect to lose and for how long, so that in addition to start-up funds, you can plan to find sufficient funding to carry the business until it becomes profitable and your cash flow from operations becomes positive.

For More Information on the Balance Sheet go to www.fasttrac.org/toolkits.

For More Information on Income Statements go to www.fasttrac.org/toolkits.

Tip Net income is calculated by deducting expenses from revenues over a given period of time.

Backyard Solutions Year-End Income Statement (Projected)		
	2005	**%**
Net Sales (less returns & allowances)	$775,175	100.0%
Cost of Goods Sold	542,623	70.0%
Gross Margin	**232,552**	**30.0%**
Operating Expenses		
Advertising	-	0.0%
Bad Debt Expense	-	0.0%
Bank Charges	-	0.0%
Depreciation & Amortization	14,095	1.8%
Dues & Subscriptions	220	0.0%
Insurance	2,700	0.3%
Licenses & Fees	215	0.0%
Marketing & Promotion	11,300	1.5%
Meals & Entertainment	1,000	0.1%
Miscellaneous	1,200	0.2%
Office Expense	1,800	0.2%
Office Supplies	-	0.0%
Outside Services	1,640	0.2%
Payroll Expenses		
Salaries & Wages	44,000	5.7%
Payroll Taxes	3,600	0.5%
Benefits	12,000	1.5%
Professional Fees	4,000	0.5%
Property Taxes	-	0.0%
Rent	50,400	6.5%
Repairs & Maintenance	720	0.1%
Shipping & Delivery	-	0.0%
Telephone	3,840	0.5%
Training & Development	-	0.0%
Travel	5,000	0.6%
Utilities	7,400	1.0%
Vehicle (includes mileage)	1,440	0.2%
Leased Equipment	4,800	0.6%
Other	-	0.0%
Other	-	0.0%
Total Operating Expenses	**171,370**	**22.1%**
Operating Income	**61,182**	**7.9%**
Interest Expense	3,477	0.4%
Other Income (interest, royalties)	-	0.0%
Income Before Taxes	**$57,705**	**7.4%**
Income Taxes (if C Corp)	-	0.0%
Net Income	**$57,705**	**7.4%**

Although the Income Statement does report the profitability of the business, Net Income doesn't always indicate positive cash flows. One reason is that non-cash expenses such as Depreciation and Amortization are included in the Income Statement. In some instances, particularly in real estate and other high-investment enterprises, large depreciation or amortization charges can result in a loss—no profit—yet the firm is flush with cash.

Another reason for the disconnect between the Income Statement and the actual cash flow of the business is that you might have significant cash outflows for debt repayments, purchases of inventory, and payments to the owners of the business (dividends or draws) and cash inflows from borrowings from banks and other funding sources that will not show up on your Income Statement. Remember, a business cannot have a negative cash balance.

These discrepancies between what is allowed to be reported on the Income Statement and what is actually flowing into and out of your business make the third financial statement, the Cash Flow Statement, another crucial financial tool on your journey to business success.

Cash Flow Statements

Entrepreneurs usually use one of two cash flow documents to assist them in financial decision-making: the Cash Flow Report or the traditional Cash Flow Statement. Both can be used to report or project the cash that flows in and out of a business for a specific time period. The difference between the two documents is the way in which this information is prepared and reported.

Both these documents include the cash flows received and paid out for loans and owner investments, as well as the purchases of fixed assets. But the primary difference is that the Cash Flow Report records cash activity as it relates to the individual revenue and expense categories such as you would find on an Income Statement. The traditional Cash Flow Statement reports cash activity as it relates to the operating, investing, and financing activities of the business.

Cash Flow Report – The monthly Cash Flow Report is one of the most important planning and reporting tools you use during the start-up phase of business.

Compare the Cash Flow Report to your personal checkbook register. Every time you deposit money into your account or write checks out of the account you record the transaction and keep a running total. In the same way, the Cash Flow Report records every cash entry into your business and cash payment out of the business on a monthly basis. These inflows and outflows are grouped by categories that will affect the other financial statements, such as equity contributions, inventory purchases, or operating expenses.

The advantage of the Cash Flow Report over your regular checkbook register is the way it displays monthly financial activity over time, making it easy to analyze past fluctuations in cash flow during the year and predict future fluctuations.

The Cash Flow Report can help you with day-to-day cash budgeting. You need cash flow analysis because a delay usually occurs between the time you pay out cash to generate sales (for example, purchasing inventory or paying employees' salaries) and the time you actually receive cash from those sales—also called the *cash cycle*. Since typical sales transactions have a cash cycle of days, weeks, or even months, you will need to locate additional funds to keep the business running while waiting for the cycle to be completed.

Fortunately, cash flow planning is simple in concept, although coming up with the numbers can involve considerable diligence. Cash flow is exactly what its name implies: the anticipation of cash as it flows into and out of the company. Only cash transactions are included in this analysis. You can ignore non-cash accounting entries such as depreciation and amortization on the Cash Flow Report.

The Cash Flow Report lists the sources of cash you expect to receive on a monthly basis. This list includes cash sales, collections from accounts receivables, equity contributions from owners, and loans from either owners or outside sources. The cash you expect to receive is added to the cash balance remaining from the prior month to total the cash available for that month.

Backyard Solutions Cash Flow Report (Projected)		
2005	**JAN**	**FEB**
Cash In		
Cash Sales	-	-
Collections from Accounts Receivables	15,504	13,798
Equity Received	-	-
Loans Received	20,000	-
Other Cash In (receipts from other assets)	-	-
Other Cash In (interest, royalties)	-	-
Total Cash In	**35,504**	**13,798**
Total Cash Available	**45,504**	**27,000**
Cash Out		
Inventory Expenditures		
Inventory/Raw Material (cash)	8,363	8,363
Inventory/Raw Material (paid on account)	-	-
Production Expenses	2,256	2,256
Operating Expenses		
Advertising	-	-
Bank Charges	-	-
Dues & Subscriptions	-	-
Insurance	225	225
Licenses & Fees	215	-
Marketing & Promotion	3,500	200
Meals & Entertainment	1,000	-
Miscellaneous	100	100
Office Expense	150	150
Office Supplies	-	-
Outside Services	70	70
Payroll Expenses		
Salaries & Wages	2,000	2,000
Payroll Taxes	300	300
Benefits	1,000	1,000
Professional Fees	1,200	200
Property Taxes	-	-
Rent	4,200	4,200
Repairs & Maintenance	-	-
Shipping & Delivery	-	-
Telephone	300	350
Training & Development	-	-
Travel	5,000	-
Utilities	500	500
Vehicle	120	120
Leased Equipment	400	400
Other	-	-
Other	-	-
Paid on Account	-	-
Non-Operating Costs		
Capital Purchases	-	-
Estimated Income Tax Payments	-	-
Interest Payments	309	306
Loan Principal Payments	594	598
Owner's Draw	500	500
Other Cash Out	-	-
Total Cash Out	**32,302**	**21,838**
Monthly Cash Flow (Cash In – Cash Out)	**3,202**	**(8,040)**
Beginning Cash Balance	**10,000**	**13,202**
Ending Cash Balance	**$13,202**	**$5,162**

For More Information

on the Cash Flow Report go to www.fasttrac.org/toolkits.

You deduct all items paid for with cash from the total cash available to identify the cash balance at the end of the month. This amount must always be above zero. In fact, you should try to maintain a healthy cushion to cover unexpected differences between projected cash flow and actual cash transactions.

Your business may have a lot of money coming in next month, but that may not save it from insolvency if you have to pay out a lot of money tomorrow. Prepare to finance any expected negative balances.

Backyard Solutions Statement of Cash Flows for the Year Ending 2005 (Projected)	
Cash Flows from Operating Activities	
Net Income	$57,705
Adjustments to reconcile Net Income to Net Cash provided by operating activities:	
Depreciation & Amortization Expense	14,095
Decrease in Accounts Receivable	2,650
Decrease in Inventories	5,730
Decrease in Accounts Payable	(6,834)
Net Cash Provided by Operating Activities	73,346
Cash Flows from Investing Activities	
Purchase of Property, Plant, & Equipment	(25,000)
Net Cash Used by Investing Activities	(25,000)
Cash Flows from Financing Activities	
Proceeds from Loans	40,000
Principal Payment on Loans	(7,026)
Payment of Owner's Draws	(6,000)
Proceeds from Issuance of Stock	25,000
Net Cash Provided by Financing Activities	51,974
Net Increase in Cash	100,320
Cash at Beginning of Year	10,000
Cash at End of Year	$110,320

Cash Flow Statement – The traditional Cash Flow Statement prepared by accountants reconciles the changes that occur within the Balance Sheet accounts with the cash provided from the operations of the business. The cash flows from investing and financing activities are also reported. These statements are more effective at reporting actual cash activity than projected activity. Therefore, you may find that the traditional Cash Flow Statement becomes more useful to you after your start-up phase.

Instead of projecting a traditional Cash Flow Statement, this program relies on the Cash Flow Report that will help you track the same information in a more user-friendly format.

Screening for Financial Feasibility

When you decide you want to visit a new vacation spot, do you just jump in the car and drive there? Of course not. You learn about the costs of the visit: how long, how far, how much? You look at your bank balance and your work schedule and then make some decisions. In the same way, you should plan ahead, research, and evaluate your new business venture.

You have already established your personal financial goals and learned some of the financial language of business. Now let's focus on the business itself and its ability to fulfill those goals by using the financial statements as business planning tools.

As you explore your business concept to determine its financial feasibility, investigate three components—start-up costs, profitability, and cash flow. Here are the steps in the process:

1. Start-Up Costs – Determine how much money you need to get your venture off the ground.
2. Profitability – Gauge whether the concept is profitable or at least has a profitable future.
3. Cash Flow – Understand the cash flow needs of the venture and have funding sources identified to meet those needs.

This process will begin with an initial screening in this module against your personal financial goals. Then you will determine start-up costs. Module 8 will focus on profitability, and Module 9 will concentrate on cash needs and potential sources to obtain the cash.

Start-Up Costs

Before you start, you need to have some idea of what costs you will incur even before you make your first sale. Identifying the start-up costs for a venture helps you know the amount of money needed prior to opening your doors for business.

What Are Start-Up Costs?

Start-up costs can be either *expenditures*—one-time costs for capital assets or vendor deposits—or *expenses*—costs for operations that will continue throughout the existence of the business.

You need to understand the difference between expenditures and expenses because you will record them differently on your financial statements, and they can affect your business's financial position and tax liability. See if you can apply these concepts on a small, relatively simple business.

Start-Up Expenditures – Imagine that you are setting up a pet grooming business. What are some of your expenditures during the start-up phase? Remember, expenditures are assets purchased to operate the business and generate revenue such as computers, grooming tables, and shears. They can also include upfront payments for security deposits required by utility companies or landlords. These deposits will be recorded as assets on the Balance Sheet because as long as you perform all the requirements of your agreement, you expect to receive that money back. So, in essence, you have given them money to hold on your behalf.

TiP Keep in mind that start-up costs are only incurred in the start-up phase of business. Once your business engages in sales opportunities, it has progressed through start-up and into the on-going operational phase.

Another type of start-up expenditure is the cost of purchasing your opening inventory such as dog food, leashes, or other supplies you might want to sell to customers.

Examples of possible start-up expenditures include:

Capital Expenditures
- Equipment
- Furniture and Fixtures
- Leasehold Improvements
- Vehicles
- Buildings
- Land

Security Deposits
- Rent Deposit
- Telephone Deposit
- Utility Deposits

Other Expenditures
- Inventory

Start-Up Expenses – When you pay out cash during the start-up phase for costs to operate your business and those purchases do not retain value, they are expenses. These expenses include all costs of running the business. Keep in mind that you are currently only concerned about those costs occurring while the business is in the start-up phase. Most expenses will continue to occur throughout the life of the business. For now, focus on the expenses you expect to have only during the length of time it takes you to complete the start-up phase.

Examples of possible start-up expenses include the following:
- Rent
- Computer Repairs
- Legal and Consulting Fees
- Accounting Fees
- Salaries and Wages – Training/Setup
- Benefits and Taxes – Training/Setup
- Office Supplies
- Business Supplies
- Printing – Business Cards, Stationery, Brochures
- Pre-Opening Advertising

Check Your Knowledge ✓

Expenditures vs. Expenses

Reinforce your understanding of the differences between start-up expenditures and expenses. Identify each start-up cost below as an expenditure or expense by placing a check in the appropriate box. Or, check your knowledge online at www.fasttrac.org/toolkits.

	Expenditure	Expense		Expenditure	Expense
Accounting Fees	❑	❑	Marketing	❑	❑
Building	❑	❑	Office Expense	❑	❑
Equipment	❑	❑	Office Supplies	❑	❑
Filing Fees	❑	❑	Payroll Benefits	❑	❑
Furniture	❑	❑	Pre-Opening Advertising	❑	❑
Land	❑	❑	Printed Materials	❑	❑
Leasehold Improvements	❑	❑	Rent	❑	❑
Legal and Consulting Fees	❑	❑	Vehicles	❑	❑
			Wages	❑	❑

Where Do I Find Start-Up Costs?

You need to estimate start-up costs as accurately as possible based on research you began in Module 2 about your industry and local conditions. If actual costs differ significantly from your expectations, then your business could experience cash shortages even before its doors open.

TIP When estimating start-up expenses, be as realistic and accurate as possible. Entrepreneurs always discover hidden costs after start-up.

You will practice estimating start-up costs for a sample business when you complete Activity 3a. One method of identifying start-up costs is to do a mental walk-through of what your business will look like by answering some important questions in the Reality Check *Start-Up Planning*. Answers to these questions will help you determine the type of expenditures and expenses you need to estimate. When you identify these estimates, you can record them on the Start-Up Costs Matrix in Action Step 3.1 on p. 108.

How Do I Keep Track of Start-Up Costs?

Now that you have identified certain aspects of your business concept that will have costs associated with them, you can begin to estimate the actual amounts. Your initial estimates will be a "best guess" based on your past experiences or just a hunch. If you know other entrepreneurs, you may be able to ask them for cost estimates. Or maybe you have run across cost information in your market research and can supply industry averages for now. Because these costs and amounts must ultimately be accurate, think of ways to research your estimates to either corroborate them or to make them more accurate.

What Else Shall I Consider About Start-Up Costs?

TIP Alter your start-up plans, not your start-up cost estimates.

Ideas for launching new companies are everywhere, but your business concept must match both your personal vision and your pocketbook. To assure that your business concept matches the available money, you must be as realistic and accurate as possible in start-up estimates. Some entrepreneurs inadvertently underestimate start-up costs, just as the magazine publishers did who had to abandon their business after just three issues. Some entrepreneurs try to force the budget process to match the amount of money they have available. Your start-up cost estimates—not your currently available funds—should reveal to you how much money the business concept needs at start-up.

Start-Up Estimates Matter

Often a primary portion of start-up costs is used to support the ongoing activities of a business until revenues reach an adequate level to provide the needed cash. One statewide magazine in the Midwest underestimated its start-up costs by basing research on numbers supplied by a neighboring state's magazine. This magazine had been in business for thirty years and had a slightly different market focus. When advertising and subscription sales came in at lower-than-expected rates, and graphic design, paper, and printing costs posted higher than expected, the magazine faced an immediate cash shortage. After calculating its additional funding needs, the owners went looking for an investor only to discover that most magazines cannot attract funding in the first three years of business. The magazine was forced to fold after only three issues or risk heavy debt for its owners.

Reality Check ✔

Start-Up Planning

The following questions will help you further define the start-up costs necessary for your particular business concept.

Where will my business be located?

What size will my business be initially?

What will the facilities look like? What improvements are necessary?

What furniture and fixtures will I need?

What equipment will I need for the office or for production?

What types of signs will be required for the facility?

What type of inventory and how much will I need prior to opening the business?

What kinds of security deposits will be required? For instance, how much will deposits cost for telephone, utilities, and rent—first and last month?

What types of governmental (local, state, federal) requirements must I comply with?

What type of marketing will I be doing prior to opening the business such as brochures, advertising, stationery, and business cards?

What staff members need to be hired and trained prior to opening?

Do Your Homework

When Danny O'Neill decided to launch The Roasterie, he took a leave of absence from his corporate job and spent nearly seven months investigating the specialty coffee business and determining his start-up costs.

O'Neill approached this research like a full-time job. "I was relentless," he admits, noting that fear was a key driver. "I was afraid that I might fail and have to go back to my corporate job. But instead of being paralyzed by fear, I let it motivate me."

One of O'Neill's first moves was to join a specialty coffee association, which proved to be his single biggest source of information. The association pointed him to a number of industry experts—and the right questions to ask.

Traveling across the United States and to Costa Rica, O'Neill visited coffee growers, exporters, brokers and other industry players. He also called on potential customers in his own backyard to find out what kind of coffee they currently bought, how much they spent, and if they would be willing to upscale.

As a result of O'Neill's extensive research, he confronted no real surprises in terms of start-up costs. In fact, as he gathered information, O'Neill was able to significantly reduce costs and fund the company entirely on personal savings—with his largest expenditure being a $12,000 roaster.

The most dramatic savings came from a decision to start the business in his home instead of commercial space. Then O'Neill sliced infrastructure costs even further. He needed to retrofit his basement into a "cleanable, washable" environment that would pass governmental codes, and contractors had estimated the remodeling job would cost between $10,000 and $20,000. Yet with a little creativity—and a lot of sweat equity—O'Neill did the work himself for $800. "My goal was to save as much money as possible and eke out an existence until I could get cash flow coming in," he explains.

"Many entrepreneurs lose their shirts because they haven't spent enough time researching costs and putting a good plan in place," says O'Neill, who believes in leaving no stone unturned. "Most people are glad to help, and if they don't know the answers to your questions, they'll usually refer you to someone else. But it's strange how often leads drop in entrepreneurs' laps and they don't pursue them."

Avoid projecting a lower start-up amount just to get a loan from a bank. Redefine your concept rather than start a business with too little money. If the costs of starting the business under your current business model are too high, consider another approach to starting the business or another business altogether.

If you find it necessary to reduce start-up costs, first consider altering your business concept to one that has a more flexible entry and still matches your personal vision. For example, an entrepreneur whose initial business concept is to renovate a historic building into a banquet facility in the downtown district of a major city may find that starting an event planning business targeting individuals provides the same type of personal satisfaction. This alternative business concept would also be more flexible and require far less in start-up funds.

CHECK YOUR KNOWLEDGE ANSWERS FROM P. 94

	Expenditure	Expense		Expenditure	Expense
Accounting Fees		X	Marketing		X
Building	X		Office Expense		X
Equipment	X		Office Supplies		X
Filing Fees		X	Payroll Benefits		X
Furniture	X		Pre-opening Advertising		X
Land	X		Printed Materials		X
Leasehold Improvements	X		Rent		X
Legal and Consulting Fees		X	Vehicles	X	
			Wages		X

If you cannot adjust your entry strategy, but still need to reduce start-up costs, consider ways you can lease, barter, or alternatively provide for goods or services you have initially identified as necessary. For example, Alex Putnam of Backyard Solutions, whose financial statements you have been seeing as examples in this module, projected start-up costs at $15,000. Trying to protect his cash reserve, Alex re-examined his projections and decided he could lease his equipment instead of buying it, saving him about $8,000 at start-up. Then he considered bartering with an attorney, one $1,000 shed for $1,000 worth of legal advice, assuming of course, his attorney agreed to the swap and it was properly recorded for income tax purposes. Finally, he discovered that he could eliminate the cost of a second phone line for his fax machine by using a free fax-to-e-mail service for the few times he might need fax capabilities. The total of these adjustments reached $9,300, dropping his start-up projection to $5,700, well within his range to begin.

The level of flexibility and options you have for start-up may mean the difference between starting a business and just thinking about it. Also, the length of the start-up process and level of involvement will mean more money out of your pocket. For example, a catering business has a great deal more flexibility than a restaurant. It could be started on a smaller scale, in a shorter time frame, targeting a smaller market, with limited start-up costs. Consider how you answered the first question in the Reality Check *Personal Goals Worksheet*, "What aspects of owning and operating your own business especially appeal to you?" What flexibility have you designed into your business concept?

Another way to reduce start-up costs is to reconsider ways to cover the expenditures and expenses needed. Here are some ways to reduce these costs:
- Lease instead of purchase equipment
- Sub-contract instead of hire
- Start in your home
- Delay hiring dates
- Reduce inventory costs by having manufacturers drop ship
- Reduce your salary with the expectation of increasing it later

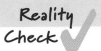

Business Concept Flexibility

Before you estimate start-up costs, you must have a solid business concept established. As you collect the information you need for this estimate, ask yourself these questions:

How flexible are my options for start-up based on my business concept?

How long and involved is the start-up process?

How critical is it to obtain 100 percent of my costs prior to initial start-up?

Reduce Your Costs, Not Your Potential for Success

When Danny O'Neill of The Roasterie resigned from his corporate job, he had to turn in his company car. In need of transportation but wanting to save money for his business, O'Neill bought an old Chevrolet for $700. "I remember parking blocks away whenever I went on sales appointments because I was so embarrassed by that car," he recalls.

Despite his company's success, O'Neill still embraces a frugal mentality. Although he won't skimp on quality equipment or coffee beans, he finds plenty of other ways to save money. For example, when importing beans from South America, The Roasterie has reduced shipping costs from 20 cents to 5 cents per pound by using a central warehouse in California.

"Whenever we need something, we challenge ourselves to think of ways to get it cheaper," O'Neill says. When the company needed special "cupping" tables for coffee tastings, O'Neill was able to build his own, using tabletops one customer was about to throw away and swapping another customer a grinder in exchange for pedestals. "Instead of spending $7,000, we got what we wanted for less than $200 by using a little creativity," O'Neill says.

As you screen for feasibility, estimating your start-up costs helps you keep in mind your personal vision. Remember, a business concept that cannot reach your personal financial goals is not a feasible business for you. Accurately predicting start-up costs will affect another aspect of your business that you will screen for: profitability.

Profitability

One of the primary goals of every business is to become profitable. You may have enough cash to get your business started, but do you have enough to keep it going?

Only with adequate profits will you have the cash to pay debts, purchase inventory, fund future growth, and reward investors.

Profit is what is left over after the expenses of your business have been deducted from the revenues generated by the business:

Revenues – Expenses = Profit or Net Income

You will screen for profitability by comparing your business against profitability criteria in Action Step 3.2 Evaluate My Business Concept Against My Financial Goals. This test should give you the confidence to make changes and move forward with planning your business start-up. Testing for profitability will continue in Module 8.

Revenue

Revenue is money, or the promise of money, you receive when you provide customers with products or services. You calculate revenue by taking the total number of products or services sold and multiplying them by the price:

Revenues = Number of units sold x Price (per unit)

TiP Even nonprofits must consider profitability. Profits generated from their operations can be re-invested to grow current programs or start new ones.

Reality
Check ✓

Revenue and Pricing

Describe the revenue-generating activities of your business.

What products will you offer?

What services?

What product/service combinations?

How will your products/services be priced?

The price you charge often affects the number of products or services you can sell. Most often, the lower the price, the more products or services sold. In some cases, however, increasing the price gives the customer the idea of increased value and you sell more products or services.

Expenses
The other major contributor to calculating Net Income is Expenses. Expenses on the Income Statement are classified into two main categories: Cost of Goods Sold and Operating Expenses.

Cost of Goods Sold – Cost of Goods Sold/Cost of Sales includes all costs directly related to a product or service you sell. For example, a custom lawn chair business records all the costs of building its chairs, including labor, materials and overhead related to production. These costs appear in the Inventory account on the Balance Sheet until the chairs are sold. When the chairs sell, the Inventory amount related to the chairs that are sold is transferred out of the Inventory balance and into Cost of Goods Sold on the Income Statement.

Cost of Sales is a term used by service-based businesses instead of *Cost of Goods Sold*. Cost of Sales usually refers to service labor costs, but may also include costs for materials or supplies.

Even if a business is owned and operated by only one person, a portion of the owner's salary relates to the cost of providing that product or service and, therefore, is included in Cost of Sales.

TiP Retail stores often mark up merchandise 100 percent of cost. This markup means that every time a retail store sells something, up to 50 percent of the money collected covers the actual cost of the item. The remaining 50 percent covers operating expenses and provides a profit.

of Cost of Goods online at
www.fasttrac.org/toolkits.

When you subtract the Cost of Goods Sold or Cost of Sales from Revenues on the Income Statement, the result is the Gross Margin:

Gross Margin = Revenues - Cost of Goods Sold (or Cost of Sales)

Gross Margin is a critical number to understand because it reflects the amount of money you have left to cover your operating expenses.

Operating Expenses – Operating expenses are the costs associated with keeping your business up-and-running. They include all of the expenses of operating the business. Sometimes called *overhead*, these expenses are necessary to support the selling, administrative, and general operations of your business venture. You subtract the Operating Expenses from the Gross Margin on the Income Statement to identify Net Income.

Sales
- *Cost of Goods Sold (or Cost of Sales)*
= *Gross Margin*
- *Operating Expenses*
= *Net Income*

What types of expenses do you anticipate for your business? You will consider many of these expenses on the Start-Up Costs Matrix in Action Step 3.1 Estimate Start-Up Costs. Which expenses on that matrix will be ongoing and will directly relate to your Cost of Goods Sold or Inventory? If you are a service business, what expenses will you include in your Cost of Sales? Complete the Reality Check *Business Expenses* to start thinking about start-up costs.

Reality Check ✓ **Business Expenses**

Check the expenses below that you expect to be ongoing in your business.

- Cost of Goods/Inventory
- Advertising
- Bank Charges
- Dues & Subscriptions
- Insurance
- Licenses & Fees
- Marketing & Promotion
- Meals & Entertainment
- Miscellaneous

- Office Expenses (for example Postage)
- Office Supplies
- Outside Services
- Payroll Services
- Professional Fees
- Property Taxes
- Rent
- Repairs & Maintenance

- Shipping & Delivery
- Telephone
- Training & Development
- Travel
- Utilities
- Vehicle
- Other
- Other
- Other

You will research the business expenses that relate to your business concept. As you complete each subsequent module and the corresponding section of the Business Plan, you will develop financial assumptions on the Financial Facts Worksheets. These worksheets will help you project the cost associated with each aspect of operating your business. See the Financial Facts Worksheets in this module on pp. 128 – 136.

Monitoring profitability means keeping an eye on revenues and expenses—both Cost of Goods Sold and Operating Expenses. When testing your business concept for feasibility, you need to ensure that your predicted costs of doing business can be more than adequately covered by projected revenues. One way to maintain this balance is by projecting cash flow.

Cash Flow

Just as you would not begin a trip without knowing how much it was going to cost, you would not spend money while on that journey without keeping an eye on the cash in your pocket. The same principle applies in business. Profitable or not, your business must maintain a positive cash balance.

If profitability tells you about your business's ability to generate income, then cash flow tells you about your business's ability to pay obligations and still maintain a cash reserve. Using your financial statements as a tool, you can forecast the ability of your company to achieve your cash flow objectives.

You can use the Cash Flow Report not only for reporting but also for projecting cash activity in your business. When you test your business concept for feasibility, you will want to try to project its cash flow accurately.

As you have seen, the Income Statement reports the profitability of the business; however, Net Income does not always result in positive cash flows. For example, if you allow customers to pay for purchases, not at the time of the sale, but ten to forty-five days later, you have just granted them credit terms. You record the revenue from the sale when you deliver the product or provide the service, and you have more than likely already paid for the costs associated with the sale. But you do not receive the cash until later.

The delay between when you spend cash to generate a sale and when you receive cash from the customer is called the *cash cycle*. This interruption in cash flow can have significant impact on the cash available to your business, especially when your business is experiencing significant growth in sales.

Many businesses rely on outside cash sources, in addition to profits, to make sure cash is available when they need it.

TiP Customers who pay late can have a significant effect on your business because if you do not receive cash when you expect it, your business may run into cash shortages.

Business Funding Needs

Businesses often need different kinds of funding during each stage of development in the business life cycle—start-up, operational, and growth. An accurate projection of cash flow over three to five years of business can help you predict your funding needs.

Funding Stages

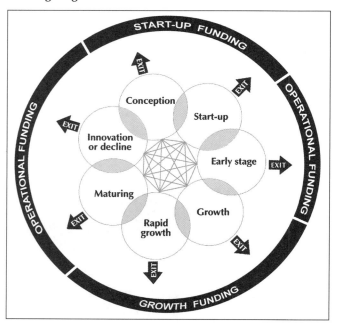

Start-Up Funding – Businesses generally need start-up funding because sales have yet to take place. If you have no sales, then you have no profits or cash generated from those profits. During this time, you'll need to find funding for the cost of developing your concept, purchasing assets, and paying expenses such as salaries, rent, and advertising. After you have prepared the Start-Up Costs Matrix in Action Step 3.1 Estimate Start-Up Costs, you'll have a better idea of the amount of money you need to get your business started.

Operational Funding – Operational funding will cover cash needs during the early stage of operations (post-start-up) and when the business enters the maturing stage. During these business stages, cash flow is more predictable, but there may be a need to update equipment or cover seasonal cash flow shortages.

After you complete the projected Income Statement and Cash Flow Report in Modules 8 and 9, you will be able to more accurately estimate the amount of operational funding you may need.

TiP A business can operate for a long time at a loss—many do—but no company can operate without cash. No cash…no business!

Growth Funding – Businesses seek growth funding when they experience or expect to experience high growth rates. Growth usually creates significant cash needs. Growth usually requires additional equipment, employees, locations, and inventory to increase the output of products or services to meet increased market demand. The growth stage is not the final phase of the business. You can expect the business's growth to plateau, and it will enter a mature operational stage.

In each of these business stages, your funding needs will be unique. Carefully predicting start-up costs and then keeping a wary eye on profitability and cash flow will provide you with accurate information about how much money you will need. Now let's consider where you might find that money.

Funding Sources

Raising money is an art. Fortunately, it's an art you can learn. To become an expert at raising money, you need to know about sources of money, how to find them, and how to evaluate them to determine which source is the best fit for your business. Even if you do not need outside funding in the start-up stage, you may discover a time when outside money is necessary. Whether you can get the money will depend on how well you have prepared for it and how you deal with the money sources.

The majority of financing for entrepreneurial ventures comes from the business owner and informal investors—meaning your family and friends.

By downsizing his original concept, Danny O'Neill was able to launch The Roasterie on his own, without outside financing. Yet he continued to meet with bankers, showing them monthly progress reports about The Roasterie's customer base and cash flow. Building those relationships helped O'Neill secure a $100,000 Small Business Administration loan within six months of start-up, which enabled him to move into commercial space and buy new equipment.

Equity vs. Debt

All funding for your business will come from either equity or debt sources. During the life of your business, you may use a combination of each of these. When you think about getting funding, think about it as a give-and-take relationship. You get the money. The funder expects to receive something too.

Equity financing – Remember the Balance Sheet term *owner's equity*? Equity means ownership. To become an owner of a business, typically you have to pay money to the business. For corporations and limited liability companies, owners purchase stock or ownership units. The money received from these transactions can be used to fund the activities of the business.

These are examples of equity financing:
- Entrepreneur contributions
- Private investors, including angels and venture capitalists
- Earnings retained in the business
- Initial Public Offerings

Equity gives owners the rights to a certain amount of control and a share in the profits. If you are a single equity holder, you clearly hold all the rights to the business. As you add equity holders, you share rights with them and your business can become more difficult to manage.

Debt financing – Debt takes many forms. The essence of debt is that the borrower must repay the funds along with agreed-upon service charges such as interest and loan origination fees. If the money is not repaid as promised, the lender can start collection proceedings. This process can become very uncomfortable for the entrepreneur, who could stand to lose the business and any non-business assets pledged to secure the loan.

These are examples of debt financing:
- Loans from entrepreneur
- Loans from friends and family
- Bank financing including short- and long-term loans and lines of credit
- Small Business Administration-backed loans

The decision to borrow money should not be taken lightly. The borrower assumes a serious obligation. A basic lesson of finance is that money should not be borrowed unless it will earn more than it costs. You will estimate your funding needs in Action Step 3.3 Consider Potential Funding Sources.

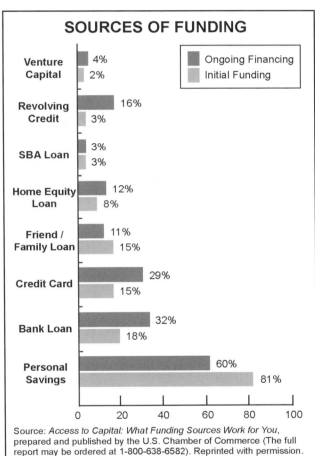

SOURCES OF FUNDING

Ongoing Financing
Initial Funding

Venture Capital: 4% / 2%
Revolving Credit: 16% / 3%
SBA Loan: 3% / 3%
Home Equity Loan: 12% / 8%
Friend / Family Loan: 11% / 15%
Credit Card: 29% / 15%
Bank Loan: 32% / 18%
Personal Savings: 60% / 81%

Source: *Access to Capital: What Funding Sources Work for You*, prepared and published by the U.S. Chamber of Commerce (The full report may be ordered at 1-800-638-6582). Reprinted with permission.

Business Concept Analysis

Throughout these first three modules, you have analyzed your business concept from three perspectives:

- How well the business concept will help you reach your personal and professional goals
- Whether the business concept represents a market opportunity
- How well the business concept will help you meet your financial goals

In each module, one of the three screening checklists helps you examine your business concept and decide if it passes your criteria.

In this module, Action Step 3.2 Evaluate My Business Concept Against My Financial Goals guides you as you screen your business concept for financial feasibility. The final action step, Action Step 3.4 Complete My Business Concept Analysis, gives you a comprehensive tool to evaluate your concept before you begin working on your Business Plan. This action step combines criteria from the previous three screenings into an overall business concept evaluation tool. Remember to come back and repeat this action step each time you make significant changes to your concept to make sure it still passes your personal, professional, and financial goals.

Passing this screening is your green light to continue planning your business. Keep these results in perspective. Passing does not guarantee that your business will be successful; rather, it tells you your business concept is potentially feasible and that additional planning is appropriate. As you conduct further research, gather more information, and apply it to your business concept, you will be in a better position to gauge the feasibility of your proposed venture. After you complete your Business Plan, you will be in a great position to decide whether to launch the business.

Summary

This module introduced the financial aspects you must consider when evaluating your business concept—start-up costs, profitability, and cash flow. You also discovered the key relationship between researched information and accurate projections. This module concludes the concept analysis portion of this program with an overall evaluation of your business concept. This evaluation will help you determine if your next steps should be to use or modify your business concept, continue the business planning process, and write your Business Plan.

Key Things to Remember

- Financial goal setting includes the key aspects of analyzing and planning for sufficient start-up funds, profitability, and cash flow.

- Effectively estimating start-up costs by obtaining accurate, timely information is critical to achieving a successful start-up.

- Understanding key financial concepts affects your overall success as an entrepreneur.

- The finalized business concept statement should be a match with your personal vision, the market needs, and financial goals.

- Screening tools can make the business concept assessment process easier.

In Module 4, you will learn what goes into an effective Business Plan and begin the planning process with a closer look at your product or service.

Activity 3a Start-Up Costs

Practice the process of identifying start-up costs and adjusting them to reflect available funds.

Directions

Using one of the following sample business concepts, identify potential start-up items (both expenses and expenditures). Estimate the amount of money needed for each item as well as a grand total. Make assumptions when necessary.

Midtown Bicycle will be located in the celebrated Midtown area within a 6,500 square foot historic building. The business, offering bicycle sales, service, and training in the 3,000 square foot training facility, will open on July 1 after the historic redevelopment of the building is complete. Opening inventory will include premium quality bicycles, parts, accessories, clothing, safety equipment, and books. Services will include cyclist training, classes, service, and repairs. Facilities and fixtures can be installed six weeks prior to opening. Staff will be hired and trained one month prior to opening. Signage will be provided by the property manager, but paid for by Midtown Bicycle. Marketing prior to opening will include television and radio advertisements, as well as an endorsement by an Olympic medal-winning cyclist.

Plant Care, Inc., will provide fresh flowers, plants, and trees to businesses located in downtown's new corporate Pinnacle Office Park. The unique aspect, stemming from the entrepreneur's horticulture degree and lifelong love of plants, is the source of the flowers and plants—Plant Care's own 15,000 square foot nursery and green house located outside the city limits on Highway 99. Plant Care will use uniquely painted delivery vehicles and maintain a small warehouse facility near the office park with a small office and room for daily deliveries from the greenhouse. Because Plant Care is providing its own flowers, plants, and trees, the start-up process will take nearly eighteen months. Marketing will include providing free flower arrangements and plants to potential clients.

Start-Up Item	Cost Estimate
EXAMPLE *Equipment*	*$15,000*

Note: Exact amounts cannot be determined without research. Estimates are fine for this activity.

Action Step 3.1 Estimate Start-Up Costs

Identify my start-up costs so that I can analyze the feasibility of my business concept.

Directions
Follow the steps below to fill out the Start-Up Costs Matrix and identify research necessary to estimate start-up costs.

A. **Estimate expenditures and expenses.** Using your Reality Check *Start-Up Planning* and other sources you may have discovered, estimate the expenditures and expenses associated with your particular business concept.

B. **Record start-up costs on the Start-Up Costs Matrix.** Use the Start-Up Costs Matrix on p. 108 to capture the start-up items and money needed. Be sure to include all costs you expect to incur *only* during the start-up phase.

C. **Research your estimates.** Knowing that these costs and amounts must be accurate, think of ways to research your estimates to either corroborate them or to make them more accurate. Fill in each blank next to your estimated amounts with possible research sources.

D. **Prove the accuracy of your estimates.** The final step to complete the matrix is to contact the research sources and prove the accuracy of your initial start-up cost estimates. Your final estimates will be entered into the Financial Template when you write your Financial Plan in Modules 8 and 9.

Action Step 3.1 **Estimate Start-Up Costs** continued

Start-Up Costs Matrix

Expenditures	Estimated Amount	Sources for Research
Security Deposits		
Rent Deposit		
Telephone Deposit		
Utility Deposits		
Other Deposits		
Capital Expenditures		
Computer Equipment		
Equipment & Machinery		
Furniture & Fixtures		
Vehicle (includes mileage)		
Leasehold Improvements		
Buildings		
Land		
Other Capital Expenditures		
Other Expenditures		
Inventory		

Expenses	Estimated Amount	Sources for Research
Accounting Fees		
Activation Fee		
Corporate Fees & Taxes		
Federal Tax ID		
Fictitious Name Costs		
Insurance		
Legal & Consulting Fees		
Marketing		
Meals & Entertainment		
Office Expenses		
Office Supplies		
Payroll Expenses		
Salaries & Wages		
Payroll Taxes		
Benefits		
Pre-Opening Advertising		
Printing		
Rent		
Sales Tax Permits		
Other Start-Up Expenses		
Total Estimated Start-Up Costs		

Action Step 3.2 **Evaluate My Business Concept Against My Financial Goals**

Evaluate my business concept and its potential to help me meet my personal financial goals.

Directions

Follow the steps below to review your personal financial goals and the business's financial feasibility and compare them to your business concept using the charts on p. 110 – 114.

A. **Review your personal financial goals.** Take a minute to review your *Personal Goals Worksheet* from the Reality Check on p. 87. Make any changes you feel are necessary to adequately define what financial success means to you.

B. **Identify non-negotiable criteria.** Read the criteria in the first column of the charts on pp. 110 – 114. Some criteria relate directly to your own personal goals, such as *Start-up costs are within my investment goal*. Others relate to the business's ability to be financially feasible, such as *Revenue stream is continuous*. Check the box in the corner of each lettered item to indicate which criteria are most important to your personal financial success. For example, your personal salary requirements may be non-negotiable. A indicates that this criterion cannot be compromised.

Some essential criteria are based on your answers to the following questions from the Reality Check *Personal Goals Worksheet*:
1. How much are you willing to invest in the business?
2. How much of your investment will come from savings and from borrowing?
3. What salary do you require? Want?

C. **Rate how well your business concept matches your personal financial goals.** Identify the level that your business concept meets your personal financial goals using a scale of 1 to 5. A 1 means that the business concept does not at all meet the criterion (or that not enough information is yet available) and a 5 means that the concept perfectly meets the criterion. If a criterion does not apply to your business, skip it. Circle the numbered response to each lettered criterion statement that best describes your concept.

Action Step 3.2 — Evaluate My Business Concept Against My Financial Goals
continued

Business Concept Analysis Checklist

Personal Financial Goals	1. Does not meet my financial goal.	2. Somewhat meets my financial goal.	3. It might meet my financial goal.	4. Meets my financial goal very well.	5. Meets my financial goal perfectly.
a. I am willing to invest money in my business.	1. I have no money to invest.	2. I have money to invest, but I'm not sure I want to risk putting it into my business.	3. I have a small nest egg that I'm pretty sure could be used for my business.	4. I have sufficient money in other investments that could probably be used.	5. I have been putting aside money for this purpose for several years.
b. A portion of the money I invest will come from my personal savings.	1. I have no personal savings.	2. My personal savings are so small that using the money would not matter.	3. I am considering using a portion of my savings.	4. I am fairly confident that I can use a portion of my savings.	5. A portion of the money I invest will definitely come from my savings.
c. A portion of what I invest will be borrowed.	1. My credit is too negative to borrow.	2. My borrowing limits are fairly low.	3. I'm not certain how much I would be able to borrow, all things considered.	4. I am fairly sure I can borrow what I need.	5. Borrowing is not a problem at all.
d. The business will generate enough salary for me to meet my personal needs.	1. I don't anticipate being able to take a salary for many years. This is a big problem.	2. I know I won't draw a salary for awhile and will try to figure out how to pay my living expenses.	3. I think I can squeak through.	4. I will be able to draw a salary before my savings run out.	5. The salary I can draw will be fine from the very beginning.
e. Other					

Action Step 3.2   Evaluate My Business Concept Against My Financial Goals
continued

Business Concept Analysis Checklist

Start-Up Criteria	1. Does not meet the criteria.	2. Somewhat meets the criteria.	3. It might meet the criteria.	4. Meets the criteria very well.	5. Meets the criteria perfectly.	
f. Start-up costs have been identified.	1. I know very little about the start-up costs.	2. I have begun to research start-up costs.	3. I have identified and researched most of my start-up costs.	4. I have identified most of my start-up expense and expenditure categories, estimated amounts, and need more research to validate the figures.	5. I have identified all start-up expense and expenditure categories, estimated amounts, and conducted research to validate the figures.	☐
g. Start-up costs are flexible and can change if necessary.	1. Once the start-up is underway, the costs are set in stone.	2. There may be some way that a few of the start-up costs could be modified.	3. I'm not clear how flexible the concept is.	4. The concept is a little flexible in that the length of the start-up process, the initial investment, and the target market can all be reduced.	5. The concept is extremely flexible in that the length of the start-up process, the initial investment, and the target market can all be reduced.	☐
h. The start-up process is short/minimal.	1. There will be a long start-up process for this business.	2. The start-up process is average for this business.	3. I'm not sure how long the start-up process will take.	4. The length of the start-up process is somewhat short from initial idea to business start.	5. The length of the start-up process is very short and uninvolved from initial idea to business start.	☐
i. Start-up costs are within my investment goal.	1. This will cost much more than I anticipated investing.	2. Start-up costs are just outside my investment goal.	3. My start-up costs and/or investment goal is not clear to me.	4. The start-up costs are fairly close to the amount I would like to invest.	5. The start-up costs are the same or lower than the amount I am willing to invest, whether the money comes from my own savings or from borrowing.	☐
j. Other						☐

Action Step 3.2 continued — Evaluate My Business Concept Against My Financial Goals

Business Concept Analysis Checklist

Profitability Criteria	1. Does not meet the criteria.	2. Somewhat meets the criteria.	3. It might meet the criteria.	4. Meets the criteria very well.	5. Meets the criteria perfectly.
k. Revenue stream is continuous.	1. I never know what's going to come in because of seasonality, large contracts, and other factors.	2. Monthly sales will fluctuate significantly but are somewhat predictable.	3. Our sales vary somewhat from month to month due to sales cycles and products offered.	4. Most of the time, sales will be steady from month to month.	5. We can always count on steady sales from month to month.
l. Hiring and retaining employees is easy.	1. Turnover will be high. The cycle of hiring and training will be continuous.	2. I will spend lots of time and money hiring and training employees.	3. For now, I can control labor costs by using sub-contractors as the company grows.	4. I will have well-qualified employees and expect a low turnover rate.	5. This is great! I will have top employees and expect a zero turnover rate!
m. Inventory/Service providers are dependable.	1. I do not have a clue where to get most of the inventory/supplies I need.	2. I'm not completely sure about where I'm going to get the inventory/supplies I need.	3. I've found inventory and supplies, but only a few companies can give me what I need.	4. Many companies can supply what I need.	5. No problem! Numerous companies with good reputations can supply what I need.
n. Market will allow price adjustments to increase profitability.	1. Prices are set by law.	2. I have very little flexibility in pricing.	3. I cannot tell whether sales to potential customers are affected by price increases, which would improve profitability.	4. Sales to potential customers are somewhat unaffected by price increases.	5. Sales to potential customers are unaffected by price increases.
o. Other					

Action Step 3.2 **Evaluate My Business Concept Against My Financial Goals**
continued

Business Concept Analysis Checklist

Cash Flow Criteria	1. Does not meet the criteria.	2. Somewhat meets the criteria.	3. It might meet the criteria.	4. Meets the criteria very well.	5. Meets the criteria perfectly.	
p. Funding will be easily obtained as I have collateral to pledge and the ability to take on more debt.	1. I have no idea how I will fund this. Or, I will have to borrow a huge amount, more than I should comfortably take on.	2. I have a few ideas about how I will fund this but my collateral is weak.	3. I have to further investigate funding.	4. Borrowing may be okay. I have some collateral to pledge against the loan and the ability to take on a little more personal debt.	5. Borrowing is easy. I have the required collateral to pledge against a loan and the ability to take on more personal debt. Or, I already have the money needed to start my business, and I can comfortably risk it.	☐
q. My personal credit is excellent.	1. My personal credit is abysmal.	2. I am working on repairing my personal credit, but it isn't perfect yet.	3. I have doubts about my personal credit.	4. I can borrow some of the money necessary for start-up costs and working capital.	5. I can borrow as much money as necessary for start-up costs and working capital.	☐
r. The business has a short cash cycle, which will help create a healthy cash flow.	1. The cash cycle is very long. We will routinely send out a bill for products/ services and wait over 30 days for customers to pay.	2. The business has an average cash cycle, which will hamper a healthy cash flow.	3. Customers pay at the time of service or when they receive the product.	4. The cash cycle is relatively short. The customer may make a deposit that covers the direct costs of the product/service.	5. The cash cycle is very short. The customer may pay for the product/ service prior to delivery.	☐
s. Other						☐

Action Step 3.2 **Evaluate My Business Concept Against My Financial Goals**
continued

D. Evaluate how well your business concept matches your personal financial goals. Pay close attention to whether or not those items you marked with a   in the non-negotiables box received high scores. If not, is there any way the business concept can be altered to improve its ability to meet your essential criteria? If such adjustments cannot be made, should you continue to pursue this business concept or search for another? Summarize your results below:

Business concept's match to personal financial goals.

Action Step 3.3 **Consider Potential Funding Sources**

Identify a list of potential sources of financing for start-up and ongoing money needs to help me throughout the planning process.

Directions

Fill out the Potential Funding Sources Grid on p. 116 using the steps below to determine what types of funding you may need for your business at which stage in operations.

A. **Review your estimated start-up costs.** Using Action Step 3.1, review the total amount needed to start this business. Consider that you will also need additional funds to operate and/or grow the business after start-up.

B. **Identify available funds.** Enter the amount of money potentially available from each Source of Funding in the first column. Don't forget that 90 percent of start-ups use the entrepreneur's own funds. Keep in mind that each of these sources has certain risks that need to be evaluated.

C. **Classify equity and debt funds.** Identify each source as equity or debt in the second column, because this characteristic often affects costs of funding, the control desired, payback time frame, and other variables.

D. **Record the next action needed.** List the action needed in the third column, such as research, identifying specific contacts, comparing sources.

E. **Use the form throughout the program.** Update this form throughout the program as information is made available. In Module 9, you will make funding decisions based on this information and completed financial projections.

Action Step 3.3 Consider Potential Funding Sources continued

Potential Funding Sources Grid

Source of Funding	Estimated Amount	Type: Equity or Debt	Action Needed
Entrepreneur			
❏ Personal savings			
❏ Home equity loan			
❏ Take on second job			
❏ Personal credit cards			
❏ Withdrawal from retirement account			
Friends and Family			
Name			
❏			
❏			
❏			
❏			
❏			
Financial Institution			
Name of bank			
❏			
❏			
❏			
❏			
❏			
Other Sources			
❏			
❏			
❏			
❏			
❏			
Total Estimated Funding Available			

Action Step 3.4   **Complete My Business Concept Analysis**

Screen my business concept and decide if this concept is right for me.

Directions
The following checklist combines the screening tools you used in the first three modules and tests for:
- How well the business concept will help you reach your personal and professional goals.
- Whether the business concept represents a market opportunity.
- How well the business concept will help you meet your financial goals.

Use the following checklist to evaluate if you have learned anything new through research or made any modifications to your concept since you first completed the screening checklist. You may skip any of the three sections for which no changes have been made since you completed them previously.

Remember to come back and repeat this action step whenever you make significant changes to your concept to make sure it will still meet your screening criteria.

Refer to the directions for using this checklist in Action Step 1.3 if necessary.

Action Step 3.4   Complete My Business Concept Analysis continued

Business Concept Analysis Checklist   **A. Screen the business concept to see if your personal and professional goals are met.**

Personal Criteria	1. Does not meet my criteria.	2. Somewhat meets my criteria.	3. It might meet my criteria.	4. Meets my criteria very well.	5. Meets my criteria perfectly.
a. Aspects of owning and operating my own business appeal to me. □	1. I am unsure about whether this is a good idea for me. It might not be.	2. I've considered this and believe it might be right for me.	3. The good aspects of owning a business clearly outweigh the negative ones.	4. I'm fairly sure that owning a business is what I would like.	5. I've wanted to own my own business since I was a child.
b. The number of hours per week I will need to work in the business is acceptable. □	1. I don't know how I will find the time for this business, given my other commitments.	2. I will need to manage my time better if this is going to be successful.	3. I'm not sure how many hours I will need to work, but I think this will work out.	4. I am fairly confident that the number of hours I will need to work will be acceptable.	5. I will work the number of hours that are needed to succeed.
c. The degree of flexibility of my work hours suits me. □	1. I see potential conflicts with the daily routine of this business.	2. I am concerned this schedule may not be right for me.	3. I think the work schedule will be okay.	4. The schedule required for this business will be good for me.	5. I have always dreamed of this type of schedule.
d. I will be able to operate in a location that works well for me. □	1. This is a terrible location.	2. The location is not the best.	3. I think this location will work for me.	4. This location should work well.	5. I couldn't ask for a better location.
e. The amount of business travel required matches my desired level of travel. □	1. This is way too much/little travel for me.	2. This is probably not the best level of travel for me.	3. The amount of travel is okay.	4. I think I'm looking forward to traveling this much/little.	5. This is my travel dream. Just the right amount.
f. This type of business is in keeping with my morals, beliefs, and standards. □	1. I will be embarrassed for people to know I'm doing this.	2. I may have to change my standards for this business to work.	3. I'm not certain how in line with my beliefs this business is.	4. This business is pretty much in line with my morals, beliefs, and standards.	5. This business is in perfect sync with my morals, beliefs, and standards.
g. The physical requirements of the business are within my capability. □	1. I don't believe I have the physical strength or stamina for this work.	2. I can probably handle the physical requirements for a little while.	3. I think I have the physical capability for this.	4. I am very sure I can handle the physical requirements.	5. The physical requirements of the business appeal to me. I can't wait to start.
h. The level of support I will receive from my family is satisfactory. □	1. My family thinks I've lost my mind.	2. My family may come around eventually.	3. My family will probably support me after I get going.	4. My family is always supportive, so they will be now also.	5. My family is super supportive and can't wait to help me out.

Action Step 3.4   Complete My Business Concept Analysis continued

Business Concept Analysis Checklist

Professional Criteria	1. Does not meet my criteria.	2. Somewhat meets my criteria.	3. It might meet my criteria.	4. Meets my criteria very well.	5. Meets my criteria perfectly.
i. The business will provide me with a level of status and power that I will value. ☐	1. I will probably keep this business a secret. The fewer who know the better.	2. I will probably become accustomed to the step down in status and power.	3. I'm not sure if this provides me any status and/or power.	4. I think I will appreciate the status and power my new business will give me.	5. I have dreamed about this level of status and power. Now I will have it.
j. The amount of time I will need to be involved in daily operations suits me. ☐	1. I never dreamed I'd have to do anything in daily operations.	2. I'm not going to like spending the time needed in daily operations, but I can stand it.	3. I'm not sure how much time I'm going to spend. It might be okay.	4. My time in daily operations will suit me to some extent.	5. The amount of time I will need to be involved in daily operations suits me perfectly.
k. My skills and abilities match those needed to make the business successful. ☐	1. I don't have any skills or ability for this business.	2. I can probably improve my skills to make this business work.	3. My skills and abilities are largely untested.	4. This business is a pretty good match for what I do well.	5. My skills and abilities perfectly match those needed to make the business successful.
l. I will have a sense of job security in my business. ☐	1. I will worry about the lack of job security in my business.	2. I will have minor concerns about job security in my business.	3. I'm not certain how secure I will feel about job security.	4. I will have no worries about job security in my business.	5. I will have a strong sense of job security in my business.
m. I believe that the business will help me reach my long-term goals. ☐	1. I see little connection between this business and my long-term goals.	2. This business may be a little useful in helping me reach my long-term goals.	3. I'm not certain if this business will help me reach my long-term goals.	4. I believe that the business will be somewhat helpful in reaching my long-term goals.	5. I believe that the business will help me tremendously in reaching my long-term goals.
n. The business matches my desire to own a certain type of business, for example, lifestyle or growth. ☐	1. This type of business does not suit me at all.	2. This business is marginally close to the type I would like to have.	3. I don't really know what type of business I would like.	4. This business is very close to the type I would like.	5. The business perfectly matches my desire to own a certain type of business.

Action Step 3.4 Complete My Business Concept Analysis continued

Business Concept Analysis Checklist   B. Determine if the business concept responds to a market opportunity.

Market Feasibility Criteria	1. Does not meet the criteria.	2. Somewhat meets the criteria.	3. It might meet the criteria.	4. Meets the criteria very well.	5. Meets the criteria perfectly.
a. Customers perceive a need for product/service. ☐	1. Customers are totally clueless about my type of product/service.	2. Customers must be educated about my products/services before they see a need for them.	3. Customers must be convinced to buy from me instead of my competitors.	4. Customers need my products/services and will often select them over competitors'.	5. Slam dunk! My customers need my products/services and want to buy from me.
b. Market can be recognized and measured. ☐	1. My customers could be just about anyone, so targeting a certain group may not be easy.	2. I have many potential customers, so I need to do more research to find my target market.	3. I have identified my potential customers, but they will be somewhat difficult to reach because of their demographics/buying patterns.	4. With some effort, I can use my customers' demographics/buying patterns to find them.	5. My potential customers are easy to find because of their demographics/buying patterns.
c. Existing competition has identifiable weaknesses. ☐	1. I have lots of competition who have been in this business longer than I.	2. I have no competition! Hmmm, I wonder why?	3. I have identified my competition, but I do not know its weaknesses.	4. I know my competition and its weaknesses, but I need more research.	5. I have limited competition, and I know its weaknesses.
d. Distribution system is established and receptive. ☐	1. I must develop a brand new distribution system.	2. My current distribution system offers only limited options.	3. I've found a distribution system already established with several options.	4. Several distributors seem receptive to carrying my products/services.	5. Unbelievable! Distributors are calling me wanting to carry my products/services.
e. There is an identifiable competitive advantage in the marketplace. ☐	1. A competitive advantage would be hard to find.	2. There is a small competitive advantage in the marketplace.	3. I'm not sure a competitive advantage exists.	4. A small, identifiable competitive advantage exists in the marketplace, and I am in a somewhat unique position to use it.	5. There is an identifiable competitive advantage in the marketplace, and I am in a unique position to use it.

Action Step 3.4 **Complete My Business Concept Analysis** continued

Business Concept Analysis Checklist

Market Feasibility Criteria	1. Does not meet the criteria.	2. Somewhat meets the criteria.	3. It might meet the criteria.	4. Meets the criteria very well.	5. Meets the criteria perfectly.
f. There are few competitors to serve the needs of the market. ☐	1. There are many competitors to serve the needs of the market.	2. There are quite a few competitors to serve the needs of the market.	3. The competition is not clear.	4. There are a few competitors to serve the needs of the market.	5. There are almost no competitors to serve the needs of the market.
g. The business concept can be modified to serve the needs of a specific, underserved market niche. ☐	1. The business concept cannot be modified to serve the needs of a specific, underserved market niche.	2. The business concept can be modified with some difficulty to serve the needs of a specific, underserved market niche.	3. The business concept might be modifiable to serve the needs of a specific, underserved market niche.	4. The business concept can be modified to serve the needs of a specific, underserved market niche.	5. The business concept can easily be modified to serve the needs of a specific, underserved market niche.
h. The customer profiled would respond favorably to the current business concept. ☐	1. I don't think the customer profiled would respond at all to the current business concept.	2. The customer profiled would respond somewhat unfavorably to the current business concept.	3. How the customer would respond to the current business concept is unclear.	4. The customer profiled would respond somewhat favorably to the current business concept.	5. The customer profiled would respond very favorably to the current business concept.
i. There is a sufficient market for the business. ☐	1. There is an insufficient market for the business.	2. There is a relatively small market for the business.	3. The size of the market is not clear.	4. The size of the market seems sufficient enough.	5. There is a perfectly sufficient market for the business.
j. Customers purchase frequently. ☐	1. Customers will only buy once from me, so I must find new customers all the time.	2. Most customers will only buy once from me.	3. Customers will buy more than once, but not frequently.	4. Some customers will purchase products/services frequently.	5. Wow! Customers currently purchase similar products/services very frequently.

Action Step 3.4   Complete My Business Concept Analysis continued

Business Concept Analysis Checklist

C. Screen the business concept against your financial goals.

Personal Financial Goals	1. Does not meet my goal.	2. Somewhat meets my goal.	3. It might meet my goal.	4. Meets my goal very well.	5. Meets my goal perfectly.
a. I am willing to invest money in my business. ☐	1. I have no money to invest.	2. I have money to invest, but I'm not sure I want to risk putting it into my business.	3. I have a small nest egg that I'm pretty sure could be used for my business.	4. I have sufficient money in other investments that could probably be used.	5. I have been putting aside money for this purpose for several years.
b. A portion of the money I invest will come from my personal savings. ☐	1. I have no personal savings.	2. My personal savings are so small that using the money would not matter.	3. I am considering using a portion of my savings.	4. I am fairly confident that I can use a portion of my savings.	5. A portion of the money I invest will definitely come from my savings.
c. A portion of what I invest will be borrowed. ☐	1. My credit is too negative to borrow.	2. My borrowing limits are fairly low.	3. I'm not certain how much I would be able to borrow, all things considered.	4. I am fairly sure I can borrow what I need.	5. Borrowing is not a problem at all.
d. The business will generate enough salary for me to meet my personal needs. ☐	1. I don't anticipate being able to take a salary for many years. This is a big problem.	2. I know I won't draw a salary for awhile and will try to figure out how to pay my living expenses.	3. I think I can squeak through.	4. I will be able to draw a salary before my savings run out.	5. The salary I can draw will be fine from the very beginning.

Action Step 3.4   Complete My Business Concept Analysis continued

Business Concept Analysis Checklist

Start-Up Criteria	1. Does not meet the criteria.	2. Somewhat meets the criteria.	3. It might meet the criteria.	4. Meets the criteria very well.	5. Meets the criteria perfectly.	
e. Start-up costs have been identified. ☐	1. I know very little about the start-up costs.	2. I have begun to research start-up costs.	3. I have identified and researched most of my start-up costs.	4. I have identified most of my start-up expense and expenditure categories, estimated amounts, and need more research to validate the figures.	5. I have identified all start-up expense and expenditure categories, estimated amounts, and conducted research to validate the figures.	
f. Start-up costs are flexible and can change if necessary. ☐	1. Once the start-up is underway, the costs are set in stone.	2. There may be some way that a few of the start-up costs could be modified.	3. I'm not clear how flexible my concept is.	4. The concept is a little flexible in that the length of the start-up process, the initial investment, and the target market can all be reduced.	5. The concept is extremely flexible in that the length of the start-up process, the initial investment, and the target market can all be reduced.	
g. The start-up process is short/minimal. ☐	1. There will be a long start-up process for this business.	2. The start-up process is average for this business.	3. I'm not sure how long the start-up process will take.	4. The length of the start-up process is somewhat short from initial idea to business start.	5. The length of the start-up process is very short and uninvolved from initial idea to business start.	
h. Start-up costs are within my investment goal. ☐	1. This will cost much more than I anticipated investing.	2. Start-up costs are just outside my investment goal.	3. My start-up costs and/or investment goal is not clear to me.	4. The start-up costs are fairly close to the amount I would like to invest.	5. The start-up costs are the same or lower than the amount I am willing to invest, whether the money comes from my own savings or from borrowing.	
i. Other ☐						

Action Step 3.4 Complete My Business Concept Analysis continued

Business Concept Analysis Checklist

Profitability Criteria	1. Does not meet the criteria.	2. Somewhat meets the criteria.	3. It might meet the criteria.	4. Meets the criteria very well.	5. Meets the criteria perfectly.
j. Revenue stream is continuous. ☐	1. I never know what's going to come in because of seasonality, large contracts, and other factors.	2. Monthly sales will fluctuate significantly but are somewhat predictable.	3. Our sales vary somewhat from month to month due to sales cycles and products offered.	4. Most of the time, sales will be steady from month to month.	5. We can always count on steady sales from month to month.
k. Hiring and retaining employees is easy. ☐	1. Turnover will be high. The cycle of hiring and training will be continuous.	2. I will spend lots of time and money hiring and training employees.	3. For now, I can control labor costs by using sub-contractors as the company grows.	4. I will have well-qualified employees and expect a low turnover rate.	5. This is great! I will have top employees and expect a zero turnover rate!
l. Inventory/ Service providers are dependable. ☐	1. I do not have a clue where to get most of the inventory/supplies I need.	2. I'm not completely sure where I'm going to get the inventory/supplies I need.	3. I've found inventory and supplies, but only a few companies can give me what I need.	4. Many companies can supply what I need.	5. No problem! Numerous companies with good reputations can supply what I need.
m. Market will allow price adjustments to increase profitability. ☐	1. Prices are set by law.	2. I have very little flexibility in pricing.	3. I cannot tell whether sales are affected by price increases, which would improve profitability.	4. Sales to potential customers are somewhat unaffected by price increases.	5. Sales to potential customers are unaffected by price increases.

Action Step 3.4   Complete My Business Concept Analysis continued

Business Concept Analysis Checklist

Cash Flow Criteria	1. Does not meet the criteria.	2. Somewhat meets the criteria.	3. It might meet the criteria.	4. Meets the criteria very well.	5. Meets the criteria perfectly.
n. Funding will be easily obtained as I have collateral to pledge and the ability to take on more debt.	1. I have no idea how I will fund this. Or, I will have to borrow a huge amount, more than I should comfortably take on. ☐	2. I have a few ideas about how I will fund this but my collateral is weak.	3. I have to further investigate funding.	4. Borrowing may be OK as I have some collateral to pledge against the loan and the ability to take on a little more personal debt.	5. Borrowing is easy as I have the required collateral to pledge against a loan and the ability to take on more personal debt. Or, I already have the money needed to start my business and I can comfortably risk it.
o. My personal credit is excellent.	1. My personal credit is abysmal. ☐	2. I am working on repairing my personal credit, but it isn't perfect yet.	3. I have doubts about my personal credit.	4. I can borrow some of the money necessary for startup costs and working capital.	5. I can borrow as much money as necessary for startup costs and working capital.
p. The business has a short cash cycle, which will help create a healthy cash flow.	1. The cash cycle is very long. We will routinely send out a bill for products / services and wait over 30 days for customers to pay. ☐	2. The business has an average cash cycle, which will hamper a healthy cash flow.	3. Customers pay at the time of service or when they receive the product.	4. The cash cycle is relatively short. The customer may make a deposit that covers the direct costs of the product / service.	5. The cash cycle is very short. The customer may pay for the product/ service prior to delivery.
q. Other					

Action Step 3.4 Complete My Business Concept Analysis continued

D. Evaluate how well the business concept matches your criteria. Pay close attention to whether or not those items you checked in the non-negotiables box received high scores. If not, can the business concept be altered to improve its ability to meet your criteria? If such adjustments cannot be made, should you continue to pursue this business concept or search for another? Summarize your results below:

Business concept analysis results

Action Step 3.4 **Complete My Business Concept Analysis** continued

E. Make necessary modifications. Write your new business concept statement below.

Business concept statement

Inventory

You will use the Inventory Financial Facts Worksheet to accumulate notes and information as you research the types of production expenses you expect to have in your business. You will want the information you document to be as detailed as possible, so that when you begin inputting your Inventory expense information into the Financial Template, you'll have complete and accurate estimates. Be sure to include the following information:

1. What is the estimated amount of monthly or annual expense? Or if the expense will only be paid once during the year, which month?
2. Do you expect a seasonal variation for the amount of each expense?
3. From what source did you get your information?
4. What is the name of the expected vendor (whom will you write the check to)?

Freight-In & Trucking

Insurance

Payroll Expenses – Include in this box only the payroll related to production of inventory.

    Salaries & Wages

    Payroll Taxes

    Benefits

Rent

Inventory continued

Repairs & Maintenance

Rework

Subcontracting

Utilities

Other Production Expenses

Operating Expenses

You will use this Operating Expenses Financial Facts Worksheet to accumulate notes and information as you research the types of operating expenses you expect to have in your business. Subsequent modules will help you identify which expenses will need to be researched. You will want the information you document to be as detailed as possible, so that when you begin inputting your Operating Expenses information into the Financial Template, you'll have complete and accurate estimates. Be sure to include the following information:

1. What is the estimated amount of monthly or annual expense? Or if the expense will only be paid once during the year, which month?
2. Do you expect a seasonal variation for the amount of each expense?
3. From what source did you get your information?
4. What is the name of the expected vendor (whom will you write the check to)?

Advertising	*Yellow Pages $90/mo.* *30/mo internet* *1x/wk.*

Bank Charges	*$150.00/yar checks Fees*

Dues & Subscriptions	*$100/yr — Auction Assn.*

Insurance	*$30/mo.*

Financial Facts Worksheet

Operating Expenses continued

Licenses & Fees
$20/yr $100/yr BOND

Marketing & Promotion
START up. $500.— $ Web site : $1000

Meals & Entertainment
$50/mo.

Miscellaneous

Office Expense
$45/mo tel. $25/mo stationery

Office Supplies

Operating Expenses continued

Outside Services

Payroll Expenses – Include in this box all payroll expenses for your business, except production.

Salaries & Wages

$ 5000 /mo.

Payroll Taxes

Benefits

Professional Fees

Operating Expenses continued

Property Taxes   no

Rent   no

Repairs & Maintenance   100/mo.

Shipping & Delivery

Telephone

Training & Development

 **Operating Expenses** continued

Travel   *NO*

Utilities   *NO*

Vehicle

Other

Other

Other

Financial Facts Worksheet

Post Start-Up Fixed Asset Purchases

You will use this Post Start-Up Fixed Asset Purchases Financial Facts Worksheet to accumulate notes and information as you research the fixed assets you expect to purchase. These purchases will take place after you have exited the start-up phase. You will want the information you document to be as detailed as possible, so that when you begin inputting your fixed asset purchases information into the Financial Template, you'll have complete and accurate estimates. Be sure to include the following information:
1. When do you expect the purchase to take place?
2. Why is this purchase necessary?
3. From what source did you get your information?
4. What is the name of the expected vendor (whom will you write the check to)?

Computer Equipment

New Computer 1000.—

Equipment & Machinery

Speakers, microphone
SIGNS.

Furniture

Vehicles

Leasehold Improvements

Financial Facts Worksheet

Post Start-Up Fixed Asset Purchases continued

Building

Other

Planning the Product/Service

Customers buy products and services for an endless number of reasons. In this module you will describe your product or service in terms that are the most meaningful to others: customers, investors, lenders, members of your management team, and employees. You will consider each feature of your product or service according to its benefit to customers. To be successful, your product or service should have a competitive advantage. Why will your potential customers purchase from you instead of competitors?

In addition to the product or service itself, how you define your business model will have an impact upon many aspects of your business. Similar products and services can be supplied by many different business models. Some models will be more effective than others in protecting intellectual property and helping you comply with governmental regulations. As you work through the planning process in this module concerning your product or service description, you will be developing the Product/Service Plan of your Business Plan.

Key Questions
- What are the unique features and benefits of my product/service?
- What is my business model?
- What intellectual property does my business have and how do I protect it?
- What governmental regulations apply to my business and how do I comply with them?
- What are the financial implications of my Product/Service Plan?
- How do I get started writing my Business Plan?

Action Steps   Due Date
- ❏ 4.1 Create My Product/Service Plan   _____
- ❏ 4.2 Write My Product/Service Financial Assumptions   _____
- ❏ Read Module 5 Researching and Analyzing the Market   _____
- ❏ _____   _____
- ❏ _____   _____
- ❏ _____   _____

Defining the Product/Service

You created and refined your business concept in the first three modules of this program. During the next seven modules, you will focus on planning your business and writing your Business Plan. The first step is defining your product or service.

Before you can do anything about your new business, you need to know exactly what you are selling. What is your product? What is your service? This module will not only help you think through the aspects of your product or service, it will also enable you to write down your thoughts and keep track of them as you refine them.

T¡P Investors will be wary of any venture in which all possible problems have not been addressed or solutions for possible future problems have not been devised.

Writing the Business Plan is a final test of feasibility before you begin your business; your Product/Service Plan should be completed after all product or service problems have been worked out. If a product or service is not workable, the business concept is not feasible. Your plan should make clear that your product works and is ready to go. All other technical information can go in an Appendix for readers who want technical specifications.

How much should you say in your Business Plan about your product or service? You should describe the product or service just enough to demonstrate that you have sufficiently considered its details, worked out the bugs, and addressed potential problems.

Inventors are notorious for developing elaborately technical product descriptions in their Business Plans. Instead, you should include only enough information to help the reader understand the product and highlight proprietary characteristics, limitations, liabilities, and other operational aspects. These issues help the reader understand your plan to make products or services available to potential customers.

The description of your product or service includes both its *functional* and *operational* attributes. Functional attributes are those characteristics most observers can see right away—the features and benefits of the product or service. The operational attributes of your product or service are those beneath-the-surface characteristics that you, your management team, or investors must pay attention to, such as its limitations, liabilities, production needs, and financial demands.

You must be able to clearly and concisely communicate both the operational and functional aspects of your product or service. Readers of your Business Plan must understand the exact nature of your product or service to understand your entire plan.

Before you begin writing your Business Plan, however, you will want to consider all the major aspects of your product or service, including its purpose, features, benefits, competitive advantage, stage of development, limitations, liabilities, production and supply issues, and spin-off potential. All of these factors will help you determine the best business model for making your product or service available to the market.

What Is the Purpose of My Product/Service?

What problem is your product or service solving for your customers? This question gets at the core of your product or service description. If you can, describe the purpose of the product or service in terms of the problem it solves from the customer's standpoint. Emphasize the benefits or value your product or service creates. Testimonials or results from marketing surveys and focus groups can highlight the problems that the product or service will solve.

Reality Check ✔

Problem Solving

What problems does my product or service solve for customers?

Customer's Problem	Product's/Service's Solution
a.	
b.	
c.	

Remember, one of the tests of market feasibility in Module 2 is whether your business concept solves a problem or meets a need in the marketplace. If your business solves a problem for customers, you should highlight that aspect in your Business Plan.

What Are the Unique Features and Benefits of My Product/Service?

Features are what the product or service does or has. *Benefits* are the reasons customers buy it.

Unique features, highly valued by customers, result in increased marketability. And marketability leads to profitability.

Tip Features *tell*. Benefits *sell*.

The uniqueness of a product or service sets it apart from its competition. Unique features are important. They help explain what a product or service does or has that other products do not do or have. Unless a product or service is a necessity, however, customers will focus primarily on benefits when making a purchase.

Once you have identified each feature of your product or service, you should describe it in terms of the benefit the customer receives or the way it solves customer's problems or meets their needs. For instance, if you own the only dry cleaning business in the area offering home pick-up and delivery, you would describe this service in terms of the benefit to the customer: convenience. A carpet company does not sell floor coverings; it sells an attractively decorated interior. A garment maker doesn't sell clothes; it sells self-esteem, image, social acceptance, and career advancement.

COMPROSE, Inc., a St. Louis software company, conducts in-depth client interviews and performs additional market research to identify and understand its most important markets. By having this information, they can more effectively develop products and product upgrades that solve their target market's business problems.

Focus on the Benefits and Value. Entrepreneurs succeed when they redefine what they are selling to their customers in the terms of the benefits customers are buying.

Reality Check ✔	**Features and Benefits**
List features of your product/service (what it does) in the left column.	List benefits of your product/service (why people will buy it) in the right column.
Features of my product/service	**Benefits of my product/service**

TIP Focus on the benefit that the product or service creates for customers. They will easily see your product or service features. Benefits may not be obvious.

From your list of features and benefits, you may soon discover one important element of your product or services description—your competitive advantage.

How Is My Product/Service Different from My Competitors?

Successful businesses differ in meaningful ways from their competitors. You will not succeed just by copying competitors' products or services. A significant difference in what you offer creates built-in motivation for customers to buy your product or service.

Your venture's success depends upon its *competitive advantage*. What advantage do you have over your competition? Some businesses compete on price. Can you sell the same product or service for less than others? Perhaps you can, but generally not, especially for a start-up business. If you can't compete on price as a start-up, then you should establish your *market differentiation* as your competitive advantage. Your differentiator is the unique difference which influences consumer demand by setting your product or service apart from others offering the same product or service.

Maybe your location sets you apart. Perhaps you have discovered a process by which you can produce the product or service more quickly than your competition. Or maybe you have discovered a new way to offer the same product or service more conveniently. The customer must perceive some difference in the features of your product or service that provides benefits not available from competitors. Why will a customer purchase your goods or services rather than another's? Whatever your competitive advantage, you must emphasize it in your Business Plan, because others reading the plan will be looking for it.

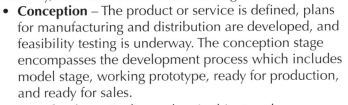

Stand Out from the Crowd

"If you can't do it better or different than your competitors, then you are wasting your time," maintains Carol Frank, founder of Avian Adventures, Inc.®, of Dallas, Texas, a provider of high-end cages for exotic birds.

After owning a pet shop and distributing bird products for several years, Frank saw a need for a better birdcage. To create a unique design that could not be confused with competitors', she hired a bird curator who had a master's degree in landscape architecture and years of experience at the Dallas Zoo.

Launched in January 1996, today Avian Adventures generates more than $2 million in annual revenue.

Source: Carol Frank. *Do As I Say, Not As I Did!: Gaining Wisdom in Business Through the Mistakes of Highly Successful People*. Entrepreneurial Adventures, 2005. Used by permission.

How do you discover your competitive advantage? Think about your own preferences. Why do you buy groceries where you do? You probably have many choices but most likely do most of your shopping in one particular store. Does that store have a greater selection? Is its produce fresher? Is it more convenient for parking? Are the employees more helpful or more cheerful?

You must consider how to differentiate what you are selling from others in the same business and communicate that difference in your Business Plan. Most successful businesses sell a product or service to an established market differently than others offering the same thing. For example, Dominos® revolutionized the pizza business, not by making a better tasting or cheaper pizza but by offering delivery at no additional charge.

What Stage of Development Is My Product/Service In?

Just as businesses go through stages, so do products and services. If you are still defining and planning your product or service, you are in the conception stage. At each stage of the life cycle your product or service will produce different levels of sales and require different approaches to marketing. The product or service life cycle is determined by how long that product or service is marketable. The common stages that a product or service may go through during its life are the conception, introduction, growth, maturity, and innovation or decline stages.

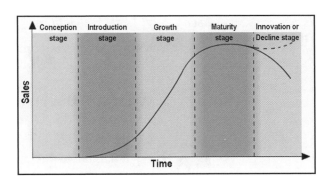

- **Conception** – The product or service is defined, plans for manufacturing and distribution are developed, and feasibility testing is underway. The conception stage encompasses the development process which includes model stage, working prototype, ready for production, and ready for sales.

- **Introduction** – Profits are low in this stage because research and development, production, and marketing costs are high. Prices are set high on the product or service to recoup some of the development and introduction costs.

- **Growth** – Sales generally increase with the demand for the product. Cash flow improves and profits are at their peak.

- **Maturity** – Sales may continue to increase or level off. Profits decrease since prices are continually lowered to compete. Still, a great amount of cash flow is generated through sales in this stage.

- **Innovation or decline** – Sales drop rapidly even though prices continue to fall. Profits are extremely low at this stage, but the product or service has generated sufficient cash flow during its life. The company needs to redevelop, remarket, or discontinue the product or service before losses eat into the cash flow generated by sales.

TIP Even the simplest change, such as increasing the size of a candy bar by 33 percent, can start the life cycle of a product or service over again.

Instead of eliminating a product or service once it hits the decline stage, many entrepreneurs reintroduce the product or service with a new feature or create a new benefit.

This section of your Product/Service Plan should include a history of your product's or service's development, the current stage of development, the projected dates for achieving the next stage of development, and how the product or service can be regularly improved to remain competitive.

What Are the Limitations of My Product/Service?

The ideal product or service will not suffer limitations. Its demand will go on and on. In the real world, factors such as rapidly changing consumer-driven trends, new innovations, and technological advances limit the amount of time most products or services are marketable.

TIP In many start-up service businesses, a major limitation is the amount of time you can spend on the business. If you have thirty hours available each week for billable work, that is the maximum amount of income you can generate. When your time is used up, you cannot serve additional customers.

The shorter the marketable life of a product or service, the less attractive it is. High-tech ventures often face this difficulty. The economic life of these products or services is sometimes so short a company cannot make enough money on them to be profitable. A product with a long shelf life can be stored until a profitable market can be found for it.

These attributes, followed by examples, create product or service limitations:
- **Fashion trends** – Cars, clothes, music
- **Technical difficulties** – Software applications, computer hardware
- **Perishability** – Food, flowers
- **Assembly or installation** – Satellite TV, water purifiers
- **Legal restrictions** – Prescription drugs, building contractors

If you cannot overcome the limitations of your product or service, you should openly discuss them in your Business Plan.

What Are the Liabilities of My Product/Service?

Some people don't like to talk about liabilities. They want to think positively and only focus on the strengths of their product or service.

Legal liability is the responsibility that you must bear for the safety and fitness of what you sell for the purpose intended. Smart entrepreneurs think about liabilities, so that they can overcome them or limit their effect. In your Business Plan, you will want to clearly define your product's or service's potential liabilities and your plans to address them.

Liability is not limited to product-centered companies. Any company—service provider, manufacturer, wholesaler, distributor, or retailer—can be liable for the use or misuse of a product. Service companies are also at risk if the services involve any exercise of professional judgment, such as medicine or law. Other services share in liability risk as well, such as fulfillment businesses and suppliers. Every product or service should be carefully evaluated as to its potential liabilities.

You may be liable for:

- Negligent product design or packaging.
- Inadequate product/service testing.
- Failure of the product to be safely used for its intended purpose.
- Failure to adequately warn against misuse.

Equally as important as identifying a liability is to outline plans to protect your business and personal assets against a potential lawsuit. Trade associations can be a good source of liability exposure and protection information. Consult an experienced attorney to fully understand the warranties both expressed and implied in product or service liability. In addition, you should have, at a minimum, a general business liability policy. A good independent insurance agent or risk consultant can help you define your particular needs. Openly discuss all actions you plan to take in this section of your Business Plan.

TIP Everyone in the distribution chain (manufacturer, wholesaler, distributor, and retailer) can be sued and may be liable for personal injury or property damage caused by any defect or negligence of anyone in the chain.

Reality Check ✔

Costs for Product/Service Legal Liability

Take a moment to think about costs associated with your business for product/service legal liability. Put a check by each of these costs that might apply. Indicate whether you already know these amounts or need more research.

	Already Know	Need to Research
❏ Expert consultation regarding liability prevention	❏	❏
❏ Product/Service warranty	❏	❏
❏ Insurance:		
❏ Workers' compensation coverage	❏	❏
❏ Commercial automobile coverage	❏	❏
❏ Health coverage	❏	❏
❏ Key person life insurance	❏	❏
❏ General property coverage	❏	❏
❏ Liability insurance	❏	❏
❏ Operational coverage		
❏ Bonds	❏	❏
❏ Business interruption	❏	❏
❏ Cargo and transportation	❏	❏
❏ Errors and omissions	❏	❏
❏ Fidelity	❏	❏
❏ Flood	❏	❏

Action Step 4.2 asks you to estimate these costs on the Financial Facts Worksheets introduced in Module 3, pp. 128 – 136.

Financial Facts Worksheet

What Are My Production and Facility Needs?

When writing the production and facilities portion of your Product/Service Plan, you will describe the production process, the need for facilities, and the amount of product or service to be produced internally, and the amount to be subcontracted out. You will want to include your production capacity and project the need for future capital to build facilities.

TIP The production and facilities section of your Business Plan is not just for product-based businesses. It is just as important to clearly define the process and people involved in providing a service.

Consider selecting competitors with superior performance as benchmarks when designing your production processes. Look at the competitors' production processes to identify areas you can match or surpass their performance. Outline these processes in your Business Plan.

Production performance can be rated on these bases:
- Production capacity
- Absence of errors or reworks
- On-time processes and delivery
- Inventory reduction
- Cost reduction
- Other criteria relevant to the product/service

When you discuss facilities in your Business Plan, describe what facilities you require such as manufacturing, office, or retail. Then describe your facility's layout, capacity, and future expansion needs. A diagram of the facilities can also be very helpful.

Reality Check ✓ — Costs for the Production Process

Think about costs associated with your business for production. Put a check by each item that might apply after the doors are open for business. Do not consider start-up costs. Indicate whether you already know these amounts or need more research.

	Already Know	Need to Research
❑ Production salaries, payroll taxes, and benefits	❑	❑
❑ Subcontracting some/part of the production process	❑	❑
❑ Rent and utilities for production facilities	❑	❑
❑ Production equipment & machinery, including repairs and maintenance	❑	❑
❑ Freight-in and trucking out	❑	❑
❑ Production vehicles	❑	❑
❑ Insurance related to production employees and facilities	❑	❑
❑ Product rework	❑	❑

Financial Facts Worksheet

Action Step 4.2 asks you to estimate these costs on the Financial Facts Worksheets introduced in Module 3, pp. 128 – 136.

Who Are My Suppliers?

You will spend a lot of time planning your business and working towards success. Do not risk your success on the performance of an unknown supplier.

Some business owners don't put much effort into checking out suppliers—a costly mistake. Before signing suppliers, understand if they operate with the same basic values you do, if they make good on their promises, and if the supplies will be available when you need them.

One way you can improve your chances of finding good suppliers is to plan a supplier selection process. Ask and answer these questions before you set up any long-term relationship with a supplier:

- Who else does this supplier do business with?
- What is the supplier's strategic plan?
- How is the company doing financially?

If companies want to do business with you, they may be willing to provide basic financial information to help you evaluate their long-term viability. If they are not willing to provide this information, you can check on their credit ratings or obtain information from the Better Business Bureau or commercial rating agencies such as Dun & Bradstreet. Don't ignore what you find out. It may mean the difference between success and failure for you.

In this portion of your Business Plan, list your major raw material, inventory, and service suppliers. Describe the relationship you expect with these suppliers. How often will they supply goods and services? What is your contractual agreement with them? What are your contingencies? Who are your backup suppliers and how will you use them? Answering these questions in your Business Plan puts readers' concerns about these issues at rest concerning your overall ability to do business.

What Are My Related Products, Services, or Spin-Offs?

Rarely is one product or service, or even one product or service line, sufficient to keep a company profitable over time. You will want to continually reevaluate the products or services of your company for possible enhancement or discontinuation. In addition, you can look for ways to expand your product or service line and bring in new products or services.

Put Some Spin on It

Rebecca Smith expanded A.D. Morgan Corp., her Tampa, Florida, commercial construction company, by offering in-house expertise in a different, albeit related capacity—a strategy Smith calls "slight shifting." The new unit, A.D. Morgan Building Services, provides consulting services to help companies assess how their buildings are aging and what needs to be done to restore them to optimal condition.

The consulting division has enabled Smith to use existing resources. Her staff can just as easily spend forty hours reviewing the condition of an existing facility as overseeing the construction of a new one, she explains. The new unit also required very little capital expense. In fact, Smith only had to hire one additional staff person, an individual with mechanical expertise.

"As a boutique commercial construction company, we compete with entities many times our size," Smith says. "It is imperative that we offer something extra, and our advantage is customer service. The consulting arm is a natural extension of this orientation. It also helps shore up our company during inevitable downturns."

You should consider whether a spin-off enterprise may result from a successful venture. A spin-off is an enterprise started from an existing company. Spin-offs are common in high-technology industries. If potential spin-offs could meet market needs in the industry, clearly define them in your Business Plan.

What Is My Business Model?

In Module 3, you finalized your business concept and screened it for feasibility. Now you will extend it to become a business model. Your business model will explain who your customers are, what they value, and how you'll profit from providing them that value in your product or service. In other words, how are you going to make money?

Two businesses that sell the same product or service can have quite different business models. For example, both Dell®, Inc., and CompUSA® sell computers and peripherals. Dell Computers receives orders via the telephone or online, receives payment from the customer/user before the computer is even built, builds the computer, and ships it directly to the consumer. CompUSA is a retail operation, selling various brands of computers it has purchased from manufacturers or distributors. The choice of business model has a profound effect upon all aspects of their businesses.

The Customer Comes First

In 1991, CarMax® surveyed shoppers to find out what they liked and disliked about the car-buying process, and then built their business model around consumers' responses. They are a bricks and mortar business, with both franchises and a strong Internet presence. Customers at CarMax pay a fixed price for a car, because their market research told them that consumers hate haggling over price. Because of their size, CarMax is able to buy a customer's car at a discounted price even if that customer is not purchasing another car from them. They can turn around and sell that car, then, to a different customer for a profit. This unique combination of business models arose through customer surveys and market research.

Look at existing business models to evaluate which model is best for your business concept. What components of each model make it work? How would you improve it? How can it be adapted to make your business better than the competition? With this type of evaluation, you can unearth the unique attributes of your business model.

Let's look at some common business models, keeping in mind that most businesses use hybrid models and not purely one or the other.

Bricks and Mortar – The most basic business model is the storefront model, more recently referred to as the *bricks and mortar model*. You set up a store in a location where you display your products to potential customers. Customers come to you to buy at that location. In recent years, many store owners have modified their business model and also sell their products on the Web to increase revenues. This practice is commonly referred to as the bricks and clicks model.

Bait and Hook – Years ago, Gillette® came up with the idea to hook customers with the purchase of an initial low-cost product and then supplement this initial item with the sale of high-priced accessories. This model is often referred to as *bait and hook* and is implemented with products such as cell phones and airtime, printers and ink cartridges, and cameras, film, and prints.

Subscription – A business model originally developed for magazine and record clubs is now finding many new applications. The *subscription* business model allows a company to generate recurring revenues, usually on a monthly or yearly basis. Other industries that have adopted this model include cable and phone companies, newspapers, Internet providers, software providers, and cell phone companies. While this model can generate a constant stream of revenue, subscriptions can sometimes be difficult to manage and track. Another reason this model is popular is convenience for the customer.

Direct Sales – The *direct sales* business model eliminates the middleman and increases the sale-to-delivery speed of a company's products. In the model popularized by Dell, Inc., having customers pay for products before they are built provides a good cash flow position. This business model reduces the number of layers in the distribution channel which in turn lowers costs and brings the customer closer to the seller. For some businesses, however, middlemen help streamline the sales process, reducing costs and increasing profits.

Auction – While the *auction* business model has been around for ages, the Internet has provided new uses for it. The traditional auction-house business model is usually associated with antiques and collectibles such as stamps, coins, classic cars, and fine art. The world's largest online auction site, eBay®, has generated countless new auction business opportunities for entrepreneurs. Specifically, eBay provides an online auction Web site where people from around the world buy and sell all kinds of goods and services.

Service – The service industry is a main category of our economy and presents the most complex and challenging business models. The service sector consists of such industries as insurance, tourism, banking, education, franchises, restaurants, transporation, healthcare, consulting, investment, and legal services, among others. The problem that many service providers face is how to deliver quality services, efficiently

Change with the Times

Olin B. King founded Space Craft, Inc., in Huntsville, Alabama. King started his business in the basement of his home in 1961 with two friends whose goal was to design and build satellites. They had built only three before that program was transferred to NASA from the U.S. Army. Later they set out to manufacture subsystems for the Apollo missions, completing fifteen systems before the Apollo program came to a halt.

Back to square one, SCI then began to manufacture subsystems for F4 jets for the Department of Defense, building thousands before it found itself, once again, searching for a new market need to fill. In the late 1970s and early 1980s, SCI made computers for IBM® and evolved into a Fortune 300 company.

In just a few years, SCI grew from a handful of people to thousands of employees working in plants all over the world. Some industry analysts dubbed Mr. King the "Father of Contract Manufacturing."

Mr. King will tell you it was not easy; in fact, he found he had to reinvent his company and his business model a number of times. Although SCI began with an engineering services business, it continued to adapt until it evolved into a contract manufacturing business model.

In 2001, when SCI Systems, Inc., was acquired by Sanmina® for $6 billion, SCI was a publicly-traded company operating forty-nine facilities in nineteen countries and employing more than 35,000 people. Analysts projected this merger would create one of the most respected and successful companies in the $130 billion global electronics contract manufacturing industry.

and effectively, every time. A typical service business model may focus on increasing customer satisfaction, which leads to loyalty, which leads to profitability. The increase in profitability is related to customer retention. It's typically less expensive to keep existing customers than to acquire new ones.

T¡P Your business model does not have to have a name, but you should be clear about what it is and how it will produce revenue. A "fuzzy" idea will not play well with potential investors.

Internet – Internet commerce has given rise to new kinds of business models, as well as new uses for old business models. While many Web business models have been defined, they continue to evolve and new variations can be expected in the future. Here is a quick glimpse at a few Internet models:

- **Brokerage** – A broker makes a market by bringing buyers and sellers together for a transaction fee. Examples of the brokerage model include Orbitz®, Priceline®, eBay, Paypal®, Amazon®, Shopping.com®, and MySimon.

- **Advertising** – A Web site provides content services and sells advertising for a charge or incentive. The advertising revenue is in direct proportion to the volume of viewing. Yahoo!®, Monster.com®, Google®, and Marketwatch® are examples of this model.

- **Infomediary** – Independent sources, typically Web-based, offer consumers a place to gather information about specific products and companies before they make purchasing decisions. For example, DoubleClick Inc.® analyzes Internet consumption habits and sells its data to firms for use in targeting a market. Edmunds.com® provides consumers extensive research, reviews, and prices on new and used cars.

Today's global economy creates more competition than ever. The business atmosphere is tough and entrepreneurs are constantly challenged to understand the ever-changing needs and wants of their customers. A well-thought-out business model gives your company a position ahead of its competition. But as customers change over time, you can rethink your model and adapt to stay in the game.

Check Your Knowledge of business models online at www.fasttrac.org/toolkits.

The success of a company is directly related to how well its business model matches its customers' priorities. The CEO Refresher's *Establishing a Continuing Business Model Innovation Process* by Donald Mitchell and Carol Coles reports that successful high-growth companies revise their business models according to customer preference as often as every two to four years.

Reality Check ✓ **Business Model**

Based on your product or service description, which of the following business models have possibilities for your business?

❏ Bricks and mortar	❏ Direct sales	❏ Internet advertising
❏ Bricks and clicks	❏ Auction	❏ Internet infomediary
❏ Bait and hook	❏ Service	❏ Other
❏ Subscription	❏ Internet brokerage	

Which of the above models might serve as a secondary choice or future model for your business?

Protecting the Product/Service

Protecting intellectual property is critical to the growth, value, and stability of your company. Intellectual property gives you a competitive edge in the marketplace and builds value. Intellectual property takes three forms: *legal* such as patents, trademarks, copyrights, and trade secrets; *people* such as employees' knowledge and skills; and *relationships* such as customers, suppliers, independent contractors, and consultants. You should plan to protect your proprietary assets.

Check Your Knowledge ✔

Intellectual Property

Find out if you know what the following legal terms (right) mean by matching them with their definitions (left).

1. Issued to new and useful inventions, discoveries, and designs. The work must be completely new, useful, and not obvious.

2. Given to "original works of authorship" such as written works, musical works, visual works, or performance works.

3. Protects a name or symbol, which is used to distinguish one person's goods or services from those of others.

4. Describes some information or process that provides a commercial advantage, which is protected by not disclosing it to others.

a. Copyright
b. Trade Secret
c. Patent
d. Trademark / Service Mark

Being familiar with intellectual property and strategies for protecting it will help you comprehend the ramifications of business decisions related to intellectual property. It will also help you strategically use intellectual property to create new profit centers and increase the value of your company. For example, patenting inventions keeps competitors from using the same technology for a period of time. On the other hand, obtaining a patent takes time. If you want to establish a dominant position in a new market immediately, you can skip the patenting process and take a product directly to market. An intellectual property attorney or other advisers can help you to determine whether getting a patent, rushing to market, or pursuing a trade secret is the best strategy for your business concept.

Coca-Cola® has protected its intellectual property for a long time by using a variety of approaches:
• The artwork of the can/bottle is copyrighted.
• The brand name and logo are trademarked.
• The formula for Coca-Cola is a trade secret.

The formula for Coca-Cola could have been patented, but that would have made it a matter of public record within just a few years. Without protection after the patent expired, anyone could have copied their secret recipe for the cola syrup. Keeping it a trade secret for so many years has helped Coca-Cola preserve its domination of the market.

Once intellectual property is properly protected, you must guard and maintain its rights zealously. If you do not defend your rights, you will lose them. If your company allows others to use its trademarks or copyrights without legal challenge, your intellectual property rights may slip into the public domain and become public property.

One of the biggest mistakes entrepreneurs make is not recognizing their intellectual property. Your business name, logo, brochures, product, service procedures, and much more are proprietary and can be legally protected from competitors.

TiP Strive to build proprietary assets for the future success of your company.

Success alone can eliminate the value of your intellectual property. A name can become so dominant it takes on a generic meaning. For example, Kleenex®, Xerox®, and Ketchup, although brand names, have become synonymous with a generic product rather than a specific brand.

Unfortunately, protecting intellectual property rights takes time and money, but defending those rights is what maintains their value for the business. Each form of protection has its own set of processes and regulation. You should consider how each might apply to your business concept and then incorporate its use into your plan.

Patents

A *patent* is a grant of a legal right to certain property by the United States for a term of seventeen years. What is granted is not the right to make, use, sell, or import, but the right to exclude others from doing so. Any person who invents or discovers a new and useful process, machine, product, or compound can apply for a patent. When a patent expires, anyone is able to use that previously protected knowledge. All of the patent holder's rights are gone.

Plan to Protect

When one of Carol Frank's best customers called to say that one of Frank's largest competitors was trying to sell Avian Adventures birdcages to them, Frank was stunned—and certain it was a mistake. The customer explained that Frank's competitor had made a deal with a manufacturer to copy Avian Adventures cages.

At first she was angry with the manufacturer, but then Frank became angry with herself because she hadn't invested the time or money to patent her birdcage design. "My intellectual capital had been stolen, and I could have prevented it," she says.

Patent law is a complex field that requires the assistance of a patent lawyer to navigate. Not all patent lawyers have the same expertise; they specialize in various fields. Most patent attorneys have very specific product or service experience reflected in their fields of specialization.

TiP Spending money to obtain a patent for an unmarketable product is foolish. Don't consider a patent unless you can verify that it will pay off over time.

Getting a patent is a very long and expensive process. It includes a search of existing patents, an application, probably at least one rejection, and then, even after it is issued, defending it. A patent can cost as much as $20,000 or more and take eighteen months or longer to obtain. After all that, you only have the right to defend it against claims of others. Many companies hire engineers and patent attorneys to do nothing more than design around existing valuable patents so the real core of the invention can be used and the original patent holder can do nothing about it.

Spending the money to receive patent protection for a product or service is not always appropriate. Usually you should retain the services of a patent attorney to determine if an idea should be patented. Before hiring an expensive patent attorney, be aware of these patent realities. The product or service may not be patented if:

- Another party already has patented the product/service. Preliminary patent searches can help to identify similar patents that have already been issued.
- The product/service may not be useful. Patent law requires that the patent will only be granted for a useful product/service.
- The product/service was in the public use or offered to the public before the application.
- The product/service is just an idea without a workable device or process.
- The inventor disclosed it to another person more than a year before applying for the patent.

Running a Patent Search

Before investing in an intellectual property attorney's advice, run an online search for prior patents at www.uspto.gov, www.delphion.com, or more traditionally, at the Search Room of the Scientific Library of the Patent and Trademark Office, which is located at 2021 Jefferson Davis Highway, Arlington, Virginia, 22202-3513. An attorney can make this search on your behalf for a fee.

TiP It is unlawful to put "Patent Pending" or an abbreviation to that effect on a product unless you have applied for a patent.

Trademarks and Service Marks

Trademarks (TM, ®) or *service marks* (SM, ®) are important marketing tools that help distinguish the goods or services of a venture from those of its competitors. They add value to a company as intellectual property. Trademarks apply to goods and service marks apply to services.

A trademark is any word, name, device, symbol, or combination of those used by a business to identify its products and distinguish the products from those offered by others. Probably the most recognizable trademark in the United States is the Nike® swoosh. Brand names are one form of trademark. Distinctive packaging, unique color schemes, unique designs, and slogans can also be trademarked.

Service marks are often titles, slogans, or phrases used in the sale or advertising of services as opposed to products. For example, FedEx® uses an easily identified service mark to distinguish its parcel delivery service. A service mark is used in advertising while trademarks appear on packaging.

CHECK YOUR KNOWLEDGE ANSWERS FROM P. 149

a.	Copyright	2.	Given to "original works of authorship" such as written works, musical works, visual works, or performance works.
b.	Trade Secret	4.	Describes some information or process that provides a commercial advantage, which is protected by not disclosing it to others.
c.	Patent	1.	Issued to new and useful inventions, discoveries, and designs. The work must be completely new, useful, and not obvious.
d.	Trademark/Service Mark	3.	Protects a name or symbol, which is used to distinguish one person's goods or services from those of others.

151

In the eyes of many business experts, trademarks or service marks can be far more valuable than patents in protecting a business's market share. In practice, trademarks continue for the life of the business and are transferable.

TIP You can enforce trademark infringement much more easily and with more certainty than patent theft.

Trademark and service mark rights may be used to prevent others from using a confusingly similar mark, but not to prevent others from making the same goods or from selling the same goods or services under a clearly different mark.

You may protect intellectual property with trademarks and service marks at the state or federal level. Federal registration is much more advantageous because it gives nationwide protection and permits greater damage recovery. Until the mark has in fact been registered, one cannot legally use the ® symbol.

Trademarks and service marks are an affordable way to obtain protection for intellectual property. You can search registered marks at www.uspto.gov.

Copyrights

Copyright protection is automatic. It exists the moment an original work is created, but the work should be registered with the Register of Copyrights at the Library of Congress in order to prove when the material was created and to identify its contents.

Copyrights protect the property of the author who created the work. Copyrights protect original works of authorship from unauthorized copying or use. They are good for the life of the creator plus seventy years. Literary, musical, dramatic, choreographic, pictorial, graphic, sculptural, audiovisual, and architectural works can all be protected through copyrights. Copyrights do allow limited use of the material by others for criticism, comment, news reporting, teaching, scholarship, and research.

Every company owns copyrightable material developed within the scope of business. Many businesses include copyright notices on all such materials as a matter of routine practice. Copyright notices should contain all of the following three elements:
• The symbol ©, the word "Copyright," or the abbreviation "Copr."
• The first year of publication.
• The name of the owner or company.
For example: © 2005 John Doe.

When employees produce work for a company, the company owns the copyright on the materials. Work produced by an independent contractor belongs to the contractor unless the contract specifies that it is "work made for hire" and belongs to the company. You must develop clearly written agreements with employees and subcontractors concerning who owns the copyright on the materials produced.

Licenses and Royalties

Another strategy some companies use is to license their intellectual property to another company. Such an agreement might limit the licensed usage to a particular category of product or service or to permit its use without limits. Since intellectual property is actually property, it can be sold completely just like any other property. When you license intellectual property, you retain ownership but another business or person may use it in accordance with the contract. Generally, you receive a license fee paid up front or over time, and you receive periodic payments based on use or sales called *royalties*.

You can issue a license for a specific period of time or key it to performance quotas. Many times the licensor (the owner) will insist upon minimum royalties regardless of sales or use. A license can be exclusive for the intellectual property, exclusive or non-exclusive for a particular market or territory, or otherwise restricted by the contract. The variations are limited only by the imaginations of those involved.

Don't Tread on Me

Licensing provided an effective way to saturate the market for Teva® founder Mark Thatcher. After a layoff from Citgo®, Thatcher combined his love of river rafting and technical ingenuity to create an amphibious utility sandal.

Without the resources to manufacture and market the Teva sandal himself, he entered into an oral licensing agreement with a sporting goods company. When sales began to climb, the partner tried to squeeze him out. Fortunately, Thatcher found another licensee and a good lawyer and managed to regain his rights. Thatcher grew the company into a leader in the sports sandal market.

You can be the *licensor* and profit by licensing products or services to others, or you can be the *licensee* and gain the rights to use or sell other companies' products. Whether you are the licensee or licensor, carefully consider the contents of the license agreement. Asking these questions may help:

- Will any money be paid up front for the license?
- What royalty will be paid? Will it be based on time, units, or a percentage of sales?
- Will a minimum royalty be paid regardless of sales or use?
- What type of exclusivity will be negotiated? In most cases, if entrepreneurs can find one licensee, they will probably be able to find more.
- What level of involvement do the licensor and the licensee want in marketing the product or overseeing its production?
- What is the performance standard?
- What is the duration of the license?
- Does the licensee have the right to assign or sub-license others?
- Who will own any modifications or improvements to the licensed intellectual property?
- Who pays for any further research and development of the intellectual property?

TiP License agreements are complex. As with all legal documents, licenses should only be entered into with the advice of an experienced attorney.

Some organizations that deal with licensing issues include the Licensing Industry Merchandisers Association, the National Association of Small Business Investment Companies, and the National Venture Capital Association. Local chambers of commerce, Small Business Development Centers, venture capitalists, and banks can also assist with licensing leads.

Trade Secrets

A trade secret is something an entrepreneur or firm knows that others do not know. Trade secrets include techniques, designs, materials, processes, and formulas the public does not have access to. They can be licensed in the same way as a patent. A supplier or customer list, manufacturing process or technique, or merchandising or promotional system may also be trade secrets. Such trade secrets can be very valuable.

TIP Always obtain a confidentiality agreement before disclosing information that may be protected under trade secret or patent law. Even with such an agreement, the information is at risk of being disclosed and used improperly.

You may want to keep a process, technique, or formula a secret to all but the upper levels of your venture's management. You may not allow even the employees to learn it. For example, only a few top executives of the Coca-Cola Company know the secret formula for the Coke® syrup.

You must be particularly careful that your employees do not divulge trade secrets. Employees should sign a non-disclosure agreement that legally prohibits them from disclosing the secret information during or after their employment. Further, the secret must be zealously guarded and disseminated only on a need-to-know basis. If employees leave the information lying around, available to anyone in the business, courts are not likely to enforce confidentiality agreements. Sometimes, only portions of a formula or process are shared with individuals so no one person can disclose the entire thing.

Team Defects

"Ever taken a punch to the stomach when you weren't ready?" asks Michelle Lemmons-Poscente, president of International Speakers Bureau® (ISB), Inc., in Dallas. That's how she felt when a longtime employee announced he was joining three colleagues and launching a business that would compete with ISB.

Lawsuits began, based on the non-compete and non-disclosure agreements employees had signed when they joined ISB. But then Lemmons-Poscente discovered the four defectors had removed those records from the company's on-site personnel files—and she had no back-up copies. Fortunately, forensic computer experts were able to reconstruct the deleted files, along with incriminating communications. The four employees settled out of court, and Lemmons-Poscente absorbed their new company into her own.

Source: Carol Frank. *Do As I Say, Not As I Did!: Gaining Wisdom in Business Through the Mistakes of Highly Successful People*. Entrepreneurial Adventures, 2005. Used by permission.

TIP Many entrepreneurs' most valuable trade secret is their customer list. Consider ways to protect this valuable asset.

Employees at all levels of a business may have specific skills or knowledge that are immensely valuable to that business. Perhaps it's a salesman who knows the customers, whom to meet with, when and where to call on them, and their internal procedures. That salesman doesn't need a written list; it's all in his head. Suppose one day he decides to work for the competition or start his own business? What about the plant manager who knows every detail of how to produce your product?

Those are both examples of intellectual property that need to be protected. Employees cannot be forced to continue to work unless an employment contract requires it, and even then, when the contract expires, they are gone. Non-compete clauses in their employment contracts, reasonable as to duration and scope, can provide protection for a period of time.

Trade secrets often are the most valuable asset of a business. Just as with patents, the protection of trade secrets needs the attention of an experienced attorney.

Using Intellectual Property Attorneys

Intellectual property issues can quickly become expensive and time-consuming. If your business concept launches you into these waters, find an attorney who specializes in the type of intellectual property law applicable to your business to help you navigate.

Reality Check ✔

Costs of Developing and Protecting Intellectual Property

Think about costs associated with protecting intellectual property. Put a check by each one that might apply. Indicate whether you already know these amounts or need more research.

	Already Know	Need to Research
❏ Consulting with an intellectual property attorney	❏	❏
❏ Establishing agreements concerning:		
❏ Who owns copyrightable materials	❏	❏
❏ Non-compete/non-disclosure	❏	❏
❏ License agreements	❏	❏
❏ Identifying and designating a trade secret	❏	❏
❏ Registering trade or service mark	❏	❏
❏ Hiring a graphic artist for logo and product design	❏	❏
❏ Defending intellectual property	❏	❏

You can have valuable rights stolen from you and be unable to do much about it for a number of reasons:
- The cost of correcting the problem is prohibitive.
- You lack proof of theft.
- No legal cause of action is apparent.

It costs money to file patent claims and even more money to protect the intellectual property rights of a company. Patenting an invention could easily cost as much as $20,000 or more. Defending a patent against infringement is even more expensive.

An intellectual property attorney can do much, however, to prevent problems. First, attorneys can spot intellectual property in your business and devise ways to protect it more readily than you can. Certainly attorneys can prepare the appropriate documents, but they can also advise you on protective measures in matters such as hiring, firing, administration, and operations. Prevention is cheaper than cure.

For assistance, ask your general business lawyer to recommend an intellectual property attorney and then interview prospective candidates. When screening candidates, ask yourself the following questions:
- Can you and the attorney effectively communicate with each other?
- Does the attorney explain advice in terms you understand?
- Do you feel confident in the attorney and the advice?
- Does the attorney adequately explain the fee and billing procedures?
- Is the attorney accessible by phone?
- Does the attorney return phone calls within twenty-four hours or have a procedure in place that others from the office will call you and see if they can help?
- When you do speak with the attorney does he or she appear knowledgeable about you, your business, and the status of the matter at hand?

Financial Facts Worksheet

If the answers to any of these questions are negative, work on changing that answer by telling your attorney directly what is negative about your relationship. If several are negative, find another attorney.

Action Step 4.2 asks you to estimate these costs on the Financial Facts Worksheets introduced in Module 3, pp. 128 – 136.

Complying with Governmental Regulations

As you are planning your Product/Service Plan for your Business Plan take into account what kinds of governmental regulation your business concept may incur.

TiP Entrepreneurs who own 100 percent of their business may not realize that they still have partners—the federal, state, and local governments.

Complying with all federal, state, and local regulations and obtaining all licenses and other permissions before beginning operations is essential. Most of these requirements were created to put people on the various tax rolls, such as income, sales, Social Security, workers' compensation, unemployment, and personal property (inventory). Other requirements were established to prevent people from doing dangerous or undesirable things.

Federal Government

Unless your enterprise plans to make or sell alcohol, firearms, explosives, pharmaceutical drugs, nuclear devices, or other controlled substances, your main concern is with the Internal Revenue Service (IRS).

The IRS wants to know where a business is and what it does. Thus, you most likely must file form SS-4 with the IRS to register your business. If a sole proprietor has no employees, an SS-4 form may not be required. When you file the form, you will receive an employer's kit containing information about the types of taxes owed, when to pay them, where to pay them, and how to compute the amounts due.

You will also receive an Employer's Identification Number (EIN) (sole proprietors use their Social Security number) to identify your business. All communications with governmental agencies must include this EIN. The EIN is also needed to open business bank accounts and brokerage accounts and to deal with others who report your business's actions to any governmental agency. The government identifies your venture by its EIN, not by name.

TiP You can find out more about the federal guidelines that pertain to your business from the Small Business Administration www.sba.gov or a Small Business Development Center www.asbdc-us.org.

If your business has employees, you must withhold portions of each employee's earnings and contribute your share as well. These funds are deposited to special accounts at designated banking facilities. The regulations regarding withheld wages are very strict and must be complied with. Failure to make the required deposits in a timely manner usually brings swift action by the government. Agents can padlock your business and arrest you until you make the deposits. The reason for such drastic action is that the money involved belongs to your employees. Your business is simply a temporary custodian or trustee of it.

Occupational Safety and Health Administration (OSHA) has very specific requirements concerning health and safety, which apply to many businesses. The enactment of the Americans with Disabilities Act (ADA) affects businesses both in hiring practices and customer accommodations.

State Governments

While federal regulations are the same for everyone in the United States, each state has different regulations, and may require additional licenses and sales tax collection.

The selection of the state in which to locate a business is not a minor matter. Where you choose to do business greatly affects the cost of operations, markets, and profits. Granted, circumstances are often beyond your control and force you to do business in a certain state. Still, you should be keenly aware of all regulations required by the state in which you do business.

One of the primary requirements of many state governments is that businesses collect sales tax from their customers. Although most states have a sales tax, the method of each state for handling the tax differs. Some states tax certain products and services differently. You can find out about your state's sales tax on the secretary of state's Web site, from local chambers of commerce, or by contacting your closest Small Business Development Center.

If you conduct business in several states, your venture may have to be authorized to do business in all of them. Companies that plan to resell goods use a state sales tax identification number when purchasing goods that will be resold. This way, the company does not pay sales taxes, but collects them when it sells the product or service to the final user. The business must still pay sales tax on the things it buys to use such as plant equipment, office supplies, and plant-maintenance supplies.

Sales taxes should not cost you anything. The intent is for you to collect money from your customers for sales tax at the time of sale. You turn in this money to the state sales tax division. Still, some entrepreneurs get caught in the trap of spending the collected sales tax money before it is due. Then they must scramble to come up with additional funds to pay the sales tax division. All state governmental agencies frown upon this practice.

Many state governments also require a business to register with the secretary of state. Corporations will file their articles of incorporation while sole proprietors may be required to file a fictitious name registration. A quick call to the secretary of state's office will reveal the regulations for companies doing business in that state. Also, many states have established Web sites with answers to frequently asked questions about starting a business and links to the appropriate agencies.

Local Governments

Local governments (county and city) regulate licenses, permits, and zoning. When you apply for a local license you will probably be asked to get inspected by the fire department, building officials, and zoning authorities. The fire department wants to know if you are doing anything that could be a potential fire or chemical hazard. It also wants to know if the building meets all fire codes. The building inspection department may inspect the property to make sure it is safe and up to code, and the zoning department will determine if your intended use is permitted in the zoning classification.

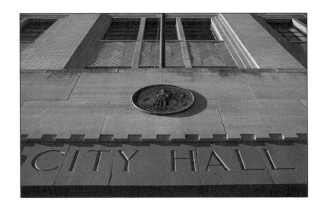

Reality Check ✓ | **Costs of Governmental Compliance**

Think about costs associated with your business to comply with governmental regulations. Put a check by each that will or might apply. Indicate whether you already know these amounts or need more research.

	Already Know	**Need to Research**
❏ Inspection fees	❏	❏
❏ Site modifications	❏	❏
❏ Signage	❏	❏
❏ License fee	❏	❏
❏ Business licenses	❏	❏
❏ Zoning variances or rezoning applications	❏	❏

Financial Facts Worksheet

Local governments can impose changes to existing and new buildings. For example, a new plant was forced to cut a large hole in the middle of its floor for another stairway from the basement, even though the basement was unused. The stairway added a significant expense of $9,500. Although the plant had been built to local building-code specifications, the local authorities still had the ability to order the extra stairway.

A home-based business can sometimes avoid zoning regulations. Other entrepreneurs avoid such problems by locating themselves in rural areas or small towns without excessive requirements. A call to city hall or county government will reveal the requirements in your region.

Action Step 4.2 asks you to estimate these costs on the Financial Facts Worksheets introduced in Module 3, pp. 128 – 136.

Starting My Business Plan

The purpose of the business planning process is to investigate all aspects of a potential business. It is not a rigid, step-by-step blueprint to follow. Instead, planning is more like a road map that leads you in a desired direction. A business plan will help guide your business as you maneuver through detours and rough roads.

Business plans are living documents that will change as you receive new information about the performance or external environment of your business. In many industries, business plans may need to be revisited and reevaluated every few months, not years.

Writing business planning documents is essential if you are serious about your business. It focuses thinking. It forces you to take an objective, critical, and unemotional view of your business. The discipline of writing business planning documents is a learned process you will use again and again.

Polish the Plan

When serial entrepreneur William J. Link founded Chiron Vision, he and his team spent several months—and hundreds of edits—crafting a business plan to attract investors. Their goal was to focus the company on ophthalmic surgical products, primarily for cataract and refractive surgery, and position it for eventual sale.

Their top-notch plan demonstrated the market for their products and included information about the competitive landscape. It also described research, development, and risks associated with the product.

A good business plan doesn't have to be long, Link says: "Complete information communicated thoroughly but with brevity is more important to success than extraneous information added for no reason other than increasing length."

Plans that grab Link's attention are those that raise a question in readers' minds and then go on to answer it. "For example," he explains, "if there are some major risks related to the competition, mention them and then address them directly."

Reality Check ✔

Benefits of Business Planning

Business planning creates many benefits. Place a check beside the benefits you are seeking from the business planning process.

❑ Develops a successful start-up plan and guides the start-up process.

❑ Forces me to consider all aspects of feasibility, even some I may otherwise overlook.

❑ Highlights strengths and exposes flaws in my business concept.

❑ Uncovers hidden opportunities.

❑ Provides guidelines to follow when operating the business.

❑ Communicates the business concept to others.

❑ Clarifies financial requirements.

❑ Becomes a powerful tool for convincing investors to provide money.

What Are the Major Parts of My Business Plan?

Your Business Plan is a written document that articulates your business model, opportunities, management team, potential market, and financial requirements. It also identifies potential risks, problems, and trade-offs.

You might use several types of business planning documents as your business develops. The Business Plan for a start-up business used in this program includes these sections:

Cover Page
Table of Contents
Executive Summary
Management and Organization Plan
Product/Service Plan
Marketing Plan
Financial Plan
Appendix

You will actually complete the first three sections last. The Executive Summary is a brief compilation of the major aspects of the business such as management and organization, product or service description, marketing, and finances.

Business plans are written for many different reasons. Entrepreneurs often write business plans for their own personal reasons. At other times internal and external forces necessitate a written plan. For example, William Link sought funding with his Chiron Vision plan, so he needed to make sure it communicated how much money he needed to raise, what the money would be used for, and what the investors could expect to gain in return. The exact purpose of your plan will determine the type of information you include.

A business plan for an existing business includes the same sections as a start-up plan plus additional sections that include plans for operating and control systems and growth.

An existing business's plan also includes documents that reflect the financial history of the business. These additional sections—operations, growth, and historical financials— are not discussed in this program. To learn more about programs and tools for creating a Business Plan for an existing business, visit the FastTrac® Web site at www.fasttrac.org.

Who Is My Audience?

You will write your Business Plan for a variety of reasons and might present it to many different audiences. You might be writing to obtain financing or to attract key management team members. At a minimum, you will revise your Executive Summary for different readers. That portion of the plan communicates personally with the reader, emphasizing the sections of the plan of greatest importance to that reader and telling the reader what it is you want of him or her. Do you want a loan? If so, how much do you want, what do you intend to do with it, when and how will it be paid back, and what terms do you desire? If you are seeking critical comment on your marketing ideas, your Executive Summary will be different than if you are seeking a loan.

Specific sections of your plan may change if you are writing for different audiences. If the purpose of the plan is to gain financing, then the financial projections will be of greater importance and consequently more detailed than they would be for a marketing expert. If your plan is to be used internally for the management team members to grasp your vision, it may have substantially more proprietary information than would be passed out to external readers.

As you write each section of your plan, think about what your intended audience will want to know. It's possible that after writing your plan you may decide to use it for a purpose you did not originally anticipate. In that case, you can go back through the entire plan, revising the sections to emphasize those of greatest importance to your new audience as well as updating it to reflect more current and complete information.

Here are some things to watch for as you write your plan:

Use of *I*, *we*, or other personal pronouns – If you talk too much about yourself using *I*, *we*, and *me* in the plan, the focus is on you and not on the business. Most statements that start with *I* can be rephrased. For example, the statement "I really want to start a business that meets the needs of customers," can easily be changed to, "This business will respond to the needs of customers." This revision takes the focus off *me* and puts it on the *business*. When referring to yourself, write in third person, using your name, rather than using *I* or *we*.

TiP Developing a Business Plan involves thinking, researching, evaluating, planning, and writing. But don't get hung up on writing the plan. The writing will be easy once you have gathered what goes into each section.

Undocumented facts – Facts should drive decisions in the business planning process. Neglecting to include the sources of facts does not reflect positively upon you. It is just as damaging to the Business Plan to include facts from unreliable sources as to not include facts at all.

TiP Use facts from reputable and authoritative sources.

Negative words or phrases – The Business Plan should be a positive plan of action for a business. Whenever possible, avoid using negative phrases. Negativity sets the wrong tone for the reader of the plan. Notice how the tone changes in the following statements. The positive statements still convey the same message, but in a more upbeat way:

TiP Eliminate the negative.

– The service is easily marketed; however, a subcontractor has not yet been found to provide the technical services.

+ Marketing will begin as soon as a contract is signed with a subcontractor who will provide the technical services.

– The break-even point is 5,000 units, but the company has not been able to produce more than 3,000.

+ With current production personnel and facilities, 3,000 units are produced monthly. The break-even point is 5,000 units per month.

– Customers demand a combination of products and services our business can't provide.

+ Currently the company is offering a single service. Based on customer demand, opportunities exist to expand this service to include products.

Take the time to examine your plan to ensure you are presenting your business in a positive tone.

Check Your Knowledge ✓

Critique a Start-Up Business Plan

Before you begin writing your Business Plan, examine business plans written by others, noting what works well and what could be improved. Read a sample start-up Business Plan at www.fasttrac.org/toolkits and use the Business Plan Checklist below (pp. 161 – 164) to evaluate the strengths and weaknesses of the plan with regard to style, format, and content requirements. You will use this same checklist to critique your own Business Plan later in this program.

By evaluating your plan against this checklist, you will find changes may need to be made. These changes will make your plan more readable, concise, complete, fact-based, and error free.

Overall Readability

Yes	No	
❑	❑	Language is concise (does not read like a novel or term paper).
❑	❑	Each section stands on its own and clearly defines and satisfies its objective.
❑	❑	Facts are supported with sufficient documentation.
❑	❑	Conclusions drawn from facts are reasonable.
❑	❑	Contents are supported with sufficient charts and graphs.

Overall Spelling/Grammar/Math

Yes	No	
❑	❑	Spelling is correct.
❑	❑	Grammar is clean.
❑	❑	Math is error-free.

161

Critique a Start-Up Business Plan continued

Overall Formatting

Yes   No

- ❏   ❏   Font choice is readable.
- ❏   ❏   Spacing between lines is sufficient.
- ❏   ❏   Plan contains headings and subheadings.
- ❏   ❏   Formatting on headings and subheadings is consistent.
- ❏   ❏   Plan includes page numbers.
- ❏   ❏   Formatting on page numbers is consistent.
- ❏   ❏   Plan contains enough white space for readability.

Cover Page / Table of Contents

Yes   No

- ❏   ❏   Cover Page contains name of business.
- ❏   ❏   Cover Page contains chief executive's name.
- ❏   ❏   Cover Page contains address, telephone, fax numbers, e-mail, and Web address.
- ❏   ❏   Cover Page contains company logo.
- ❏   ❏   Page numbers in Table of Contents correspond correctly.
- ❏   ❏   Appendix includes a Table of Contents.

Executive Summary

Yes   No

- ❏   ❏   Does not exceed three pages and wholly describes the new venture.
- ❏   ❏   Describes the unique features and benefits of the product/service.
- ❏   ❏   Identifies the management team and supporting infrastructure.
- ❏   ❏   Explains the opportunities found within the industry.
- ❏   ❏   Contains plans for targeting a market segment and penetrating it.
- ❏   ❏   Specifies how much money the company needs and how funds will be obtained.

Management and Organization

Yes   No

- ❏   ❏   Explains the legal form of business.
- ❏   ❏   Lists key management positions, including primary job responsibilities.
- ❏   ❏   Identifies the board of directors/advisory board members, including primary contributions expected.
- ❏   ❏   Documents the process of recruiting and selecting employees.
- ❏   ❏   Clarifies the compensation and employee reward systems.
- ❏   ❏   Establishes credibility of the management team.

Critique a Start-Up Business Plan continued

Products/Services

Yes	No	
❏	❏	Describes product/service in plain language (not too technical).
❏	❏	Describes product/service in specific terms (not too broad).
❏	❏	Provides evidence that the product/service is technologically feasible.
❏	❏	Identifies unique features.
❏	❏	Identifies special benefits.
❏	❏	Wholly explains product/service limitations and potential solutions.
❏	❏	Wholly explains product/service liabilities and potential solutions.
❏	❏	If applicable, identifies production process and facility plans.
❏	❏	Provides backup suppliers and subcontractors.
❏	❏	Anticipates future related products/services and spin-offs.
❏	❏	Describes how intellectual property will be created and protected.
❏	❏	Lists requirements from regulatory agencies.

Marketing Plan – Industry Profile

Yes	No	
❏	❏	Focuses on current size and growth potential of the industry.
❏	❏	Discusses industry trends and opportunities associated with each.
❏	❏	Addresses geographic locations, seasonality, and industry profit characteristics.
❏	❏	Identifies existing distribution networks.

Marketing Plan – Competitive Analysis

Yes	No	
❏	❏	Identifies direct, indirect, and future competition.
❏	❏	Contains matrix to illustrate competitive position in marketplace.
❏	❏	Describes competitive advantage.

Marketing Plan – Market Analysis and Penetration

Yes	No	
❏	❏	Contains customer profile.
❏	❏	Contains target markets and size of each.
❏	❏	Fully illustrates the image of the company.
❏	❏	Describes plans to reach the market, including customer service, location, sales force, licensing and distributing.
❏	❏	Addresses plans for advertising and promotion.
❏	❏	Includes plans for marketing through technology, including the Internet.
❏	❏	Discusses other penetration strategies, including publicity, telemarketing/direct mail, Web site, and trade shows.
❏	❏	Describes plans for evaluating market penetration effectiveness.

Marketing Plan – Pricing

Yes	No	
❏	❏	Addresses pricing strategy.
❏	❏	Contains price sheet.
❏	❏	Includes volume and special pricing information.
❏	❏	Contains the company's pricing policies.

Critique a Start-Up Business Plan continued

Financial Plan

Yes No
- ❑ ❑ Sales and profit projections appear to be reasonable.
- ❑ ❑ Assumptions and projections are wholly supported.
- ❑ ❑ All operating expenses have been included.
- ❑ ❑ Hidden costs have been identified.
- ❑ ❑ Salaries and other benefits are in line with industry standards or entrepreneur's goals.
- ❑ ❑ Contingency plan seems reasonable if sales forecasts go unmet.
- ❑ ❑ Figures on various documents are consistent.
- ❑ ❑ Sources of debt or equity financing are appropriately identified.
- ❑ ❑ Exit strategy is clearly defined.

Appendix

Yes No
- ❑ ❑ Contains resumes of the management team and key personnel.
- ❑ ❑ Contains all employee contracts, stock option plans, retirement plans.
- ❑ ❑ Contains personal financial statements for each of the principals.
- ❑ ❑ Contains patent and copyright approvals.
- ❑ ❑ Contains such agreements as partnerships, sales, distributor contracts, non-compete/non-disclosure, corporate bylaws, and other legal documents.
- ❑ ❑ Contains copies of product/service brochures or other advertising samples.
- ❑ ❑ Contains copies of all logos already developed.
- ❑ ❑ Contains copies of recent reference letters, recommendations, and endorsements.
- ❑ ❑ Contains copies of market studies or articles from trade journals or other media.
- ❑ ❑ Contains professional photographs of the product.
- ❑ ❑ Contains detailed outlines of the operating and control systems.
- ❑ ❑ Contains customer-signed orders or letters of intent.
- ❑ ❑ Contains documents that support the industry study.
- ❑ ❑ Contains detailed description of high-tech products.

Summary Comments Overall

Strengths: Note specific aspects that make the plan strong.

Suggestions for improvement

How Do I Get Started?

The FastTrac® NewVenture™ program includes electronic templates to give you a jumpstart in producing your Business Plan. The templates save you time by assisting with formatting, organizing, and presenting information. You will start using the Microsoft® Word-based Business Plan Template for Action Step 4.1 and continue using it as you progress through the rest of the modules. The Excel®-based Financial Plan Template will walk you through several worksheets and then automatically generate financial statements to include in your Business Plan. Instructions for using the templates are included in the action steps.

Consider the following ways to use technology to plan your business:

- **Research** – Rely on Web sites, library databases, research reports, trade journals, magazines, and other sources that are now available through technology.

- **Evaluation** – Financial tools are available on the Web to evaluate a business against others in its industry. Such financial comparisons are invaluable in setting financial projections.

- **Financial projections** – Using a financial spreadsheet program with an electronic worksheet, such as the Financial Template provided in this program, can save hours of time in preparing financial statements. These templates allow specific financial data to be entered once to produce multiple financial statements for use in your Business Plan.

- **Writing** – Using features of word processing programs greatly improves the business plan writing process. Built-in spelling and grammar checks provide helpful corrections for finalizing your plan.

- **Design/layout** – Graphs, pictures, and other format options create a professional touch. This extra flair is necessary for plans to be distributed to individuals outside the company such as bankers, investors, suppliers, mentors, and others.

Summary

This module outlined the basics of product or service planning. Defining and protecting the new product or service and complying with all governmental regulations is extremely important in the planning process so that you do not encounter legal or financial surprises later.

Key Things to Remember

- When defining a product/service, describe its purpose in terms of the problem it will solve.

- Each feature can be described as a benefit the customer receives or as a solution to the customer's needs.

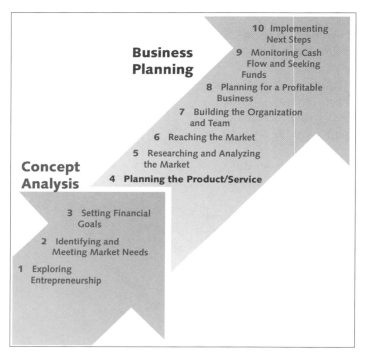

- Briefly explain the history of your product/ service development and identify its current stage of development.

- Consider and address your product/service limitations and potential liability of the product/service.

- Provide information regarding the production aspects of product/service development, as well as any potential spin-offs.

- Protecting your business's intellectual property is critical to the growth and stability of your company.

- You can protect the intellectual property of your business in the form of patents, trademarks, service marks, copyrights, licenses, trade secrets, non-disclosure, non-compete, and employment contracts.

- You must satisfy the necessary governmental requirements in order for your business to proceed.

A clear picture of your product or service and its features and benefits will greatly assist you as you move into Modules 5 and 6. These next two modules help you develop a Marketing Plan for your product or service that focuses on its features and benefits. Remember, features *tell*, but benefits *sell*!

Activity 4a Intellectual Property

Determine the types of intellectual property my business may have.

Directions
Use the steps below to determine what types of intellectual property your business may need to protect. Review pp. 149 – 156 for information on intellectual property.

Step 1 Brainstorm intellectual property. Think of a non-franchised but themed restaurant, such as Mexican or Thai, which has unique menus, décor, and recipes. Brainstorming with another participant, make a list of all the potential intellectual property that a restaurant might have and in which category each would properly be classified.

Intellectual Property Item	**Type**
EXAMPLE *Recipe for certain food*	*Trade secret*
a. _____	_____
b. _____	_____
c. _____	_____
d. _____	_____
e. _____	_____
f. _____	_____
g. _____	_____
h. _____	_____
i. _____	_____
j. _____	_____

Step 2 List three proprietary aspects about your own products or services you may want to protect.

a.

b.

c.

Activity 4a   **Intellectual Property** continued

Step 3 List three ways to protect your business's intellectual property.

a.

b.

c.

Step 4 List three questions you need to ask an attorney about protecting intellectual property.

a.

b.

c.

Action Step 4.1 **Create My Product/Service Plan**

Begin writing my Business Plan.

Directions

The Product/Service Plan is the first section of your Business Plan you will write. This action step, combined with the rest of the planning action steps in this program, will make up your Business Plan. Throughout the process of writing a Business Plan, you can continually update previously completed sections. You will probably find that you need to update the Product/Service Plan later in the program as additional information becomes available.

For this action step, you will start using the Business Plan Template at www.fasttrac.org/toolkits. Read the instructions on page 1 of the template. Then move to the Product/Service Plan in the template to insert your information.

Each section of the template contains headings with questions to prompt you to consider the type of information to include under each heading. The questions are also listed in each action step for easy reference. After you enter your answers into the template and print them out, the questions will not appear on the hard copy. You should try to incorporate enough of the question into your answer so that the reader understands what is being answered:

Product/Service Plan

Purpose of Product/Service
What is the purpose of the product/service?
How does the product/service benefit the customer?
Does it solve a problem or address an opportunity?
Is it a luxury item or a needed good?

Features and Benefits
What are the unique features of the product/service, such as cost, design, quality, and capabilities?
What benefits does the customer receive?
What problem is solved for the customer?

Stage of Development
What is the history of product/service development?
At what stage of development is the product/service (model stage, working prototype, small production runs, full manufacturing/production, or other)?
When do you plan to achieve other stages of development?
At what life cycle stage is the product/service (conception, introduction, growth, maturity, innovation, or decline)?

Product/Service Limitations
What are the inherent product/service limitations, if any?
Include perishability, limited shelf life, installation needs, legal restrictions, staff availability, or other relevant limitations.

Product/Service Liability
What are the liabilities this product/service may pose?
What are the insurance requirements and costs?
What other factors may reduce or eliminate product/service liability?

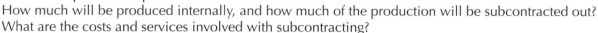

Action Step 4.1 **Create My Product/Service Plan** continued

Production

What is the production process?

How much will be produced internally, and how much of the production will be subcontracted out?

What are the costs and services involved with subcontracting?

Who are the backup subcontractors; what are their costs, and who supplies the services?

Include shipping, billing, inventory, stocking, and payment terms.

Facilities

What are the plans for facilities (manufacturing, office, retail)?

Include manufacturing facilities, production capacity, and future capital required to build facilities.

Suppliers

Who are the major raw material/service suppliers, and what are the significant purchasing contracts with them?

Are there backup suppliers?

Related Products/Services and Spin-Offs

What related products/services will be provided, and how will they increase or enhance the profitability of the venture?

What new product/service (spin-offs) could be developed to meet changing market needs in this industry or others?

Trademarks, Patents, Copyrights, Licenses, Royalties

How will you protect intellectual property?

What patents, trademarks, or copyrights have been obtained or which ones will be pursued?

What licenses or royalty agreements are associated with the product/service, and what plans have been made for future agreements?

What distribution rights have been obtained or given away?

Governmental Approvals

What governmental agencies regulate businesses in your industry?

What governmental approvals are necessary, and what is the status of such approvals?

Some examples of agencies providing governmental approvals include the FDA, EPA, FCC, USDA, OSHA, IRS, secretary of state, State Department of Revenue and Taxation, Workers' Compensation Division, health departments, planning and zoning commissions.

Action Step 4.2   **Write My Product/Service Financial Assumptions**

Project how much money I will need for the product/service aspect of my business.

Financial Facts Worksheet

Directions

Use the Financial Facts Worksheets to estimate costs for the product or service aspects of your business. Each worksheet heading in the list below suggests possible costs to consider. Not all headings will apply to all businesses. Think about how each one applies to your business and, in particular, to your vision of that business.

Write your assumptions on the Financial Facts Worksheets on pp. 128 – 136 or from your electronic toolkit at www.fasttrac.org/toolkits. Base your answers on facts and document sources for each assumption. Allow enough time to do your research. You might want to talk with experts in your industry, suppliers, and professionals who serve the industry to determine appropriate costs. For example, you can research typical costs for inventory and supplies and industry-standard payment terms. Also, plan for increases over time.

Completing your Financial Facts Worksheet now while you work on your Product/Service Plan will save you time later when you fill out your Financial Template and make your financial projections.

Operating Expenses Worksheet

Insurance – Product/Service liability, business premises, and general business liability

Licenses & Fees – Local inspection fees and business licenses. Intellectual property filings

Professional Fees – Consultations with attorneys about protecting intellectual property such as obtaining a patent, registering a trade or service mark, preparing non-disclosure and non-compete agreements, or "work made for hire" contracts. Accountant's fees for setting up accounting records for sales tax and withholding. Attorney or risk management consultant regarding warranties and liability protection

Rent – Production facilities

Repairs & Maintenance – To production facilities and equipment

Utilities – For production

Other – Research and development for new or improved product/service

Inventory Worksheet

Insurance – Against casualty loss of raw materials as well as finished goods. Workers' compensation

Payroll Expenses – Salaries, wages, and payroll taxes of workers involved in production

Benefits – Health, retirement, and death benefits for workers involved in production

Rent – Storage of raw materials and finished goods

Rework – Costs to rework sub-standard finished goods or services provided

Subcontracting – Cost for work performed by others outside the business

Action Step 4.2 **Write My Product/Service Financial Assumptions** continued

Post Start-Up Asset Purchases Worksheet

Financial Facts Worksheet

Computer Equipment – For doing the work of the business as well as administration, include software and peripherals

Equipment & Machinery – For production. Might be anything from a 100-ton press to a cash register

Furniture – Desks, chairs, file cabinets, waiting room, display cases, bookcases, and other furnishings

Vehicles – Those used in and owned by the business

Leasehold improvements – The walls, ceilings, floors, or fixtures the business must pay for in rented space to decorate, make the space suitable for the business, or to comply with governmental laws or regulations such as OSHA, ADA, health and safety codes, or zoning regulations

Building – If buying or building, the cost of labor and materials as well as permit and inspection fees

Note: Once you complete the financial assumptions for the marketing modules (Modules 5 and 6), compare them with these product/service financial assumptions to make sure your projections are consistent. If you plan to sell 10,000 widgets in your Marketing Plan, for example, make sure you have planned production accordingly.

Researching and Analyzing the Market

Since you began market research in Module 2, you should have quite a collection of information about your product or service and its industry, customers, and competition. How do you best use this information as it applies to your business? This module and the one that follows will help you analyze your research to make decisions about your business.

Market analysis can help you confirm or modify your business concept and its assumptions. This analysis is used as a basis for moving forward and making decisions—about distribution, promotional, and pricing strategies for your product or service. These strategies will affect sales and profits. Using the information you analyze in this module, you can begin to write the marketing sections of your Business Plan.

Key Questions
- What common distribution channels does my industry use?
- What success factors are critical to my industry?
- Why is a competitive advantage important to my business?
- Who is the ideal target market for my product/service?
- Which pricing strategies allow me to compete and be profitable?
- What is a marketing plan and why is it important to my business?

Action Steps   Due Date

❏ 5.1 Create My Marketing Plan – Industry Profile   _____

❏ 5.2 Create My Marketing Plan – Competitive Analysis _____

❏ 5.3 Create My Marketing Plan – Market Analysis   _____

❏ 5.4 Create My Marketing Plan – Pricing   _____

❏ Read Module 6 Reaching the Market   _____

❏ _____   _____

❏ _____   _____

❏ _____   _____

Analyzing the Market

By now you should be fairly comfortable with many aspects of your industry and its market. In this module you will delve more deeply into market analysis. Industry and customer characteristics, especially your options for distribution should come into focus. You will define your competitive advantage and analyze your competition. The customer profile you developed in Module 2 is the starting point for your analysis of market segments and your target market. Finally, this module introduces you to the relationship between your market and finances by asking you to think about pricing your product or service.

You will have an opportunity to record the results of these various analyses—your industry profile, your competitive analysis, market analysis, and pricing strategies—in the Marketing Plan section of your Business Plan, which you will consider in detail at the end of the module. Let's begin by looking at industry distribution channels.

Industry Profile

One industry characteristic not yet fully covered by your market research is the distribution channels businesses use to get products to market. As you consider positioning your new business in its industry and market, you should have firmly in mind the means by which you will distribute your products or services.

Although distribution channels for products are usually very different than those for services, some will work for both, including:

- Retail outlets operated by your company or by a franchise (for example, H&R Block® is a service business that uses retail outlets)
- Internet marketing and Web sites
- Direct mail using a catalog, brochure, or flyer
- Sales force compensated by salary, commission, or both
- TV and cable direct marketing and special shopping channels
- Telemarketing implemented on your own or through a contracted firm
- Educational seminars

Research the following questions about your industry's marketing and distribution channels:

- What are the most common distribution channels for this industry and why? Do businesses like yours sell directly to their customers, through retail stores that they own, through retail stores where shelf space is purchased such as a consignment store?
- Which distribution channels are the most cost effective for your new business? Are certain channels better suited to you because they do not require a large cash output to start?
- Is there a new channel for your product/service that might reach the customer better or differently than current industry distribution channels? Does new technology such as the Internet offer channels your competitors have not explored?
- What are the typical barriers or challenges for entering this industry? Does this industry require so much resource allocation that it is difficult to enter? Is an exceptional amount of technical knowledge or capital necessary?

Keep these questions in mind as you read the following discussion concerning typical distribution channels for most industries.

Product Distribution Channels

Entrepreneurs sometimes struggle with how to get their products to market. Most often, they can develop their products and prove that customers will purchase them, yet they do not know how to distribute them. For many new concepts, the key to long-term success lies in an ability to either build an effective distribution system for products or introduce them into existing distribution channels.

A *distribution channel* refers to the people and processes that bring a product to the market. A business may sell its product or service directly to the end user or it may be sold through a number of intermediaries. The distribution channel may include wholesalers, retailers, or both. It may include *middlemen* who act as agents, brokers, or manufacturers representatives, find customers, or negotiate contracts. Middlemen sometimes operate between the manufacturer and wholesaler and sometimes between the wholesaler and retailer. The term *distributor* may refer to the wholesale middleman who sells either to the retailer or to the end customers.

Activities in a Typical Product Distribution Channel

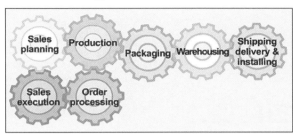

The easiest way to get a product to market is to place it in an established distribution network that already serves the desired market. Make it easy for distributors to sell your goods by furnishing their sales force with sales literature, training, demonstration units, price sheets, point-of-purchase displays, Web sites, and anything else that will help make the sale. Sometimes, entrepreneurs decide to build a new distribution system unlike their competitors'. This choice may be influenced by the type and size of the business and the target market, so not all channels are feasible for every type of business. Examine all possible channels of distribution available to you before making a final decision as to which you will use.

TiP Although established distribution systems reach the customer easily, such systems may not welcome recent entrants as readily as newer systems.

Service Marketing Channels

Service entrepreneurs can also find getting their services to market a challenge. In a service business, *distribution* channels are often referred to as *marketing channels*. These channels, as with products, are also influenced by the type of service you want to sell, the customer you want to sell it to, and the distribution processes available to you. Consider those three factors before beginning to develop a marketing channel for your new service business.

How do potential customers expect to find and engage your services? For example, when customers need a plumber, the first place they may look is the Yellow Pages where, if you are a plumber, you would want to have a presence. Someone with a plumbing problem might come directly to you through this advertisement.

Not all potential customers will seek you out directly. Children, for example, might connect with a professional service provider such as a physical therapist, speech pathologist, or tutor through a number of referral sources. These might include teachers, other professional specialists, or medical personnel who recommend services to the parent. The elderly in need of at-home care might obtain it through the efforts of family members with the advice of social workers, medical professionals, or geriatric care agencies. The referral source, not the end user, may be the key element in your marketing channel.

As with product sales, determining the correct marketing channel is your first step. Do you wish to sell through referral agencies, through individuals who are in informal positions to refer, or directly to the end user of your service?

Communication is also important to promoting your service. You may be able to open your doors by working with people who are already familiar with your work. Furnish potential clients with literature outlining the scope of your services including prices, a portfolio of creative works, or anything that will help them make a decision to use your services. Phone calls to keep in touch and remind potential clients of available services help gain and retain relationships with clients. Make it easy for customers to use your services.

Since one of the keys to successfully marketing a service business is communication, service companies are also finding ways to sell their services through the Internet. Communication as a marketing strategy is not new, but using the Internet as a tool for communication is relatively new.

One entrepreneur saw the potential of starting a home-based business by developing a Web site she could run from home. She started Webcertificate.com for people who like to shop online and want to give gift certificates. After signing up, a customer picks the amount of the gift certificate and pays a service fee of $3 to $5. Webcertificate.com e-mails the recipient a gift certificate along with an identification number and a link to its site, where an account has been set up. The recipient can use the account like a debit card, shopping at a range of Web retailers. Online purchases are instantly deducted from the recipient's account, and the remaining balance can be viewed any time.

Whatever your marketing channels, it is important that you analyze, plan, and monitor how customers learn about and use your service.

TiP The Internet is an effective distribution source or communication tool for some products or services. Many existing distribution systems have slightly altered themselves to operate online. What seems like a new distribution method, such as an electronic auction, is really just a new spin on an old method.

Combined Product/Service Distribution Channels

Some distribution models may include both products and services. Since distribution systems for products and services vary considerably, this combination adds complexity to an already involved process. Consider establishing your business by concentrating efforts on either products or services to start. Then, as you perfect distribution or marketing channels, you can add new products or services that respond to changing market needs.

Some businesses, such as a bicycle shop or computer repair, must offer both a product and service component from the start. In these cases, look for the primary distribution method of the business. For example, a bicycle shop is primarily in the product distribution business and a computer repair shop is primarily a service business. In starting a business that could have a combination of distribution models such as the bicycle shop, concentrate on selling bicycles and bicycle accessories. Providing bicycle repairs may become a necessary service you can add based on market demand. As the business grows, opportunities may arise to establish additional distribution for the service side of the business.

The same principle applies to many service businesses. A computer repair company should concentrate on the service side of the business initially. As this business model is established, computer products may be added as a result of customer demand.

Expanding into a combined product and service distribution model may be the best way for you to reach the needs of your market. For instance, when customers buy Xerox equipment, they can purchase a service plan to cover regular maintenance on the machine. This strategy applies to many high-ticket items—cars, computers, and multimedia textbooks that offer training to enhance teachers' abilities to use the products.

You can introduce additional services or products to an established business to increase profit potential. For example, Ann Wylie, of Wylie Communications offers business communications consulting services to public relations departments of national and international companies. In addition, she has written several "learning tools"—books about business communication—which she sells on her Web site or provides to clients who purchase her services. She holds electronic teleconferences over the Internet, conducts public and private seminars, and offers writing, editing, and training services all on general business communications topics in addition to her custom consultations.

For many entrepreneurs, distribution of their products/services is managed directly by their companies. These entrepreneurs use an internal sales force and operational capabilities to meet the demands of their customers. Distribution in these companies resembles the illustration below:

TIP Before developing a business concept with both product and service distribution needs, consider the financial demands they will place on your business. By analyzing these demands first, you can more accurately allocate resources to meet them.

Offering the Same Products/Services to Multiple Customers

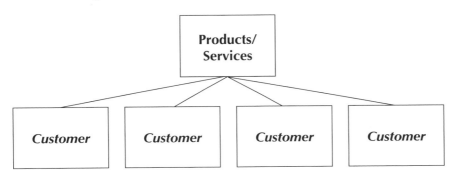

Some entrepreneurs prefer to expand their capabilities by using intermediaries as their distribution channels to reach their intended audience. These intermediaries may be independent representatives, wholesalers, or distributors. For these entrepreneurs, their distribution may resemble this following illustration:

Offering Products/Services Through Intermediaries

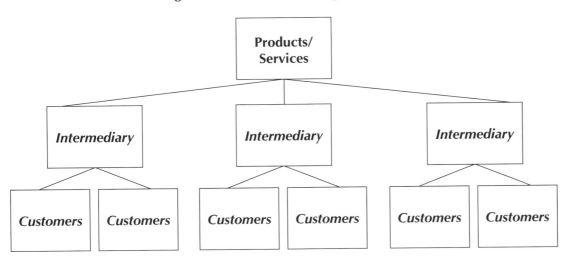

Many high-growth entrepreneurs use intermediaries in locations other than their home-base because they can provide these benefits:
- Reach more customers without hiring additional internal sales staff
- Share the risk of sales and doing business in the market
- Advertise at the local level
- Receive and monitor customer feedback in the market
- Break down bulk shipments for resale
- Move goods throughout the market efficiently
- Consolidate goods and services for distribution
- Manage point-of-purchase promotions
- Finance purchases
- Provide customer service and support on a local level

Distribution capability gives you access to many potential customers. Of course, distribution alone does not guarantee success in meeting your goals. It does make success more possible since it creates awareness of what you offer and provides venues for customers to buy your product/service. Customers still have to see the value of what you offer and consider buying it from your company. Distribution is an important component of your Marketing Plan as it places your offer when, where, and how prospective customers want it.

Reality Check ✔ Distribution Channels

My business concept is primarily:
- ❏ A product
- ❏ A service
- ❏ Both a product and service

The distribution channels most commonly used in my industry are:

Product:
- ❏ Wholesale
- ❏ Internal sales force
- ❏ Retail (store front)
- ❏ Mail order
- ❏ Internet
- ❏ Licensing/Franchise
- ❏ Other_____

Service:
- ❏ Yellow Pages
- ❏ Web site
- ❏ Sales calls
- ❏ Word of mouth
- ❏ Other_____

The distribution channel I think will work best with my business concept is _____ because

Activity 5a will offer some questions for you to answer concerning what you know about your industry, including distribution and/or marketing channels. In Action Step 5.1 you will include this information in the marketing section of your Business Plan.

Competitive Analysis

Understanding as much as possible about the competition helps you define your position in the marketplace. When you determine how to enter the market with your product or service, you'll want to feel confident about how you will differentiate your business from competitors. This distinction is called your *competitive advantage*, which was introduced in Module 2.

In conducting market research, you identified real or potential competitors that may be threats to your business's success. Now, you will analyze these competitors' strengths and weaknesses, and determine how you can compete against them effectively.

In Activity 5b you will use a Competitor's Strength and Weakness Worksheet to compare your business to its direct competitors using a set of factors that you believe are critical for success. From there, you can refine your competitive advantage and consider how best to position your business in the market. You will record the results of these activities in the Competitive Analysis section of your Marketing Plan.

Competitive Advantage

In any industry, businesses can develop a competitive advantage through *price* or the *market*. A price or cost advantage is tied directly to production costs, efficiency, or available technology. A competitive advantage in the market requires you to develop *market differentiation*—the aspect of your business that sets you apart from the competitors in your industry.

Your industry research should reveal to you which arena is central to the competition in your market. As you learn the basis for competition in your industry, analyze your competitors' strengths and weaknesses to better position your own competitive advantage.

Your competitors will not likely volunteer this information. You will need to employ some creativity to find it out. For example, ask a friend to call or visit some competitors with a specific need in mind. Suggest that your friend find out what the service will cost, how quickly the service may be performed, and whether service providers exhibit distinctive characteristics that separate them from their competition.

After conducting your research, pinpoint your competitive advantage before developing your marketing strategy in Module 6. All your marketing energies will be directed at reminding potential customers why they should buy from you instead of someone else. Consider the following ways to define your competitive advantage through market differentiation or price.

Competing by Market Differentiation

If your business can offer superior service, quality, or benefits to the customer that your competition does not provide, you have developed market differentiation—your competitive advantage that separates you from others in your market. Your product or service may have special features that appeal to customers and help them decide to buy it for reasons other than price. As a result, your business may be able to sell more units or charge a premium price. Customers may also be more loyal because they value the service, quality, or perceived benefits.

TiP Before pursuing a market differentiation strategy, determine if customers value the differentiator.

You can achieve competitive advantage through a variety of means including:

Perceived quality – The perceived quality of the product is so superior to competitors' products that the customer will pay more money for it.

Customer service – The treatment the customer receives from the business is more important to them than the price.

Benefits – The customer perceives greater benefits from the product and, therefore, will pay more to purchase it.

Reputation – The business has a good reputation in the marketplace.

Brand equity – The business has established a brand that people trust or that indicates a quality product or service.

Niche focus – The business chooses to serve a niche, a narrow portion of the market, where the customers have special needs or preferences that do not appeal to the broad market. This niche could be defined by geography, serving customers in a specific area. It could also be defined by how the product or service is used or other benefits perceived by customers.

Each of these well-known brands has grown because of a competitive advantage strategy centered on an alternative uniqueness.

> **Tip** A business will achieve market differentiation only if its product or service offers to the customer a benefit greater than its cost.

Unique Product/ Service	Unique Combination of Products/Services	Unique Way to Meet Needs of Target Group	Unique Method of Delivery
Apple® (Macintosh®) First commercial computer with a graphic user interface	**FedEx Kinko's®** Suite of office products and services	**Subway®** Fast food for the health conscious	**Amazon.com®** Books, music, and much more via the Web
MP3 files A music file that can easily be moved and stored on computers	**Logitech®** Extensive line of computer peripherals	**Starbucks Coffee®** Relaxing hangout for coffee aficionados	**XM® Radio** Satellite radio service to subscribing customers

By positioning its toothpaste as a natural product, Tom's of Maine created a new category in the toothpaste market. At the time, no other toothpaste filled this need, so the company was able to charge a premium price and consumers who buy organic or all natural products gladly paid for it.

Consider how you can develop a competitive advantage for your product or service—through market differentiation.

Competing on Price

You can also create a competitive advantage when you offer a similar product or service and benefits to customers at a lower price than other businesses. Be aware, however, that many new businesses cannot compete solely on price because a strong competitor can copy methods and regain the advantage. Large, established product-based competitors are often better at being low-cost providers because they buy items in bulk.

If you want to explore the possibility of competing on price, businesses use a variety of means:

Efficient production – Your business produces products or services more efficiently and in less time than competitors. This cost savings is passed on to the customer in the price.

Technology – Your business uses the most up-to-date technology and has developed more efficient processes with vendors, customers, shipping and distribution, online sales, or in other operational areas. You pass on the cost savings to the customer in the price.

Innovation – Your business invests in innovation and continues to develop a better product or service at a similar or lower price. Innovation may help improve technology as well as productivity and, therefore, affects the price to customers.

Lower overhead – Your business experiences lower overhead costs in the area of rent, employee turnover, salaries, benefits, or other operational costs. This savings could be dependent on location, type of employees (part-time vs. full-time), or outsourced functions. You pass on the cost savings to the customer.

A newcomer cannot usually compete directly against the market leader on price. For example, it would be next to impossible for any new start-up to compete with Wal-Mart® on price. Many consumers are price sensitive, however, and will shop around. Using other techniques such as coupons, frequent buyer clubs, financing, or a hassle free, money-back guarantee, you could offer price benefits to the consumer that Wal-Mart does not. The result could attract new customers.

Reality
Check ✔

Competitive Advantage

Your new business will have many of the characteristics below. Pick the one upon which you will base your competitive advantage. You will use this one element in your marketing materials to separate you from your closest competitors.

Competing on Market Differentiation
- ❏ Perceived quality
- ❏ Customer service
- ❏ Benefits
- ❏ Reputation
- ❏ Brand equity
- ❏ Niche focus
- ❏ Other _____

Competing on Price
- ❏ Efficient production
- ❏ Technology
- ❏ Innovation
- ❏ Lower overhead
- ❏ Other _____

Explain precisely how you see your competitive advantage in the area identified. What specifically is different about your product/service in that area?

How will this competitive advantage affect the research you do on your market and competition?

Although not all business concepts can compete on price, consider in the planning stage whether or not price can be your competitive advantage. If you rule out price, then you will need to determine what competitive edge you have in the market based on market differentiators. Use the Reality Check *Competitive Advantage* to think about your own advantage in the marketplace.

Another way to determine your competitive advantage is to look at the critical success factors in your industry and develop a competitive advantage based on one of those factors.

Critical Success Factors

Critical success factors are the basic activities your company must do well to compete effectively in your market. They are the characteristics of businesses that customers look at when they are choosing where to buy. Critical success factors directly impact customer satisfaction. Satisfied customers become loyal customers who prefer to buy from you. You may have a clearly defined competitive advantage, but learning the critical success factors in your market improves your chances for success.

The market will determine your company's critical success factors. For example, an auto repair shop may find that most customers choose auto services based on price, reliability of repairs, and convenience. Knowing that these are the most important factors to prospective customers, this auto repair shop must meet customers' basic expectations for each factor to stay competitive. It may develop a competitive advantage based on one of these factors, but at the minimum it must maintain and manage all of the critical factors. The auto repair shop might offer a competitive advantage that benefits customers above and beyond these critical success factors, but if it does not at least provide reliable and convenient repairs at a good price, its competitive advantage as the shop owners have defined it will be irrelevant. Their ability to compete in the market will slip away.

To determine the critical success factors in your market, consider the following questions:
- How do prospective and current customers perceive or rate my competitors?
- What factor seems to be the most important to customers who buy this product/ service?
- How do competitors compete for business in the market? Do they compete on price, product/service quality, convenience, location, or other factors?
- What do competitors say is unique about their product/service? How do they differentiate themselves from others?

The most common critical success factors important to customers across industries include:
- Perceived quality
- Convenience
- Price
- Reliability
- Availability
- Treatment by staff
- Reputation in the market
- Variety of products/services
- Skill or expertise
- Guarantee

You will notice that many of these critical success factors are also listed in the previous section as possible competitive advantages, depending on your product or service and its market. The question to ask about critical success factors is *what does the customer value?* Then you will know which of these factors is critical to success and which you can build on as your competitive advantage over others who provide similar products or services.

Reality Check ✔

Critical Success Factors

What factors about my product or service do I think are most important to my customers? Rank the factors below in order of importance to your potential customers.

____ Quality   ____ Availability   ____ Skill or expertise

____ Convenience   ____ Treatment by staff   ____ Guarantee

____ Price   ____ Reputation in the market   ____ Other

____ Reliability   ____ Variety of products/services

How can I find out what customers really want?

Once you know which critical success factors are important to your prospective customers, what your competitive advantage is, and how other competitors rate, you can compare the strengths and weaknesses of competitors in your market. From there, you can determine how to enter the market. You can promote your company's strengths and develop a plan to improve its weaknesses.

Competitive Profile

You do not do business in a vacuum. While you focus on your competitive advantage and sharpen your business's response to critical success factors, your competition is doing the same. Just as athletes learn how competitors train, what their approach to the sport is, and where their weaknesses lie, so do businesses. This information is your *competitive profile*.

To compile a competitive profile, explore key information for every significant competitor that poses a threat to your business. Some competitors might react very aggressively to any challenge to their market position. Other competitors may take a more tolerant view of newcomers in the industry. Identify which companies will provide the most significant competition and anticipate what they will likely do if a newcomer enters their market.

Every competitor has strengths and weaknesses. Study them. Your competitors' weaknesses may become your competitive advantage. Many larger competitors are not able to make rapid decisions, allocate resources, and respond to changing market needs as quickly as smaller ones. Because of this weakness, smaller companies can often gain market advantage until larger companies respond.

On the other hand, smaller companies have a hard time competing with the financial resources of larger competitors. For examples, a local beverage manufacturer may not offer as many flavors or new products as larger soft drink companies. The smaller company may need to focus on unique flavors and depend on local strategic alliances with restaurants to keep its market share.

TiP A successful entrepreneur recognizes the need to change in order to stay ahead of the competition. Entrepreneurs plan for change.

To find more information about your competition, refer to the market research section of Module 2, using the new questions you have encountered in this module. Remember, your local librarian may be the best resource for finding additional secondary sources.

Once you have gathered information about your competition, you will want to compare that information to the needs and wants of your target market. The key is to research which advantages are critical success factors, and which other factors are important enough to your target market that they would choose to buy from you. Once you have discovered what advantages are important to your target market, you can build on and promote a competitive advantage the market values and your competition does not deliver.

Business Plan

Activity 5b will help you analyze the information you have gathered about your competition. Action Step 5.2 will direct you to incorporate this analysis into your Business Plan.

Now let's look at the ways you can further research and analyze your market to gather information you can use concerning your customers.

Market Analysis

You may have a product or service you want to sell and that will sell easily, but you do not know who will buy it. If you cannot readily identify a group of potential customers, then how will you reach them? Although you may want to sell your product or service to the largest possible market, that isn't always the path to success. It's difficult to market to everyone and you need resources—time, money, and people—to sell to every person possible.

Because you do not have the money, time, or energy to market your product or service to the whole world, you will want to analyze the greater marketplace to find a well-defined customer base that is most likely to buy from you. This module and the one that follows will help you complete your analysis.

In this module you will review the customer profile you developed in Module 2 and refine it. Then you will look at the market segments in which you will find the customers you have profiled, consider any niche markets you may discover for your product or service, and define a target market to focus your start-up marketing strategies. You also have the opportunity to identify future markets you may not have the time or resources to reach today but plan to target later. Module 6 builds on this information to help you develop a marketing strategy for start-up, including marketing tactics, specific activities that will reach your target market, and a schedule for implementing them.

Customer Profile

If you are a B2C (business-to-consumer) entity, then customers in your profile may have things in common such as age, occupation, gender, geographic location, or outside interests. If you are a B2B (business-to-business) entity, your profile may indicate that your customers share company size, type of industry, or distribution channels.

Customer profiles include descriptions or characteristics you believe to be important in describing your ideal customer. For example, the customer profile of a locally owned travel agency might be like the following:

> **Customer Profile**
> Professionals in Jefferson County between the ages of 35 and 55 with household incomes of $100K or more/year, who travel frequently and who appreciate the quality and customized service of working with a travel professional to manage all their arrangements.

Your customer profile is a description of the customers you expect to reach with your product or service. But even this well-defined group may be too large a population for you to reach at start-up. One way to further refine your market is to look for market segments within the customer profile so that you can focus your efforts more effectively.

Market Segments

Since people with similar tastes often develop similar social habits, you can use your customer profile to define possible market segments for your product or service. Where will you find groups of people like the one you have described in your customer profile? Exploring market segments may help you find them. Then you can choose among the segments you have identified to determine your target market.

A market segment is any smaller, identifiable group within your larger market. These smaller market segments may be distinguished by demographic, geographic, psychographic, behavioral, or level of usage variables you used when producing your customer profile. You may also distinguish market segments by the way they will use your product or service or the benefits they receive from it.

Reality Check

Customer Profile

Using Activity 2a and the customer profile example above, describe your potential customer by writing a short customer profile.

American Gardenscapes sells a variety of standard—as well as antique, rare, and heirloom—plants, seeds, and fresh-cut flowers. Initially, the founder had some difficulty identifying the characteristics of the customers she expected to purchase her products. She started out by identifying one group—gardeners. After research, she was able to segment the business's primary customer profile of "owners of horticultural-related businesses who sell unusual and rare plants, seeds, and flowers" into segments that included gardeners, landscape designers, business owners, and local nurseries/garden centers owners.

Market segments may be grouped by what prospective customers have in common. For example, the travel agency whose customer profile appeared above may identify the following market segments:

	Market Segment 1 Consumer	Market Segment 2 Consumer	Market Segment 3 Business
Demographic Age, Sex, Family size, Family life cycle stage, (Industry, company size for B2B)	• Married • Professionals • Children • Income $100K + • Own home • 25,000 families	• Married or single • Professionals • No children • Income $100K + • Own home • 15,000 professionals	• 500+ employees • $5M revenue/yr • Diverse industries • 500 companies in area
Geographic Region, County size, Climate	• Jefferson County	• Jefferson County	• Jefferson County
Psychographic Social class, Lifestyle, Personality	• Liberal • Trendy • Travel • Family-oriented	• Liberal • Trendy • Innovative • Travel	• Employee/ customer-oriented • Innovative
Behavioral Occasions, Benefit, Loyalty	• Quality-conscious • Service-conscious • Convenience	• Quality-conscious • Service-conscious • Convenience	• Quality-conscious • Service-conscious • Outsource suppliers
Usage and Usage rate	• Book travel 2 to 3 times/year • Travel packages	• Book travel 4 to 6 times/year • Travel packages	• Book travel for employees, contractors • Travel packages

Ultimately, you want to choose market segments in which your product or service will have the most buying potential. A well-constructed matrix can display the various identifiable markets for your product or service. For each market segment, you can break down critical success factors into features and benefits and determine how your product or service will meet each segment's needs or expectations.

For example, each of the market segments selected by the travel agency value quality and service. These are critical success factors. Market Segment 1, professionals with children, may be more price-conscious than Market Segment 2 without children, because travel costs for four people per trip are higher than for one or two people. Market Segment 3 involves booking travel for many employees, so the companies in this market may also be price-conscious.

A sample market segmentation matrix is shown here for the golf ball market. It focuses on four potential markets. Each of those markets can then be classified as to its demands. For example, the high handicap golfer might be most interested in a durable golf ball with a low cost. Yet, the corporate market might want a ball with a recognizable brand name. The makers of a new golf ball concluded from this matrix that the professional golfer would be the least likely to accept its product and the recreational player would be the most likely because the features of their new ball most accurately matched the features most desired by the recreational player. Thus the manufacturer targeted the recreational player.

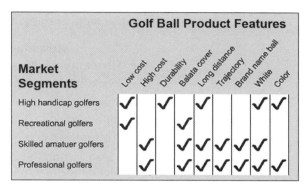

Market Segments	Low cost	High cost	Durability	Balata cover	Long distance	Trajectory	Brand name ball	White	Color
High handicap golfers	✓	✓	✓					✓	✓
Recreational golfers	✓			✓					
Skilled amatuer golfers		✓		✓	✓	✓	✓		
Professional golfers		✓		✓	✓	✓	✓	✓	

Golf Ball Product Features

As you analyze your customer profile and market segments, you may discover a potentially lucrative market, called a *niche market* that your business may be in a unique position to serve.

Niche Markets

Within your customer profile, you may be able to identify some specific needs or benefits a particular market segment wants and you are in a unique position to provide. This narrower group of potential customers and its characteristics might be your niche market—a specialized group demanding certain features or benefits that other members of your market may not require. You may find niche marketing more cost effective or it may become your competitive advantage. It may be that the size of this group is too small to be of interest to your larger competitors or that you have some unique technical knowledge or experience that your competitors do not have.

For example, if the travel agency wanted to focus on a niche market, it could focus on adventure travel for professionals, including cruises, safaris, and exotic destinations. Although this niche market is smaller and more specialized, customers will generally go on longer vacations and spend more money for customized arrangements.

TIP Most products or services offer many features and benefits. Make sure you know which benefits are important to your customers.

Reality Check ✓   **Market Segments**

Here are three market segments I can identify based on my customer profile from Module 2:

a.

b.

c.

Of these three market segments, which one can I most easily afford to reach with current resources?

Advantages and disadvantages of niche markets include:

Advantages	Disadvantages
• Fewer competitors	• Smaller customer base
• Market may be underserved	• Customers who don't fit niche may be turned away
• Possible to charge a higher price	• Niche customers must have higher transactional value or be repeat buyers
• Customized offering	
• Easier to find those interested in niche products/services	
• Infrequent direct competition from large competitors	

As you continue your market research, you should consider what possibilities your business concept has for niche marketing. If you cannot identify a niche market right now, you will still need to define the target market you believe you can reach right away.

Target Markets

The most successful entrepreneurs recognize that they have the resources to reach only a limited number of people in the general market. They know that trying to reach everyone described by their customer profile is impossible and even reaching everyone in just one market segment may be cost and resource prohibitive. For this reason they "target" their marketing efforts and resources toward potential buyers specifically chosen for a particular time.

The best target markets exhibit the following characteristics:
• Easy to identify
• Easy to enter
• Significant profit potential
• Identifiable weaknesses in the competition

During the life of your business, you will define many target markets and develop marketing strategies to reach them. At this point in your venture, you are looking for the market you want to target during the start-up phase of your business. Once you have made inroads into that target market, you may want to develop a new strategy for reaching another target market or you may want to modify your strategy for the same target market. Module 6 provides more information about marketing strategies. In this module, you will focus on defining the target.

Designing, pricing, positioning, and promoting your product or service is easier, more effective, and less costly when the target market is small and well defined. Most important, a well-chosen target market will be small enough to permit its members to be reached several times, a more effective strategy than reaching many people once.

Use your customer profile and market segmentation to find a target market you can reach by a specific strategy. For example, the travel agency in the sample on p. 185 defined their customer profile as "professionals in Jefferson County between the ages of 35 to 55 with household incomes of $100K or more/year, who travel frequently and who appreciate the quality, and customized service of working with a travel professional to manage all their arrangements."

For their next marketing strategy, they may identify a target market for their spring South American Eco-Tour package as "A compiled list of individuals who have purchased three or more international airline or cruise tickets of more than $1,000 each from the agency during the last three years." If the list they compile from their customer records is too large to reach more than once, they could change the criteria. They could, for example, raise the ticket price criterion to $1,500. Notice that their strategy for defining this target market was to compile a list of individuals from their customer records who fit a specific set of criteria. You will consider other strategies in Module 6.

For target marketing to be successful for your new business, keep the following objectives in mind. Good target markets should be:

- Within your capability to identify. People "thinking about" purchasing something are hard to spot.
- Large enough to provide a sufficient customer base but small enough to be affordably reached several times.
- Profitable.

TiP The more narrowly a target market is defined, the fewer the number of potential customers. Is your target market large enough to sustain your business?

As you focus on your target market, you may discover a future market—a market that has possibilities for later stages of your business.

Target Market

Since I probably can't reach everyone in the market segment I identified in the previous Reality Check, how would I define my target market for the first year of my business?

Future Markets

Whether your company's goal is high growth or stability, consider planning for opportunities in the future. You can develop future markets by adding a product or service, improving a current product or service, or by selling to a new market with an existing or new product or service. The search for future markets should be driven by customer demand. Ask these questions to consider future markets for your business:

- Does adding a product/service to meet customer demand make sense with my overall vision?
- Will a new product/service fit within the existing organizational structure?
- Will daily operations of the new product/service mirror the operations of existing product/service lines?
- Will additional research and development be necessary before launching the new product/service?
- Will the same profit margin apply to the new product/service?
- How much do I stand to lose if sales of the new market do not meet sales goals?
- When would be the most opportune time to offer this new product/service?

The answers to these questions will help you determine whether entering a new market is the right thing to do. The future success of your business may depend on your ability to be flexible while meeting the needs of the customers and identifying new markets.

Business Plan

Activity 5c will help you more clearly define your target market. Action Step 5.3 will incorporate your market analysis into your Business Plan.

Setting Prices

Pricing decisions affect almost everything about your business—your product or service's image, its sales, and your financial projections. Every product or service has a range within which to set your price. The highest price you can ask is called the *ceiling price*, which is usually set by customers. The lowest price, called the *price floor*, is determined by your costs. Between the two is the reasonable range of prices you can ask for your product or service. So, how will you know how to set prices? Your pricing strategies will support your Marketing Plan. These strategies can help you reinforce a premium image or break into a new market. In this section, you will explore the pricing process and other considerations before actually setting prices for your product or service. You will learn more about formulas to calculate prices for both products and services in Module 8.

What is Your Market Price?

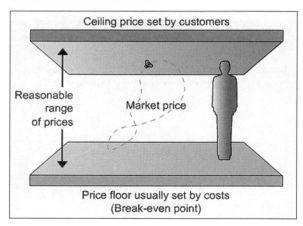

To maximize profits, try to price your products or services within the market's price range, to yield a targeted net profit that more than meets fixed and variable costs, and to position your company competitively. Price and sales correlate. Decisions you make about price will have an impact on sales.

Keep these three general rules in mind when you evaluate your pricing strategies:

1. **The lowest price you can charge depends on your costs** – If you or your competitors can develop a product/service for less or have access to resources at lower costs, then the cost provides a pricing advantage in the market.
2. **The highest price you can charge depends on your competitors and your position in the market** – If your products or services are not much different from your competitors', you may have constraints on how much more you can charge

than they do. If you serve a niche or special market, or have few competitors in the same market, you may have an advantage for pricing and position.

3. **Customers ultimately decide if your price matches the value and benefits your product/service provides** – The customers' perceptions of your competitive advantage determine how much customers are willing to pay to buy your products or services.

TiP In general, costs determine the minimum price a business can charge, and the competition determines the maximum price you can charge.

Many factors in the market influence how you set your prices, which then affects almost every aspect of your business. How you price your product or service has a direct impact on these six factors:

Sales volume – Sales volume correlates with the prices being charged for products or services. Higher prices often mean lower volume, whereas lower prices generally result in higher volume. Some entrepreneurs can charge more because of additional or perceived benefits of their products or services.

Sales revenue – Prices set for products or services will affect the total revenue projection. If prices increase, sales volume may decrease, causing an associated reduction in total revenue. Products or services priced effectively, however, can increase revenue and profit. It's important to know what customers are willing to pay.

Market share – How products or services are priced and the pricing position of companies will determine their market share. Sometimes, lower pricing can command a higher market share.

Competitive advantage – Pricing plays an important role in how companies create and maintain a competitive advantage in the market. Much of the advantage depends on how competitors price their products or services and how they respond to price variances in the market.

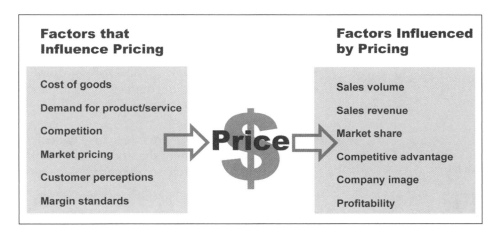

Factors that Influence Pricing	Factors Influenced by Pricing
Cost of goods	Sales volume
Demand for product/service	Sales revenue
Competition	Market share
Market pricing	Competitive advantage
Customer perceptions	Company image
Margin standards	Profitability

Company image – The prices for products or services create a perceived image in customers' minds. Customers perceive some companies as the lowest-priced provider while they believe others are the market leader for quality products with high-end margins.

Profitability – Pricing affects companies' Gross Margin and Net Profit. Aligned with sales volume and revenue, how products or services are priced will determine overall profitability.

The Pricing Process

As part of the business planning process, evaluate how pricing will affect your position in the market, and whether your pricing strategies will yield the desired results. You may need to make adjustments to how you price your products or services after you start your business. Successful entrepreneurs understand the market, the role of pricing, and how to position their products or services to compete effectively.

Although pricing is not an exact science, you can use this three-step pricing process to make the task easier:

1. Evaluate pricing position and constraints
2. Consider pricing strategies and policies
3. Set prices

The Pricing Process

1. Evaluate pricing position and constraints
2. Consider pricing strategies and policies
3. Set prices

Evaluate Pricing Position and Constraints

How you price your products or services can differentiate you among competitors in the market. When products and services are not highly distinguishable by their attributes or uniqueness, then pricing and service become the differentiators.

As you develop a Marketing Plan, determine how your pricing position can reinforce your competitive advantage in the market. Your pricing position should support your overall business goals and contribute to sales and profitability. Essentially, you can take one of three pricing positions in the market.

Lower prices compared to the competition:
- Aims for a high volume of sales with low profit margins.
- Purpose is to expand the market, to steal market share from other competitors, to remain competitive in the market, or to keep competition from entering the market.
- For example, a retail store offers novelty items and souvenirs and charges 10 to 20 percent less on items than other stores in the area because it is owned by a larger entity that purchases items in bulk at lower prices.

TIP To be able to charge more than the competition, you have to clearly differentiate yourself from the competition and build value in the mind of the consumer to justify the difference.

Higher prices compared to the competition:
- Aims to maintain a quality position in the market with high profit margins to support production costs and promotional activities.
- Purpose is to offset development costs for a product with a short life span, substantiate a quality image, take advantage of a high-demand and low-supply situation, or to charge more because the product or service is hard for competitors to copy.
- For example, an award-winning landscape company prices services at a premium level to align with the high quality, unique, and environmentally-conscious designs it is known for in the community.

Parity prices compared to the competition:
- Aims to have a portion of the market without being the highest- or lowest-priced competitor.
- Purpose is to stay in the game when little differentiation in the product or service exists or when price is the basis of competition.
- For example, a bed and breakfast inn prices its rooms within the same range as other bed and breakfasts in the area.

Consider these benefits and drawbacks of the pricing position strategies:

Benefits of lower pricing position strategies	**Benefits of higher pricing position strategies**	**Benefits of parity pricing position strategies**
• Forces competitors to keep prices low. • Attracts customers to take advantage of special or low prices. • May increase sales and frequency of buying.	• Profit margins are high; fewer transactions needed. • Brand has a higher perceived value or image. • Customers think products/ services are better than others in the market.	• Forces competitors to keep market prices fair. • Creates industry standards for costs and margins.
Drawbacks of lower pricing position strategies	**Drawbacks of higher pricing position strategies**	**Drawbacks of parity pricing position strategies**
• Must be the market leader for the lowest prices or best deals. • Competes at very low margins. • Attracts price-sensitive customers.	• Attracts a small, niche portion of the market. • Sales volume or number of transactions may be lower than other providers in the market.	• Must maintain prices that are the same as other competitors. • Competes at low or fair margins. • May not differentiate from other competitors.

Pricing constraints are those things that keep you from having much flexibility in your pricing position. Constraints are often industry specific. In some cases, **costs may control price**. The pricing floor, for example, will always be determined by costs. Once costs are covered, however, other factors may limit your ceiling price.

In some industries, the **government regulates prices**. Sometimes this is helpful and sometimes it is not. Airlines might prefer to return to the time when the government set their prices, because they made more money that way. Now that they must compete for market share, many airlines have discovered they cannot keep up.

In most industries, **constraints are set by the competition**. It is difficult to get much more for a product or service than what the marketplace dictates. For instance, an entrepreneur with a gas station that has three competitors in the same area may not be able to charge more for the gasoline. This is often common in markets in which products or services are not easily differentiated from one another. Profits are difficult to come by in such situations unless the business has some distinct cost advantages.

Customer demand is often price sensitive. *Elasticity* refers to the degree that a change in price affects the quantity of demand. If demand is very elastic, a lower price means the amount purchased increases significantly. If demand is inelastic, the amount purchased does not vary much with price changes. Understanding the elasticity of demand for a market helps you recognize opportunities in managing your prices.

Reality Check ✓ — Pricing Position and Pricing Constraints

What pricing positions do my closest competitors use?
- ❏ Lower
- ❏ Higher
- ❏ Parity

How does their pricing position align with their competitive advantage?

What pricing position is consistent with the image I want to have in the market?
- ❏ Lower
- ❏ Higher
- ❏ Parity

What pricing constraints have I found in my industry?
- ❏ Costs control prices.
- ❏ Price is regulated by the government.
- ❏ Competition dictates pricing constraints.
- ❏ Customer demand is price sensitive.

How will these issues affect my pricing position?

The Pricing Process

1. Evaluate pricing position and constraints
2. Consider pricing strategies and policies
3. Set prices

TIP Remember, the price of the product must be consistent with its image. The same is true for service businesses: being the cheapest consultant may create a misperception about your ability.

Consider Pricing Strategies and Policies

Your pricing strategies depend heavily on the market position you want for your product or service. Your pricing strategies reinforce your pricing position. Your strategy dictates how you will price products or services to be competitive and make a reasonable profit. They also take into account customers' thresholds. Consider your target market before selecting or changing a pricing strategy. You may position and price your product or service based on customers' attitudes or perceived benefits, special niches or applications, specifically targeted users, or the level of quality you offer your customers.

Pricing can send a message to your target market. Some companies target a high-end buyer and are successful pricing their product or service higher than competitors. For example, Lexus® and Land Rover® charge more for their cars because their customers think these cars offer prestige and better value than Ford® and Chevrolet®.

Consider the most common pricing strategies in Reality Check *Pricing Strategies*. Notice how they support the three pricing positions—lower, higher, and parity pricing.

Pricing Strategies

Reality Check ✔

Check the strategy that represents a pricing strategy used by your closest competitors.

Lower Pricing Position Strategies	Higher Pricing Position Strategies	Parity Pricing Position Strategies
❏ **Penetration pricing** Price products/services at a loss to gain market share. Offer lower prices to get larger volume sales. Use to enter a new market or to position a commodity product. *Examples: car and computer accessories, food, supplies, household items*	❏ **Image, value, or quality pricing** Price matches customer's enhanced perception. Customers see brands as status symbols, in high demand with limited quantities. *Examples: signed, limited editions, luxury perfume, cars*	❏ **Going rate pricing** Create pricing wars between competitors who offer the same or similar products/services. No one charges more to prevent loss of market share. Few competitors control pricing. *Examples: gasoline, airfare, hotels/motels, electrical goods*
❏ **Predator pricing** Deliberate price-cutting to prevent others from entering the market. Forces competitors to compete on price and low profit margins. Offer free gifts and bundling of products/ services that competitors can't meet effectively. *Examples: computer and software packages, cell phones and special provider service plans*	❏ **Opportunistic pricing** Set premium prices for products/ services in high demand with short supplies. *Examples: fresh fish, pharmaceuticals*	❏ **Keystone or target pricing** Set prices to reach or maintain specific profit levels. Mark-up is standard over cost. *Examples: clothing and department store items*
❏ **Expansionistic pricing** Set low prices to establish mass markets. Exaggerated form of penetration pricing. May offer temporary price reductions to increase sales. May offer lower-cost version to gain acceptance and then switch to higher-cost version after purchase. Prices hurt other competitors. *Examples: magazine and newspaper subscriptions, CD music and DVD clubs, software*	❏ **Market or price skimming** Premium pricing on high-demand products in the early stage of its life cycle. Gain maximum profit from the market for high-tech or new inventions. *Examples: plasma or high-definition TVs, video games, PDAs*	❏ **Contribution or marginal pricing** Set prices to cover variable costs and a portion of fixed costs. Follows industry standards for costs and profits. *Examples: seminars, airfare, catering*

Which pricing strategies will most likely help me achieve my goals?

To support their pricing strategies, many entrepreneurs use additional pricing policies to respond to trends and industry practices, and to create incentives or influence customers' buying behaviors. Use the Reality Check *Consider Your Pricing Policies* to determine which of the most popular pricing policies you will use to market and sell your product or service.

Reality Check ✓ — Consider Your Pricing Policies

Which of the following pricing policies will help you to respond to trends, follow industry practices, and/or influence customers' buying behaviors?

- ❏ **Volume Pricing** – Studies show that small orders are costly, and many are sold at a loss. Entrepreneurs can encourage larger orders by providing volume discounts, or tiered pricing, on larger orders.

- ❏ **Bundled Products and Services** – By selling related products or services together, entrepreneurs increase the amount of sales per purchase and profitability.

- ❏ **Fixed Price Bid** – Instead of working for an hourly rate, entrepreneurs give the customer a fixed price bid for the job. This protects the customer and provides an incentive to the entrepreneur to work efficiently. The customer is paying for results, not time.

- ❏ **High-Margin Products** – Different products usually have different gross margins. Entrepreneurs can offset sales of lower margin items by selling sufficient products/services with higher margins.

- ❏ **Discounts for prompt or early payments** – By offering term discounts, entrepreneurs can improve cash flow and collect on receivables earlier. For example, entrepreneurs may provide a term of 2/10, n/30, which allows a two percent discount on invoices that are paid within 10 days of invoice and that are due in 30 days.

- ❏ **Payment options** – Allow customers to spread out their payments over time, with or without paying interest. Provide coupon books if payments are stretched out for six months or more, invoice a portion over two or three months, or charge an automatic payment on customers' credit cards.

- ❏ **Pricing conflicts** – Price wars are generally costly, so you should plan ways to avoid them. If a price war develops, try to respond creatively without matching the competitor's price cuts penny for penny. See Wayne Hampton's story on p. 197 for an example of how to avoid pricing conflicts.

The Pricing Process

1. Evaluate pricing position and constraints
2. Consider pricing strategies and policies
3. Set prices

TiP If the quality of a product is not apparent, price is usually the major element by which buyers determine it. Buyers often assume that high price equals high quality.

Set Prices

Once entrepreneurs have reviewed their pricing positions and strategies, and explored how their competitors are pricing similar products or services, they set or refine their own prices. Depending on the products or services offered, entrepreneurs may choose different pricing strategies for each product or service offered.

Most likely, you will set your prices based on the following:

Costs – Consider the actual costs for producing or creating the product or service. Include fixed costs such as space and equipment leases, salaries, and insurance and variable costs such as utilities, gas, supplies, and bonuses.

Market price – Review the price floor and price ceiling for similar products or services in the market. Consider how much customers are willing to pay for your product or service. For customers to pay the price ceiling or more, a product or service must have perceived benefits that equal or exceed the asking price.

Price positioning – Ensure that pricing is consistent with the pricing position you want in the market.

Return-on-investment – Factor in the profit margins you expect by a predetermined time.

Market Pricing

What is the price range in the market for the product/service I offer?

What is the estimated ceiling price for our product/service?

Are there any competitors that sell products/services above the price range? If so, what is the increased perceived value by customers?

Price it Right

When Wayne Hampton launched Waco Composites, Ltd., in 1996, four other companies were making bullet-resistant and bulletproof panels for the construction industry. Hampton carefully researched those firms and decided to match prices of the industry leader.

"We didn't want to come in with lower prices, for fear that would spark a price war," Hampton explains. "No one wins a price war—except perhaps the customer." Unfortunately, his major rival didn't see things the same way. As Waco Composites gained market share, the competitor began to slice prices, moving from about $15 to $13 per square foot on its bestselling panels.

In response, Hampton lowered his prices—and watched his gross profit margin plunge from 28 percent to 18 percent. A few months later, the competitor slashed prices again, moving to $10.50 per square foot. Hampton followed suit, but knew he couldn't survive further decreases. Instead, he began to find ways to differentiate his product, such as:

- Offering free cutting for all custom orders—something no one else was doing
- Offering same-day shipping on all orders received before 2 p.m.
- Implementing a new manufacturing process to fireproof panels
- Securing approval from Underwriters Laboratories® (UL) in eight areas
- Determining ratings for specific product characteristics, such as acoustical quality, tensile strength, and heat resistance

Becoming UL–listed was the biggest expense—about $20,000 and it cost another $10,000 to determine product ratings. "Yet this data was very important to engineers and architects—the people who specify our products for projects," Hampton says. "Since no one else was offering this information, we became the industry benchmark."

Differentiating itself in both product and service enabled Waco Composites to raise prices, restore its profit margin, and continue growth, generating $4.5 million in revenue.

Granted, some of the changes were about perceived value rather than tangible value. "Yet perception is as important as real value in the mind of the customer," Hampton says. "And, unlike competitors' pricing, your company's perceived value is something you do have control over."

Price List

Your price list is an important marketing tool. Customers may be motivated to purchase a product or service just by reading a price list. Remember, that a price list should be attractive, informative, easy to read, and easy to use for ordering. Most entrepreneurs make the mistake of including only their prices on the list. A price list should clearly identify all the different products or services, how much each costs, and the terms of the sale.

The basic principle is to make ordering or requesting products or services as easy as possible for customers. Here are some ideas to ensure that your price list remains an effective marketing tool:

- Use easy-to-complete order blanks that can be entered online, faxed, or dropped into the mail.
- Obtain a toll-free telephone number and feature it on the price list.
- Display products/services on the reverse side of the price list.

Help keep your price list out of the customers' files by placing it on some useful advertising-specialty item such as a calendar, business card holder, or paper pad holder. Don't forget to include information on where and how the goods can be purchased. Experts recommend you provide at least three different ways of placing an order including traditional mail, Internet ordering, fax, phone, or e-mail.

Activity 5d will help you think more about setting prices for your products or services. In Action Step 5.4 you will add your pricing policies to your Business Plan.

For More Information

on price lists go to www.fasttrac.org/toolkits.

Business Plan

Marketing Plan

A key component of every Business Plan is its Marketing Plan. The purpose of the Marketing Plan is to define your market—customers and competitors—and identify how you will reach prospective customers to promote your products or services. The Marketing Plan is the bridge that allows you to reach your intended audience and sell your products or services.

Now that you have completed some market research and analyzed it according to your business goals, you can begin to write your Marketing Plan.

A primary purpose of your Marketing Plan is to capture your competitive advantage, customer profile, target market, and pricing strategies, in written form. The plan can be used to answer the what, who, where, when, and how questions that arise in your marketing strategy.

A strong Marketing Plan answers the following questions and describes marketing and sales activities for your business:

- **What** are the significant characteristics of my industry?
- **Who** is described in my customer profile and target market?
- **What** is my competitive advantage?
- **Where** will we spend our marketing resources?
- **When** will we spend our marketing resources?
- **How** much sales and profit do we anticipate?

What Is Your Marketing Plan?

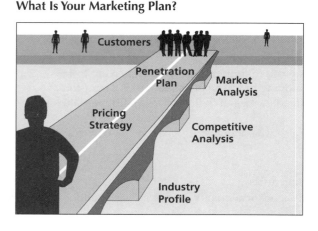

Because many of the financial projections in your Business Plan are based on the assumptions you make in your Marketing Plan, each part of your plan should address the costs of implementation.

Take Market Analysis Seriously

Only after spending time and hard work researching her market, did Sally Smith decide to open Iowa Chops. You encountered her story about researching markets before choosing a business to start in Module 2. She talked to potential customers, suppliers, and industry officials to understand the industry. Sally also located, read, and analyzed information from libraries, trade associations, and Internet searches to discover trends, identify competitors, and determine her strategic position. Because she had invested time to understand the industry and the local market and developed a marketing plan, Sally felt confident about her new business's potential.

TIP One purpose of your Marketing Plan is to demonstrate you have the strategies and budget resources to generate sufficient customer awareness, trial, and use of your product or service to meet your sales and profit goals.

Approach your Marketing Plan with determination. When asked if there is a section in a Business Plan that entrepreneurs usually leave incomplete, one banker answered, "By and large, the marketing section—the most important section—is usually the weakest." She went on to explain the reasons for this planning error:

- Marketing is a skill just like accounting. Entrepreneurs may think it should come naturally, but it doesn't. It needs to be studied and praticed just like any other skill.
- Entrepreneurs must go into the marketplace and research the industry, which requires time and effort. Sometimes they don't know how to research. Other times they don't want to take the time.
- Entrepreneurs must make important, difficult decisions when writing a marketing plan. They need to answer the question, "What is the right way to market my concept?" They may find many alternatives from which to choose, each with pros and cons. This uncertainty sometimes discourages entrepreneurs from making a decision.
- Entrepreneurs wrongly assume that the market will come to them. Instead, entrepreneurs must determine how the product/service will get to customers.

The five components of your Marketing Plan are listed below. This module focuses on market analysis and addresses all components except market penetration, which you will explore in Module 6.

TIP When writing your Marketing Plan, cite your sources. Citations add credibility to your Business Plan and allow you to update it with more current information as it becomes available.

- **Industry Profile** – Defines the current size, growth potential, current and future trends, distribution channels, and any other industry characteristics.
- **Competitive Analysis** – Identifies direct, indirect, and future competition, the critical success factors for your industry (for example, price, quality, promotion, service), and your competitive advantage.
- **Market Analysis** – Analyzes potential markets to determine an ideal target market, describes the customer profile, and considers future markets for your product/service.
- **Pricing** – Explains the pricing strategy, structure, and policies you will use to position the business in the market and be profitable.
- **Market Penetration** – Details the brand and image of your business, its location, the marketing strategies, tactics, and activities you will engage in, and the sales force and distribution channels you will use.

After conducting market research since Module 2 on your industry, prospective customers, and competition, you can now analyze your results and determine which marketing strategies are best for your business. In Module 6 you will consider how you will communicate your product or service to those who are most interested in buying it.

Summary

Market analysis is critical to developing a sound and feasible Business Plan. Because market analysis requires time and additional research, many entrepreneurs often overlook it. The best ideas for launching a new business often unravel in this section. Marketing strategies you will develop in Module 6 are based on your understanding of your industry, competitors, and customers. Take market analysis seriously as it becomes the foundation for developing assumptions for your sales and profit projections.

Key Things to Remember

- To create an industry profile, you will want to analyze the size, growth potential, profitability, trends, and distribution channels of your industry.

- Your competitive advantage affects the success of your business in a specific market area.

- Conducting a competitive analysis helps you understand how well the current competition is meeting the expectations of customers and how you can position your product or service to compete successfully.

- Market segmentation helps you focus the potential customers described in your customer profile into a target market of customers who are more easily reached and likely to buy from you.

- You can use pricing strategies to position your product/service within an acceptable range for the market.

- Your Marketing Plan is essential to your business planning process because it affects sales and profits.

The next module explores strategies to reach your target market. Based on the results of analyzing your market, you will develop the Market Penetration section of your Business Plan in Module 6.

Activity 5a **Industry Profile**

Identify what I know about my industry and what I still need to research.

Directions
Industry information can be invaluable to you as you learn how to enter the market, position your business in its industry, and respond to trends. Record the information you have been collecting below:

1. How many companies are in the industry?

   Nationally

   Regionally

   Statewide

   Locally

2. What is the total number of units sold or revenue realized?

   Nationally

   Regionally

   Statewide

   Locally

3. How would you describe the growth pattern and potential growth projected for the industry?

4. What is the expected gross margin and net profit for the industry?

5. What are the current trends of the industry?

6. What are some of the future trends projected for the industry?

7. What are some common distribution channels in the industry?

Activity 5b   Competitors' Strengths and Weaknesses Worksheet

Evaluate current competitors based on research about my competition and market.

Directions

Follow the steps below to compare and contrast your business with its competitors.

Step 1 List critical success factors. On the first row of the chart, fill in the critical success factors that are important to prospective customers of your product or service. If you do not know what factors are most important to your prospective customers, you may need to collect additional information through surveys or focus groups.

Step 2 Identify current competitors. Remember that direct competitors are ones who offer the same product or service as your business. List the name of a direct competitor under the labels Competitor A, Competitor B, and following. You have space for five competitors.

Step 3 Rate how well you and your competitors meet each critical success factor. Using your research about competitors, rate each business including your own, against each critical success factor. A 1 or 2 indicates a weakness in the critical success factor. A 3 indicates adequate performance in that critical success factor. A 4 or 5 indicates superior strength in the critical success factor. For future reference, you may want to write in each box the specific ways each competitor meets that particular critical success factor.

If you cannot determine a rating, you may need to research further. You might talk to people (for example, suppliers or customers) who can rate these categories for each competitor, or conduct focus groups or interviews with those who have been customers of any of the selected competitors.

Competitors' Strengths and Weaknesses Worksheet

Critical Success Factors	Your Business	Competitor A	Competitor B	Competitor C	Competitor D	Competitor E

Activity 5b **Competitors' Strengths and Weaknesses Worksheet** continued

Step 4 Analyze your competitive advantage. Based on this analysis of competitors' performance on critical success factors and other market research you have conducted, answer the following questions about your competitive advantage.

Who are your stronger competitors? Why?

How do you compare?

What is your competitive advantage?

Activity 5c **Target Market**

Identify characteristics of my target market.

Directions

Use Activity 2a Customer Profile Worksheet and prior research on your market and competitors to determine your market segments and target market for start-up by following the steps below. If you need additional research, you may wish to interview potential customers.

Step 1 Brainstorm potential market segments. Brainstorm a list of potential market segments for your product or service. Use your research about the competition to help determine which segments have unmet needs or problems relevant to your product or service. Write your answers below.

Potential Market Segments

EXAMPLE

Electrical contracting – The market segments I have identified are based upon the type of work performed, which is a demographic criterion: commercial construction, residential construction, remodeling, and repairs.

Market segments for my business could be:

I have chosen these market segments based on:

Activity 5c   Target Market   continued

Step 2 Identify key characteristics of each market segment related to your product or service. On the chart below, list the market segments you identified above in the left-hand column. Across the top, list the major features or benefits of your product or service. You may want to review the Reality Check *Features and Benefits* in Module 4, p. 140. Then check each feature or benefit that is most valuable to each market segment to determine which segment is your most likely target market. See the example of the golf ball manufacturer on p. 187 for an example.

Features and Benefits

Market Segments						
Segment 1						
Segment 2						
Segment 3						
Segment 4						

Activity 5c **Target Market** continued

Step 3 Select a target market. Which of your market segments in Step 2 appears to be the best fit for your product or service? Using this segment, choose a target market. You may choose this target market because its members are easy to identify, it is easy to enter, it offers a significant profit potential, or competitors have identifiable weaknesses.

Target Market

EXAMPLE

> *My target market is the owners of commercial construction companies who will use an electrical subcontractor to build new homes. I have chosen this market because I can create a list of construction company owners who are members of my building industry association and who are known to my fellow subcontractors in other trades.*

My target market is:

I have chosen this market because:

Activity 5d **Pricing Process**

Determine a preliminary price for your product or service.

Directions

Follow the steps to practice using the pricing process to set a price. Remember to check and adjust your price after projecting your sales, cost of goods, and operating expenses in Module 8. Answer the following questions and then discuss your answers with a partner.

Step 1 Evaluate pricing position and constraints. List the pricing position of your strongest competitors (lower, higher, parity). What pricing position do you want for your product or service? List the pricing constraints for your product or service.

Step 2 Consider pricing strategies and policies. Which pricing strategies will you use to support your pricing position and goals for your business? What policies will you use to influence customers' buying behavior? How do your choices affect the estimated number of units sold and total sales dollars?

Step 3 Set prices. What will you charge for your product or service? If the price you calculated is not within the high/low range of competitors, your price is probably not realistic. Note any information you need to research before you finalize your price.

Action Step 5.1   **Create My Marketing Plan – Industry Profile**

Complete the Industry Profile of my Business Plan.

Directions

Use the Business Plan Template to complete an Industry Profile for your business concept. This profile describes the industry you will be entering by identifying growth potential, trends, and opportunities.

A. Describe your industry. When you describe your industry, document your sources so that readers will recognize your enthusiasm for the industry is substantiated with facts. Also, use quantitative information when available. It's much more helpful to cite a source saying that industry sales are "projected to grow at a 20 percent rate annually over the next three years," according to such-and-such industry expert, than to note that the industry is "in rapid growth."

B. Use the template. Read the instructions on page 1 of the template. Then move to the Industry Profile section of the template to insert your information.

Each section of the template contains headings with questions to prompt you to consider the type of information to include under each heading. The questions are also listed in each action step for easy reference. After you enter your answers into the template and print them out, the questions will not appear on the hard copy. You should try to incorporate enough of the question into your answer so that the reader understands what is being answered.

Industry Profile

Current Size
What is the current size of your industry for this product/service?
What is the size of your industry at the national, regional, state, and local levels?
How many dollars are spent annually and/or how many units are consumed annually in the industry?
Cite the sources of information.

Growth Potential
How much is the industry growing, stabilizing, or declining?
Cite the sources of information.

Industry Trends
What are the trends in the industry?
What effect does technology have on the business?
How is the Internet affecting your industry?
Cite the sources of information.

Other Characteristics
What seasonal issues affect your industry?
What is the average profit for businesses in the industry?
In what area of the country are most businesses in your industry located?
Cite the sources of information.

Distribution Channels
What distribution channels currently exist to support the sale of your product/service?
Cite the sources of information.

Action Step 5.2   **Create My Marketing Plan – Competitive Analysis**

Complete the Competitive Analysis section of my Business Plan.

Directions

The Competitive Analysis section of your Marketing Plan is your opportunity to demonstrate that you have identified the competition, understand its key attributes, and know how your product or service compares. The research you completed for Activity 5b is a good foundation for this section. Include this matrix in your Marketing Plan.

A. Define your competitive advantage. The most important question you will answer in this section of the Marketing Plan is "What is my competitive advantage?" Be sure you understand on what terms your product or service will compete and that you clearly explain your competitive advantage from the customers' point of view in the Marketing Plan.

B. Use the template. Read the instructions on page 1 of the template. Then move to the Competitive Analysis section of the template to insert your information.

Each section of the template contains headings with questions to prompt you to consider the type of information to include under each heading. The questions are also listed in each action step for easy reference. After you enter your answers into the template and print them out, the questions will not appear on the hard copy. You should try to incorporate enough of the question into your answer so that the reader understands what is being answered.

Competitive Analysis

Direct Competition
What direct competition exists for your product/service?
What companies sell similar products/services to the same target market?
Cite the sources of information.

Indirect Competition
What indirect competition exists for your product/service?
What companies sell different products/services that fill the same need as your product/service?
Cite the sources of information.

Future Competition
What future competition do you expect to have for your product/service?
Cite the sources of information.

Competitive Analysis
What is your competitive advantage?
Include a competitive analysis chart and summarize key points.
How will your product/service compete in the areas of price, quality, unique features, distribution system, marketing/advertising, geographic location, and strengths/weaknesses?

Action Step 5.3 Create My Marketing Plan – Market Analysis

Complete the Market Analysis section of my Business Plan.

Directions
The Market Analysis section of the Marketing Plan verifies that you have identified several market segments and determined which provide the best opportunity for your product or service. The information to determine a target market in Activity 5c is a good foundation for this section. Include this analysis in your Marketing Plan.

A. **Identify your market.** The most important question you will answer in this section of your Marketing Plan is, "What market provides the best opportunity for my product or service?" Be sure you describe the different market segments and why your product or service is best positioned to compete in this segment.

B. **Use the template.** Read the instructions on page 1 of the template. Then move to the Market Analysis section of the template to insert your information.

Each section of the template contains headings with questions to prompt you to consider the type of information to include under each heading. The questions are also listed in each action step for easy reference. After you enter your answers into the template and print them out, the questions will not appear on the hard copy. You should try to incorporate enough of the question into your answer so that the reader understands what is being answered.

Market Analysis

Target Market Profile
What target market will be selected?
How many potential customers and/or potential dollars are available in this market segment?
What is your share of the market?
What other markets, if any, will be targeted and at what stages of the business?
Note that the target market might be firms in the distribution channel instead of the end user.

Customer Profile
What is the profile of the intended customer, including age, gender, profession, income, and geographic location?
What attitudes, values, belief systems, and social status define this customer group?
For business customers, what is your customer's business type, SIC and NAICS codes, intended use for the product/service, geographic location, and size of organization?

Future Markets
What opportunities could occur in future markets, including market size, method of market penetration, projected date of entry, and approximate costs?

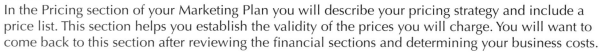

Action Step 5.4   Create My Marketing Plan – Pricing

Complete the Pricing section of my Business Plan.

Directions

Business Plan

In the Pricing section of your Marketing Plan you will describe your pricing strategy and include a price list. This section helps you establish the validity of the prices you will charge. You will want to come back to this section after reviewing the financial sections and determining your business costs.

A. Determine your pricing strategies. The most important question you will answer in this section of your Marketing Plan is, "What pricing strategies should I use for my product or service?" When you explain your pricing strategy, be sure to explain your rationale for setting these prices. In your rationale, reference the industry, competitors, your pricing position, and policies.

B. Use the template. Read the instructions on page 1 of the template. Then move to the Pricing section of the template to insert your information.

Each section of the template contains headings with questions to prompt you to consider the type of information to include under each heading. The questions are also listed in each action step for easy reference. After you enter your answers into the template and print them out, the questions will not appear on the hard copy. You should try to incorporate enough of the question into your answer so that the reader understands what is being answered.

Pricing

Pricing Strategy

What are your short-term and long-term pricing strategies?
Why have you selected these strategies?
What are the competitors' pricing strategies?
What pricing constraints and sensitivities exist for your product/service?

Price List

What is your price list, including purchase price, quantity discounts, introductory offers, shipping costs, and warranties/maintenance contracts?

Pricing Policies

What are your pricing policies, including volume pricing, avoiding price conflicts, and bundling products and services?

Reaching the Market

With literally thousands of things you could do to promote your business, what will you base your marketing decisions on? Who is most likely to buy what you're selling? What image, strategies, and techniques will create a connection with your market? You have already begun to answer some of these questions with market research in Modules 2 and 5. In this module, you will plan ways to reach the markets you have identified. You can determine how to sell your product or service by exploring various strategies used by other entrepreneurs. You can develop a mix of advertising, publicity, or promotions to fit your business's needs. After you have identified how you will penetrate the market, you will write your findings into your Business Plan and determine the estimated costs to implement them. These projected costs will be useful when you build your budget in Module 8.

Key Questions
- How do I define my company's brand?
- How does my location enhance marketing?
- What marketing strategies and activities will I use to market my product/service?
- What is the most effective way to sell my product/service?
- How will I know my marketing strategies are working?
- What are the financial implications of my Marketing Plan?

Action Steps   Due Date

❏ 6.1 Develop a Marketing Activities Schedule   _____

❏ 6.2 Create My Marketing Plan – Market Penetration   _____

❏ 6.3 Write My Marketing Financial Assumptions   _____

❏ Read Module 7 Building the Organization and Team   _____

❏ _____   _____

❏ _____   _____

❏ _____   _____

Creating a Brand

To attract customers who fit your customer profile, your business's image should align with your customers' needs and expectations. An image makes a company distinctive, or unique, compared to others in the market. By emphasizing your competitive advantage as part of your image, you can position your products or services to stand out in the market and attract more customers.

What's an image? An image describes how customers feel about your business. But you don't want to leave this emotional response to chance. You can have some influence on your business's image by creating a brand.

A brand establishes an identity for a product, service, or business. It creates a visual, emotional, and cultural connection between customers and the company. A brand conjures up powerful images for customers, both consciously and subconsciously. It paints a picture about the company, the product or service, and the type of customer it represents. For example, Disney® has a strong brand as the family entertainment leader. It strives to portray a positive business image and ensures that customers' experiences keep them coming back. Disney communicates messages of family fun, clean environments, and service excellence. Employees are referred to as "cast members" and attend Disney University to learn their roles, responsibilities, and service standards.

TIP If you don't intentionally create a brand, you still create an unintentional image.

When customers buy a brand, they buy its values and promises, and feel that their expectations are aligned with the company. The product or service the customers buy and the quality experience they receive is what persuades them to buy the same brand again. The product or service and brand have a direct reflection on one another.

A number of companies have successfully created a brand that stands out in customers' minds. A successful brand has a positive association, a recognized name, and a higher perceived value than its competitors. For example, Apple® commands higher prices than its competition because it has a loyal following that appreciates its innovative, counter-culture image. The Volvo® brand is identified with a widely sought vehicle attribute—safety. This strong, focused image has guaranteed it steady sales.

Check Your Knowledge ✔

Brand Awareness

Think of a company—local or national—whose image you admire. Check which of the following components most attract you to that company's brand image.

Name of Company _____

- ❏ Ads
- ❏ Color scheme
- ❏ Company name
- ❏ Customer experiences

- ❏ Customer service
- ❏ Jingles or musical signatures
- ❏ Logo
- ❏ Packaging designs

- ❏ Physical layout or environment
- ❏ Product names
- ❏ Taglines and slogans
- ❏ Uniform or dress code

What do I want my brand to say about my product/service, my company, and me?

Create a Brand

In 2002, Erika Feinberg and her husband, Larry Fugleberg, bought a small business in Scottsdale, Arizona, that sold medical products to seniors, primarily through a low-grade Web site with limited capabilities. They knew immediately that they needed to create a brand in order for the business to grow.

Using the business planning process, they thought through each aspect of the business. To give their Web site credibility, they decided to open a retail store located in a medical complex just half a block away from a major retail center. Sales increased five-fold, thanks to medical industry recommendations and the company's "guaranteed lowest price" promise.

They also initiated a complete re-branding. "We wanted to expand the business beyond its elderly image," Feinberg says. She and her husband admit to sharing a "save the world mentality" and wanted to focus on preventative and active care. They adopted the tag line, "solutions for daily living," to highlight their creative approach.

Brainstorming with a technology team, Feinberg and Fugleberg carefully considered how to communicate their new image beyond Scottsdale on the Web. "Name construction is very important so that search engines and link pages put you at the top of the list," Feinberg says. Their new logo—*ActiveForever.com: Product Solutions For Medical, Rehab, Accessibility, Convenience*—conveys the company's mission at a glance.

They also beefed up and redesigned their Web catalog, contracting the programming from outside the company but keeping its design and marketing in-house. "To do it right," Feinberg says, "the design people have to live and breathe the business. It's essential to our marketing strategies."

Utilizing the company's prior twelve-year history on the Web, the couple defined their target market as baby boomers, aged 40 to 55, with disposable incomes, and a willingness to spend money on themselves and their parents. They also studied market size in the medical products industry. Insurance billing turned out to be an already crowded and highly regulated field, so they chose to go cash pay, standing behind their belief that, as Feinberg puts it, "people deeply appreciate good service and thoughtful products."

Components

A number of things go into creating a brand. Most people think of branding as visual components such as logos and stationery. *Marketing collateral*, a general term for marketing materials, refers to brochures, business cards, and Web sites. Although branding often results in marketing collateral, branding encompasses more than what customers see. You can create branding for your company by thinking through the many points of contact you have with your customer. The list in Check Your Knowledge *Brand Awareness* gives you a good starting place for building your brand.

Notice that ActiveForever worked on almost every aspect of the branding process in their refocused marketing efforts. They developed a name, logo, and tag line that define their mission at first glance. They carefully positioned both their bricks and mortar location and their Web presence for maximum impact. They chose a well-defined target market and worked to fulfill that market's needs. They networked in their industry to establish partnerships with other businesses to increase their visibility and image among consumers by getting referrals from the medical community. All of these activities enhanced their image and reaped many of the benefits of branding for their company.

Benefits

A brand can represent you, your product or service, and your business. A brand conveys what types of customers you want to attract. Businesses with strong brands often see these benefits:

- Enjoy a higher perceived value for their products or services.
- Maintain higher margins over their competitors.
- Create loyal customers who don't switch to competitors easily.
- Cross-sell other products and services more easily.
- Develop new products/services quicker and more cost-effectively.

Name

A memorable name is a valuable part of a company's brand. An entrepreneur should select a name that will be appropriate for the company throughout its business life. When Marion Luna Berm started her own automobile dealership in Corpus Christi, Texas, she chose the name Love Chrysler, Inc. She uses the tag line, *Love keeps you going* and a heart as part of her logo. Berm's savvy ability to create a strong brand helped her succeed. She was recently inducted into the International Automotive Hall of Fame.

When selecting a business name, consider these elements:

Names of competitors – Your name should distinguish your business from its competitors, but still fit within the industry. For example, in many locations law firms use only the last names of the partners. The name *Legal Ease* is creative, but it may set a new law firm too far apart from its competitors.

Message it communicates – Your company name should fit with your business image. The name *Curl Up and Dye* might be a creative name for a hair salon in writing, but potential customers may not be impressed when they call to make an appointment and are greeted with, "Curl up and die."

Uses of the name – Will the customer's primary experience with the name be written or oral? Your business may have a cool sounding name, but if customers can't spell it, they may not be able to find your phone number or Web site to contact you.

Business it describes – Organized Living® and Holiday Inn® are more descriptive of their products or services than Xerox® and Fuji®. A descriptive business name can help create the image you desire.

In Module 4, you learned that your company name, product names, logos, and taglines are intellectual property and should be trademarked or registered. Remember to talk with an attorney about protecting them.

Location

TIP Many retailers believe their success depends on three things: location, location, location.

Today's business environment offers you more options for choosing a location than ever before. In Module 4 you gave some thought to your business model—bricks and mortar, bait and hook, direct sales, and others. Your business model will be the primary determiner of your location. Will you need a storefront for customers to come to? Will you choose an office suite or a home office? Location, accessibility, parking, and visibility all have an impact on your ability to reach your market.

Product-based businesses may need warehouse space in addition to administrative areas such as accounting and customer service. Many service businesses start out in the entrepreneur's home and then expand to commercial office space as needed.

Here are some of the many location options available to you:

Home office – Can you start your businesses using space in your home? This option is the most cost-effective and allows you to use existing space, furniture, and amenities without incurring too many additional expenses. Check with your accountant on home office tax deductions you may be able to take.

Executive suites – You may want to sublet office space on a temporary basis. This type of commercial arrangement usually offers a phone line, mailbox, shared receptionist, business equipment, such as fax and copy machines, lunchroom and vending services, and conference rooms. Depending on the monthly fee for services, the receptionist can answer your business calls, take messages, or page someone for assistance. Most executive suites also offer a virtual tenant option for entrepreneurs who want a physical location for mail and a phone line, but choose not to rent office space.

Commercial leases – You can lease office, production, and warehouse space based on square footage. Monthly lease rates depend on the going market rate in your area and the size of the space you lease. Long-term contracts are generally required. Some leases allow for entrepreneurs to sublet extra space to other companies. There's a lot to know about negotiating commercial leases. Read the fine print about policies on subletting space and early lease-terminations. Do not sign a lease before consulting an attorney experienced in business leases. Many items in a lease are negotiable. Neighboring businesses can help you learn about the customers who frequent the area and how satisfied they are with the traffic flow and the landlord.

> **TiP** Don't select a space just because the rent is low. The low price may reflect low desirability. The location won't seem like a bargain if your customers don't want to come to it.

Buying or developing a building – Although it's not always a feasible option for a start-up business, you can buy an existing office building or have one custom built to meet your needs. One of the big advantages of owning your own building is that, in the long run, your business has real estate equity and can lease out space to other companies. Depending on the cash flow of your business, buying may be the best option. Talk with your accountant before making this decision and compare the tax advantages of leasing or buying the space you need.

> **TiP** Your local Small Business Development Center and chamber of commerce may be able to direct you to information on traffic counts and demographics for a specific business location.

If customers will be coming to your business location, select a location that matches your marketing strategy to reach your target market. Are you expecting walk-by traffic? Will people drive out of the way for your products or services?

Considerations about your business location should include the following:

Cost and lease terms   Parking availability
Suitability of physical space   Image of the space
Demographics of the area   Competitors' locations
Customer traffic in the area   Neighboring businesses
Visibility to potential customers   Availability of employees
Ease of access for customers

When you have settled these marketing issues that have long-term impact on your brand, such as your name and location, then you can turn your attention to specific marketing messages you want to communicate to reach the customer you have identified as most likely to buy from you.

Reality Check ✔   Business Location

What is my business model (see Module 4)?

How will customers find my business?

Where is my competition located?

Based on the answers to the above questions, what type of location should I consider?

❏ Home office   ❏ Commercial lease   ❏ Other _____

❏ Executive suites   ❏ Owning/Building

Tip The visual image of a business is reinforced through its Web site, signage, and printed materials.

Communicating the Brand

Your image encompasses the total experience customers will have with your company from the first sale. It is more than the company's name, tagline, and advertising. The image is projected in how the phone is answered, what the invoices look like, the company's involvement in civic organizations and causes, and so much more. In essence, everything you do communicates your image.

The bad news is that once you establish an image, it is difficult to change the way customers view your company. The good news is that you can build a strong image without breaking the budget. Investing forefront thinking into how you communicate your brand will save you time and money and your business's reputation in the long run.

Define the Message

Before you create marketing collateral, define what you want your brand to communicate to your target market. Maybe you want to communicate more than one message to your target market, or the same message to more than one target market.

Many entrepreneurs start by identifying the core values they want to communicate to customers. Core values are important characteristics that entrepreneurs personally possess and want reflected in their business. Common core values include integrity, responsibility, reputation, and community service.

Define the Message

What can my customers expect from doing business with me? (for example, honesty, dependability, quality, exceptional service)

Why will customers choose my products/services rather than my competitors'?

What core values do the people in my business share in common (for example, owners, partners, employees)?

How do I want customers to describe my business (for example, fun, professional, chic, safe)?

The core values of your business can be communicated in a variety of ways. Marketing messages may be humorous, professional, focused on safety, or geared toward customers' desire for status or prestige. As the business owner, you can set the tone of your business and link your products or services to your intended target market by the type of message you communicate in your marketing materials.

TIP Test your brand ideas on members of your customer profile. Your perspective is not as important as theirs.

Convey the Message

The next step in building your image through branding is to decide how to convey your message. Once you have identified your company's core values, you can create a mission statement that describes what customers and employees can expect from doing business with you. A mission statement highlights your core values and states a promise to meet customers' expectations. You may already have written the essence of your mission statement in your business concept statement from Module 1. Look it over now and consider what you could use from it to turn into a branded mission statement.

Your message to the public might take the form of a story. To communicate his passion for his coffee business, Danny O'Neill of The Roasterie® includes his entrepreneurial story on each packet of coffee beans he sells. It starts with "I can tell you when I fell in love. It was November 22, 1978. On that day, as a foreign exchange student in Costa Rica, I picked my first coffee bean in the mountainous, volcanic, coffee-growing region around the Poás volcano. I fell in love with the country, the people, and the coffee. Especially the coffee. Fifteen years later my passion for great coffee could no longer be denied and The Roasterie was born…."

Similar messages may be communicated in employee handbooks, company policies, and in marketing materials. Some companies create guarantees or statements that highlight their competitive advantage, particularly when the advantage promises superior service or a high-quality product. For example, one company's Web site states, "We are committed to building value not only for our customers and our business, but also for the communities that our company and our employees call home. We strive to participate responsibly in the global marketplace in which we operate."

These examples may help you identify messages you intend to communicate to customers through your brand:

- We hire the best, deliver the best, and stand behind our work.
- We appreciate your business and work to surpass your expectations.
- We treat our customers and employees like family.
- Quality you can trust. Guaranteed.

 Reality Check | **Convey the Message**

What messages do I want my business to communicate to customers?

How will I communicate these messages? (Where will they appear in my business's marketing materials?)

How will these messages support my competitive advantage?

Every aspect of your business communicates a message about your image to the customer, including cleanliness, landscaping, hours of operation, employee appearance, and customer service.

Design Marketing Materials

Once you have defined your message and decided how your brand should be communicated, you are ready to design marketing materials to promote your business and build your brand. You can spend a lot of money designing and developing marketing materials to build your brand. Depending on your budget, you may choose to start with a few items and then add others when you have more to invest.

Determine which marketing materials to start with by thinking about how you are most likely to reach your target customer. Will flyers, brochures, or a Web site be a better approach for your audience? If you think you may change the marketing content on a frequent basis or are trying to reach a plugged-in market, perhaps a Web site or electronic marketing is a better path to pursue. The following discussion outlines common marketing materials businesses use to promote their brand.

Logo

Your logo is usually the first thing potential customers notice and is a critical part of your company's brand. The purpose of the logo is to identify the company, communicate a message, and leave a lasting, positive impression with the customer. Nike® and Coca-Cola® can be identified by their logos only, reflecting the power of a well-designed logo.

A successful logo design will be:

- **Timeless** – A logo, like classic clothing design, does not become dated over time. Stay away from trendy designs and colors. Consider a logo that will identify your company's look ten or twenty years from now.
- **Symbolic** – The logo should convey some type of symbolic meaning that contains literal or metaphoric imagery. A candle, for example, may symbolize eternity, light, or leadership. Colors also convey symbolism. For example, blue represents loyalty and bravery, while white communicates purity.
- **Simple** – A logo should be readable and reproduce clearly in both color and black-and-white images. An ornate logo may not communicate your message quickly.
- **Unique** – A logo should be identified with a specific company. Use distinctive features such as vivid or contrasting colors, interesting design elements, or an optical illusion that is easy to distinguish.

You may think using a professional designer for your collateral materials is cost prohibitive. Although doing it yourself may appear to cost less, it may take you longer, and the results may be less than professional. Stick to your strengths and use outside help when it's appropriate.

TIP Remember that your company name, logo, marketing materials, physical environment, policies, and personal appearance all send messages to customers. Ensure that your target customers actually see, hear, and feel the message you intend to communicate.

Business Cards and Stationery

Once your logo is designed, incorporate it into your business card and stationery design. Today, a variety of options exist for these collateral materials in color choices, paper texture, and graphics. Although the initial design costs may seem high, business cards and stationery are often the most cost-effective marketing pieces you can use to promote your business.

Consider these options and guidelines before designing your business card and stationery:

- What are the benefits of putting your photo on the business card?
- Do you want prospective and current customers to be able to write on the back of the business card?
- How will you use business stationery as part of your regular correspondence (for example, letters, proposals, thank you notes, follow-up, inquiries)?
- Will you need additional pages of stationery for longer letters or proposals?
- Will you use note cards for handwritten correspondence (for example, thank you notes, invitations, staying in touch with customers)?
- What do you want imprinted on the envelopes (for example, logo, business name, tagline, mailing address)?

Brochures and Flyers

The purpose of a brochure or flyer is to provide overall information about a company or a specific product or service. Depending on how you plan to reach your target market and its preferences, decide if you need a brochure or flyer to market your business. Not every business needs a brochure. Some businesses such as dry cleaners or car washes use flyers to promote their services. Consultants and engineering firms may use brochures to send to prospective clients. If you market to a younger target market, you may find that this audience prefers electronic marketing and online resources. In that case, you may be better off investing your resources in a Web site rather than print materials. Consider these questions before producing a brochure:

- How will the brochure be distributed (for example, trade shows, proposals, letters, sales presentations)?
- How many brochures do you estimate using monthly, quarterly, or annually?
- How often will brochures be updated to reflect changes?
- Can flyers or postcards be used in place of brochures? If so, when and how will this substitution change the quantity you need of each?

Web Site

Web sites are standard for doing business in many markets. Most customers will expect you to have one. Your Web site should be more than another piece of collateral marketing material; it should earn its keep by opening a new avenue of sales. Done correctly, a Web site will work hard for your business and help you build your brand, your customer list, and your business.

The look and feel of your Web site should align with your brand image. Make sure that your Web site and collateral materials are consistent. Because the Web site is a dynamic environment, you can use it everyday to help promote your business and keep it in the public eye. Information on your site can be changed in seconds to promote your latest press release or to tout your new product offering. If you add a well-known person to your board, you can mention it on your Web site almost immediately. If you win a big contract, the news can be posted in a flash.

Many companies believe they should build their own Web site to save money and maintain control, but this is not necessarily true. If you have a graphics person or Web designer on staff and can afford to pay for their time as an overhead cost, building it yourself might make sense. If the designer is billing hours to clients, however, having them stop to build the company site may actually cost you money.

Hiring a professional design firm, a freelance Web site designer, or even an online Web design site, through elance.com or a search engine such as Yahoo!® may turn out to be a better option. No matter who builds the site, maintain control over the process—including content, design, layout.

Creating an effective Web site entails more than just hiring a designer to put up a pretty homepage. The actual design is just a small piece of the puzzle. A Web site should be designed to quickly satisfy a customer's needs and expectations, not impress them with flashy graphics.

Use the questions below when you discuss your Web site with a Web designer:

Who is my target Web audience? Just as in other marketing avenues you need to know your target Web audience.

Why will this audience visit my Web site? Prospective customers using the Web will visit your site for one of two reasons: to learn or to buy.

What does my target audience expect to find at my site? Product reviews and descriptions, pricing and delivery information, customer testimonials, a client list, a company info page, a press release, a downloadable product spec sheet: these are just a few types of information Web users may be looking for.

TIP Hire a graphic designer to achieve a distinct identity and professional look for all your materials. And don't forget the Web site. Customers should know they are at *your* Web site by the overall look.

What other visitors might my site attract? Consider the needs or intentions of prospective employees, potential partners, investors, news media, and competitors. But be cautious. Never put anything on the Web that may give competitors information you do not want them to have.

What's the competition doing? You will find yourself competing for Web site visitors in the same way you compete for other customers. Search similar businesses in your industry and click around their Web sites. How are they designed? What messages do they convey? What do you like about their Web sites? What don't you like? Take notes and share your findings with your site designer.

How will people find my site? Search engines are a big part of online marketing. Studies have shown that the vast majority of Web surfers use search engines to find what they're looking for. Google® and Yahoo! dominate the search industry, so it is imperative that you try to establish a presence there. You have two options for search engine listings: free and pay per click.

- **Free search engine listings** – Many companies hire experts who spend enormous amounts of time trying to get the company's Web site listed high on Google and other sites. Search engine optimization (SEO) experts can work with you to make sure your Web site is coded correctly and that keywords are used wisely, but in the end free search engine optimization is not something you should depend on. If the SEO does their job well and the Google algorithm doesn't change, you might find yourself listed one day, but it will be later rather than sooner.

- **Pay per click search engine listings** – One of the fastest, albeit more costly, ways to get your Web site on Google, Yahoo!, and other search engine sites is to use pay per click (PPC) advertising. PPC ads are the text ads you see along the right side of a Google results page. Advertisers there have set up a Google Adwords account and have placed bids on certain keywords. For example, you may choose the keyword *oranges* and pay to have your ad appear each time someone searches on *oranges*. If the person then clicks your link to go to your Web site, you are charged a nickel. You can find more in-depth information on pay per click advertising by doing an online search for "PPC marketing."

What sales and operational functions do I want my Web site to handle to save time or resources? Consider your Web site an "online branch" of your business. It can offer basic information and automate many business functions, such as adding or making changes to the database, monitoring sales transactions, checking on the status of orders, and even paying bills. Will you sell products/services online? If yes, consider e-commerce capabilities and security issues.

Who will manage and maintain my Web site once it has been launched? Effective Web site marketing has far less to do with buzz words than with real and accurate information. Making timely adjustments keeps the Web site working for you. Do you want to access your Web site internally to make small changes as necessary? If so, maintain an in-house Web expert or outsource the task to a reputable firm. Many firms will make your updates in less than an hour. If it takes more than twenty-four hours for you to get a Web update, hire a different firm.

My site is launched, now what? The marketing begins. Think of the launch of your Web site as the opening of a store. Send out press releases, e-mail customers and partners, call everyone you can think of. Do anything to get the word out that your site is open and ready for business. Some companies will actually start the marketing process before the site is launched to build anticipation and have customers waiting at the electronic door when the site is launched. Recently, a savvy Internet marketer used online marketing to build anticipation for the release of his new DVD and book product. On the day the product was made available online his gross sales were over a million dollars.

For most entrepreneurs, marketing materials provide visual images of their brand to the target market. These materials should reflect a consistent look and message. A brand is reinforced when customers recognize the business when they see its materials.

Reality Check ✔

Make Your Image Visual

Check which marketing materials you could use to make your brand visual. Then indicate whether you already know the costs of these materials or need further research.

	Already Know	Need to Research
❏ Business cards and letterhead	❏	❏
❏ Brochures	❏	❏
❏ Flyers	❏	❏
❏ Web site	❏	❏
❏ Point-of-purchase displays	❏	❏
❏ Publications	❏	❏
❏ Product packaging and labeling	❏	❏
❏ Physical décor (for example, themes, colors, patterns, icons)	❏	❏
❏ Uniforms	❏	❏
❏ Promotional products or advertising specialties	❏	❏
❏ Signage	❏	❏

TIP Listen to your customers. Customer feedback cards can keep you in touch with what your customers expect. The most valuable ones are those with complaints. If you follow up with customers who have quit buying, you may get valuable feedback and encourage them to come back.

Enhance Customer Service

As part of your Marketing Plan, customer service strategies can build the reputation you desire for your business and for your products or services. No matter how carefully your company operates, sometimes customers will be unhappy. If you can resolve customer problems, you may win a customer for life. As part of your customer service strategies, establish policies for warranties, guarantees, and customer complaints. Industry standards for returns and service costs can serve as a baseline for determining what you might encounter and how others have handled these issues.

Employees are the face of the business to a customer; they comprise part of the brand image and its message. Train employees so they know exactly how you want them to treat customers. Most businesses do not adequately empower their employees to handle problems. An unhappy customer does not want to be told to wait until the employee can check with the owner.

Most customers like to feel appreciated or recognized for their patronage. Frequent-buyer punch cards and special sales for preferred customers are some of the ways businesses build customer loyalty. Consider how you will build on each first-time sale and create reasons for customers to buy from you again. As your business grows, you may also want to create incentives for customers to provide referrals. Don't forget to calculate the financial impact of these incentives on your cash flow and profitability.

Reality Check ✓ **Customer Service**

How will I encourage customers to buy from me again?

How will I encourage customers to provide referrals?

What policies will I have about returns or complaints?

What types of warranties or guarantees will I offer?

Exploring Marketing Strategies

As a new entrepreneur, you have a lot to do with few resources. It's important that you focus your marketing energies on target markets where you have the greatest opportunity to succeed and on marketing activities that fit your budget.

Your market analysis in Module 5 enables you to prioritize opportunities in your market and use your resources to get the biggest return possible. If you have too many strategies and associated action plans, you may feel overwhelmed and not accomplish any of them. Develop a marketing strategy that focuses on:

- Selected target markets you are most able to reach during your first year of business.
- Specific market and selected products/services that best meet those needs.
- Your competitive advantage.

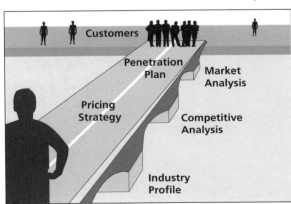

What Is Your Marketing Plan?

Marketing strategies focus on a target or niche market, offer a specific product or service as an opportunity to meet unmet market needs, or use specific strengths as an advantage. Sometimes you will want to think about more than one target market to reach the same end-users in your marketing strategy. For example, a security business could target architects, developers, and high-end homeowners in selected zip codes with the goal of being the preferred business for security systems in a geographic area.

The marketing strategy you develop in this program will focus on the target market you have decided to reach during the start-up phase of your new business. Once you have been in business for six months to a year, you may want to develop additional marketing strategies based on the information you gather about customers' buying patterns, market responses to your product or service, or reactions of your competition.

The Marketing Map

The best marketing plans work from a focused strategy, through a set of carefully designed tactics, outward to an array of specific activities to implement. Call it the Marketing Map. *Tactics* define the marketing message and the way is should be communicated. *Activities* are the specific actions that must be implemented for the tactics to be successful. Activities are concrete action items with deadlines and responsibilities. Strategies have little meaning or effectiveness without tactics or activities to support them.

For example, if your strategy is to target a specific, well-defined market, then your tactics may include using salespersons from within that market, communicating directly to that market, or emphasizing the core values of that market in your brand or image. The activities related to these tactics would include hiring the people you defined in your customer profile and training them in your business; creating and placing collateral marketing materials specifically for that market; and holding focus groups to determine the markets' core values or selecting community leaders from that market as your spokespersons. A sample Marketing Map is shown on p. 227. Using Activity 6b you will create a Marketing Map for your marketing strategy. If you have more than one marketing strategy, use the same format to create additional maps.

Before you determine which marketing activities to undertake, it is important to understand how they relate to your marketing strategies, and why they are the best activities to select. The next section on Marketing Activities will give you some ideas of specific activities you may want to include in your marketing strategy.

Marketing Activities

The philosophy "if you build it, they will come" may have worked for Kevin Costner's character in the popular movie *Field of Dreams*, but it won't work for your new business. Registering with the secretary of state and printing business cards doesn't mean customers will magically appear with cash in hand.

To reach your target market, you will promote your products or services over and over again and convince potential customers that your product or service meets their needs. The marketplace is highly competitive and your potential customers have many options to choose from, including your new business. You have to convince them that your product or service is as good, if not better, than the other choices available.

Marketing Map for Johnson Security Systems

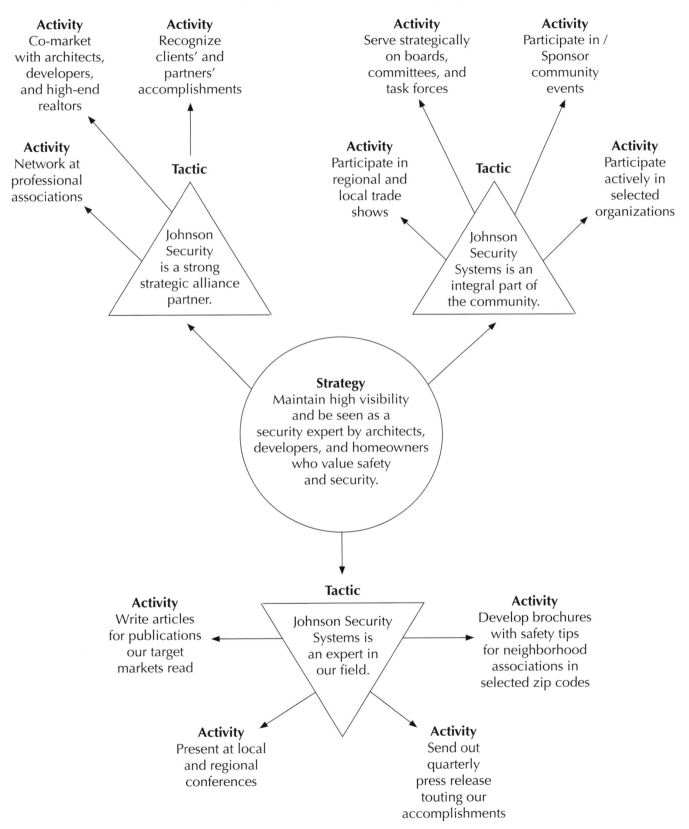

Activity
Co-market with architects, developers, and high-end realtors

Activity
Recognize clients' and partners' accomplishments

Activity
Serve strategically on boards, committees, and task forces

Activity
Participate in / Sponsor community events

Activity
Network at professional associations

Tactic
Johnson Security is a strong strategic alliance partner.

Activity
Participate in regional and local trade shows

Tactic
Johnson Security Systems is an integral part of the community.

Activity
Participate actively in selected organizations

Strategy
Maintain high visibility and be seen as a security expert by architects, developers, and homeowners who value safety and security.

Tactic
Johnson Security Systems is an expert in our field.

Activity
Write articles for publications our target markets read

Activity
Develop brochures with safety tips for neighborhood associations in selected zip codes

Activity
Present at local and regional conferences

Activity
Send out quarterly press release touting our accomplishments

Reaching the target market successfully involves using a combination of approaches. In this section of the module, you'll explore a mix of marketing options and determine which ones are most appropriate for your business. As your business grows, you will analyze your marketing mix and revise your marketing strategies to implement the options that will best meet your goals.

A good marketing mix incorporates *advertising, publicity*, and *promotional strategies* to support your business. Advertising alone is ineffective. Publicity can provide great company visibility, but is difficult to sustain without using other effective marketing strategies, and the media will only do so much for any one company. Promotions bring in the crowd intermittently, but require ongoing time and investments. If you offer incentives too often, customers may wait until the next incentive before buying again.

Technology has changed the way businesses promote products and services. Internet marketing, when used as part of a comprehensive marketing plan, can build sales and target a large customer base inexpensively. Business Web sites can show and explain your product or service, take orders using e-commerce or secured transaction protection, provide customer support for your product or service, and in some cases even deliver the product or service over the Internet. For example, people can buy an e-book and download it within minutes of purchasing it. You can use e-mail to contact new customers, promote products or services, offer special discounts, or remind customers about a specific product or service now available. Keep these electronic options in mind as you consider the marketing mix that is best for your business.

This section explores examples of advertising, publicity, and promotions. You can decide how to create a marketing mix to best reach your target audience and fit your budget. Keep in mind that marketing always involves time, money, or both. You can't do everything on your wish list at once. You will need to prioritize your marketing investments.

Advertising

Advertising is one way to get information about your product or service to potential customers. Because advertising can be expensive, you will want to limit your reach to a very narrow target market—which means getting in front of specific prospects most likely to be interested in what you offer. For example, if you have a day care center, advertising it in selective local publications that target parents with young children may be more effective. Or you could consider advertising in school newsletters that reach families within a ten-mile radius of your center. Advertising is only effective if it reaches the eyes and ears of your intended audience. Think about how ActiveForever.com positioned its name and tagline for maximum exposure on the Web, through Web links on healthcare-related Web sites most likely to attract their target market.

Find out which media are most likely to reach your target market. Then, use your competitive advantage and brand messages in your ads. Focus on what's unique about your business, product, or service and how customers will benefit from doing business with you.

Print and Media Advertising

Print and media advertising sites include newspapers, magazines, television, radio, and the Internet. If you are considering advertising in these venues, you need to ensure that the advertising will yield the results you desire. The medium needs to produce quick results and rapid sales. Consider the advantages and disadvantages of each of these advertising venues:

Medium	Advantages	Disadvantages
Newspapers	Reach a large audience Fit various budgets depending on size and frequency of ads Have short deadlines that make placing or changing ads easy Offer special feature sections and articles	Short life span of ads Uncertainty that the target audience will see ads placed for a specific date Clutter of other ads
Magazines	Reach a more specific audience based on well-defined geographic, demographic, or lifestyle variables Have a longer life and more exposure since readers look through it more than once Provide a superior production quality Offer unsold spaces at deeper discounts Provide extra services such as reader-response cards which allow you to build a mailing list Delay fee collection until ad appears in print	Long lead time between placement and printing Higher costs for production and ad placement Fewer options for ad sizes and formatting
Television	Reaches a large number of people in a short time Conveys messages using visuals, language, sound, and motion Offers the option of spot ads in one market with one station or cable television advertising	High costs Short exposure Need multiple exposures to be effective Competition from national and larger companies
Infomercials (cable television show)	Demonstrate how a product or service works Reach large population bases where high sales can result	Up-front expenses such as setting up a toll free number and purchasing television time before generating sales
Radio	May reach a larger audience than print or television Allows you to target a very narrow segment of the market by advertising during a specific time block or program Offers cheaper rates and shorter deadlines than print advertising	No visual impact on the target market Branding more difficult Less time to convey messages Repeat exposure for ads to be effective
Internet	Can reach a global audience Allows targeted messages to certain interest groups through search engine optimization or pay per click Provides links from the advertising directly to an online site for ordering; potentially minimal time lapse between message and result	Must compete with lots of clutter Up-front expenses for designing and placing an ad before sales are generated Links can be ignored

TiP Don't expect results from a single ad. Marketing experts believe average consumers need to hear or see a message at least seven times before they act.

When a Boston public radio station needed office relocation assistance, entrepreneur Gretchen Fox saw an opportunity to get the message out about her new company. Instead of a fee-for-service arrangement, she swapped her relocation services for radio spots promoting Fox Relocation. The market synergy was perfect; top executives of professional and financial firms in Boston listened to the station. The urbane, understated announcements positioned Fox's firm as professional and civic-minded, educated the market about the new service she was offering, and gave the impression of a more established firm.

Advertising in traditional media can be costly. If you plan to promote your business this way, consider:

- Purchasing small blocks of local radio or television time at a reduced rate.
- Buying pre-emptable time. If timing is important, however, this won't work.
- Selecting a smaller local newspaper, radio station, or television station that reaches your market.
- Working with a media-buying service that provides expertise in buying various types of media.

Other Forms of Advertising

Other popular advertising venues include direct mail, Yellow Pages®, flyers, catalogs, and ads as well as new and creative advertising options that are just emerging

Direct mail – Direct mail means sending marketing information and sales literature to potential customers by mail. Direct-mail marketing provides a way to reach a large number of customers quickly. It is selective and accountable because it allows you to easily measure the response. The accuracy of the mailing list makes a major impact on the effectiveness of your campaign. Many lists are only updated annually and the contact information may be outdated quickly. Some lists are one-time-use only and suppliers can track how often the labels are used by planting fictitious names and addresses throughout the list.

TiP The effectiveness of a direct mailer is only as good as the actual mailing list, followed by the right offer and multiple exposures.

Thoughtfully designed direct mail pieces can produce the results you desire. Research has shown that more than 90 percent of Americans have bought at least one item as a result of direct mail. The disadvantage of using direct mail is that the cost is front-loaded. The mailing piece, mailing lists, and postage are paid for up front without any guarantee that sales will be generated. Response rates for direct mail are low and average about 1 to 3 percent. Carefully targeting the recipients can improve your response rates.

Your best mailing list comes from actual customers. If you keep track of names and addresses via receipts and order forms, you automatically have a list. Asking customers to sign a list or enter e-mail information enhances your customer mailing list.

Postcards are one way to stand out above the clutter of direct mail while keeping costs down. Most consumers will glance at a card and its message while they trash multiple page letters or brochures without reading them.

The Yellow Pages – Many entrepreneurs find that advertising in the Yellow Pages is a necessity, while others discover it isn't. Some of the advantages of advertising in the Yellow Pages include the ability to select a well-defined neighborhood as well as an entire metropolitan area, the various ad sizes and color options, and a relatively low cost for production and target reach. Disadvantages to using the Yellow Pages include the infrequency of placement—ads can only be placed once a year, the clutter caused by competitors' listings and ads, and lack of creative flexibility compared to other media options.

Flyers – You can use handouts or flyers at networking events or trade shows. They often contain a discount coupon to attract customers. This method can be a cost-effective way to reach a small market since you can design them on a personal computer and have a printing service print hundreds of them fairly inexpensively. You can also trace how many customers are attracted to your business by counting the redeemed coupons.

Catalogs – The catalog industry has grown significantly. Firms such as L.L. Bean®, Orvis®, and Lands' End® have all enjoyed tremendous growth and success. Catalogs, however, are expensive to produce and send, and these costs are incurred prior to sales. Develop a targeted customer list before investing in catalog production.

Web banners – You can place advertisements for your company, product, or service on other companies' Web sites. Some banners appear along the top or sides of the Web page, while others open separate windows.

E-commerce catalogs – Electronic catalogs can be made available to customers on your company Web site. The advantages include no printing or mailing costs and product or service descriptions and prices can be updated anytime.

T*i*P Although flyers are inexpensive to design and produce, they should maintain the look and feel of your other marketing collateral. Avoid too many type fonts, sizes, or colors. Stick to the image you have set for your business.

The Not-So-Ordinary Options
Entrepreneurs are exploring newer options for advertising that allow them to target customers based on behavioral variables. Ads can be placed in airports, on ski lifts, and even on television monitors in grocery stores. By using creativity and "why not?" approaches to accessing customers where they shop and play, you are more likely to be seen and heard by your intended audience.

Reality Check ✔

Advertising Options

Which advertising options would be best to use in marketing my product/service?

How often would I consider using these options?

- ❏ Newspaper _____
- ❏ Magazines _____
- ❏ Television _____
- ❏ Infomercials _____
- ❏ Radio _____
- ❏ Direct mail _____
- ❏ Yellow Pages _____
- ❏ Flyers _____
- ❏ Catalogs _____
- ❏ Web banners _____
- ❏ E-commerce catalogs _____
- ❏ Other _____ _____
- ❏ Other _____ _____
- ❏ Other _____ _____

Through the design of your advertising, you can build your brand image. Once you know which medium you want to use for advertising, you can decide on the format that works best and the message you want to present. You can find experts for each medium who can help you design advertising that fits your goals and budget. Effective media advertising meets the following criteria:

- Creates awareness, arouses curiosity, and persuades the audience that your product or service meets its needs.
- Educates the audience about the benefits and uniqueness of your product or service in a way they can understand. The ad provides contact and purchasing information.
- Uses illustrations, metaphors, or analogies conveyed through words, images, or sounds that grab and hold the audience's attention.

Activity 6a will help you consider basic information to include when you advertise your product or service.

Publicity

Besides paid advertising, you can get the word out about your business through publicity. Publicity is known as "free advertising" because stories or notices about businesses, products, or services are published by the media at no cost. You can use publicity to market your business when it's new and once it's established.

Feature Story – One way to stimulate publicity is to be featured in news stories or other media coverage. You can contact newspapers, magazines, radio, and television stations to learn their guidelines for submitting ideas for stories. By building relationships with programmers and editors, you might be interviewed or profiled on shows and in publications as an expert in your industry. Many publications might also accept interesting or educational articles that you or someone from your company writes.

If you are trying to use publicity to gain awareness about your business, be prepared to present an interesting angle or fact about your business's uniqueness. Programmers and editors look for information that is timely, important, and interesting to a large segment of their audience.

TiP "Free advertising" or publicity can be expensive in terms of the time and resources you invest in it. When planning publicity efforts, consider the time requirements as well as the financial costs of contacting editors and submitting information.

Five years after their launch, the founders of Three Dog Bakery® spotted a man snooping around their shop, taking notes. He turned out to be a *Wall Street Journal*® reporter interested in doing a story on the makers of "canine confections extraordinaire." Sales went to warp speed! Ever since, publicity rather than advertising has been the cornerstone of their marketing mix—so much so that their paid advertising costs were less than $1,000 the next year.

Press Releases – Another way to make publicity work for you is to submit press releases on a regular basis to local and regional media sources. Press releases should be as short as possible. Most editors and media representatives prefer them to be no more than one or two pages. Examples of press releases can be found on the Internet or in books that focus on publicity or public relations.

Press releases include these common elements:

- **Identification** – The press release should feature your company name or be printed on company letterhead. The name and phone number of the contact person should be displayed at the top of the page.
- **Release date** – Press releases indicate when the information can be released. Generally, the release date is "Immediate" or "For use upon receipt." Specify the release date if the press release covers an event, a speech, or news announcement you want reported after-the-fact.
- **Appearance** – Margins should be wide on each side of the page, usually an inch or more. This space allows the editor to make notes and edit the sentences, if needed. Because of the space needed for editing, most editors prefer the press release to be double-spaced. It should be printed on white paper or e-mailed. Ask the media outlet how it prefers to receive press releases.
- **Headline** – The headline should summarize the press release. Many times, media outlets will create their own headlines for publication, so yours should emphasize the point of the press release.
- **Error-free** – Press releases should be proofread and free of spelling and grammatical errors. Errors in a press release reduce the credibility of the news.

about press releases, go to www.fasttrac.org/toolkits.

TiP Your work is not finished when you send a press release. Follow up with a phone call or e-mail. Don't give up if your first effort does not result in a story. It may take several attempts to get coverage. If nothing results, ask the editor or reporter for suggestions.

Media sources are most interested in press releases that create news angles, especially those that feature these components:

Controversial issues   Links to current local, regional, or national news
New trends   Celebrity or well-known personalities
Shock value or hard-to-believe facts   Timeliness

Community Recognition – Other ways you can gain positive publicity are by sponsoring an award or community event or donating your product or service as a prize for a local charity. This recognition provides visibility to your business as well as for the charity or causes you sponsor.

Contests – Publicity is about learning to make your own noise in the marketplace. Another way to create awareness and excitement about your business is to stage a contest. You can create the title of the contest, develop a theme, make categories for entries, and offer awards or prizes to the winners. For example, if you are a photographer, you could stage a "Best Vacation Shot" contest and set the criteria for winning. Of course, you or a celebrity panel can be the judges, and you can display the entries on your Web site.

By staging a contest, you can generate publicity from various media sources, be interviewed about the winning entries, and position yourself as the expert in the area. The contest is another reason to create press releases—for the contest, the winners, sponsors, and your business.

Contests do not have to be conducted on a large scale. If you own a restaurant, you can ask customers to place a business card in a bowl for a chance to win a free lunch. You can hold monthly drawings and contact winners by mail or phone. Offering this type of contest also helps you collect contact information from customers to use in future promotions.

Reality Check

Publicity

Which publicity options would be the best to use in marketing my product/service?

How often will I consider using these options?

Feature story

_____

Press release

_____

Community recognition

_____

Contest

_____

Other _____

_____

Other _____

_____

What is unique or compelling about my product/service that would interest the media's audience?

Promotions

You have to find ways to promote your products or services to the same buyers or target market over and over again. Do not underestimate the importance of staying in front of potential or existing customers to create interest to buy again or to refer a new customer. Promoting your business consistently does not always have to cost a lot of money. It does, however, require forethought and some creativity to find new and cost-effective ways to market your business.

The most common promotional activities to market your business include premiums, coupons and rebates, and product or service demonstrations. Telemarketing, trade shows, and networking also may be ways that you get the word out about your business and stay in front of your target market. Emerging technologies also offer avenues for promotion.

Premiums – Premiums or gifts offer prospects or customers something at no extra charge and reinforce your brand. Also called *promotional products* or *advertising specialties*, premiums have been around for quite a while. They include t-shirts, mugs, magnets, or cool gadgets that capture people's attention because they are unique.

The objective behind premiums is to provide value to customers and visibility for the business. When using premiums, consider choosing items that customers will want to use and keep. You can buy premiums from representatives whose catalogs feature thousands of items and who can help you select items that meet your budget. Keep in mind that premiums require camera-ready logos and artwork, minimum volumes to place orders, and space to store the inventory. Premium dealers offer discounts for different volumes, so it pays to order in larger quantities.

Coupons – Coupons provide a variety of options to promote your business. Coupons may offer a price reduction, two-for-one offer, or limited incentive for purchasing products or services. An incentive can be anything from a free gift, an opportunity to win a grand prize, or discounts on future purchases.

Rebates fall into the same category and are redeemed by the customer or by the vendor who sold the product or service. Only a small percentage of customers use coupons or rebates. The average redemption rate for coupons placed in newspapers is between 1 and 5 percent. Other coupons placed in magazines, direct mail pieces, and enclosed with products still average less than 10 percent redemption.

Demonstrations – Demonstrations, or *demos*, allow prospects and customers to try a product or service before they purchase it. Although demos may be expensive since they require planning, labor, and other hard costs, they allow people to sample what they normally might not buy, and studies have shown that up to 80 percent of shoppers buy through this form of promotion. Demos may offer a product sample, initial free trial period for using a service, or a coupon or rebate to create an incentive to buy at that time.

Telemarketing – The telephone has emerged as a major sales tool with the advent of automatic dialers and computerized-screening sales pitches. No matter the scale, the modern marketer should make maximum use of the telephone. One advantage of telemarketing is its low cost. The disadvantage is that staffing and managing a telemarketing salesroom can be stressful. Rejections occur often, and customers are not always pleased to be called by telemarketers.

Networking – Word-of-mouth marketing through networking is the one of the best means of promoting a business. Face-to-face opportunities with prospects allow you to use your personality and passion to market what you offer. Networking provides opportunities for you to respond to questions, build rapport with prospective customers, and market your business with little or no financial investment.

When starting a new business, check out networking opportunities through chambers of commerce, association meetings, and community events. If you are not comfortable with your networking skills, consider taking a class on developing those skills, or start with groups that are smaller and more comfortable for you to talk with a handful of people. Practice using your one-minute marketing speech from Module 1 until you feel confident about trying it out in larger networking scenarios.

TIP No-call laws prohibit certain types of telemarketing calls to consumers who register on a no-call list. Before using telemarketing to promote your products or services, you should check with the state attorney general's office.

Strategic Partnerships

Partnerships—with customers, health-related organizations, and non-profit foundations—form the cornerstone of ActiveForever's marketing strategy. Not only does the company strive to offer outstanding customer service, they also establish online initiatives by courting alliances with health-related Web sites that attract millions of visitors.

As business grew, Feinberg kept asking, "How can we build this smart?" To create a print catalog, they partnered with major pharmaceutical companies and condition-specific foundations, that pay for and distribute the catalog. In return, ActiveForever requests customers' permission to sign them up for educational programs offered by their marketing partners. "We do no mass mailings—only 100 percent permission marketing," Feinberg says.

ActiveForever's advertising dollars are spent primarily on donations to nonprofit organizations and major art centers who do the advertising for them. "We're interested in how we can best leverage foundation dollars, promote nonprofit organizations, and reach our target market," says Feinberg.

What looks like a simple Web-based medical products business is growing into a business-to-business marketing company. Feinberg says, "The way we see it, the bigger we get, the more of an influence we can have on healthcare—period."

Trade Shows – Another face-to-face opportunity to interact with prospects is to participate in trade shows. They are used frequently in marketing products or services to businesses and consumers. Spending a few days attending or exhibiting at the right show can reach a large number of high-quality prospects. Studies indicate that 50 percent of people attending trade shows do so for the purpose of seeing new products or services.

Literally hundreds of trade shows span the country, as well as local events planned by associations, chambers or commerce, and civic organizations. Trade show organizers can provide lists of past exhibitors and attendees to help you find shows that match your business. Managing a trade show effectively requires a specific set of skills such as attracting prospect traffic to the booth, building rapport, and following up with good leads. It's important to set goals for trade show participation and follow-up on all leads and contacts immediately after the trade show ends.

E-Newsletters – Stay in touch with customers, educate them about new products or services, and offer incentives that can be downloaded and used for their next purchase through your company's e-newsletter. This form of communication costs less than the print version because it eliminates the costs of printing and postage.

Electronic Media – Send an interactive CD-ROM or DVD instead of a print brochure. This relatively new marketing technique allows customers to view diverse forms of information on their own time. Using e-mail to communicate with customers, suppliers, employees, and colleagues can be a good marketing and communication tool because of its speed, lower cost, reliability, and efficiency. With today's technology, electronic communication is faster and, sometimes, more reliable.

Reality Check ✓ | Promotions

Which promotional options would be the best to use in marketing my product/service?

How often will I consider using these options?

- ❏ Premiums
- ❏ Coupons
- ❏ Demonstrations
- ❏ Telemarketing
- ❏ Trade shows
- ❏ Networking
- ❏ E-newsletters
- ❏ Electronic media

_____

_____

_____

_____

_____

_____

_____

_____

What other promotional ideas would help me create awareness and generate sales?

Marketing Activities Schedule

Once you know your marketing strategies and activities, you can create a schedule of which strategic activities you will implement on a weekly, monthly, quarterly, or annual basis. Before creating the schedule, you should list all your marketing ideas. You won't have enough time to do everything on the list or enough money to budget for them. But from this list you can make a plan.

Once you have created the list of ideas, estimate the amount of time or expense involved with each item. Then prioritize which ones you want to implement for the first six months of the year. Depending on the outcomes of these activities, you can determine which ones to repeat or try for the first time in the second half of the year. See the example of Johnson Security Systems' strategic marketing activities schedule below. Action Step 6.1 will assist you in developing your own Marketing Activities Schedule.

Marketing Activities Schedule for Johnson Security Systems

Activities	January	February	March	April	May	June
Advertising						
Yellow Pages	$500	$500	$500	$500	$500	$500
Industry publications	$500	$500	$500	$500	$500	$500
Printed brochures	$5,000					
Direct mail postcards		$1,000		$1,000		$1,000
Publicity						
Feature stories	X		X		X	
Press releases – quarterly	X			X		
Articles, stories for newsletters		X		X		X
Community recognition – paid		$1,000		$1,000		$1,000
Promotional						
Premiums		$5,000				
Coupons for new products, specials			$2,500		$2,500	
Trade shows	$5,000			$5,000		
E-newsletters	$500	$500	$500	$500	$500	$500

The X signifies activities requiring time but no additional expense.

Developing Sales Methods

All the marketing strategies in the world will be ineffective if they do not result in sales. No business will survive without sales. Without sales, you cannot pay for overhead and operating expenses. No sales—no profits. Sales methods vary almost as widely as the products or services being sold. What works for you might not work for your competitor. Whatever your sales methods, the sales process will be nearly the same. You should master this process or hire sales representatives who have.

Comparison of Sales Strategies

	Internal Sales Team	External Sales Team
Employment Status	Employees	Subcontractors; sales team
Supervision	Your company can direct their sales effort.	Call their own shots
Compensation	Your company pays salary, salary plus commission, or straight commission.	Commission
Impact on operating expenses	Salary is an expense regardless of sales effectiveness.	Commission is an expense only when a sale is made.
Sales reach	Limited to your company's resources and relationships.	Sales agents can be engaged in many territories.
Knowledge of customers	Based on your company's knowledge or personal relationships	May have pre-existing customer relationships
Products sold	Only your company's	Often sell products of more than one company
Customer service	Provided by your company	Provided by the sales agent

You can use internal or external sales methods to sell your products or services. The type of sales method you use depends on the industry, type of product or service, the sales volume you need to grow your business, and the resources you are willing to invest in sales. When deciding on the best sales method for your business, research how competitors are selling their products or services and consider learning additional methods used by other businesses outside your industry.

Internal Sales Methods

In an internal sales method, teams of employees market and sell your company's products exclusively. The advantage of using an internal sales method is that your company has control over the sales process, pricing, customer service, and relationships with the customer. The primary disadvantage of using internal sales methods is that your company carries the sales costs until the customer pays for the product or service. Another disadvantage is that your sales revenue depends on the size of the internal sales team. If you use a solo approach, all revenue depends on you.

These are the most common types of internal sales methods:

Solo Approach – You sell the products or services yourself. Initially, you may do so out of necessity, if you don't have enough profit to pay commissions or salaries. With the many roles you need to play in your business, you will eventually consider other methods to increase your sales volume.

Direct Sales Force – Internal salespeople, also known as a *direct sales force*, work directly for you and are paid straight salary, salary plus commission, or straight commission. The advantage of using a direct sales force is that they are full-time employees. You can orchestrate their sales efforts and monitor their activities closely. You have more control in training them to sell, price, and support the product or service. The disadvantage is the expense involved in maintaining a full-time sales force. You have to pay salary, travel, office support, and benefits for each salesperson.

Internet – Many entrepreneurs have been successful selling products or services over the Internet or on Web sites. Technology is quickly changing industry distribution patterns, specifically for books, music, and software products. Using this method initially allows some sales functions to be done electronically. Over time, this sales method will increase the need to hire other staff in operations or to outsource entire functions such as sales processing and fulfillment.

External Sales Methods

The advantage of using an external sales method is that your company does not incur any sales costs until the customer pays for the product or service. You hire another company to do the selling for you. This method allows you to utilize a large sales force and sell more products or services locally, regionally, and nationally. The primary disadvantage of using external sales methods is that these entities usually sell other products or services. External sales teams tend to push the products or services that are easiest to sell and that already have a large customer following. Another related disadvantage is that you have no control over external sales teams since they are subcontractors and do not work directly for you. Therefore, they can be harder to manage in regard to pricing, follow-up, and service.

TiP Using external sales methods may be a good strategy during your start-up phase. Paying commission after the customer pays for the products or services helps you manage cash flow.

The most common types of external sales methods include the following:

Licensing – Many entrepreneurs seek companies or people to whom they can license their products. In addition to up-front and annual fees, licensees typically pay the licensor a royalty percentage for each product sold. In some cases, other entrepreneurs can launch their business faster and more economically by buying the rights to your existing products than by developing their own. If you have a solid product, you can grow faster by licensing the rights to your product or service to other entrepreneurs. Going rates for you as the licensor for licensing your product or service are 5 to 12 percent of wholesale revenues over the life of the agreement.

TiP Both the licensee and the licensor should seek professional advice from an intellectual property attorney before signing a licensing agreement.

Reality Check ✓   **Sales Methods**

What sales methods are most often used by competitors in my industry?
- ❏ Solo
- ❏ Direct sales force
- ❏ Internet
- ❏ Licensing
- ❏ Existing distribution channels
- ❏ Sales or manufacturer's reps

Which methods would work best for my business? _____ Why?

Opus®, makers of bird feeders in Bellingham, Massachussets, secured a license to use the Disney name to help tap the kids' market. Opus invested $50,000 upfront in design, merchandising, and promotion, consulted with Disney during the year-long process, and was ultimately able to place the Opus/Disney feeders in about 3,000 stores.

Existing Distribution Channels – Your industry may have existing distribution channels that could market and sell your products or services. Many manufacturers use wholesale distributors to reach both business and consumer markets. Food and toys are some common products that have well established wholesale distributor channels. You looked at potential distribution or marketing channels in Module 5. In this context you can see why distribution is a marketing issue because it affects your approach to sales.

Sales or Manufacturer's Representatives – External salespeople, also known as representatives, sales agents, or sales reps, are engaged as subcontractors for your business. You pay these agents by commission, which is calculated as a specified percentage of the wholesale price. They receive their commission after you collect from customers. The sales agent pays for expenses incurred in selling your product or service such as product samples, travel, office, telephone, and supplies. You save the cost of full-time employees.

The Sales/Service Process

TiP Periodically document your actual sales process to identify how well you or your sales team follow each step. Determine what changes should be incorporated and define a new sales process.

The *Sales/Service Process* refers to the steps you take to prospect, sell to, and retain customers. By adapting this process, you can create a pattern to follow, improve, streamline, and replicate successful sales. You can train others to use the same process. If your sales begin to drop, you can use this process to diagnose whether one aspect or another of your sales process needs particular attention. Planning your sales process from the beginning of your venture will help you address deficiencies in the future more quickly to keep your business running smoothly.

Using the Sales/Service Process illustrated on p. 241, determine how prospects in your industry turn into a first sale and then become repeat customers and referral sources. By anticipating each step in the process, you can prepare your approach, learn customer's needs, highlight features and benefits of your products or services, overcome objections, close sales effectively, and build long-term relationships with customers.

Define Target Market

In Module 5, you defined your target market. Remember, your target market is a specific group of customers you have identified as the best fit for your product or service. Your target market is relatively easy to enter, it offers a significant profit potential, or your competitors have identifiable weaknesses.

Generate Sales Leads

Once you know your target market, consider methods for generating sales leads. You can use marketing to reach your sales leads and generate interest for your products or services.

A Sales/Service Process

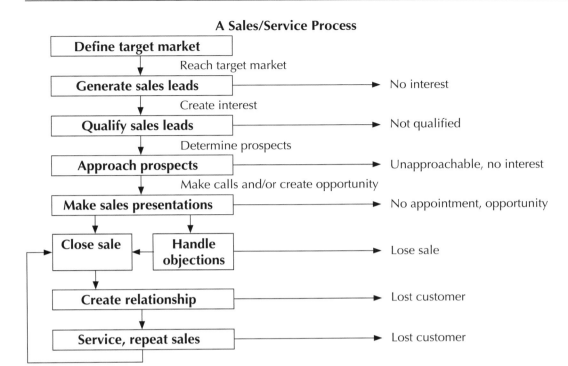

Another way to generate sales leads is to join local clubs or networking groups created for business owners or sales people to share sales leads. Chambers of commerce often have several such groups and others are listed in the local newspaper.

TiP Check with your library to find out what lists they may have available at low or no cost.

You can also purchase mailing lists that match your customer profile to generate sales leads. List brokers usually price lists by the number of names and sort them by zip codes or other demographic variables. Find local list brokers in the Yellow Pages or check with sales or marketing organizations for suggestions. You can develop your own mailing lists from Yellow Page listings, professional association directories, or other local sources.

Qualify Sales Leads
In this step of the Sales/Service Process, you determine whether the sales lead matches your customer profile. If leads were generated by a listing service—a firm that gets paid to sort out potential customers in a target area that matches pre-selected demographic variables—or comes your way through a referral, you may consider these leads as potential customers.

TiP Do your homework before contacting prospects. Collect as much information as you can beforehand. If you know people who have insights or information about the prospect, call them first.

If sales leads have not been generated by a professional list broker or referral source, then you will need to develop a process to determine their suitability through further research. Create a set of questions that may help you determine if a lead matches your customer profile and then answer these questions by conducting more market research. This research may be as simple as asking others who may know more about the consumers you are considering contacting.

Approach Prospects

In order to make sales, you have to approach potential customers. For many businesses, this step usually means that the sales representative makes an initial contact with the prospect in person or by phone. For some entrepreneurs, approaching prospects is a daunting task. If contacting people you don't know makes you uncomfortable, you may consider signing up for sales training or hiring a sales coach. If you still can't get over the fear or if you decide that you don't like selling, you will need to consider hiring a sales representative.

TIP If you need to brush up on selling skills, don't hesitate to take a class at the local Small Business Development Center or a community college.

Prospects may also initiate the approach by coming to your business or by calling, mailing, or e-mailing with requests for information. Part of your sales/service process is to create a standard for greeting prospects, making them feel welcome, and responding to their requests or visit. With some businesses, the prospect is usually the one initiating the approach. For example, retail stores and restaurants generally have prospects coming to them.

Regardless of who initiates the approach, the objective is to establish rapport with the prospect and determine the level of interest in your product or service. You will spend a great deal of effort, time, and money marketing your products or services. Interacting effectively with prospects is critical to making sales.

Make Sales Presentation

In this step of the Sales/Service Process, prospects learn more about your products or services and how they align with their needs. Although some sales presentations are pitched formally using a script or pre-determined format, many entrepreneurs have found that using either *consultative selling* or *relationship selling* is more successful. Concentrating their focus on each client's particular situation, needs, and vision, a sales staff can create opportunities to increase business. Consider how your company and product/service can provide meaningful value to a client, and include that in the sales presentation.

Reality Check ✔ **Sales Presentations**

Which selling approach do I prefer when I am the customer?   Consultative selling   Relationship selling
Why do I prefer this approach?

Which selling approach would work best for my business?   Consultative selling   Relationship selling
Why do I think this approach will work best?

Consultative Selling – In a consultative selling approach, sales representatives diagnose each customer's particular situation and needs. The goal is to find out if the benefits the sales representative can provide match the needs. They ask questions to learn more about the prospects' problems and then collaborate with prospects to consider solutions. This approach is also called *solution selling*. The emphasis is on the prospects' needs and not on the product or service. The sales representative's objective is to provide the prospect a solution with the company's product or service.

TiP Focus on the benefits of your product or service. If the benefits match the customer's needs, you should have a sale.

Relationship Selling – When using the relationship selling approach, sales representatives first focus on building a relationship with a prospect. Once rapport and trust have been developed, sales representatives provide valuable solutions to meet the prospect's needs and problems. This approach is focused on connecting with people profitably, not on persuading them to buy. By creating and nurturing relationships with prospects, sales representatives can build long-term customers and generate more referrals. Recognize that if *your* product or service does not meet a customer's needs you can create future opportunities by referring them to another product or service that does.

Handle Objections

During the Sales/Service Process, you might encounter obstacles that could prevent the sale from closing. Customers may express objections to the price, features or benefits, or their perceived need. The best way to prepare for this step is to anticipate possible objections and be prepared to address them.

Use the *Yes, and* technique when prospects raise objections. Agree with the objection (the *yes*) and then offer additional information that will influence the sale (the *and*). Avoid acting defensively. Objections are part of the sales process and provide opportunities to close the sale.

Reality Check ✔

Handling Objections

What are three objections I expect to encounter when I am selling my product/service?

How would I respond to each of them?

a. _____   _____

_____

b. _____   _____

_____

c. _____   _____

_____

T i P Know when to stop talking and ask a closing question, such as, "Will you be paying by check or credit card?" or "Would you prefer it in red or blue?"

Close the Sale

The next step in the Sales/Service Process is about recognizing buying signals made by prospective customers and asking for their business. Buying signals may include body language, comments about delivery or quantity discounts, or other statements that show readiness to buy. The best way to close a sale is by asking questions that indicate you are ready for the transaction. If prospects raise an objection, then you will need to respond to those concerns before closing the sale. Consider these sample questions for closing:

- "How many cans of paint do you want to take with you today? If you need more to finish painting the fence, you can call us, and we'll have it available before you come down."
- "What day would you like it delivered to your home?"

Create Relationships

Although the sales transaction is complete when the prospect buys the product or service, you want to maintain ongoing relationships with your customers. You want customers to buy again. Many companies only focus on marketing to customers and closing sales. Very few businesses concentrate on creating long-term relationships with customers. Several studies have documented, however, that it costs as much as five times more to get new customers than it takes to keep them.

By developing strategies to create relationships with first-time customers, you are more likely to generate repeat sales and referrals. In fact, repeat customers may become a strong competitive advantage for your new business.

Reality Check ✔

Closing the Sale

What three questions can I use to close sales in my business?

a.

b.

c.

What buying signals or questions from a prospect will I use to determine that it's time to close a sale?

a.

b.

c.

Reality Check ✓   **Creating Relationships**

How will I thank first-time customers for buying from me?

How have other companies rewarded customers for buying from them?

How can I create and develop long-term relationships with my customers?

Service and Repeat Sales

Depending on your business model, you may perform services after the sale. For example, if a house cleaning company makes a sale and schedules the service, the actual service occurs after the sale. If your business involves service after the sale, take this step even further by contacting customers after transactions are completed to check on their satisfaction and to determine if additional opportunities exist. Most businesses overlook this step and lose repeat sales and referral opportunities.

TiP Follow up all first-time sales with a note card to say "thank you" for the business.

Go the Extra Mile

"I want to keep taking things off customers' to-do lists," says O'Neill, founder of The Roasterie, whom you met in Module 3. "That way, if a competitor slashes prices, our customer says, 'Yeah, but we can't leave The Roasterie—they do this and this *and* this for us.' "

To provide that peace of mind, O'Neill asks himself two simple questions: What are we doing for customers *today* that we didn't used to do? And what can we do that will mean more to them? For example, about 45 percent of The Roasterie's customers are restaurants and coffee shops—frantic environments where ordering supplies is either a last-minute activity or a downright emergency. "You can hear the stress in customers' voices when they call," says O'Neill. So he tried a new twist on "don't-call-us-we'll-call you." To keep accounts well stocked, The Roasterie makes weekly phone calls to see what customers need.

"Customers love it because it takes one more thing off their to-do list," says O'Neill. "They know The Roasterie is going to call and check on supplies, so they don't have to think about it."

Besides sparking customer loyalty, the new process has another payback, enabling The Roasterie to better organize its production and deliveries. "Before, we never knew when we would be making deliveries," says O'Neill. Going the extra mile in customer service after the initial sale has provided benefits for both customer and retailer.

245

For many companies, this part of the sales and service process is more about being responsive to customers when they contact them. If sales and company representatives respond favorably to customers, they have a higher likelihood for repeat business and referrals. In almost every industry, building a strong business depends on repeat sales and referrals. If current customers and their referrals generated 20 or 30 percent of your company's new business, you would spend less on marketing costs and build a strong loyal base of customers. Activity 6c will help you design a sales process that fits your business concept.

Checking Marketing Effectiveness

How will you know if your marketing efforts are paying off? You keep track of the performance of each marketing activity so you know which ones are producing results and which ones aren't. Remember, though, that it may take some time before marketing initiatives show results. For instance, it may take two or three months before networking efforts generate appointments or sales.

For each item in your marketing mix, determine how you will measure whether the item or activity was effective. For example, if you pass out coupons for a discount to buy your product, you can count how many coupons are redeemed. If you place an ad in a local organization's newsletter, you may consider every phone call or e-mail that results from the ad as a response to that effort.

	A	B	C	D
1	**Promotion Comparison**			
2				Booth at
3				Business
4	Media Type	Radio	Mailings	Expo
5	Dates	2/10 - 3/2	4/3 - 5/10	8/14 - 8/18
6	Cost	$12,000	$11,000	$3,200
7	Reach (Touches)	250,000	11,000	16,000
8	Responses	204	228	168
9	Cost per Touch	$0.05	$1.00	$0.20
10	**Cost per Response**	**$58.82**	**$48.25**	**$19.05**
11				
12	Sales	24,072	26,904	19,824
13	Net Sales	$12,072	$15,904	$16,624
14				

Checking Effectiveness. In this example, all three promotions resulted in positive Net Sales. Although the business expo had the lowest cost-per-response, it required the most time.

You may have to use the same marketing activity for you to know if it is worthwhile to continue. It may take up to seven or more exposures with the same target market before customers buy a product or service. If consistent exposures over time yield better results, you may choose to repeat the marketing activity several times for six months or even a year before making a decision to try something new.

Tracking the performance of marketing activities is important. It helps you measure how well your product or service has penetrated the market. To determine the market penetration effectiveness of each marketing activity, you may want to record the following aspects of the effort:

Media used	Responses generated
Timing of the promotion	Sales generated
Cost	Return on sales (the sales generated minus the cost)
Reach (the number of persons exposed to the promotion)	

You can measure the effectiveness of a marketing activity by a variety of methods, including these:

- Asking customers how they heard about the business
- Counting coupons used for purchases
- Conducting a focus group to review ads, offers, and incentives and measuring responses
- Interviewing potential customers to determine where they buy similar products/services
- Reviewing the number of hits to a Web site
- Offering a special gift with each purchase and tracking how many were distributed
- Videotaping prospects' reactions to product sampling

TiP If a promotion is a disappointment, analyze what went wrong. Was it the message, the medium, the timing, or something else?

Reality Check ✔

Marketing Costs

Think about costs associated with marketing your business. Some of the costs are one-time only, such as designing the company logo, while others, such as advertising may occur monthly or quarterly. The following are possible costs. Put a check by each that might apply to your business. Indicate whether you already know this amount or need to research it.

	Already Know	Need to Research
❏ Consulting with a graphic designer or Web designer	❏	❏
❏ Creating and printing marketing materials		
❏ Business cards	❏	❏
❏ Stationery package	❏	❏
❏ Brochure	❏	❏
❏ Web site	❏	❏
❏ Postcards	❏	❏
❏ Ads	❏	❏
❏ Advertising placements	❏	❏
❏ Memberships and dues to associations	❏	❏
❏ Marketing events	❏	❏
❏ Premiums	❏	❏
❏ Contests	❏	❏
❏ Coupons	❏	❏
❏ Flyers	❏	❏
❏ Direct mailings	❏	❏
❏ Yellow Pages ads	❏	❏
❏ Newsletter or e-newsletter	❏	❏
❏ Trade shows	❏	❏
❏ Electronic media promotionals	❏	❏
❏ Networking lunches, coffee, phone calls	❏	❏
❏ Sales team	❏	❏

Before undertaking an extensive or expensive promotion, you should test the promotion on a limited basis. You can use the results of the test to improve the promotion before expanding it. For example, a printing company can send out a direct mail campaign to a hundred local businesses and measure the results before mailing out 5,000 postcards.

Action Step 6.2 will help you begin to write the Market Penetration section of your Marketing Plan.

Business Plan

Creating a Marketing Budget

You will create a marketing budget in Module 8 that summarizes your marketing mix and the various marketing activities you plan to implement. Although some items on your Marketing Activities Schedule may be free, each one that is not will have a financial impact on your business.

Some entrepreneurs determine how much they will spend on marketing each year for their business and then create their Marketing Activities Schedule based on how much they are willing to spend. Others create a list of marketing activities and include those items as part of their overall budget for the year. In either case, you will need to recognize the cost of marketing and anticipate the return-on-investment.

Action Step 6.3 will ask you to estimate these costs on the Financial Facts Worksheets introduced in Module 3, pp. 128 – 136.

Summary

This module introduces the concepts you need to reach your target market. Marketing is not an exact science. You can market your product or service many ways; thus, you must make many decisions about your marketing strategy, tactics, and activities. You considered the marketing mix you may want to use to bring your products or services to market. You have literally thousands of alternatives from which to choose. This module should help you develop a sales process and an awareness of the need to ensure market effectiveness.

Key Things to Remember

- Whether you intend to or not, you will create an image of your business in the minds of potential customers. It is better to be in control of this image through branding.

- Location can be a critical component in your business's image.

- Marketing your business includes setting a strategy, developing tactics, and planning specific activities to implement the strategy.

- A successful marketing mix will include a blend of advertising, publicity, and promotions.

- Your schedule of marketing activities will have a direct impact on your budget and should be tracked to ensure its effectiveness in penetrating the market.

- Following a sales process can help you or your sales team close sales, build relationships with customers, and ensure repeat sales.

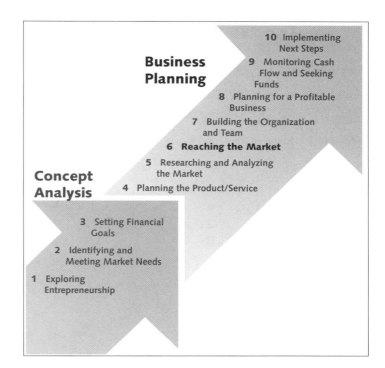

Congratulations on completing the marketing section of your business planning process! This major component of your plan touches many areas of your business, and has a significant impact on your ability to project its financial situation. Before you delve back into financials, however, you will turn your attention to your organizational structure, management needs, and legal form of doing business in Module 7.

Activity 6a   Advertising

Focus on the message for an advertisement for your product or service.

Directions

Use the steps below to design an advertisement for your product or service. Feedback from other participants will help you determine the effectiveness of your advertisement.

Step 1 Select a medium to reach your target market. Based on the results of the Reality Check *Advertising Options* on p. 231 select one of the following media to reach your target market:

Newspaper – A local or national newspaper

Magazine – A local or national magazine that your target market reads

Radio – A local station, program, and time your target market listens

Television – Network or cable programming appropriate to your target market

Web banner – Web sites with content most likely to attract your target market

Step 2 Set a goal for the advertisement. What do you want it to accomplish? Who is your audience for this ad? What question will you answer or problem will you solve for this audience? Write this goal in Box A.

> **A**   **Goal for advertisement**
>
>
>
>
>
>
>
>
>

Step 3 Determine what the advertisement should say. What is your marketing message for this ad? Focus on benefits, not features, of your product or service. Write your copy in Box B.

> **B**   **Advertisement copy**
>
>
>
>
>
>
>
>
>

Activity 6a **Advertising** continued

Step 4 Sketch out illustrations. What images are useful in illustrating your ad copy? Include such details as the color of the ad, the headline style and size, the wording you might use, or the music you might select.

C Sketch of advertisement

Step 5 Ask others for feedback on your advertisement. If possible, seek feedback from persons in your target market. Modify your advertisement based on this feedback.

251

Activity 6b **Marketing Map**

Develop a Marketing Map for marketing my product or service.

Directions
Follow the steps below to create a Marketing Map for your business that includes strategies, tactics, and activities.

Step 1 Determine marketing strategies for your business. Respond to the following questions to determine which marketing strategies are best for your business.

a.   Which target markets are you most able to reach over the next year?

b.   What specific needs does your target market have that are not currently being addressed well?

c.   What products or services can you offer to best meet these needs?

d.   How does your competitive advantage meet these needs (See Activity 5b)?

e.   What tactics should you employ to connect your competitive advantage with the need of the target market?

f.   What activities will best help you implement these strategies (for example, advertising, publicity, promotions, sales methods, or other activities)?

Step 2 Create your Marketing Map. Identify one marketing strategy in the circle. In each of the three triangles, identify a tactic that will support this strategy. Then list two or more activities for each tactic that you can use to support this strategy. Refer to the sample Marketing Map on p. 227 if you need ideas.

Activity 6b **Marketing Map** continued

Activity   Activity   Activity   Activity

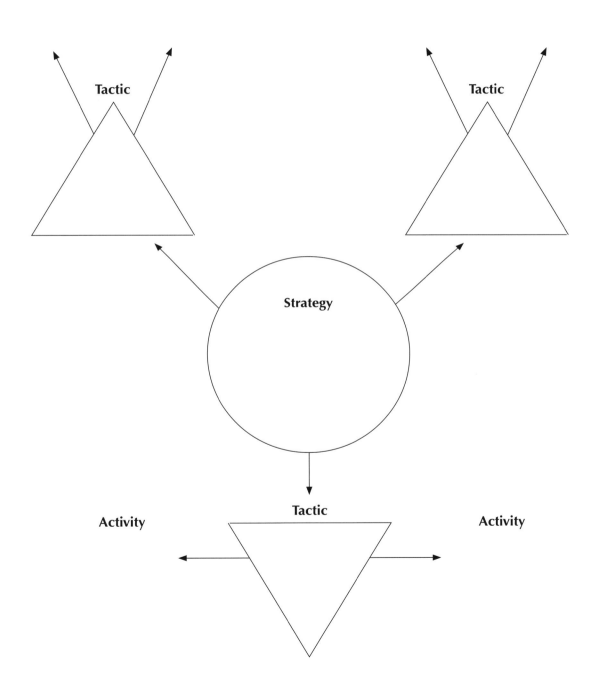

Activity 6c **Sales/Service Process**

Design a Sales/Service Process for my business.

Directions

Using the following steps, write out how you anticipate selling your product or service. Feedback from other participants will help you refine these steps.

Step 1 Describe your target market. Describe your target market based on Activity 5c Target Market.

Step 2 Generate sales leads. Describe the actions you will use consistently when a) prospects initiate the contact or b) you or a sales representative initiates the contact with prospects.

Activity 6c **Sales/Service Process** continued

Step 3 Qualify sales leads. Describe how you will match sales leads to your customer profile. Do you want to make sales presentations to the user, the decision maker, or the buyer?

Step 4 Approach prospects. Describe the means by which you or your sales team will approach qualified prospects.

Step 5 Make sales presentation. Describe the actions you will use consistently when a) making a sales presentation to prospects or b) describing or showing prospects your products or services.

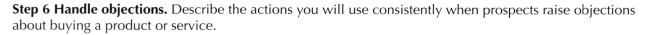

Step 6 Handle objections. Describe the actions you will use consistently when prospects raise objections about buying a product or service.

Step 7 Close the sale. Describe the actions you will use consistently when a) prospects show buying signals or b) you or a sales representative ask for the business.

Step 8 Follow-up after the sale. Describe the actions you will use consistently when a) service after the sale is needed or b) you or a sales representative follow-up with a customer after completing the sales transaction.

Action Step 6.1 **Develop a Marketing Activities Schedule**

Determine which advertising, publicity, and promotional activities I will use to market my business for the next six months to a year.

Directions
Using your Marketing Map from Activity 6b and the sample on p. 258, create a Marketing Activities Schedule. Select a mix of marketing tactics and activities from your Marketing Map and the module discussion of advertising, publicity, promotions, and sales methods, as well as other marketing techniques. Refer to the sample Marketing Activities Schedule on p. 237 for ideas. Include costs if you know them. If you don't, plan time to research them in the near future.

Action Step 6.1   **Develop a Marketing Activities Schedule**   continued

Marketing Activities Schedule

Activities	Month 1	Month 2	Month 3	Month 4	Month 5	Month 6	Month 7	Month 8	Month 9	Month 10	Month 11	Month 12

Action Step 6.2   Create My Marketing Plan – Market Penetration

Complete the Market Penetration section of my Marketing Plan.

Directions
For this action step, you will explain exactly how customers will be told about your product or service and how it will get into customers' hands. Use Reality Checks, activities, and action steps from this module complete this action step.

A. Define your marketing options. If you are planning for more than one target market, address how you will penetrate each one. By carefully explaining your market penetration strategies, you will convey that you have thought through how and when each marketing activity will be accomplished.

B. Use the template. Read the instructions on page 1 of the template. Then move to the Market Penetration section of the template to insert your information.

Each section of the template contains headings with questions to prompt you to consider the type of information to include under each heading. The questions are also listed in each action step for easy reference. After you enter your answers into the template and print them out, the questions will not appear on the hard copy. You should try to incorporate enough of the question into your answer so that the reader understands what is being answered.

Market Penetration

Company Image
What is the image of your company?
How will you portray that image?
How will your image be noticed by potential customers (for example, how the phone is answered, what the invoices look like, the company's involvement in civic organizations and causes)?

Customer Service
What are your customer service strategies?
What policies will you establish for warranties and guarantees concerning your product/service?
What will be your policy for returns and service costs?

Location
Where will the business be located?
How will this site promote your business?
What are the demographics of the surrounding neighborhood?
How long do you plan to be at this location?

Direct Sales Force
Will an internal sales force be used for selling the product/service to the end user?
How many sales persons will be hired?
What will a direct-sales force cost (compensation package, training, support staff, contests, bonuses, meetings, sales aids, displays, samples, training materials, catalogs, and brochures)?

Sales Representatives
Will external sales representatives be used to sell the product/service to the end user?
How many representatives will be used?
What will be the cost of using sales representatives (compensation package, allowances, catalogs, brochures, and samples)?

Action Step 6.2 **Create My Marketing Plan – Market Penetration** continued

Licensing or Distributors

To whom, if anyone, will you license your product/service?

What upfront, annual, and royalty fees will you charge?

What companies will be used to distribute your products/services? List the name and address of the distribution company, contact person, geographical area assigned, and a brief description of the distribution contract.

Advertising and Promotion

What advertising/promotion will be used for the distribution system and customers?

What media will you use to promote your business?

What will the advertising/promotion cost?

Publicity

What strategies do you have for obtaining publicity for your business?

What events will you promote through press releases?

What media will you attempt to solicit publicity from?

Telemarketing/Direct Mail

Will telemarketing/direct mail be used to sell the product/service to the end user?

Where will you obtain a mailing list?

What is your schedule for telemarketing/direct mail and estimated response rate?

What will the telemarketing/direct mail cost (mailing list, print materials, postage, and cost per contact)?

Internet

How will you use the Internet to market your services?

What features will you have on your Web site?

Will you use e-mail to communicate with customers?

What will it cost to build and maintain a Web site?

Trade Shows

What trade shows do you plan to use to exhibit your product (name of the trade shows, location, date, size of booth, cost to attend, the projected number of contacts, and other information)?

What trade shows do you plan to attend without an exhibit?

Market Penetration Effectiveness

What activities are planned for penetrating the market?

When will they begin and end?

Who is responsible for each activity?

How will you measure the effectiveness of each market penetration tactic?

Action Step 6.3 **Write My Marketing Financial Assumptions**

Begin accumulating financial data to project how much money I will need to market my business.

 *Financial Facts Worksheet*

Directions

Refer to the Marketing Activities Schedule you developed in Action Step 6.1. After calculating the frequency of the advertising, publicity, and promotional activities, estimate how much it will cost to implement them.

Use the Financial Facts Worksheets to estimate costs for all the marketing aspects of your business. Each worksheet heading in the list below suggests possible costs to consider. Not all headings will apply to all businesses. Think about how each one applies to your business and, in particular, to your vision of that business.

Write your assumptions on the Financial Facts Worksheets on pp. 128 – 136 or in your electronic toolkit. Be sure to cite sources for the facts that are the basis for your assumptions. For example, you can research the expected costs for designing logos and marketing materials and what ranges you should expect to pay by talking with persons in your industry, suppliers, and professionals who serve the industry. Also, plan for annual cost increases for expenses such as advertising or Web site maintenance. Prices go up in every industry.

Completing your Financial Facts Worksheet now while you work on your Marketing Plan will save you time later when you fill out your Financial Template and make your financial projections.

Operating Expenses Worksheet

Advertising – All costs for ads, including newspaper, radio, magazines, newsletters, television, direct mail, billboards, Web banners, catalogs, and any other media selected

Dues & Subscriptions – Costs for membership in chambers of commerce, trade or professional associations, for subscriptions to magazines, journals, newspapers, and monthly, quarterly, or annual service fees for online services such as survey software or anti-virus fees

Licensing & Fees – Costs for using licensed products and logos, distribution fees associated with marketing and selling other companies' products, special license or fees to market, sell, and distribute specific products

Marketing & Promotion – Costs for printing collateral materials such as business cards, brochures, and flyers; promotional products, coupons, rebates, contest prices, sponsorships, demonstrations, trade show booths, focus groups, surveys, and customer appreciation activities

Meals & Entertainment – Costs associated with events, networking, outings with clients, tickets to concerts and sporting events to entertain clients, and meals for trade shows and conferences

Miscellaneous – Any miscellaneous or minor costs that do not fall into other categories

Outside Services – Costs associated with outsourcing, that are distinctly different from those classified as Professional Services. Such outsourced costs may include staffing or temporary employment fees, distribution of flyers, and direct mail services

Other – Significant costs that do not fall into other categories. Identify the category associated with these costs by entering a description next to Other

Payroll Expenses – Costs for salespersons or marketing staff, includes salaries, benefits, commissions and bonuses

Action Step 6.3 **Write My Marketing Financial Assumptions** continued

Professional Fees – Fees paid for services such as Web site design, development, and updates; graphic design fees, consultants, and other costs associated with outsourcing work. If specific costs are associated with customer projects, those costs should be categorized under Cost of Goods

Financial Facts Worksheet

Shipping & Delivery – Costs associated specifically for marketing such as sending samples, direct mailings, or products and material shipping costs for trade shows. Costs may include postage, insurance, or courier fees

Telephone – Costs associated with making calls for marketing

Travel – Costs associated with marketing such as airfare, hotel, car rental, and taxicabs expenses to call on prospects and customers and to attend conferences and trade shows

Building the Organization and Team

Before you meet your first customer or make your first sale, you will want to choose a legal structure for your business. Then you will want to plan how to manage the business—its people and operations. This module discusses ways to organize your business and manage its tasks. It will help you decide whether you need to build a management team, form an advisory team or board of directors or both, hire outside contractors, or rely on your own skills and energy. It will provide you with insights about critical tasks that must be accomplished if your business is going to succeed.

Almost all entrepreneurs need other people to accomplish the work of the business. Whether you are dealing with employees, contractors, partners, or advisers, the way you manage these relationships will bring you success or failure. This module will introduce you to creating the right team for your business and developing an organizational culture that will drive productive work.

Key Questions
- What is the best legal form of doing business for my concept?
- How will I manage key business functions?
- Will I have a board of directors or advisory board?
- What do I want my organization to be like?
- Where and how will I find the right people for my organization?
- What outside professionals and contractors will I use?
- What are the financial implications of my Management and Organization Plan?

Action Steps   Due Date
- ❏ 7.1 Create My Management and Organization Plan   _____
- ❏ 7.2 Write My Management and Organization Financial Assumptions _____
- ❏ Read Module 8 Planning for a Profitable Business   _____
- ❏ _____   _____
- ❏ _____   _____
- ❏ _____   _____

Choosing a Legal Form of Business

Business must be done within some kind of legal framework. The law insists on it. If you do not take legal action to structure your business, the law will make those decisions for you—and that can be dangerous.

Factors to Help You Choose

While you should consider many factors in choosing the legal structure of your business, not all factors apply to every business. Several key issues, however, apply to most:

Control – Who is the decision maker? The decision maker will control management, determine who receives profits, decide whether to get loans or solicit investors, and be solely responsible for the company's financial losses. If control is important to you, choose a legal structure that protects your standing in the company.

Taxes – Taxes are a major concern for business owners. The amount of taxes your business pays yearly can make or break it.

Liability – Liability is another key concern. Some legal structures do not protect your personal assets from business debts. If you do not want to personally pay the debts of your business, consider a legal structure that will protect your personal property.

Transferability of ownership – Depending upon the legal agreement, one person's ownership in a business may be transferred to another owner in whole or in part simply by the exchange of a piece of paper. Consider whether transfer of ownership is important to your business concept.

Longevity of the business – Not all business forms are perpetual. Some forms of business cease when the entrepreneur exits the business. Do you want the business to continue after you leave it?

Raising capital – Simple entities such as sole proprietorships and general partnerships are restricted in their ability to raise capital. If you expect to raise funds to grow your business, consider the legal structures that make investment attractive to others.

Most often, entrepreneurs are concerned with all of these important issues. The key is to identify the legal structure that best meets your needs and the needs of your business. In an ideal world, you would select a legal form of business, understanding every legal and tax implication. The reality is that you must rely on the advice of attorneys and accountants to help you make this decision. They can anticipate your concerns based on their experience and on information you provide. Still, the legal structure of the business is your decision to make and live with.

Before we get to the nitty-gritty regarding six legal forms of doing business, Check Your Knowledge to see if you can help some other entrepreneurs. Don't expect to know all the answers, but make your best guess. You may not be familiar with all of the terminology; it will be explained in this module. These stories come from the experiences of real entrepreneurs. You will see what happened in each case as the module unfolds.

Now let's focus on six legal forms of doing business. Keep your own business concept in mind as you read.

TiP States typically view undeclared businesses as sole proprietorships or partnerships, leaving you personally responsible for debts and injuries. Select the best legal structure for your business after consulting an attorney and accountant.

TiP Your legal decisions should not be made without adequate counsel from an attorney, an accountant, and other advisers.

Check Your Knowledge ✔   **Legal Forms of Doing Business**

Cortez Consulting – Anna Cortez is a very successful business consultant with ten years' experience. When she started her business, she was fully advised as to the advantages and disadvantages of doing business in the different legal structures. She made a decision at that time to be a sole proprietor. She knew that the nature of her business would create only a very small risk of liability. She needed very little in the way of supplies or equipment. She worked alone or with others, all as independent contractors on specific projects, and she had no employees. In these ten years, she has never been sued, and she has always been profitable. Cortez is now considering changing to a corporate structure to be absolutely sure that she is free from risk and liability.

What would you recommend that she do? Circle one.
a. Keep things as they are, because they seem to be working well.
b. Form a corporation to insulate herself from liability.
c. Take money out of her business to protect herself.

James and Tyrone's Fire-Fighting Repair Shop – James and Tyrone own a highly profitable repair shop for fire fighting equipment. The business has never adopted any form of doing business, but the two owners have always split the profits 50/50, even though Tyrone contributed nearly all of the assets to the business including the land and building. Lately, they have been wondering if they ought to formally structure their business.

What would you recommend that they do? Circle one.
a. Keep things as they are, because they seem to be working well.
b. Write up an official partnership agreement, to make sure that the business rules are clear.
c. Form an LLC or an S corporation, even if it is time-consuming and expensive.

Software Solutions, Inc. – Software Solutions, Inc., began as an S corporation. Within five years of starting the business, founders Alexei and Nina Vladimir wanted to go public—that is, issue and sell shares of stock to the general public.

What do you recommend that they do? Circle one.
a. Become an LLC and then go public.
b. Become a C corporation and then go public.
c. Go public as an S corporation to avoid the expense and paperwork involved in switching.

The Doctors' Office – A group of highly skilled and successful doctors originally formed a partnership. They liked the flexibility of management; none liked to be told what they could or could not do by others. Recently, however, they have become terrified of losing individual property because of a potential malpractice claim against any one of their partners. Skyrocketing insurance costs have become nearly prohibitive.

What would you recommend that they do? Circle one.
a. Keep things as they are—there is little danger in this situation.
b. Dissolve the partnership and form an LLC with the doctors as members.
c. Dissolve the partnership and become sole proprietors.
d. Dissolve the partnership and become a corporation.

Six Forms of Doing Business

Six legal forms of doing business are:

- Sole proprietorship
- Partnership
- Corporation
- S corporation
- Limited liability company (LLC)
- Nonprofit

Let's look at their characteristics, advantages, and disadvantages individually. Remember, you want to make an informed decision about your business's legal structure.

Sole Proprietorship

A *sole proprietorship* is a business owned by only one person and operated for his or her profit. It is the easiest entity to form and maintain, requiring little to no paperwork or approvals to begin.

In a sole proprietorship, you alone control the entire business. You can either manage it or hire managers. All the profits and losses belong to you. You *are* the business.

Taxes for a sole proprietorship are relatively easy to file using Schedule C of the 1040 form. As a sole proprietor, you do not worry about double taxation, excessive compensation, or excessive retained earnings.

In a sole proprietorship, you are liable for any debts of the business. Because the business and the business owner are the same, your personal assets are available to pay the debts of the business and your personal obligations may be satisfied by business assets.

You can sell a sole proprietorship as a business or close its doors and sell its assets. Fractional sales to allow new owners or investors are not allowed. The business ends upon the death of the owner and may end upon the owner's permanent disability or prolonged absence.

The ability of a sole proprietorship to raise capital is limited. You cannot sell shares of the business. Generally, these entities obtain loans after fully collateralizing them with personal assets.

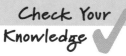
Check Your Knowledge   **Cortez's Consulting Business**

What did you recommend that Cortez do?
a. Keep things as they are, because they seem to be working well.
b. Form a corporation to insulate herself from liability.
c. Take money out of her business to protect herself.

What Cortez did: Cortez continued to operate as a sole proprietor and has never had any regrets. She does protect herself with some inexpensive liability insurance. She has enjoyed the absolute freedom to control every aspect of her business and the lack of governmental regulation. For Cortez, forming a corporation would likely have caused more headaches than it was worth—given the yearly reporting requirements.

What you should know: For some businesses, being a sole proprietor is perfectly acceptable—and often easier. Of course, not all sole proprietors will have such low risk as Cortez. Those with employees or those working in higher-risk enterprises may not fare so well.

Partnership

A *partnership* forms when two or more entities join together for a common business purpose. Two or more people, a person and a corporation, two corporations, or even two partnerships may form a partnership. A partnership can be *general* or *limited*. Although no written document is required to form a partnership, for all partners' sakes a partnership agreement should be written. This document should spell out matters such as division of profits or dissolution of the partnership.

The partners control a partnership according to their agreement. They have a great deal of flexibility. If they have no other agreement, the law assumes that partners share control equally. In a limited partnership, the general partner controls the operations and the limited partner is simply an investor.

Some experts recommend avoiding a partnership, corporation, or LLC that splits ownership 50/50. What happens if the owners do not agree? Nothing. A majority cannot be achieved. Instead of a 50/50 ownership, a third party in whom the partners have complete trust, could have a very small percentage of ownership or a written agreement to resolve tie votes. If the partners agree, that person never hears from them. If the partners cannot agree, this third party votes so the business can act.

Partnerships have a fairly simple tax structure. Income and loss earned by the partnership passes through to the partners, and they report it on their respective tax returns. The partners then pay the tax on their share of the profits. The partnership itself does not pay any tax on profits.

Some authorities strongly advise against using the general partnership form of organization for most types of businesses because liabilities are personal and unlimited. Moreover, each partner is fully personally liable for the actions of any other partner. In a limited partnership, only the general partner is personally liable. The limited partner's liability is limited to the amount of investment.

Since a partnership is a voluntary association, you or any partner can end it at any time. Partners can simply say they no longer wish to be a partner. The death of a partner also automatically ends a partnership. Therefore, a partnership agreement should include provisions for dissolution. The agreement also covers the payment or performance of partnership obligations, division of assets, continued use of the name and ownership of intellectual property.

TiP A creditor will usually seek to collect from the partner with the most accessible assets. If you are that partner, seeking reimbursement from the partners who did not pay can be a long and sometimes futile process.

Think through all the aspects of your business before deciding on a partnership. One land development partnership in Virginia was initially funded by three equal partners to develop land near a new center for horse breeding, training, and racing. The partnership contracted to develop the land with the only modern hotel and restaurant near the new horse facility. The partners planned to sell the properties to a hotel management company. Their investment was primed to reap huge profits for the partners.

When land development costs exceeded the initial estimates and the partners needed to make additional contributions, only one of them had the funds to do so. Since the partnership was contractually bound to complete the buildings, everything would be lost if they did not perform. The partner with the funds purchased the interests of the other two partners for far less than their initial investment and made all the profit himself when the land was eventually sold. The partnership structure wasn't right for the two partners who had to sell at a loss. Under a different structure they might have been able to maintain their share in the company and then had the entity raise the needed funds.

Technically, ownership in a partnership cannot be transferred since the addition of a different owner constitutes a new partnership. Provisions can be made in the partnership agreement, however, for the addition of new partners, the retirement or resignation of old partners, and the continuation of the old partnership, at least in name. Law firms sometimes use partnerships with these kinds of provisions.

A partnership is primarily dependent upon the individual assets of the partners to raise additional capital. Adding investors requires converting from a general to a limited partnership. It would create a new entity. Lenders will look for a fully collateralized loan to be personally guaranteed by the partners. Since limited partners are generally investors whose liability is limited to their investment, it is unlikely that they would be willing to personally guarantee a loan.

Check Your Knowledge ✔   **James and Tyrone's Fire-Fighting Repair Shop**

What did you recommend that James and Tyrone do?
a. Keep things as they are, because they seem to be working well.
b. Write up an official partnership agreement to make sure that the business rules are clear.
c. Form an LLC or an S corporation, even if it is time-consuming and expensive.

What James and Tyrone did: They continued as a partnership without a formal agreement. One day, James's teenaged son was returning to the shop with parts he had picked up in another town as a favor to his father. On the way, he was involved in an automobile accident that killed two people. The boy was not an employee of the business and was not to receive any compensation for the favor. In a law suit against the boy and the two owners of the business, the business was declared to be a partnership, and they were all found liable. In order to pay the judgment after the insurance limits were exhausted, all of the assets of the business were sold. Tyrone, who had contributed nearly all of the assets, was left with nothing.

What you should know: Decide what business entity is best for you. Decide soon. Look to protect yourself. If you determine that you have risk, protect yourself by forming your business as a corporation or LLC.

Corporation and S Corporation

A *corporation* is a legal entity created under state law. A corporation can manage its own affairs, hold property, borrow money, and legally do nearly anything an individual can do. Stockholders may be, but need not be, employees, officers, and/or directors of the corporation as well.

TiP If you're doing business as a corporation, follow the rules to maintain your corporate protection.

An advantage of corporations is that they insulate you from liability. If the corporation operates according to laws and regulations, creditors only have access to the corporate assets for business debts. Your personal assets are not at risk. The law requires corporations to operate separately from the owner and to file all governmentally required reports and taxes. All too often, however, a one- or two-person corporation keeps inadequate records and fails to strictly segregate corporate and personal assets and liabilities. Failing to operate the business as a corporation separate from the owners results in a loss of insulation from liability.

For example, a small corporation, solely owned by a wealthy businessman, was sued as the result of an automobile accident. The corporate vehicle driver was unquestionably at fault. The corporation had virtually no assets that were not subject to valid creditors' liens, and it had only the minimum required insurance.

The corporate owner had great personal wealth but was insulated from liability by the corporation. The corporate vehicle was a minivan which seemed unusual to the plaintiff's attorney. Upon investigation, the attorney was able to prove that the minivan, although owned by the corporation, was used frequently by the owner's wife to transport their children to Little League and soccer games. Upon questioning, the plaintiff's attorney proved that no vehicle log was maintained as is required for a multi-use vehicle. The court ruled that the corporate veil (its shield from liability) had been pierced and that the owner's assets were available to satisfy any judgment. The case was quickly settled for much more than the value of the corporate assets and insurance.

If a creditor can show that your business has not been properly operated as a corporation, the creditor can then reach both your corporate and personal assets.

Corporate insulation from liability does not shield you from liability for your own negligence causing harm to another. You may be liable along with the corporation. Nor does it prevent the corporate owners and officers from being sued. Even if you are individually determined not to be legally liable, defending the action filed against you can cost thousands of dollars. For these reasons, many corporate owners and officers obtain individual liability insurance coverage.

Corporations have a three-tiered control system. Stockholders elect the directors of the corporation. In turn, directors elect the officers. Other than electing directors and expecting dividends, stockholders generally have no other function. The directors make primary decisions for the corporation, and the officers direct day-to-day operations.

Some states permit one person to fill the roles of stockholder, director, and officer. Others permit only one owner but require two officers minimum. All states' requirements are based on the concept that the corporation is a separate legal entity from those individuals who own and operate it.

All corporations start the same. They obtain a charter from the state, generally the one in which they intend to do the most business. Unless the corporation elects to be treated as a partnership for tax purposes (the subchapter S election), it files a corporate tax return. After paying taxes, most corporations distribute money to their stockholders in the form of dividends. The stockholders must pay taxes on the income received. This practice results in double taxation.

To avoid double taxation, assuming certain requirements are met (no more than seventy-five stockholders, all stockholders are U.S. citizens, and all stockholders agree), your corporation may elect to be treated as if it were a partnership at tax time. In that case, the corporation pays no tax and the profits pass through to the stockholders who pay income tax on what they receive. If you make such an election, your corporation is an *S corporation* or a *Subchapter S corporation*. The S comes from the subsection of the Internal Revenue Code, which permits this election. A corporation that has not made the election or is ineligible to make it is known as a *C corporation*.

Shares of a corporation represent ownership of the corporation. While you may restrict shares through the by-laws of the corporation, you may transfer ownership of all or part of the corporation relatively easily. A corporation can exist forever apart from its founders. When you want to sell your business, the corporation provides a much more salable package than a sole proprietorship or partnership.

The corporation is the only entity that can deduct as business expenses many benefits such as health care and retirement plans. These expenses reduce the taxable profits of the corporation and give employees valuable benefits which are not taxed as income.

TiP *Double taxation* occurs when the earnings of a corporation are taxed twice, both as the Net Income of the corporation and again as the dividends distributed to the stockholders. Your accountant can advise you on ways to avoid double taxation.

TiP Not all companies are eligible to be every type of corporation. Some states require specific businesses such as banks, railroads, public utilities, health care, or law to be specific types of corporations. Consult an attorney and accountant before making a decision about which type of corporation is permitted and right for your business.

Incorporating a business carries many advantages. One of the most significant advantages is tremendous financial flexibility in raising capital. A corporation has the ability to provide you the capital structure you need to accomplish your goals.

Once investors, lenders, or stockholders get involved, you need to protect your own interests from those who might seek to take control, ownership, or profits. Even though you start a corporation, nothing guarantees you can continue as a director, officer, employee, stockholder, or even recipient of dividends. Nothing guarantees you will continue to be included in the inner workings of the business. You can be squeezed out in many ways, some direct and others very subtle. To recognize the various squeeze-out methods and protect against them, rely on an experienced business attorney. These professionals make sure your interests are protected before you commit to take on other owners or investors. Continue to consult an attorney as time passes and the venture changes; especially if it becomes more valuable.

Check Your Knowledge ✔   **Software Solutions, Inc.**

What did you recommend that Software Solutions do?
a. Become an LLC and then go public.
b. Become a C corporation and then go public.
c. Go public as an S corporation to avoid the expense and paperwork involved in switching.

What Software Solutions did: To go public they had to give up their S status and become a C corporation. The corporation needed to have far more than the seventy-five stockholders permitted by S regulations. LLCs cannot sell shares, they can only take on additional members.

What you should know: Determine from the beginning whether you will need to raise funds in the future, how much and what kind, and choose a corporate structure that will best allow you to do so.

Limited Liability Company (LLC)

The LLC is neither a corporation nor a partnership. This type of business entity, when properly structured, is designed to combine the benefits of corporate liability protection with the "pass through" tax treatment and management flexibility of a partnership.

TiP An LLC operating agreement, a critical document, should be written by an attorney. Its terms have a profound long-term effect and need to be carefully thought out.

Because it is the newest form of doing business, the laws concerning LLCs differ from state to state. You need to seek the guidance of an attorney before adopting this form of business.

To form an LLC, you must file articles of organization with the secretary of state. In addition, an operating agreement must detail how you will operate the business, share profits and losses, induct new members, and treat retiring and resigning ones.

The control of an LLC is in the hands of the owners, called *members*, and should be defined in your operating agreement. Members elect managers from among the membership or from outside. The operating agreement will determine not only how your management is selected but also the extent of the manager's authority. It could be that only day-to-day operations are within the control of the manager and that the members as a whole will make all other decisions. The required number of members varies from state to state. Some states require at least two members to use this legal structure while other states permit only one.

One principal advantage of an LLC occurs at tax time. The LLC may elect to be treated as a partnership. Like a partnership, then, the income and loss earned by the LLC are passed through to the members and reported on their respective tax returns. If no election is made, the LLC is taxed like a corporation.

The advantage of an LLC compared to a partnership is that the members' liability for the debts of the LLC is limited to the extent of their investment in the business.

Transfer of ownership in an LLC requires the unanimous consent of all members unless the operating agreement provides otherwise. Thus, you have maximum flexibility regarding accepting new members and withdrawing or retiring existing members.

LLCs do not exist perpetually. Unless the operating agreement provides for its continued existence, an LLC ends upon the death of a member. Most states require a stated period of existence.

Since it is a collection of individuals, an LLC suffers from the same limitations on raising capital as partnerships. It does, however, have a method to raise modest amounts by requiring initial contributions or buy-ins by new members if your operating agreement provides this option.

Check Your Knowledge ✓   **The Doctors' Office**

What did you recommend that Doctors' Office do?
a. Keep things as they are—there is little danger in this situation.
b. Dissolve the partnership and form an LLC with the doctors as members.
c. Dissolve the partnership and become sole proprietors.
d. Dissolve the partnership and become a corporation.

What the Doctors' Office did: When the state in which they practiced finally adopted laws permitting physicians to practice in a professional corporation, they jumped at the chance. They rebelled against the corporate structure, however, hating the fact that one had to be president, and thinking the record keeping was "nonsense." Today they are happy as an LLC. They have hired a professional office manager who runs the practice administratively. They all participate in the big decisions after an executive committee appointed from their own members makes recommendations. Their personal assets are insulated from liability and income is taxed only once.

What you should know: Sometimes it is worth changing the legal structure of a business. Liability should be a critical factor in these decisions.

Nonprofit

Some of the most profitable corporations in this country are *nonprofits*. The classification as a nonprofit does not mean that the business does not make a profit nor does it mean that it tried but failed to make a profit. It simply means that the Internal Revenue Service has determined that it has filed for and meets the requirements as an organization that provides a service to the community for certain purposes. These purposes may be religious, charitable, scientific, testing for public safety, literacy, educational, fostering a national or international amateur sports competition, or the prevention of cruelty to children or animals.

TIP The nonprofit approval process is long and complex. Seek the assistance of a knowledgeable professional, generally a certified public accountant or an attorney.

TIP While professional advice may be costly, do not select your attorney or accountant based upon costs alone. Consider also the attorney's experience, area of expertise, work ethic, and compatibility with your company.

Nonprofits are prohibited from distributing Net Income to owners, members, directors, or officers but they may pay fair compensation to their employees. Contributions to nonprofits are tax deductible by the donor, which is a great advantage in raising funds.

Form a nonprofit in compliance with appropriate state laws and then seek IRS classification.

Nonprofits are controlled just as other corporations by a board of directors, but they have no stockholders. A nonprofit does not pay income tax, but it does file informational returns. Just as with profit corporations, the nonprofit offers insulation from liability to its board, officers, and employees.

Since it is not always easy to determine whether a business concept will be eligible under state and federal regulations for nonprofit status, you should contact a lawyer to learn more about nonprofit organizations.

The Reality Checks *Legal Structures* and *Costs of Selecting and Forming a Business Structure* should give you a good starting point so you can engage your attorney and accountant in a thoughtful discussion. You and they will certainly want to consider other aspects of your business structure than those suggested here, but these will give you some idea of what's most important. Don't delay making that critical decision.

Reality Check ✔

Legal Structures

Use the steps below to help decide what legal form of business is best for you. Then get help from an accountant or lawyer. The rules of each state differ so you may need assistance in your final decision. Ultimately, however, this decision is yours—you need to be informed. In Step 1, answer the questions as honestly as you can, given what you know about yourself and your business right now. This will help you think about what is important to you in choosing a legal structure. There are no right or wrong answers, only your opinion on the topic. Then use your answers in Step 1 to help you complete Step 2.

Step 1 Answer the questions on the chart below by circling *Yes*, *Maybe*, or *No*.

a. Do you want to have control over your business's direction and decision-making?	Yes	Maybe	No
b. Are you willing to give up some control for the potential of higher rewards?	Yes	Maybe	No
c. Do you care about how the profits are disbursed—whether they flow directly to you, or whether they go to shareholders, or whether they are retained in the business? Keep in mind that this decision has tax implications.	Yes	Maybe	No
d. Are you willing to be personally liable for debts or injuries caused by doing business?	Yes	Maybe	No
e. Will you need to raise money from outside sources to get your business started or help it grow?	Yes	Maybe	No
f. Do you have time to fulfill extra reporting requirements needed for some types of business structures?	Yes	Maybe	No
g. Will you need to have flexibility to change the business structure as your business changes and grows?	Yes	Maybe	No
h. Do you care if the business survives after your death or the death of one of the other owners?	Yes	Maybe	No
i. Will your profit margins be so thin or your need for profit so high that tax considerations will drive the type of business structure you choose?	Yes	Maybe	No
j. Might your business qualify to be a nonprofit organization?	Yes	Maybe	No

Legal Structures continued

Step 2 Circle the cells within the Legal Structures Comparison Table below that most reflect your concerns based on the questions in Step 1 above.

Legal Structures Comparison Table

	Sole Proprietor	Partnership	Corporation	S Corporation	Limited Liability Company (LLC)	Nonprofit Corporation
a. Do I control the business?	Yes. You are the big cheese.	Only if your share of the partnership is greater than 50%.	Only if you control more than 50% of the shares of stock.	Only if you control more than 50% of the shares of stock.	Only if your share of the LLC is greater than 50%.	Only if you control a majority of votes on the board of directors.
b. What happens to the profits?	Profits are all yours.	Profits are split between you and your partner(s) as detailed in your partnership agreement.	Profits belong to the corporation and may be paid to shareholders as dividends.	Profits go directly to the owners, split as a percentage of shares owned.	Profits are split as detailed in your operating agreement.	Profits must be retained. So in some sense, there are no profits.
c. Am I responsible for financial obligations?	Yes. You have unlimited personal liability for the business.	Yes. You and your partner(s) have unlimited personal liability.	Not directly. Liability is generally limited to the assets of the business.	Not directly. Liability is generally limited to the assets of the business.	Your liability is limited to the assets you invested in the business.	Not directly. Liability is generally limited to the assets of the business.
d. Is money relatively easy to raise?	No.	No.	Yes. Money is easier to raise.	Yes. Money is easier to raise.	Somewhat. Money can be raised from members.	If approved, nonprofits can receive tax-deductible donations.
e. Is it relatively easy and inexpensive to get started and fulfill the legal requirements on an ongoing basis?	Yes. Using this structure is relatively easy.	Yes. Using this structure is relatively easy, but a partnership agreement should be prepared by an attorney.	More difficult. Corporations require some investment in time and money to start and to fulfill legal obligations.	More difficult. Corporations require some investment in time and money to start and to fulfill legal obligations.	No. LLCs are arguably the most complex and expensive business structure because of the operating agreement.	More difficult. Corporations require some investment in time and money and the IRS approval process is complex.
f. Can I easily change the legal structure of the business?	Yes. But it requires closing the existing form and starting another.	Yes. But it requires closing the existing form and starting another.	No. It is difficult to change from a corporate to non-corporate structure.	No. It is difficult to change from a corporate to non-corporate structure.	No. It is very difficult to change from an LLC to another structure.	No. It is difficult to change from a nonprofit to a profit structure.
g. What happens if one of the owners dies?	Your business dies when you die.	Partnerships die, unless otherwise specified in the partnership agreement.	Corporations survive the death of an owner.	Corporations survive the death of an owner.	LLCs can survive if specified by agreement or vote.	Nonprofits survive the death of an owner.
h. What tax advantages and/or disadvantages exist?	Taxes are easy. Allows fewer expense deductions.	Taxes are fairly easy. Allows fewer expense deductions.	Double taxation is a disadvantage. Allows more expense deductions.	No double taxation. Allows more expense deductions.	No double taxation. Allows fewer expense deductions.	No taxes, but still must file informational returns.

Step 3 Review the circles on the table to determine which structure delivers the most positive impact for your business. Take this information to a trusted legal adviser for review.

Reality Check ✔	**Costs of Selecting and Forming a Business Structure**

Think about costs associated with selecting your business structure. The following are possible costs. Put a check by each that will or might apply. Then indicate whether you already know these amounts or need further research.

	Already Know	**Need to Research**
❑ Consulting with an attorney and accountant	❑	❑
❑ Preparing business entity documents	❑	❑
❑ Filing business entity documents	❑	❑

Financial Facts Worksheet

Action Step 7.2 asks you to estimate the costs associated with your business's legal structure on your Financial Facts Worksheets.

No matter your corporate structure, you will face a variety of managerial tasks to keep your business competitive. The rest of this module will help you determine the organizational needs that your business concept, legal structure, marketing strategies, and growth plans will require.

Managing Key Business Functions

In almost all businesses, routine functions have to be performed. You have to pay bills, track finances, recruit people, make sales, purchase supplies, and obey regulations—just to list a few tasks that enable a business to run smoothly.

Moreover, every business has some special tasks that are critical to its success. Bakeries must remember to order flour. High-tech companies must create innovative products. Manufacturing companies have to maintain inventory.

You, as the entrepreneur, need to decide how to accomplish all these tasks. Some small businesses flounder because critical tasks aren't completed. Imagine forgetting to invoice your customers or to buy raw materials to manufacture.

Keys to your success will be to figure out:

What key tasks have to be completed.

Who will complete them.

How best to complete them.

How to evaluate results.

TIP Entrepreneurs are especially prone to distraction. Figure out ways to remember your most important tasks.

One of the most important decisions you'll make is whether to manage your enterprise yourself or to hire managers to run the business with you. You may have good reasons for doing either. Some businesses are too small or too new to need a full-fledged management team. Other businesses need to ramp up quickly to meet market demand, seize a competitive advantage, build economies of scale, or meet investor recommendations.

Sometimes, adding just one or two other people will enable you to accomplish the work. Often entrepreneurs in these situations hire people who complement their own abilities, providing skills or experience they don't have themselves.

The next section will provide you with a list of the common functions businesses need. The Reality Check *Management Function Analysis* will help you identify your company's specialized needs. By thinking through your needs, you'll be better able to determine whether to fly solo or hire others.

Your role as entrepreneur will evolve as your business grows. The tasks you perform early in your business's life cycle may not be the ones you focus on as your business grows.

Your role and your management needs may change in these ways:

Stages of Business

Initial conception stage – You manage on your own, focusing mostly on identifying business opportunities to pursue.

Start-up stage – After the business is launched, cash is tight and you continue to manage things on your own. Your work focuses on modifying the products and services, experimenting with marketing tactics, and attracting customers.

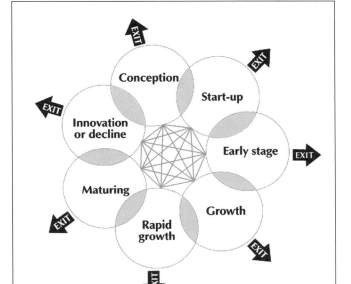

Early stage – The company has attracted customers and seeks to increase sales. You begin to rely on other management members and key personnel. You might hire a professional marketer at this point.

Growth stage – The markets are established but the company may experience continual cash flow needs. You add new investors, customers, and staff quickly. You might rely on an operations manager. Sales management becomes critical. Manufacturing companies usually need to hire a production manager in this stage.

Rapid growth stage – When the business outpaces industry growth rates and has established itself as a viable ongoing concern, you will probably need to put a professional management team in place.

Maturity stage – The company has well-established markets with multiple products and services in the maturity stage. It experiences increased competition and saturation of the market. You work with a full management team to fulfill the strategic plan of the company and preserve the business so it will continue to be healthy and increase in value.

Innovation or decline stage – The final stage of any business emerges when it must innovate or lose market share. All levels of the organization must be actively involved in innovation. You and your management team must help drive change or the organization may die.

The Reality Check *Management Function Analysis* provides an excellent way for you to ensure that you don't miss some important function you ought to cover—or plan to cover in the future.

Reality Check ✓   **Management Function Analysis**

Step 1 Determine required business functions. Look at the list of required business functions and determine when your business will need them and who will do each.

Required Business Functions

Function	Description	Needed Now	Needed Soon	Who Will Do This? *Persons or Job Titles*
Create Mission and Values	Determine the direction of the business, its mission and values.			
Overall Management	Manage all operations and be responsible for all outcomes.			
Marketing	Understand industry and customer motivations, develop brand image, create promotions and advertising.			
Sales	Organize and/or conduct sales operations, including forecasting and monitoring.			
Administration	Organize administrative functions, purchase supplies and equipment, maintain records.			
Finances and Accounting	Seek funding for business operations, handle bookkeeping, pay taxes, manage cash flow, monitor and analyze financial performance.			
Technology and Communications	Manage technology, Internet access, Web site, phones, and building security.			
Maintenance	Keep machines running, keep space clean and safe, maintain buildings and grounds.			

Management Function Analysis continued

Step 2 Identify common business functions your business will use. Look at this list of common business functions and determine when your business will need them and who will do each. If a function does not apply to your business (for example, *manufacture* may not apply to a service business), go to the next function.

Common Business Functions

Function	Description	Needed Now	Needed Soon	Who Will Do This? *Persons or Job Titles*
Product Development	Develop new products or services to sell to customers. Research, innovate, and/or develop.			
Manufacture	Manufacture items. Create products or services.			
Manage Projects	Manage client projects or in-house change efforts.			
Human Resource Management	Develop job descriptions, recruit, hire, find workspace, implement regulations, develop policies, and handle compensation and benefits.			
Direct and Motivate People	Motivate and reward, deal with performance problems, communicate direction, delegate tasks, monitor performance, create shared goals, promote teamwork.			
Training and Development	Train and develop workers so they can perform their jobs and are motivated to stay with your company.			
Distributor	Distribute or ship products. Organize service delivery.			

Management Function Analysis continued

Step 3 List your company's most critical business functions. Make a list of your company's most critical business functions based on the first two charts. Determine who will do them and when.

Common Business Functions

Function	Description	Needed Now	Needed Soon	Who Will Do This? *Persons or Job Titles*

How many managers do you need now?

How many managers do you need soon?

Management Function Analysis continued

Step 4 Write an action plan to meet the demands of three of these business functions.

Your Action Plan

What did you learn?	What will you do?	When will you do it?

Now that you have a clear idea of the management functions to cover in your business, consider what each management team member—whether a full-time employee or an occasional adviser—might cost you. Think about costs associated with the management team members your business will need over the first three years. Include not only salaries but also benefits or ownership interests you may have to give up to get them to join your team. Use the Reality Check *Costs of Management Team Members* to list the costs you need to keep in mind.

Reality Check ✓

Costs of Management Team Members

The following lists possible members you may need. Put a check by each that will or might apply. Indicate whether you already know these amounts or still need to research them.

	Already Know	Need to Research
❑ Chief operating officer	❑	❑
❑ Chief financial officer	❑	❑
❑ Sales manager	❑	❑
❑ Marketing director	❑	❑
❑ Manufacturing/production manager	❑	❑
❑ Human resources manager	❑	❑
❑ Other_____	❑	❑

Financial Facts Worksheet

Action Step 7.2 asks you to estimate the costs of your management team on your Financial Facts Worksheets. Now let's consider how your business might benefit from adding a board of directors or advisory board.

Board of Directors or Advisory Board

At every stage of your company's life, you will need input from inside and outside the company. If your company is organized as a corporation, it must have a board of directors. The board is the managing agent for your company. It makes big-picture decisions and elects officers. In many states one person can be the sole owner of the stock in a corporation and the sole director on the board. A full board of directors, however, brings the advantage of ideas from many minds. The board of directors usually includes key members of the management team, including the CEO, investors, and independent outside advisers.

Some prospective board members may be reluctant to serve since the trend by creditors or disgruntled stockholders is to sue board members for their decisions or lack of oversight. Insurance is available and perhaps necessary to persuade members to serve on a formal board of directors. Others might be persuaded to serve on an informal advisory board if they refuse to take a more formal position.

Tip After you have established a board of directors or advisory board, use it! Have regular board meetings with specific agendas, outcomes, and purposes. Talk with directors between meetings about management issues. It exists to offer guidance and direction.

Unlike a formal board of directors, an advisory board is usually a group of business experts who do not directly work for the company they are advising. Entrepreneurs use advisory boards in many ways, but the ultimate goal is to get ideas, advice, and direction from these experts.

Advisory board members may be bankers, marketing consultants, industry experts, financial consultants, customers, or other successful entrepreneurs. They may meet monthly, quarterly, or as you need them. They are usually compensated in some way, although compensation is small—a meal during the meeting or a small payment per meeting. Few advisers agree to give advice for only the money. Many entrepreneurs attribute their success to the help they received from mentors and advisers. Now, they feel it is their turn to give back and help someone else.

Loss-of-Control Phobia

Business owners may view a board as a bureaucratic hindrance or threat to their control, says Jana Matthews, founder of Boulder Quantum Ventures, a Boulder, Colorado, firm that helps CEOs become better leaders and achieve long-term growth for their companies.

"To avoid that perceived loss of control, some entrepreneurs will not appoint a board of directors at all, or they populate it with friends and family who won't give them a hard time or ask difficult questions," explains Matthews.

Failing to form a board or allowing it only rubber stamp approvals provides little value to your company. Just as you need to find and hire people smarter than you, you also need to find board members who complement your weaknesses and can help your company grow.

"The right board of directors can open new doors for you and can help you avoid trouble," Matthews says. "Yet you'll need to invest some time and effort to make sure you choose the kind of board members who can add value to your company."

An advisory board is most useful in providing strategic ideas or feedback on increasing revenue and building your business, explains Auren Hoffman, a serial entrepreneur and chairman of the Stonebrick Group, a San Francisco investment firm.

TIP *We find comfort among those who agree with us—growth among those who don't.*
— Frank A. Clark

Advisory board members are not involved in the details of your company, he adds: "You go to them, as you would an old high school friend whom you don't see often, to catch up and pick their brains—for a view of your landscape from 20,000 feet."

In contrast, a board of directors has legal authority. Members can provide guidance on a day-to-day basis about how to navigate choppy waters, such as a lawsuit or the sale of your company. "These people give you a view of your business from 200 feet," Hoffman adds.

Give careful thought to whether you need a board of directors or advisory board. Remember, certain corporate structures require a board of directors who will have legal obligations to fulfill. Use the Reality Check *Costs of Board of Directors and/or Advisory Board* to identify costs associated with the type of board your business concept calls for.

Reality Check

Costs of Board of Directors and/or Advisory Board

Think about costs associated with your board of directors and/or advisory board. The following are possible costs. Put a check by each that will or might apply. Then indicate whether you already know the amounts or still need to research them.

	Already Know	Need to Research
❏ Fees or honorariums	❏	❏
❏ Meals	❏	❏
❏ Meeting room rentals	❏	❏
❏ Travel	❏	❏
❏ Support personnel	❏	❏
❏ Materials	❏	❏

Benefiting from Advisory Boards

"Advisers are essential for most entrepreneurs, many of whom prefer not to go it entirely alone," says Barnett C. Helzberg, Jr., former chairman of Helzberg Diamonds®, a family jewelry business begun in 1915 and sold to Warren Buffett's Berkshire Hathaway® in 1995. Founder of the Helzberg Entrepreneurial Mentoring Program in Kansas City, Missouri, Helzberg shares six tips for forming and benefiting from an advisory board.

Start slowly – Helzberg started with one advisory board member, someone he had known and trusted since childhood.

Limit the terms – Asking candidates to serve for a specific tenure is a wise move. If your company's needs change or one doesn't fit, you won't have to discharge board members.

Consider board chemistry – Recruit members who will work well with each other.

Allow prospective members to meet each other – "I learned this lesson the hard way, when I named my second board member and failed to inform my old friend," Helzberg says, explaining that his original board member was upset. Happily, a lunch between the two rectified the situation.

Keep it small, flexible, and first rate – Helzberg had three board members. "Although I never had to replace anyone, I do admire those entrepreneurs who have replaced me on their boards when their business changed," he says.

Pay your advisers – Payment isn't always possible for young companies. But pay your board members when you can, because it obligates them.

"The best advice comes from knowledgeable third parties who aren't afraid to tell it like it is," Helzberg adds. "Cherish these people. Their expertise and candor will help you build your company. Play your cards right, and they will also become friends who will help you build your life."

Financial Facts Worksheet

Action Step 7.2 asks you to estimate the costs associated with an advisory board or board of directors on your Financial Facts Worksheets.

Setting Your Organizational Culture

Some companies compete on price. Others compete by having high-quality products, superior service, or unique customer support. You have a myriad of ways to create a successful company with a competitive advantage. One of the most important ways to compete is to create an organizational culture that breeds productivity, motivation, and respect. Some companies simply outperform their competition because they create such a culture.

But creating a healthy organizational culture isn't just good for the bottom line, it's also imperative for quality of life—yours, your employees', and your community. Businesses that build healthy cultures are more fun to work in, more interesting, more motivating, and provide better opportunities for all involved.

"Our people are our product," says founder Joseph Sansone, referring to Pediatric Services of America, Inc., nurses and therapists who provide care to homebound ill children.

Sansone believes that leading people is as much an art as a set of principles and tactics. Engrossed in their vision, entrepreneurs often believe people will automatically follow them. "That doesn't happen," Sansone says. "To turn vision into a company—an abstraction into a tangible—entrepreneurs must be leaders of people."

The Golden Rule of Leadership

Many ideas about developing a positive corporate culture were inspired by Ewing Marion Kauffman, successful entrepreneur and founder of the Kauffman Foundation, the world's leading foundation devoted to the success of entrepreneurs. Kauffman founded a pharmaceutical company, Marion Laboratories, Inc., by operating out of the basement of his modest home.

By 1989, when Marion Laboratories was sold to Merrell Dow, it had become a globally diversified pharmaceutical giant with annual sales of nearly $1 billion. Kauffman followed his philosophy of "treating others as you would like to be treated" in his leadership, hiring, and communication practices, which had an enormous impact upon the success of the company.

Another guiding philosophy of Kauffman's was that "those who produce should share in the rewards." Kauffman's commitment to this principle can be seen in the 300 or so millionaires created when Marion Laboratories merged with Merrell Dow. Many senior managers, plant operators, and clerical workers who had been with the company for years received great wealth from their stock ownership.

Check Your Knowledge ✔

The Art of Leadership

Pediatric Services of America, Inc., has grown from being a regional distributor of oxygen equipment to a national home healthcare provider. When founder Joseph Sansone started the company, he had to make sure that all the employees knew their job.

Which of the following offers the most important advice you could recommend to Sansone to ensure that his receptionist could do the job? Circle one.
a. Make sure the receptionist understands all aspects of the job; for example, focusing on how the phone works, how to switch calls, how to answer it.
b. Trust that the receptionist knows how to handle these simple tasks, and praise good work when it is performed as expected.
c. Role play with the receptionist, and provide feedback on exactly how to handle the responsibilities of the job.
d. Focus on how to communicate the company's business and clarify the receptionist's role in making the company successful.

Remember that employees have different perceptions of your organization. A receptionist may think only of answering phones and greeting visitors. A janitor may only see the trash. Salespeople may only look at which sales generate the highest commission. Supervisors may only consider their departmental budgets. "In contrast, the entrepreneurial leader must define each individual job as an element of the overall purpose of the company and not as an end in itself," says Sansone.

"The way the phone is answered communicates the company's business. Sales produce a profit for shareholders. Budgets ensure fiscal responsibility, and clearing the trash keeps the work force healthy and productive. The leader must instill in each worker an understanding that the end result depends upon everyone in the organization working together."

In the Check Your Knowledge *The Art of Leadership*, did you choose *d* as Sansone would have? Helping employees see their role in the business's larger mission can automatically improve how they do their jobs.

Communicating Values

Successful entrepreneurs don't take their organizational culture for granted. They build the culture they want from the very beginning by clarifying their own values, formalizing them in a written form, and remembering to live them as they make decisions in their business.

Some people think that communicating values involves telling employees what to do, creating policy manuals, and setting rules. But values are communicated more forcefully in day-to-day actions. If you want an organization that listens to customers, you have to be a role model by listening to your employees, your vendors, and your customers. If you want a business that is driven to increase revenues, you have to set sales goals, initiate brainstorming sessions on sales-related issues, and reward those who help increase the sales numbers. If you want to develop a company where teamwork is valued, you have to be a team player yourself.

Ewing Marion Kauffman's philosophy that "others should be treated as you would like to be treated" and "those who produce should share in the results" established a healthy working culture at Marion Laboratories.

Use the Reality Check *Organizational Values* to begin thinking about the values you want to pervade your organizational culture.

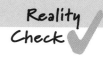 **Organizational Values**

When setting values for your business, consider customers, shareholders, employees, and the community. Values may include but are not limited to accountability, ethics, work/life balance, results orientation, or work environment.

What are the key values you want your business to embody?	How will you live this value yourself?	How will you encourage your employees to live this value?

Creating Clarity

From a firm foundation in values, organizations thrive when they create a sense of clarity about **what** needs to get done, **who** needs to do it, and **how** it should get done.

With clarity, everyone can pull together in common cause. Without clarity, wasted effort and chaos ensue. In his analysis of Ewing Marion Kauffman's company, Marion Laboratories, Gerald W. Holder attributed much of the strength of the organization to an entrepreneurial leadership team that focused significant energy on creating clarity throughout the work force, as embodied in the following four imperatives:

Clarity of purpose – People know why the organization exists. They need a reason to give their enthusiastic support. People want to be part of an organization that is the first or best at something, does what no other organization has ever done, helps people solve problems, or helps people lead better, safer, healthier, or more productive lives. Do not expect anyone else to get excited about "making you rich." As one entrepreneur put it, "I want my people to get rich because I have set up a system whereby if they get rich, so do I."

Clarity of direction – People know where the business is headed. Then they will know the kinds of skills and talent they need to bring to the company. For example, Nina and Alexei Vladimir added several new organizational team members when Software Solutions went public. To ensure that all the employees knew how they fit in the company's new high-growth phase, they held a company-wide retreat. Although the half-day retreat began with high-energy, team-building activities, Nina closed the meeting with a clearly focused presentation that communicated the leadership's vision for the company's future and each team member's role in that vision.

Clarity of structure – People know their roles and responsibilities as well as those of others in the organization. This knowledge and confidence allows them to concentrate on their own job and give it their full energy while recognizing the interdependence of the employee and management teams.

In a rapidly growing new venture, promotion opportunities are likely to abound. For example, a sales representative may become a manager in a very short time. Discuss your organization's structure and possibility for advancement with potential employees. Some may accept a low-paying position at first if they know more responsibility and compensation may occur soon.

Clarity of measurement – People know how results are measured. You should explain to your organization **what** is being measured, **how** it is being measured, and **why** it is being measured. This clarity lets them know where to focus their effort.

TiP Make sure people have access to information so they can measure their own performance. This freedom cultivates healthy productivity in which employees understand what they are working towards and why.

Setting Goals and Evaluating Results

With an eye toward clarity, entrepreneurs set goals for the organization, for themselves, and for their employees. They then measure the results and hold people accountable, including themselves. You can use many types of goals and base them at the organizational, departmental, team, or individual levels.

Organizational and departmental goals cover profitability targets, sales targets, inventory targets, financial ratios, productivity, customer satisfaction, quality, health and safety, environmental, community, employee satisfaction, turnover, human-resource targets, government regulations, and waste.

Individual and team goals may focus on the deadlines met, on-budget completion, number of units produced, specific tasks to be completed, completion rates, or time on task.

Feedback improves behavior when it is delivered in a manner that is useful. Don't set goals unless you plan to follow-up by measuring results and making improvements. One of the most important things you can do is to figure out your business's most critical goals, develop measurements for those goals, measure the gaps between desired and actual performance, and implement a strategy to close the gaps.

Goals for your business should be SMART:
- **S**pecific – Clearly defined by those who have the knowledge about their impact
- **M**easurable – Quantifiably defined in such a way as to gauge progress
- **A**chievable – Challenging and rewarding, but still within reach
- **R**elevant – Tied to current critical tasks and abilities of the team
- **T**ime-based – Linked to an agreed-upon timeline

In the Reality Check *Management Function Analysis,* you examined your organization's most important functions. The Reality Check *SMART Goal Setting* asks you to create a set of goals that can be used to guide your organization within those functions.

Reality Check ✔ SMART Goal Setting

Identify three specific goals you want to set immediately for your business. Write the first draft of the goal in the Original Goal box in the left-hand column, then check to see if it is specific, measurable, attainable, relevant, and timely. If the goal does not fulfill all these requirements, revise it in the Revised Goal box.

Goal Statement	Specific	Measurable	Achievable	Relevant	Time-based
a. Original Goal					
a. Revised Goal					
b. Original Goal					
b. Revised Goal					
c. Original Goal					
c. Revised Goal					

You will set some goals at the beginning of your venture, but you should remember to revisit those goals periodically, use them as benchmarks to measure progress, and set new goals as you accomplish previous ones.

Recruiting and Hiring Capable, Self-Motivated People

To grow your business, you will most likely want to increase the number of employees or contractors with whom you work. Your success will depend on your ability to put together a team of highly qualified people who are committed to the goals of your firm. Market demands, product or service uniqueness, or profitability goals are important. Your team will help you meet them.

You need to plan a method for recruiting and hiring the very best people you can find. They should have not only great technical skills but also the motivation to work with you to make your business a success. You need people who are willing to build things from scratch, work hard, deal with uncertainty, and be flexible. These may not be the same skills and abilities you will need from employees as your business approaches a more stable operating stage.

TiP Without an entrepreneurial organization of productive people, your business will only grow as far as your own abilities can take it.

Ewing Marion Kauffman offered his own personal twist to the talent equation with this advice to entrepreneurs, "Hire people who are smarter than you! In doing so, you prevent limiting the organization to the level of your own ability…and you grow the capabilities of your company." Kauffman also said, "If you hire people you consider smarter than you, you are more likely to listen to their thoughts and ideas, and this is the best way to expand on your own capabilities and build the strength of your company." Resist the urge to hire people just because they share your personality traits or background. You benefit from having different points of view to challenge and develop your company into the future.

If your business must rely on a productive team of individuals in addition to you, hiring self-motivated people must be part of your overall business plan. Finding qualified candidates today is difficult because of global competition, changing work force demographics, and workers' values. Employers are learning to be open-minded and more flexible regarding employment policies and working hours. New strategies include job sharing, working at home, using temporary help and contract labor, and hiring the disabled and retired.

TiP *It used to be that the head of the organization was the intellectual one who made all the decisions, who came up with the good ideas, good thoughts, and good suggestions. That's not true anymore. Today you will find ability at all levels that you should be drawing on.*
— Ewing Marion Kauffman

In a very successful medium-sized consulting firm, the managers place "making money" fifth on their list of priorities. Unsurpassed customer service and employee satisfaction are among their primary goals. They turned their management chart upside down; the management serves its employees. They hire self-motivated employees and deliberately foster innovation among them. The results are increasing profits year after year, outpacing industry averages.

These nine key steps can help you find the right person to fill a position in your company:
1. Identify your need to hire a new employee.
2. Analyze the job thoroughly.
3. Write a job description for the position based on your job analysis.
4. Determine the salary for the position.
5. Decide where and how to find qualified applicants (for example, classified advertising—both print and online, networking, temporary employment agencies, headhunters).
6. Collect and review applications and resumes and select the most qualified candidates based on the job description.

7. Check references.
8. Interview candidates, keeping in mind the interviewing and hiring suggestions below.
9. Hire the best person for the job.

Interviewing and hiring employees can be difficult and time-consuming. You can gain confidence in your final decisions by following some of these hiring guidelines:

Applications – Before interviewing applicants, consider having them complete and sign an employment application form, even if they have a resume. As a legal document, the application form must conform to state and federal regulations. For example, it generally must specify if employment with your firm is "at-will," which means that employment can be terminated at any time. The application form must give the employer permission to verify information submitted by the prospective employee. Human resources consultants can assist you with developing legal applications.

Screening – Save time conducting interviews by screening applicants beforehand using information provided on the application form. Look for unexplained breaks in employment, omissions on the application, career changes, and reasons for leaving other employers. Salary history, professional affiliations, and overall professionalism in completing the form can also give clues about the applicant.

Interviewing – Don't rely solely on the interview as the critical factor in hiring. Research shows that human beings aren't very good at making judgments about people from interviews. Determine what you are looking for and develop interview questions in advance. Develop questions that ask interviewees to tell you how they have responded to real workplace situations. Ask interviewees to describe the situation, the action they took, and the results produced. Ask every interviewee the same set of questions. Rate their answers in a systematic way. Add up the scores. Use this scoring in combination with other information.

Bias – Be aware that we tend to judge people who are similar to ourselves most highly and those who are different from ourselves least highly. This bias can cause you to hire clones who don't add anything to your organization's skill set, which creates a lack of diversity and limits the creativity and decision-making of your company. One of the best ways to determine whether applicants can do the job is to ask them to demonstrate that they can do it. Have writers take writing tests, have sales people simulate a sales call, have managers make difficult case-study decisions.

References – Always check all references and see if you can corroborate the information given with additional research. Studies show that about 30 percent of resumes contain some kind of false information. People who overstate or falsify their job qualifications may cause future harm to an organization or may be poor employees. A criminal background check can provide critical information about a prospective employee. A number of firms provide background checks on employment applicants for a fee.

The law prohibits businesses from asking potential employees certain questions or personal information on applications. Check with your attorney or human resources consultant about permissible questions. In general, questions should relate to the applicant's ability to perform the job. Document all reasons for not offering a position to an apparently qualified applicant. Maintain hiring records for at least seven years.

TiP Resumes are not legal documents. Applications are. Many resumes contain false information that cannot be verified. Information on applications should be verifiable.

Hiring Leaders

Apart from satisfied customers, a growing company needs skilled and competent managers whom founders can trust, says Donna Boone, president of the Potomac Swim School, an indoor swim facility in Ashburn, Virginia.

Boone launched Potomac Swim School in 2003 and plans to open additional swim facilities in the Washington, D.C., area. That means finding managers with whom she feels comfortable sharing authority.

"This is a classic stumbling block for entrepreneurs seeking to expand," Boone says. "In my case, I expect to promote from within, which means I must hire with an eye to developing managerial talent. No longer can I view employees merely as part-time swim instructors. Instead, I must look at them—and treat them—as potential managers, even partners. I must consider whether they are individuals as committed as I am to both swimming and the school and to learning the business from the ground up."

Helping Others Be Successful

To create a successful work environment, you'll need to make a special effort to understand the goals, dreams, and aspirations of the people you hire.

Many people are motivated by money—at least for a period of time. But successful entrepreneurs have learned that the motivational power of money often wears off over time as employees get used to their current level of compensation. Ultimately, most people are motivated more by the work they do or the environment in which they work than by the money they earn. The ability to learn new skills or advance in the company may attract and keep quality employees.

Some new ventures have capitalized upon the desire of some people to work in an informal organizational culture. One entrepreneur attributes much of her success in attracting and retaining excellent employees to the company's relaxed dress code.

Some new ventures have prospered by letting employees work flexible hours. Although this policy will not be practical for all businesses, flexibility makes employees feel valued which leads to a more dedicated workforce. Other employees will be looking for recognition, achievement, growth, autonomy, or even family time. Whatever your organizational needs, remember how greatly motivations vary from person to person and hire accordingly.

In order to respond to the interests and dreams of the people involved in your business, you must treat employees as distinct and separate individuals. Responding to individual needs allows you to create conditions in which an employee's dreams will mesh with yours.

Providing Appropriate Rewards

Many new entrepreneurs think the only rewards that really matter are monetary rewards. But effective reward systems include all forms of monetary compensation plus a wide variety of other things important to people in a work setting. You will be surprised at the benefits your company will reap when you reward good performance with job assignments, recognition, growth and learning, additional responsibility, trust, authority, and autonomy.

The effectiveness of any reward system requires two primary factors:
1. Whether or not the recipient perceives the reward as a positive event.
2. Whether the reward actually encourages the desired behavior.

TIP The people working for you will determine your success. Learn what motivates them.

TIP Employees are your most valuable asset.

To make this two-part principle work for you, try to understand rewards from the perspective of your workers, which is easier said than done. To gain this understanding you should spend time with your team and learn what's important to them. Then monitor the results of your rewards to see if they're really having the effect you want them to have. Remember, what you perceive as rewarding may not be rewarding to your team members.

In order for the reward to be effective, it must not only be seen as a positive by the employee, but it must also encourage the desired behavior. That desired behavior must be consistent with the strategic goals of the company. Your responsibility as the entrepreneur is to make sure the reward system supports the right behaviors.

Many companies reward salespeople for their efforts by basing some or all of their compensation on commission—a percentage of the dollar amount of sales revenues. This reward is a proven winner in most cases, but some companies—notably those that want to have their salespeople act as consultants to their customers—have found that poorly conceived commissions can push salespeople away from their role as consultants, making it less likely that the client will turn to the salesperson in the future, and thus making it much less likely that big-ticket projects will be developed.

Instead of relying on monetary rewards, try some of the following reward systems:

Say thank you – Acknowledge people for their good efforts and superior results. You may be surprised what sincere public acknowledgements will do.

Share the big picture – Employees work smarter and enjoy their work more when they know how their job fits into the company's success. Many companies have found success by sharing their financial performance with employees and showing them how they can help improve it.

Treat them fairly – The world isn't fair, but most people hope for it. Treating people fairly means treating everyone with respect, rewarding successful performance, and critiquing unsuccessful performance.

Create a learning attitude – You're going to make lots of mistakes as an entrepreneur, and that's okay, as long as you learn from them. Your team is going to make mistakes too. Be a role model by discussing your learning process in your mistakes. In fact, discuss learning from mistakes regularly in your meetings. If something is not working, try a new way. Successful entrepreneurs realize the importance of fostering an organizational culture in which people view failure with an experimental, learning attitude.

Three important questions to ask to learn from a mistake are:
• What did we do **right**?
• What did we do **wrong**?
• What can we **improve** next time?

Using these questions at every staff meeting and at the end of every project will help create an organizational culture comfortable with the truth, ready to acknowledge success, and open to learning and improvement.

Celebrate successes – When the company wins a big contract, finishes a large project, or reaches an important milestone, bring everyone together to celebrate. When individuals or teams do well or reach milestones, acknowledge their results as well. People want to feel part of a successful company.

Increase responsibilities – When people perform well, you can provide them with opportunities for advancement, increase their responsibilities, allow them more freedom to make decisions, or give them more budget to control. Beware, of course, not to punish people by overloading them with too much work. Remember not to pigeon-hole people as only being capable of their current responsibilities. If you don't take some risks by enabling your people to try new things, they'll take their skills elsewhere.

Trust and ask for input – When you show others that you trust them, they begin to perform on their own initiative. They create energy for your organization. If you look over their shoulders constantly, you'll get employees who will only do what they are told. Showing trust means asking for help in making important company decisions. In the early 1980s when the Ford Motor Company® changed its management approach, one of the workers said, "I've been working for Ford for twenty-seven years, and before the recent changes, not once in that time did anyone ask me what I thought should be done. For the first time, Ford is now receiving the benefits of my head, not just my hands."

Avoid micromanaging – Remember that any given outcome can be achieved a number of ways. Encourage your associates to experiment, to look for and try different ways to improve a task or solve a difficulty. Don't micromanage! Agree on the goals and let the employees figure out how to meet those goals.

Using Outside Resources

While established companies may have lots of employees, most new ventures cannot afford such a luxury. Still, if you're going to be successful, you'll need to obtain specialized and technical advice on a regular basis. This section will give you hints about the kind of help you may need and will provide you with guidance about how to contract and retain this help.

Some entrepreneurs make the mistake of trying to do everything themselves. Such bootstrapping is often worthwhile because it's economical, but it can be carried too far when you get bogged down in details. You need to find ways to use your time wisely by delegating tasks to others—even if it costs some money to do so.

Taking Time to Network

Since you're going to need to hire people and companies to help do the work, you're going to need advice on who to hire. The Yellow Pages® and online search engines will only provide lists of potential hires. Ultimately, you'll need information about whom you can trust to do what you need them to do. Because one of the best sources of this type of information is from people you know already, the wider your network of knowledgeable business people, the easier it will be for you to get trustworthy referrals, recommendations, and information.

To widen your network, you'll need to spend some of your valuable time with your local chamber of commerce, social or sports clubs, and trade associations. Think about using the Internet to connect with like-minded people or organizations. Use online forums at trade Web sites or join e-mail lists to stay in touch with valuable resources.

Tip The IRS issues specific guidelines to distinguish between a subcontractor and an employee. Information can be found at www.irs.gov.

Selecting Consultants and Contractors

Selecting external support can require lots of effort and create anxiety. New entrepreneurs especially struggle with such decisions because they lack familiarity with the process and the kind of help available. Over time, you will learn how to better assess your needs and the competencies of providers.

For example, Anna Cortez was offered a contract for a large project by a long-term client she was eager to retain. She couldn't immediately handle the work because she was already committed to another project. She considered hiring an employee, forming a strategic alliance with another consultant, selecting a contractor, or simply referring the business to a colleague. She ultimately decided that, as a short-term solution to a one-time project, she would use an outside contractor to begin the new project while she finished the one she was on. She chose an entrepreneur just entering the field whose experience and values aligned with her own company's approach. By doing so, she not only gained the value of additional help, she also retained the client and helped another entrepreneur in the process.

Don't expect to make all the right choices if you're new at selecting consultants and contractors. If one choice does not work, you can change your mind and find another provider. The chart *Selecting Consultants and Contractors* on p. 293 will assist you to think through some of the most important issues as you search for outside help. You can copy it and use it for each outside consultant or contractor as you need it.

Building Your Infrastructure

Infrastructure refers to the outside professionals who help you run your business. You will need legal advice to choose the structure of your business. You will need bankers, insurance agents, human resources support, and a myriad of other skills that you may not want to hire full time. These are the most important outside professionals you may need in your infrastructure:

Legal Professionals

In our highly regulated society, legal requirements are complex and ever-changing. Wise entrepreneurs start with a good business lawyer who can provide specialized advice. Lawyers and other legal professionals can help you deal with a myriad of issues, including selecting a legal form of business, human resource issues, health and safety, copyright and trademark, real estate leases, mergers and acquisitions, partnerships, tax and accounting rules, governmental regulations, liability protection, and contracts of all sorts. In short, get yourself a general business attorney sooner rather than later.

Accountants

Since the lifeblood of your business is money, you're going to need an accountant to help you keep things running smoothly. Fortunately, you can generally rely on the competence of Certified Public Accountants (CPAs), though non-CPAs can provide good service as well. Most new ventures use small accounting firms since they are generally more affordable and responsive than large accounting firms.

If you intend to take your business public, you may want to choose a larger accounting firm to audit the books from the beginning of the venture, to limit any questions that might arise by the Security and Exchange Commission (SEC).

Selecting Consultants and Contractors

Consideration	Questions to Ask Providers	Notes on Each Provider
a. Some external providers do one thing and do it well. Others provide a wide spectrum of services for you to choose from.	What do you typically do for your clients? How do you approach your work? How do you go about assessing my specific needs?	
b. Large external providers may have many areas of expertise but may not give you individual attention. Small external providers may give you individual attention but offer fewer areas of expertise.	What is the size of your firm? What types of accounts do you handle? What percentage of your work is done with companies the size of mine? Who will be handling my account, senior or junior associates?	
c. Firms who have dealt with your type of business, in your geographic area, in your industry, and with the same issues as yours are more likely to have the specific expertise that will help you.	I have this issue _____. How often do you deal with this issue? I'm in this state or town_____. How often do you service businesses in this area? I have this type of business _____. How often do you service businesses in my industry? I'm an entrepreneurial business. How often do you handle an entrepreneurial business?	
d. Some firms may be extremely busy and may not have time to deal immediately with your particular need. Others may generally be more responsive or may have slack in their schedule.	What timeline will you be able to keep in dealing with my work? What happens when I need you? How quickly can you work on my order?	
e. Every organization has different ways of handling its work. You'll want to make sure that the firms you select utilize processes you will be comfortable with. For example, firms differ in their approaches, their values, their concern for others, and their ethics.	Present prospective providers with one or more scenarios and ask how they would respond to those situations and issues. Evaluate their responses to determine if their methods would provide a comfortable fit with your business and your personal methods and values.	
f. Fee structures vary widely between firms, as do their flexibility.	How are you paid? What is the typical range? What special arrangements have you made in the past?	
g. Add other considerations.	Add questions related to these other considerations.	

You may want to verify your responses by checking references or asking your network.

Accountants can provide these helpful services:
- Setting up an accounting system
- Preparing financial statements
- Completing tax forms
- Advising entrepreneurs on purchasing, financing, and other decisions
- Analyzing financial information against industry standards
- Setting financial achievement goals
- Auditing financial statements for accuracy
- Handling routine bookkeeping functions

Many entrepreneurs think if they own 51 percent of the company that they control the company. Instead, the person who controls the money controls the business. To understand why this is true, consider a company that needs to expand to stay viable. If you own 51 percent but can't produce money to expand, you're stuck in a difficult position. Your business either goes under, you sell your stake at a reduced rate, or you allow other investors to come in, thus losing your control. Hire good accountants and lawyers to guide you before these types of situations arise.

Bankers

You will most likely benefit by establishing an early relationship with a banker. Many times, start-up businesses do not qualify for a bank loan because they have no assets or collateral to pledge. The bank can assist you, however, in setting up checking accounts, depositing employee payroll checks, and issuing bankcards such as VISA® or MasterCard®. They also can work with you to qualify for a commercial loan. Banks provide capital in debt form to companies with an established track record such as a company history, historical financial statements, and a good collateral base.

Business Consultants

You might want to use consultants because they are usually less expensive than hiring full-time staff, especially when you need a specific problem solved or have a project requiring an outside expert. Consultants are paid hourly or charge a fixed fee for a project.

Contract with a consultant only after carefully researching and interviewing potential candidates. The best way to find consultants is through referrals from lawyers, accountants, other entrepreneurs, business consultants, trade associations, and Small Business Development Centers.

When selecting consultants, ask for a written proposal for project work. Evaluate proposals by looking for the results the consultants say they will deliver. Interview the consultants to determine if you would be comfortable working with them.

Once you decide on a consultant, create a written agreement that specifies the consultant's responsibilities and objectives, including timeline and compensation. The agreement should address in writing what will happen if either party wishes to end the relationship before the work is finished. It should also specify who owns the completed work product.

Human Resources Consultants

Human resources consultants are helpful in establishing legally compliant employment policies and procedures, writing job descriptions, developing compensation structures, and assessing benefits programs. They can also serve as coaches to management

TiP Avoid consultants who claim they can be all things to all people. Chances are they will try, but they may not be able to provide you with the specific expertise you need.

on dealing effectively with performance problems. Many entrepreneurs also use employment agencies or executive-search firms to find and recruit qualified candidates for new positions.

Marketing Consultants

Marketing consultants are particularly useful if you do not have marketing experience. Advertising and public relations are two specialized fields you may need help with. Determining the competency of advertising and public relations consultants can be a challenge. Look at their track records as well as their costs.

Some areas of marketing require specialized knowledge and skills that general marketing consultants typically do not possess. Perhaps nowhere is this as true as in the field of direct-response marketing, in which professional consultants and operational firms can execute an entire business-to-business direct-marketing program cheaper and more effectively than you can do it yourself. Some firms will help you with total marketing plans while others specialize in certain fields such as direct mail, research, regional studies, and product and brand positioning.

> **TiP** Your new venture may not be able to afford marketing consultants, so you may need to perform advertising and public relations functions in addition to your leadership role.

Web Site Developers

Web sites are a requirement for almost all businesses today. Creating your own Web site from scratch is not for the faint of heart. Even those with programming skills sometimes find the work long and difficult. And because your Web site should reflect the image you want your company to portray, it cannot be left to amateurs. Effective Web sites involve a rare combination of marketing, technical, and graphic-design expertise. Don't just hire someone to put up a bulletin board for you on the Web. The best Web sites require constant updating and attention. Make sure your Web developer will set it up so you can make modifications easily without extensive technical knowledge. Also, make sure they'll be around to maintain it and teach you how to make it work.

Other External Advisers to Utilize

Consultants of many kinds abound in the world of business. Contracting with a consultant to advise on specific issues can be a very valuable use of resources. The following consultants may also provide insights for your infrastructure.

Risk-Management Advisers – The many risks inherent in business operations include loss from fire, flood, embezzlement, bombs, or theft, as well as other types of legal liabilities. The two major risks that owners need to cover are property loss and liability for injuries. Find and work with a good independent business insurance broker to protect your company against risk.

> **TiP** Experts forecast that more than half of all new business owners have not purchased business insurance. A good business insurance broker who can help protect your company against risk is an essential part of your infrastructure.

Governmental Agencies – The government can provide you with help and information, and the costs for this assistance are usually quite low, sometimes even free. Some agencies frequented by entrepreneurs include the National Institute of Standards and Technology (NIST), the Manufacturing Extension Partnership (MEP), the Small Business Administration (SBA), and the Patent Office. Governmental data banks and research exchanges also contain large deposits of information.

Sales Representatives – A sales force can be expensive for a new business, so many entrepreneurs contract with representatives. Using manufacturer's reps can help you keep down the cost of an internal sales force. You considered whether you need sales reps as part of your distribution channel in Module 5.

Manufacturing Subcontractors – Thousands of firms exist solely to produce goods for others. You can concentrate on marketing and sales when you hire an outside company to manufacture your goods.

Engineering or Design Firms – You can contract with engineers to solve a technical problem. You can contract with graphic designers to improve the packaging or look of a product. Contracting with outside designers or engineers saves you the cost of keeping these skills in-house if your company only needs them sporadically.

Distributors – A distributor is an existing firm that will buy your product and resell it to the intended market. Contracting with a distributor can save you time and money.

Lobbyists – If your product needs governmental approval or restrictions lifted, you may need to contact a lobbyist to represent you on critical issues.

Import/Export Brokers – To bring goods into the United States, you must comply with customs regulations. Import/export brokers, or customs brokers, take the responsibility for such goods to clear customs. They charge a commission based on shipment price. You should contract with a customs broker who has expertise in importing and exporting in the country with which you are dealing.

TIP When you need services outside the scope of your business skills, hire a professional rather than doing it yourself. You'll get a better result at a lower cost and save time to devote to more pressing issues.

Reality Check

Costs of Outside Contractors

Think about costs associated with your business for outside contractors. Put a check by each of the following costs that will or might apply. Then indicate whether you already know these amounts or need to research them further.

	Already Know	Need to Research
❏ Ongoing consultations and advice from an attorney	❏	❏
❏ Accountant:		
❏ Establish accounting system	❏	❏
❏ Tax form preparation	❏	❏
❏ Ongoing consultation	❏	❏
❏ Marketing consultant	❏	❏
❏ Web site developer	❏	❏
❏ Human resources consultant	❏	❏
❏ Bookkeeping/Payroll	❏	❏
❏ Risk management consultant	❏	❏
❏ Sales representatives	❏	❏
❏ Distributors	❏	❏
❏ Production	❏	❏
❏ Engineering and design	❏	❏
❏ Import/Export brokers	❏	❏
❏ Other_____	❏	❏

Financial Facts Worksheet

Action Step 7.2 asks you to estimate the costs of outside resources on your Financial Facts Worksheets.

Summary

This module introduces you to some of the legal structures within which most businesses operate. The legal structure will affect many aspects of your business including the extent and structure of your management team, control issues, taxes, and other concerns. This module also encourages you to think about your organizational structure including a board of directors or advisory board, internal and external management team members, and organizational culture. Attracting, hiring or contracting, and motivating strong team members is an integral component of business success.

Key Things to Remember

- Your business can assume one of several legal structures, including sole proprietorship, partnership, corporation, S corporation, limited liability corporation (LLC), or nonprofit. Depending on your needs, each has significant benefits and drawbacks.

- Your legal form of business will depend on the goals of your business, the demands of investors, control issues, tax considerations, and the amount of liability you are willing to bear.

- A formal board of directors or an informal advisory board, depending on the needs and legal requirements of your business, can provide expertise and experience as you navigate your business through start-up and growth.

- When starting a business, recognize that your role will change as the business grows. You will want to ensure that key management functions are covered, whether by acting alone or by a team of qualified people committed to the goals and objectives of the firm.

- The leadership of a new venture is responsible for setting and developing the culture and values of the organization.

- Interviewing, hiring, and retaining the best workers is crucial to building a management team.

- Although compensation is a primary motivator, persons are also motivated by their work environment, the potential for developing their skills, or advancing within the company.

- You can create an infrastructure of outside professionals to help complete the work of your business or assist with specialized support such as banking or insurance.

Think of the progress you have made so far! Having your legal structure decided and your management needs established will make the next two modules on finances a little easier. You have a better idea of what your business may need in terms of money for personnel, whether they are employees, advisers, or contract help. In Module 8 you will look at components of profitability and begin to input financial information into your Financial Template. In Module 9 you will learn about monitoring cash flow and consider your short- and long-term funding needs.

Business Planning

10 Implementing Next Steps
9 Monitoring Cash Flow and Seeking Funds
8 Planning for a Profitable Business
7 **Building the Organization and Team**
6 Reaching the Market
5 Researching and Analyzing the Market
4 Planning the Product/Service

Concept Analysis

3 Setting Financial Goals
2 Identifying and Meeting Market Needs
1 Exploring Entrepreneurship

Action Step 7.1   **Create My Management and Organization Plan**

Establish that my business will have the management expertise needed to be a success.

Directions
In answering the questions for the Management and Organization Plan, highlight both current and future management needs of the business. Current needs identify those responsibilities carried out by you and others as you start the business. Future needs identify those responsibilities that will require additional management team members. Refer to the Reality Check *Management Function Analysis* on pp. 276 – 279 if you need to.

A. Determine management needs. Think through each management function you will require, even if you are the one performing all these functions. This practice shows that you know and understand the key team members you must recruit in the future.

If you and your management team as a whole lack the needed credentials or experience, you will want to explain how these deficiencies will be overcome with assistance from a board of directors, an advisory board, consultants, attorneys, accountants, or other outside help.

B. Use the template. Read the instructions on p. 1 of the electronic template. Then move to the Management and Organization section of the template to insert your information.

Each section of the template contains headings with questions to prompt you to consider the type of information to include under each heading. The questions are also listed in each action step for easy reference. After you enter your answers into the template and print them out, the questions will not appear on the hard copy. You should try to incorporate enough of the question into your answer so the reader understands what is being answered:

Action Step 7.1 **Create My Management and Organization Plan** continued

Management and Organization Plan

Legal Form of Business
What legal form has been selected?
What are the major reasons for this selection?
What is the state of incorporation (corporations) or organization (LLCs)?
In which states will it be necessary to be authorized to do business?
Some legal forms allow for special elections for tax purposes.
What, if any, tax treatment elections will you request?

Management Team
What is the contribution of the entrepreneur?
Who are the key management team members, and what are their job descriptions and prior experiences?
What offices or titles, such as president or chief financial officer, will each hold?
What experience and qualifications are desired for future management positions?
When and how will these be filled?

Board of Directors/Advisory Board
Who are the board of directors and/or advisory board members?
Include names, compensation, and any ownership in the company.
What are their qualifications related to the business?

Recruitment and Selection of Employees
What is your plan to find and hire self-motivated people for your business?
What are the required qualifications, duties to be performed, and the interview and hiring guidelines to be followed?

Compensation and Ownership
What is the compensation package for the entrepreneur and other key management team members?
What are their salaries, benefits, and bonuses?
What portion of the business is owned by the entrepreneur and management team?

Employee Reward and Incentive Plan
What system for employee rewards and incentives will be in effect?
What is the incentive plan?
Include special recognition awards, lump sum awards, bonuses, stock options, profit sharing, deferred compensation, commissions, team work, and flexible hours.

Communication
How will you communicate your business values and expectations?
What system will you use to assure clarity of communication throughout your business?

Infrastructure
Who are the key advisers?
Include names and compensation of accountants, lawyers, bankers, and consultants.
What expertise will they provide?
Include strategic alliances, computer technology, management, marketing, and specialists in product or service issues.

Action Step 7.2 | **Write My Management and Organization Financial Assumptions**

Project how much money I need for the management and organizational aspects of my business.

Financial Facts Worksheet

Directions

Use the Financial Facts Worksheets to estimate costs for the management functions of your business. Each worksheet heading in the list below suggests possible costs to consider. Not all headings will apply to all businesses. Think about how each one applies to your business and, in particular, to your vision of that business.

Write your assumptions on the Financial Facts Worksheets on pp. 128 – 136 or in your electronic toolkit. Be sure to cite sources for the facts that are the basis for your assumptions.

For example, Jake called an accountant to research the accounting fees for his start-up business which he plans to organize as an S corporation. Jake will include the following assumptions: "Estimated cost for an accountant is $150 per month (includes monthly reconciliation of accounts) and an additional $500 for annual taxes." He would cite the name of the CPA by adding "accounting fees quote from Scott Ruther, CPA and tax attorney, Ruther and Associates, Lenexa, KS."

Completing your Financial Facts Worksheets now while you work on your Management and Organization Plan will save you time later when you fill out your Financial Template and make your financial projections.

Operating Expenses Worksheet

Licenses & Fees – Includes entity filings

Meals & Entertainment – Board of directors, advisory board, and celebrating victories

Miscellaneous – Meeting room rental and support personnel for board of directors, advisory board, or management team retreat

Outside Services – Marketing, human resources, risk management, sales representatives, distributors, engineering & design, import/export brokers

Payroll Expenses – For additional management team members

Professional Fees – Ongoing consultations with attorney and accountant as needed

Travel – For management team members, board of directors, advisory board

Inventory Worksheet

Payroll Expenses – Salaries, wages, and payroll taxes of production manager

Subcontracting – Cost for work performed by others outside the business

Post Start-Up Asset Purchases Worksheet

Add categories as a result of additional management team members

Planning for a Profitable Business

8

Business Planning

Financial success may mean different things to different people. A business's financial success, however, is always measured in its ability to cover start-up costs, to achieve profitability, and to maintain cash flow. Designing a business that meets these criteria is acritical step in reaching your own personal financial goals. In Module 3, you explored the ways entrepreneurs use financial statements as a roadmap for success and you established reasonable start-up costs for your business concept. In this module, you will concentrate on the profitability aspect of your own financial roadmap.

As with any complex system, determining profitability requires several steps First, you will finalize your sales and expense projections, using information you have already gathered throughout this program. That information will help you project your financial situation, using the Financial Template as a recording and calculating tool. Finally, you will learn how to assess your business's potential for profitability and how to monitor profitability by using your financial statements.

Key Questions
- What are the steps to profitability?
- What components affect profitability?
- How do I accurately project sales, costs of goods, and operating expenses?
- How do I use financial concepts to assess and monitor profitability?

Action Steps	**Due Date**
❏ 8.1 Project Sales	_____
❏ 8.2 Project My Three-Year Income Statement	_____
❏ Read Module 9 Monitoring Cash Flow and Seeking Funds	_____
❏ _____	_____
❏ _____	_____
❏ _____	_____

Charting Profitability

Understanding financial concepts is an ongoing process. No doubt you have a deeper understanding of your business's financial issues now than when you first started this program. This module will reintroduce and reinforce financial concepts first presented in Module 3, to assist you in developing a profitable venture.

Components of Feasibility

You began the journey when you wrote your business concept. By now you are moving quickly toward your destination—developing a feasible business concept into a full-fledged Business Plan. Modules 8 and 9 are about providing you some financial tools to use along the way. These tools will be useful in setting up your business and will continue to be important as you grow your business venture.

The financial information you have generated to this point—start-up costs estimates, personal financial goals, and Financial Facts Worksheets—will be entered into the Financial Template in Modules 8 and 9 to help you assess profitability. This template will save you hours of time in projecting financial statements for your Business Plan. The template consists of worksheets (which you enter data into), projected financial statements, and ratio analysis. The Financial Template will automatically generate the following financial statements using the information you provide:

Balance Sheet
Income Statement
Monthly Cash Flow Report

From the Income Statement, you will establish profitability goals for your business that will help support your own personal financial goals. In addition to goal setting, preparing projected financial statements that accurately represent your business will give you the information you need to manage your business and make daily profitability decisions.

You will simplify the process of projecting profits into an Income Statement using three main steps. Each step is made easier with the use of financial tools, including the Financial Template. The three steps to planning for a profitable business include:

1. **Finalize your sales and expense estimates** by researching your industry and competition. Then review the amounts you have come up with to verify they are reasonable.
2. **Create your financial projections** by entering your financial data into the Financial Template.
3. **Assess the financial information** and statements generated from the Financial Template and make changes as necessary. Prepare to monitor the profitability of your business.

Follow the Money

Ty Foose's secret weapon for running a successful business? Financial information.

Accurate, up-to-date financial data has enabled Foose to dramatically improve pricing, overhead, and profits at Monolithic Sculptures, Inc. This Boulder, Colorado, company designs and manufactures interactive sculptures and climbing structures for retail clients and fitness centers.

Gaining financial savvy has been a gradual process, admits Foose. When he first launched the company in 1999, he didn't track his project costs or even fixed expenses, which quickly took a toll. "All of a sudden I would get an electric bill, and even though it was the same amount as the previous month, I hadn't anticipated it," he explains. "Estimating per project costs also became an issue. Without knowing our costs, it was impossible to put a price on a job that made sense. We just hoped it would work."

A few months after launching the company, Foose took FastTrac®, which educated him about the benefits of financial data and how to construct financial statements. He immediately used this new knowledge to improve profitability in all areas of his business. In recent years, Monolithic's annual revenue has fluctuated between $1.2 and $1.7 million. Yet rather than revving up the top line—Sales—Foose has focused on net profits, which averaged 5 percent during his first four years. Through careful planning and monitoring, he has expanded profit margins to between 15 and 20 percent a year.

To achieve these results, Foose isolated three monthly benchmarks to track: revenue, expenses, and cost of goods. "At the end of each month, we look at our Income Statement to compare what we budgeted with what's actually happened," Foose says. "That allows us to make quick responses rather than waiting until the end of the year. For example, if revenue is below projections, we can intensify sales efforts."

Just as Ty Foose used financial statements to meet his objectives, you, too, can reach your objectives with the help of carefully prepared financial statements.

Financial statements are as essential to business management as wrenches are to a mechanic. Does a mechanic only have one wrench? Do all the wrenches work the same way? No, because different jobs require different tools and the knowledge to choose the right tool for each job.

Entrepreneurs use financial statements, such as the Income Statement, to examine and forecast the ability of a company to achieve its financial goals. They can also help you reach your personal financial goals.

Financial Statements for Entrepreneurs

Balance Sheet – Reports what the company owns, what it owes, and the net worth that remains for the owners of the business.

The Income Statement – Shows the net income or loss that the business has experienced over a period of time—in other words, a company's financial grade card.

The Cash Flow Report – Documents the cash that flows into and out of a business on a monthly basis.

Review specific aspects of these statements in Module 3, pp. 88 – 92.

TIP When reviewing or comparing financial documents and statements, remember that different businesses and industries may use different terms to describe the same types of accounts. You should know what the accounts represent and where they come from, regardless of what they are called.

Steps to Profitability

1. Finalize sales and expense estimates.
2. Create financial projections.
3. Assess and monitor profitability.

Finalizing Sales and Expense Estimates

You can only consistently reach your financial goals through business profits. As a general practice, you should project profits for three years. In order to get such a long-term projection, estimate sales (or revenues) and expenses for your first three years of operations. Then use these numbers to construct a three-year Income Statement.

The first step toward this three-year Income Statement is to finalize your sales and expense estimates. This step can be very involved as it includes researching and assembling information, assessing the information for accuracy, and selecting appropriate estimates for all areas of the business's operations. You have already begun this process. The Financial Facts Worksheets you have prepared will help you finalize your estimates.

Recognizing the Components of Profitability

The primary financial goal of your business should be profitability. Only through continued profits will you have enough cash to pay yourself, pay others, and reinvest in the business. Profit is measured by the amount of Net Income you have left over after you have deducted the expenses of your business from its revenues, or sales:

Net Income Equation

$$\begin{aligned}
&\textit{Sales} \\
-\ &\underline{\textit{Cost of Goods Sold (or Cost of Sales)}} \\
=\ &\textit{Gross Margin} \\
-\ &\underline{\textit{Operating Expenses}} \\
=\ &\textit{Net Income}
\end{aligned}$$

The only way to increase profitability, is to make a change within one of the components of Net Income shown above. For example, lowering Operating Expenses will typically increase Net Income. Increasing Sales, for example, may also increase Net Income, but solutions are not always as simple as increasing sales. You might improve profitability in the short term by purchasing cheaper materials from an alternative supplier. Later on, however, rework and lost sales caused by inferior parts might have the reverse effect and might actually lower sales and reduce profit. Regardless of your tactic, you will always observe financial responses to your business decisions, if you watch for them.

Financial Terms to Remember

Revenue – Money, or the promise of money, you receive because you provide customers with products or services.
> **Revenue Equation:**
> *Revenue = Number of units sold x Price (per unit)*

Cost of Goods Sold (or Cost of Sales) – All costs directly related to the production of a product that you sell or a service you deliver.

Gross Margin – The amount of money you have left, after the Cost of Goods Sold (or Cost of Sales) has been paid, to cover your operating expenses.
> **Gross Margin Equation:**
> *Gross Margin = Revenue - Cost of Goods Sold (or Cost of Sales)*

Operating Expenses – Costs associated with keeping your business up and running.

Net Income – Profit remaining after all Cost of Goods Sold (or Cost of Sales) and Operating Expenses have been deducted.

Each of the components of profitability—Revenue, Cost of Goods Sold/Cost of Sales, Gross Margin, and Operating Expenses—should be carefully researched, projected, and assessed. As you develop your Financial Plan, pay particular attention to the accuracy of your sales projections and the Costs of Goods Sold/Cost of Sales. These two components of Net Income play a very large role in the pursuit of profit.

How accurately you estimate Sales, Cost of Goods Sold/Cost of Sales, and Operating Expenses may mean the difference between meeting or missing your profitability goals. The profit of a business is not like a final score over which the owner or manager cannot control. Profitability can be managed through thoughtful changes in the components that go into it. Cost of Goods Sold, for example, could be reduced if efforts are made to buy in bigger quantities, find a less expensive vendor, or negotiate better vendor deals.

Reality Check ✔   **Profitability Components**

Identify steps to positively impact each of these profitability components for your business.

Profitability Component	Sales	Cost of Goods Sold/ Cost of Sales	Operating Expenses
Possible Adjustments	_____	_____	_____
	_____	_____	_____
	_____	_____	_____
	_____	_____	_____
	_____	_____	_____

If you have accurate financial projections and a very clear business concept, your only option for adjustment may be to increase sales. Consider how likely, or difficult, this might be.

Identifying and Projecting Sales

It would be nice if you could look into a crystal ball and see what the future holds when you project sales for your business. Since you can't, projecting sales requires looking at a variety of perspectives and determining how each might impact the sales and profitability of your business. Because of the importance and complexity of projecting this very critical component of profitability, many entrepreneurs use a multi-faceted approach to projecting sales.

Net Income Equation

   Sales
− *Cost of Goods Sold (or Cost of Sales)*
= *Gross Margin*
− *Operating Expenses*
= *Net Income*

<table>
<tr><td></td><td>**Sales Projections**</td></tr>
</table>

Reality Check ✓

Sales Projections

Using a multi-faceted approach to projecting sales will lead you to more reasonable sales estimates. You will need to gather the following information to help you project sales using any of the approaches outlined in this module. Indicate whether you already know these amounts or need to research them. If you already know the amount, record it on the line provided. When you determine the amount through research, come back and record it here.

	Already Know	Need to Research
a. Number of units/hours you project to sell in a year	_____	❑
b. Sales price per unit/hour	_____	❑
c. Cost to produce a product/provide a service	_____	❑
d. Estimated monthly operating expenses	_____	❑
e. Your salary requirements per year	_____	❑
f. Amount of pre-tax profit you want to make	_____	❑

Other variables:

Three common ways to project sales include the *comparative sales approach*, the *average sale approach* and the *bottom-up approach*. You will have an opportunity to experiment with these approaches during the next session when you will complete Activity 8a. Read the discussion below to prepare for this activity.

TIP Testing your estimates for *reasonableness* means that after completing the projection, you examine it to see if it makes sense. If you are not sure what makes sense, then compare your estimates to companies similar to yours or talk to someone in the industry.

Comparative Sales Approach

The comparative sales approach uses research you have done on your competitors and your industry. From your research you should be able to produce relatively accurate estimates of sales based on your competitors' annual sales and the amount of sales expected in your industry.

Keep in mind that if your competitors have been in business for a while, your first-year sales may be significantly less. Be ready to make adjustments based on the reality of your situation. After you have analyzed all of your competitor and industry data, you will want to identify a range of projected sales estimates for your business. For example, you may have been able to identify through industry research or a friend in the industry that the average annual sales for a sports memorabilia business is $500,000. After more research, you identify a competitor who sells approximately $5,000 of sport memorabilia each week during the off-peak shopping seasons and during the peak shopping season (the ten weeks leading up to the end of the calendar year) the retailer sells $15,000 per week. You will include this sales estimate of $360,000 ($5,000 x 42 weeks + $15,000 x 10 weeks) and the industry average of $500,000 in your calculation of the final range of projected sales.

You should research as many competitors and industry sources as possible. The more competitor and industry data you include in your calculation, the more accurate you can expect your sales projection to be. When formulating the final range, you should

---

also consider possible variables that might affect sales, such as the location of your business, its maturity, the expertise of the owner, and other factors. When your sales estimates, using the comparative sales approach, seem reasonable, you're ready to look at the next perspective—the average sale approach.

TIP Because your staff will only be able to produce or service a certain number of products or services, projected sales must reflect this capacity.

Average Sale Approach

To project sales using the average sale method, you will need to count the number of sales transactions you expect over a specified period. For example, a restaurant may expect sixty customers on an average day. The restaurant owner figures the *average* price of each meal sold. If the owner expects the average price per meal to be $15, then the annual sales volume is $328,500 (60 customers x $15 x 365 days). For a more accurate estimate, the restaurateur should take into consideration the number of lunch customers versus dinner customers and increases in customer counts on weekends. The restaurant might also see a significant swing in the number of customers during different times in the year. Or the restaurant may not be open every day of the week or every week of the year. All these variations affect the final estimate.

You should calculate the price of an average sale for your business and then project your sales like the restaurateur did in the example. After you have calculated sales for three years, you'll want to check your projections again for reasonableness.

Bottom-Up Approach

The bottom-up approach is more mathematical than visionary. In order to prepare this projection, you'll need to estimate your annual costs of goods sold and all of the expenses you expect in your business.

These total costs plus the amount of desired profit represent your projected annual sales. The goal is to cover costs and profit. For example, a courier service business estimates all of the cost of sales and expenses they expect in each of the first three years of the business. Then the business owner identifies the amount of profit she wants to generate each year. The projected sales for this business, using the bottom-up approach, equals the total costs of the business and the amount of profit expected. This process represents the bottom-up sales projection approach, and since covering costs and generating profits is essential to every business, this approach is a good way to check the reasonableness of the other two methods. If your bottom-up approach leaves you with a projected sales number much higher than the other two approaches, you need to consider the ability of the business to achieve that level of sales and maintain profitability.

TIP You must realize that working at full capacity does not necessarily mean producing or servicing 100 percent of the time. Your business may only be able to produce or service 50 percent of the time, with 50 percent dedicated to customer relations, marketing, and administrative duties.

Using all three approaches to projecting sales can increase your confidence in the reliability of your sales goals. You can look at the sales figures you projected using each approach and ask yourself: Which one relies on the most accurate information? Which one seems the most reasonable? Which one seems the most attainable?

In all likelihood, your actual sales will probably rest somewhere in the middle of these three estimates. Projecting sales near the low end is more conservative and will probably be more acceptable to a lender. Projecting sales at the high end is risky because the amount will be difficult, if not completely unlikely, for you to achieve. It may, however, provide a more motivating goal. Select the sales figure that seems most realistic, and be prepared to support your decision through detailed sales assumptions.

TIP When working in the Financial Template, you must condense the assumptions to fit on one line. Any additional detailed information should be included in the Appendix.

Writing Sales Assumptions

Sales projections should be based on the facts you uncover during research about your business venture and industry. You should write these facts into assumption statements that support your financial projections in your Business Plan.

Assumptions:

- Provide the reader of the plan with confidence that your projections are not just guesses.
- Help readers understand the sources of information for your financial projections.
- Remind you of the facts you used as a basis for projections.

Your assumptions should describe how you developed sales forecasts and predict growth. You should explain differences among months such as seasonal variations, number of sales days in the month, heavy marketing, repeat business, new product or service release, and expansion plans. Your assumptions should substantiate sales forecasts by including facts and figures. Assumptions may need to be very detailed to provide adequate information for the reader.

You will enter sales projections into the Financial Template when you complete Action Step 8.2 Project My Three-Year Income Statement on pp. 331 – 335.

Net Income Equation

Sales
− *Cost of Goods Sold (or Cost of Sales)*
= *Gross Margin*
− *Operating Expenses*
= *Net Income*

Considering Inventory and Cost of Goods Sold

The second component of profitability is Cost of Goods Sold/Cost of Sales, which reflects inventory that has been sold. Businesses that manufacture or assemble products, as well as those that resell products, must account for the inventory they have on hand. The same is true for businesses such as interior decorating services that provide both services and inventory. Other businesses, such as commercial cleaning services, might provide a service and not have inventory.

The way your business manages inventory has an impact on both profits and cash flow. When purchased, inventory is an asset because it has value. You record it on the Balance Sheet. At any given time, assuming a customer wants it, you can sell inventory to regain cash. You should carefully monitor your inventory by selling older inventory items, even if it means discounting sales prices. Inventory is worth cash only if it can be sold. Once you sell inventory, you transfer the cost of the items sold to the Income Statement as Cost of Goods Sold. When inventory cannot be sold, it becomes worthless to the business and you should write it off and discard it.

Manufacturing Inventory

In a manufacturing company, inventory goes through several stages before it is ready to sell. It begins as raw materials and is fashioned into work-in-progress before it is considered finished goods ready for sale. You must carefully analyze and estimate these costs to produce accurate projections of Cost of Goods Sold and also to monitor the inventory production process in the future.

Let's consider the various elements of manufacturing inventory:

Raw materials – If you are going to manufacture or assemble products to sell, you must plan for raw materials inventory. Begin by answering these questions:

- **How many types of raw materials does the product use?** If you use many types of raw materials, the costs to store or warehouse them will grow.
- **How much raw material needs to be on hand?** Purchasing larger quantities to lower costs can help increase profits, but it can also reduce cash flow.

- **How quickly can raw materials be turned into finished goods ready to sell?**
  Consider ways to streamline the production process. This efficiency allows inventory to be sold more quickly, which can bring cash into the business faster.

Production expenses – In addition to raw materials, you will spend money on production. These production expenses become part of the total Cost of Goods.

Following are some common production expenses you may incur:

- **Freight-in and trucking/shipping costs** – Represents a direct cost of having raw materials for production or products for resale.
- **Insurance** – Can only be included if the insurance applies to the production facilities.
- **Payroll expenses** – May be the highest production cost. All personnel who play a direct role in producing inventory or supervising the production process should be included. Payroll expenses include salaries, benefits, and employer-paid payroll taxes.
- **Rent and utilities** – Only includes the costs of the production facilities, which along with payroll could also be a major portion of the production expenses. If the production area is shared with office or retail space, consider only the amount used directly for production. The rest will be included in the operating expenses.
- **Repairs and maintenance** – Should be taken into account if production equipment must be periodically repaired or maintained.
- **Rework** – Consider if manufactured products need rework from time to time. This figure should include the costs to rework the products to make them salable.
- **Subcontracting** – Occurs in companies that subcontract out a portion of the production process.

TIP Adding raw materials costs and production costs together results in the total Cost of Goods Sold. This figure is critical to overall profitability.

 Reality Check ✔

Inventory

Does your business have any inventory?   Yes   No

If you answered *no*, skip this Reality Check. If you answered *yes*, continue. Your revenue may result from selling products, services or both. To prepare for the Financial Template, estimate the answers to the following questions:

a. Of all your sales, what percent do you think will be from products?

b. Of every dollar generated from sales of products, what percent will be used to pay for the product's cost?

c. Inventory can be paid for on credit or with cash. What percent of your inventory or raw materials do you think you will pay for with cash?

Base these estimates on your research and any industry averages you have been able to identify.

If you think your business will have an inventory of products or raw materials, you have a different challenge than a service business without inventory. Careful management of the inventory can add dollars to your gross margin. Sloppy management of inventory may add unnecessary costs.

You will enter inventory projections when you complete Action Step 8.2 Project My Three-Year Income Statement on pp. 331 – 335.

 Financial Plan

Check Your Knowledge

at www.fasttrac.org/toolkits to see the many ways businesses calculate their Cost of Goods Sold.

TIP Every business must invest money into the products or services it sells.

Cost of Goods Sold

As a component of profitability, Cost of Goods Sold (also called Cost of Sales and Cost of Product or Service) plays a huge role in determining Gross Margin and Net Income. Cost of Goods Sold is deducted from Revenue to reveal Gross Margin. Gross Margin reflects the amount available to cover the operating expenses of the business.

The Cost of Goods Sold is usually easier to track in product-based companies. Some service-based companies do not report a direct Cost of Sales. That is, the company is spending money and providing services, but the amount of time and money spent cannot be directly associated with specific sales in a cost-effective manner.

Consider the following businesses and their associated Cost of Goods Sold:

Type of business	Example of Cost of Goods Sold
Restaurant	Food, beverages, cooks
Residential construction	Materials, construction workers
Computer repair	Parts, technicians
Bagel shop	Food, cooks
Gas station	Fuel, retail goods
Internet service provider	Direct costs of bandwidth, technicians
Retail store	Retail goods
Landscaping	Trees, shrubs, flowers, landscaping labor
Produce grower	Seeds, fertilizer, production labor
Boat manufacturer	Materials, production labor
Bookstore	Books, videos, cards

When the Cost of Goods Sold is subtracted from Sales, the result is the Gross Margin. Understanding the concept of Gross Margin is critical because of its profound effect on your overall profitability.

You will enter elements of Cost of Goods Sold when you complete Action Step 8.2 Project My Three-Year Income Statement on pp. 331 – 335.

Reality Check ✓

Cost of Goods Sold

Accounting for Cost of Goods Sold can be very complex. Here are three basic ways to figure the cost of goods that have been sold. Check the method below that most closely resembles your business model. Contact an accountant to learn more detailed calculations for a specific industry.

☐ 1. Determine the total dollar amount spent for merchandise resold to customers (for example, a retail store).

☐ 2. Determine the total dollar amount spent for labor and supplies directly used to make the product/service available to customers (for example, a commercial cleaning service).

    Labor
 + <u>Cost of Direct Supplies</u>
    Cost of Sales

☐ 3. Determine the total dollar amount spent to buy materials, parts, and labor to make the product (for example, a cabinet shop).

    Labor
 + <u>Cost of Materials and Parts</u>
    Cost of Goods Sold

Estimating Operating Expenses

The final component to profitability is Operating Expenses. After you determine Gross Margin, you deduct Operating Expenses to determine Net Income. Some of the operating expenses of the venture are necessary to generate sales, such as sales employees, advertising, and other marketing expenses. These selling expenses can tell you a lot about how much it costs to generate revenue.

Some costs are necessary to support the overall operations of the company but cannot really be linked directly to generating sales, such as the costs of support employees, dues and subscriptions, legal fees, and accounting/bookkeeping expenses. These administrative (or general) expenses can tell you how much it costs to support the administrative activities of your company.

You have been capturing your expected operating expenses in the Financial Facts Worksheets. You will be using the estimated expenses that you have accumulated on the worksheets to complete the Operating Expense part of your Financial Plan. For those expenses you have not specifically researched, you will need to spend some time now identifying which expenses you expect to have in your business and how much each expense will cost your business each year.

Net Income Equation

   Sales
− *Cost of Goods Sold*
   (or Cost of Sales)
= *Gross Margin*
− *Operating Expenses*
= *Net Income*

Reality Check ✔

Reviewing Financial Facts Worksheets

At this time, your Financial Facts Worksheets should be complete, other than a few expense categories that still need some validation or research. Review your worksheets to determine how complete they are before continuing with the financial projection process.

Financial Facts Worksheet	Complete	Needs More Information
Operating Expenses	❏	❏
Inventory	❏	❏
Post Start-Up Fixed Asset Purchases	❏	❏

Identify the specific information you need to complete these worksheets:

Two Operating Expenses that confuse many entrepreneurs are *Depreciation* and *Amortization*. These expenses directly relate to assets you use or consume over time (fixed and other assets with more than a one-year life expectancy). You will not actually write a check to pay for either depreciation or amortization expenses. Instead, these expenses are only recorded on paper after your initial purchase, but they affect your financial statements because you move amounts from one statement to another as an item depreciates or is amortized. Also these amounts affect profitability, so you will want to understand them.

Depreciation

When Betty Cannon of Betty's Trucking, Inc., in DeSoto, Kansas, purchases a new tractor and trailer for her over-the-road hauling company, she records the purchase cost of these assets on her Balance Sheet. As time passes, these assets lose a portion of their value—they depreciate in value. As the assets depreciate, their value as reported on the Balance Sheet also declines. This decrease in value occurs because a portion of the assets' useful life has been consumed.

Another way of looking at depreciation is that the cost of using the tractor and trailer is reported during the period the equipment is used in Cannon's business. Since their useful life lasts longer than one year, the cost associated with purchasing the assets is stretched out over their estimated useful life. Each year they lose value as an asset, so their value decreases on the Balance Sheet. The amount of value lost on the Balance Sheet each year appears on the Income Statement as an expense. Then, when the assets' useful life is over, they will be fully depreciated and have a remaining value of $0.

Another important reason for depreciation is called the *matching principle*. The matching principle says that the expenses involved in generating revenue must match (or be recorded in) the same time period in which that revenue is realized. In other words, when revenue is recorded, all expenses associated with that revenue should be reported at the same time.

In reality, a business owner like Betty Cannon doesn't know exactly how long she will use the tractor and trailer she purchased in her business. But she can reasonably estimate the number of years she expects to use the equipment (the estimated useful life). By estimating the number of years she will use the equipment, she identifies the number of years the equipment will generate revenues.

The matching principle dictates that she record the expenses related to the use of the equipment such as new tires, gasoline, basic repairs, drivers' salaries, and depreciation in the same period that she records the revenue generated from the equipment. This practice provides Cannon with Income Statements that more accurately reflect her business's profitability.

Several different depreciation methods can be used to record the costs of fixed assets, but for planning purposes, straight-line depreciation is most common. This method is easy to calculate and the value of the asset is evenly distributed over its useful life. In straight-line depreciation, you estimate the useful life for each asset. Some assets are depreciated according to a pre-set industry standard of "usefulness." For example, computers are generally depreciated over no less than three and no more than five years. You may keep your computer longer, but most accountants will depreciate a new computer according to a standard rate of depreciation. You should use a reasonable estimate or talk with your accountant to determine the appropriate number of years commonly used for your assets. The Financial Template uses the following life expectancies:

Asset	Estimated Life
Computer Equipment	3
Equipment & Machinery	7
Furniture & Fixtures	7
Vehicles	5
Leasehold Improvements	5
Building	20

Straight-Line Depreciation at Work

Betty's Trucking purchased a tractor and trailer (which is classified as Equipment & Machinery). The total purchase price was $145,000. When the business purchased the equipment, the cost of that equipment was recorded as an asset in the Balance Sheet because the items retain value. Straight-line depreciation reduces the asset value of the equipment each year it is owned by the business. The business expected to keep the equipment for seven years, so it was depreciated evenly over those years. This calculation accomplishes two things. First, the $145,000 will be reduced every year on the Balance Sheet, which will more accurately reflect the use of the equipment to generate revenue over time. Second, as the value of the asset is reduced on the Balance Sheet, the amount of the reduction is recorded on the Income Statement as an expense against the revenue of the company that year. Therefore, the revenue generated by the hauling this equipment did will be recorded in the same period as the expenses (depreciation) for the equipment. Straight-line depreciation—a simple form of depreciation—works in the following way:

	Depreciated Amount on the Income Statement	Value on the Balance Sheet
Purchase Price		$145,000
Year 1	20,714	124,286
Year 2	20,714	103,571
Year 3	20,714	82,857
Year 4	20,714	62,143
Year 5	20,714	41,429
Year 6	20,714	20,714
Year 7	20,714	0

This depreciation process assumes that the tractor and trailer will retain some value for seven years. Each year, one-seventh of the purchase price is recorded as an expense against revenue on the Income Statement and the book value is reduced on the Balance Sheet. After the seventh year, the Balance Sheet will show the asset as having no value. It might in fact have market value. For example, it might still be sold to obtain some cash, but it has no value as an asset on Betty's Trucking's Balance Sheet.

Amortization

Amortization is similar to depreciation, except that it records the expense of *intangible* assets. These assets generally have no physical existence, but can have significant value to their owners. Examples of intangible assets are goodwill, patents, trademarks, and copyrights.

The value recorded on the Balance Sheet for these assets represents the cost of obtaining them. They should be amortized over their expected lifetimes on a straight-line basis. The amortization process occurs in a similar manner as the depreciation process illustrated in the Betty's Trucking example. The only difference is in the type of asset being amortized and the term *amortization* itself. If you cannot tell whether an asset should be depreciated or amortized, consult your accountant.

Writing Expense Assumptions

Operating expenses should be estimated based on facts you uncover about the business concept and industry. These facts have been captured in your Financial Facts Worksheets. You can turn them into assumption statements that support the expense estimates you will use in preparing your financial projections. The assumptions provide invaluable information to readers of your Business Plan to help them understand your financial information. The assumptions also serve as a useful reminder to you about the facts you used as a basis for your projections.

Your operating expense assumptions should describe how you estimated each expense category. You should also explain the variances between each of the months (for example, seasonal factors, number of sales days in the month, heavy marketing, exposure, repeat business, new product or service release, and expansion plans). Your assumptions should substantiate your expense estimates by including facts and figures. Your assumptions may need to be very detailed to provide adequate information to the reader. If so, include these within the written portion of the Financial Plan or as supporting documentation in the Appendix. You will need to write concise assumptions to fit on one line in the Financial Template.

You will enter operating expenses projections when you complete Action Step 8.2 Project My Three-Year Income Statement on pp. 331 – 335.

Creating Financial Projections

Steps to Profitability

1. Finalize sales and expense estimates.
2. Create financial projections.
3. Assess and monitor profitability.

You have finalized your sales estimates and researched all expenses. With information in hand, you are ready to start entering your financial data into the Financial Template. In addition to the sales and expense information, you will also be entering start-up costs, estimated in Module 3, into the Start-Up Funding and Expenditures Worksheet on the template. You must include this information, because the expenses estimated for the start-up process will reduce your first year's profitability.

Projecting Financial Statements in the Financial Template

Throughout this program, you have been working on your Financial Plan. The reading, Reality Checks, activities, and action steps have all helped you to establish financial goals along the way. Now, it is time to pull it all together. The following table identifies times throughout the program where you have been asked to consider your financial plans. If your ideas aren't fresh in your mind, refer back to these Reality Checks and action steps to help in the projection process.

After entering your start-up, sales, and expense estimates into the Financial Template, you will check this information for reasonableness and accuracy. This step will help you create financial statements you can trust to help you chart a course for financial success.

The final step is to compare your personal income goals to the business's projected profitability. This comparison will help you evaluate one aspect of financial feasibility: reaching your own financial goals. The financial statements must also show a plan for financial success that will sustain business operations throughout the coming years.

When you are working on	Refer back to
Company Information Worksheet	None
Start-Up Company Set-Up Worksheet	Module 3, Reality Check *Start-Up Planning*, p. 95 Action Step 3.1 Estimate Start-Up Costs, pp. 107 – 108
Sales Worksheet	Module 8, Reality Check *Sales Projections*, p. 306 Action Step 8.1 Project Sales, p. 330
Inventory Worksheet	Module 8, Reality Check *Inventory*, p. 309 Inventory Financial Facts Worksheet, pp. 128 – 129
Operating Expenses Worksheet	Module 3, Reality Check *Business Expenses*, p. 100 Operating Expenses Financial Facts Worksheet, pp. 130 – 134 Action Step 6.3 Write My Marketing Financial Assumptions, pp. 261 – 262
Capital Budget Worksheet	Module 3, Reality Check *Start-Up Planning*, p. 95 Post Start-Up Fixed Asset Purchases Financial Facts Worksheet, p. 135 – 136
Equity & Debt Worksheet	Module 9, Reality Check *Establish Funding Goals*, p. 347 Action Step 3.3 Consider Potential Funding Sources, p. 115 – 116
Amortization Schedule	None

Reviewing Financial Statements for Accuracy

After you have entered all of your financial data into the Financial Template, you will print off and review the financial statements generated from it. Concentrate first on the Balance Sheet and Income Statement. You will explore the Cash Flow Report in greater detail in Module 9.

You will perform a cursory review of these statements to see if you made any errors when entering your estimates. You should have a fairly good idea of the potential profit of your business. If you are surprised when reading the Income Statement for the first time, you will need to review each line item carefully. Do the individual sales and expense estimates reflect what you expected? Are any of them considerably higher or lower? Since these estimates reflect the yearly total of your monthly estimates, you will need to look back on the worksheets to verify any figures in question. Changes from one month to another are expected, but you should have documented reasons for these changes—seasonal factors, heavy marketing, and other special circumstances.

In reviewing for profitability, the primary question is whether the business will eventually generate an adequate amount of cash to support operations, pay back loans, and pay an adequate rate of return to owners. Module 9 will concentrate on this aspect of financial planning.

Now after considering the reasonableness of the financial statements and how they compare with your personal financial goals, you may want to make some adjustments to improve profitability. Make sure the changes you make are grounded in research. These estimates provide the first budget you will use to make daily business decisions. As you operate your business, you will also use this budget to assess and monitor profitability on an ongoing basis.

TIP Don't be in denial about negative financial information. It is better to spend more time researching than to risk your own personal financial well-being on negative information.

Financial Statements Review

After you have completed Action Step 8.2, verify the accuracy of your financial statements by answering these questions:

According to your Income Statement, is the business profitable? Does it show Net Income?

❑ Yes. Is the level of profit reasonable for a start-up in your industry?

❑ No. If it is not profitable and a Net Loss is reported, then how much is the loss? Is this loss expected?

Annual losses may be expected during the start-up and early stages of your business. Monthly losses may also be expected during the business cycle your business goes through each year. For example, your revenue stream may be very seasonal like many retail stores. These businesses may experience losses throughout the year until the holiday shopping begins in the fall. During this time of the year, the business will need to generate large amounts of revenue to cover the losses experienced earlier in the calendar year.

According to your Income Statement, is your required salary included?

❑ Yes. Can you reduce your salary requirements if the business does not meet projections?

❑ No. What adjustments need to be made to provide you the salary you need?

A business's financial success is directly tied to the financial goals of the entrepreneur. If your personal financial goals are not being met by the business, you should consider making changes to the business concept or explore a different concept that will produce more positive projections.

According to your Balance Sheet, is the cash account positive?

❑ Yes. You will still need to review each month's cash account to ensure that you have no periods of negative cash flow.

❑ No. How much cash is needed? Will you be able to obtain that much cash?

In reviewing for profitability, the primary question is whether the business will eventually generate an adequate amount of cash to support operations, pay back loans, and pay an adequate rate of return to owners. Module 9 will concentrate on this aspect of financial planning.

Steps to Profitability

1. Finalize sales and expense estimates.
2. Create financial projections.
3. Assess and monitor profitability.

TIP Keep your personal financial goals in mind when evaluating the financial profitability of your business. Only when these personal goals are met is your business successful. Review the Reality Check *Personal Goals Worksheet* in Module 3.

Assessing and Monitoring Profitability

Once you have finalized your sales and expense estimates and have projected your financial situation, you should review your financial statements and make changes to reflect realistic three-year profitability goals for your business. Then you are ready to assess the projected profitability of your business and monitor your results.

Assessing Profitability

Assessing profitability means reviewing the projected and actual financial statements of your business on a regular and ongoing basis to reveal areas of success and areas that need improvement. With profitability as the goal, you need to read and understand your financial statements and compare them to other businesses in your industry either through *benchmarking* or *ratio analysis*. This type of review will help you make quick decisions to improve profitability and help the business reach its true profit potential.

Statement Review

Although both statements are valuable, you will probably read the Income Statement before the Balance Sheet. The reason is that the Income Statement will give you the *bottom line* results of your business. This statement will report whether your business is profitable or not. Net Income, however, is only a summation of the entire report. To really understand Net Income, you need to be able to look at each line item and understand the amounts being reported.

It takes some time to be comfortable reading financial statements. Ty Foose of Monolithic Sculptures, Inc., continually reads information, which helps improve his financial skills. "Although I still rely on my accountants, I don't just hand things off to them," Foose says. "And the more I understand, the easier it makes their jobs."

The Balance Sheet shows the overall status of your business. It will report the current cash balance, as well as other assets owned by the business. It will also report the amount of debt the business is carrying to finance its operations and the position of the owners.

Benchmarking

Another way to assess the success of your business on an ongoing basis is to compare your financial results against companies of a similar size from your own industry. This practice is called *benchmarking*. You can use benchmarking to gain a realistic perspective of your business's current financial situation compared to other businesses. Generally, you'll be able to find financial information on similar types of businesses from industry trade organizations and financial statement guides, some of which are provided in More Info Resources 9.

Other benchmarking techniques include comparing current year financial results with your business's prior years' financial results. This comparison will allow you to assess the changes in operations between the two periods.

Ratio Analysis

You will also want to perform a ratio analysis on the financial information of your business. Financial ratios are another form of benchmarking. By measuring performance in percentages rather than raw numbers, ratios allow you to evaluate the performance of your company over a period of time, to compare the business to other companies of different sizes in the same industry, and to plan for the future. The difference is that the comparison is not of the raw numbers, but rather of calculated ratios. Although dozens of ratios exist, an understanding of a just a few simple profitability ratios will get you started. The Profitability Ratios table on p. 318 illustrates the most common profitability ratios you may want to use.

These ratios and others are automatically calculated in the Financial Template. Use the profitability ratios to compare your business to other businesses, industry ratios, or prior years. They are also valuable as goal-setting figures. For example, if a business must decrease Cost of Goods Sold in order to be more profitable, it could establish a Gross Margin goal. This figure takes into consideration the relationship between both Revenue and Cost of Goods instead of looking at a single number. Keep in mind, it is the relationship among all of the components of profitability that create Net Income or Net Loss.

Using Financial Information To Make Improvements

Once you have analyzed the profitability of your business, you should always be evaluating it for ways to make improvements, such as retooling your pricing strategy or bootstrapping to reduce expenses.

Retooling your pricing strategy – In Module 5 you identified a pricing strategy and determined a range of prices for your products or services. This decision affected the sales projections you entered in the Financial Template. As your business sells products or services at these prices, you will begin to see the results of your pricing strategy.

Profitability Ratios

Gross Margin

How it is calculated	Gross Margin / Net Sales
What it measures	Profit from the goods a company sells after direct costs are subtracted
What it tells	A rough measurement of overall profits, Gross Margin tells companies how well they are controlling direct costs. If the costs are increasing faster than sales, then the direct costs are out of control. Owners of the business should do some research to determine why costs are increasing.

Operating Margin

How it is calculated	Operating Income / Net Sales
What it measures	A company's operating profitability and efficiency
What it tells	Operating Margins show how well a company is managing its overhead costs. If the company's Gross Margins are rising while its Operating Margins are falling, management knows immediately that the company is having difficulty controlling indirect costs.

Net Margin

How it is calculated	Net Income / Net Sales
What it measures	Profitability
What it tells	The Net Margin shows how many cents on each dollar of sales are profit. A falling Net Margin may signal problems in controlling costs or setting prices.

Return on Assets (ROA)

How it is calculated	Net Income / Total Assets
What it measures	Profits against assets
What it tells	ROA can be used to compare the profitability of companies of different sizes. Assets remain fairly stable, so an increasing ROA indicates greater profitability while a decreasing ROA indicates less profitability.

Return on Equity (ROE)

How it is calculated	Net Income / Total Equity
What it measures	Income against stockholders' equity
What it tells	ROE tells whether or not the company is a good investment. As ROE increases, generally the company becomes more attractive to potential investors. Improving Net Income will also improve shareholders' equity as the profit will become retained earnings.

On an ongoing basis, you need to re-evaluate your pricing to see if it would make sense to adjust it. For example, if you're projecting a large amount of Net Income, then you should consider whether you have overestimated the price that your customers are willing to pay. How does your pricing compare to your competitors? Is it comparable or is it significantly higher? If it is higher, then ask yourself why your customers would be willing to pay more.

If your financial statements indicate that your business will not be profitable within the first three years of its existence, is it possible that you are not charging enough for your products or services? As discussed in Module 5, the biggest mistake new business owners make is pricing too low. Now that you have a better understanding of the expense structure and potential profitability of your business, you should take this opportunity to go through the pricing process again.

Keep in Mind Your Pricing Objectives

1. **Maximize Profits** – Setting prices to maximize the amount of unit sales and profits

2. **Meet a Specific Return-on-Investment** – Achieving an overall profit to meet a target ROI on total Net Sales

3. **Achieve a Target Sales Level** – Meeting Revenue projections independent of profit levels

4. **Gain or Maintain Market Share** – Attaining and keeping market share for high visibility

5. **Meet or Keep Out Competition** – Staying within average industry prices and making adjustments to be competitive

---

Bootstrapping to reduce expenses – Another way to make improvements to the profitability of the business is to reduce expenses. *Bootstrapping* means using the non-monetary resources available to you to save on costs. These resources include time, reputation, knowledge, and abilities. Consider creative ways to use all the resources you have before you rely on money. Many times a little ingenuity and creativity can save a lot of money.

For example, working out the aesthetics and mechanical details of a new product line can be expensive. Like most entrepreneurs, Ty Foose of Monolithic Sculptures, Inc., had little extra cash to fund product development. He launched the company to design and build climbing walls for fitness centers, but it soon expanded into other categories, such as artistic play equipment for schools and municipal parks and architectural facades. Instead of looking for more cash, he took a beta-testing approach of sorts: Foose found customers who were interested in the new products he wanted to develop and offered them a discounted price in exchange for their feedback and willingness to work out the kinks.

"Instead of having to set aside money for research and development, we've been able to generate it as income from a project," Foose says. Case in point: Monolithic Sculptures was creating a climbing wall for a computer company when Foose learned the client wanted some creative furniture for an employee breakroom. Foose had been considering moving into furniture and proposed building a conference table for the breakroom. As part of the agreement, Foose was allowed to photograph the table for product shots and a magazine story.

Monitoring Profitability

Once you have created your financial projections, do not file them away and forget about them. You can view these projections as your roadmap to a successful future. You need to monitor your business's actual results by comparing them with your projections. We call this process *budgeting*.

Budgeting

One of your major functions as an entrepreneur is to monitor your business's financial progress. Preparing accurate budgets and comparing the actual results against your expectations is a critical part of managing your business. A budget must be frequently revisited and analyzed to keep the business on track.

Having an annual budget and reviewing it on a regular basis can help you in these functions:
- Provide a basis to manage your business financially
- Control costs
- Reduce spending
- Predict sales
- Estimate production costs
- Set goals for payroll costs

Entrepreneurs develop their own effective system to monitor budgets. No two budget systems need be alike.

 ### Budget with Brains

Ty Foose of Monolithic Sculptures had a difficult time finding industry benchmarks when first establishing his budgets. None exactly pertained to his business.

In response, Foose created two tools of his own, beginning with an Excel spreadsheet to capture costs. This project cost worksheet, referred to as a "spend-o-meter" by Foose, tracks everything from how much material is used in various phases of a project to hotel expenses when staff members travel for an installation.

Using the spend-o-meter to collect information, Foose devised another tool, a formula for fast, accurate estimates—no simple task when sculptures can vary from $50 to several hundred dollars per square foot. The spend-o-meter identifies fifteen key factors influencing costs, so when Foose discusses a new project with a client, he assigns a score to each factor. For example, if a sculpture requires cutting-edge fabrication techniques, it scores higher on engineering difficulty than a more routine project.

Together, the fifteen factors yield an average level of complexity and detail, which are plugged into an equation along with a base price. In just a few minutes, Foose can produce an estimated quote within four or five points of his expected Gross Margin.

This project estimator and the spend-o-meter work in tandem to help Foose identify changes and take corrective action. For example, if projects begin to run over-budget, Foose can quickly determine the cause—such as an increase in raw materials—and make adjustments to the estimator's base price.

When considering the types of budgets you will need to monitor your business's financial success, review these commonly used budgets:
- **Operational Budget** – Projects the revenue and expense (and resulting profits) for the company for a one-year period. This budget is probably the most commonly used. It is a good indicator of overall financial performance since it concentrates on Net Profits.
- **Cash Flow Budget** – Details the cash collected and needed, usually monthly. Sometimes overlooked, this budget can mean the difference between success and failure. The cash flow budget details the cash sources and uses on a monthly basis to ensure the business's ability to pay out cash when necessary and to build cash reserves for future growth.
- **Capital Budget** – Assesses the equipment needed to reach the projected level of sales. This budget may be included in the cash flow budget. The importance of the capital budget is to project the overall cost of equipment and to evaluate potential sources of the funds needed.

Budgeting plays a major role in business planning. By adopting various budgetary procedures, you will successfully guide the business through the start-up, operating, and growth stages.

As you plan your entrepreneurial journey, you will use your financial savvy to make daily financial decisions that affect the future direction of the company. Your ability to evaluate financial concepts and make decisions will be a key factor in navigating your business to your own definition of success.

Throughout this program, you have been evaluating your business for financial feasibility that includes estimating start-up costs, projecting profitability, and identifying cash flow needs and potential funding sources. Equally important, these aspects work hand-in-hand to create a Financial Plan that supports financial success today as well as a foundation for future success. To be successful, start-up costs must be reasonable and fundable. Profits must be substantial enough to meet your own personal needs and the future needs of the business. Cash flow must be substantial enough to support today's cash needs as well as the continued growth and development of the company.

Spending the time to accurately project your Financial Plan now is the best way to ensure future financial success.

TIP Develop a budgeting system that meets your needs, not the needs of your accountant.

Summary

Module 8 concentrates on the components of profitability that help build financial projections and contribute to your personal financial goals. You can now project sales, inventory, and operating expenses using the Financial Template, which automatically produces financial statements and ratios. You can use the information in this module to read and understand your Income Statement to determine necessary profitability adjustments. You will also consider future profitability analyses, such as budgeting and benchmarking.

Key Things to Remember

- Understanding key financial terms and concepts will help you plan and maintain a financially successful business.

- Being able to accurately estimate the sources of revenues and expected costs of your business is the only way to project profitability.

- One way to affect profitability is to adjust pricing, which is a component of sales. This is a critical decision, because this strategy can have a positive or negative effect on sales.

- Other ways to affect profitability are to increase or decrease the components of profitability—Sales, Cost of Goods Sold, and Operating Expenses.

Once you are familiar with using the Financial Template to enter your financial information, the activities and actions steps in Module 9 will seem easier. In that module, you will finalize your numbers and look at cash flow to determine the ongoing cash needs of your business. When you complete the financial modules, you will have only one more module to go to put together a Business Plan for the business concept you have developed throughout this planning process.

Activity 8a **Pricing Strategies and Sales Projections**

Practice the process of identifying the components of profitability, concentrating on the sales component and the way pricing strategies affect profitability.

Directions
Using one of the following business narratives, estimate sales using the three sales projection methods: comparative sales, average sale, and bottom-up approaches.

Wood Brain Puzzles creates wholesale wooden puzzles and toys sold through upscale retail and mail order toy resellers. Industry averages indicate that a company with Wood Brain's production capacity could reach sales as high as $185,000. First-year sales would probably be at least 25 percent lower than that. The part-time sales manager is expected to sell twelve sets of each product (sets of four puzzles/toys distributed together) quarterly to each of the thirty-five resellers identified, although she thinks that only 75 percent of the resellers will purchase toys. Third-quarter sales should be 50 percent higher than the other quarters. The cost of production is similar to the competition, whose products are not as durable, colorful, or creative.

Competitive Information

Item/Set*	Wholesale Price/Set	Item Cost	Retail Price / Item
Small puzzles	$20/set	$5	$ 9.95
Large puzzles	$30/set	$7.50	$14.95
Toys	$40/set	$10	$19.95

* Sets of four puzzles/toys distributed together

This business is projected to operate at a cost of $3,000 per month. In addition, the entrepreneur will be taking a $50,000 salary the first year and wants to achieve $30,000 in profits for future growth.

Motivate & Celebrate, Inc., (M&C) plans annual motivational conventions and award ceremonies for corporate sales departments of Inc. 500 companies across the United States.

Competitors in the region are generating nearly $1 million in sales. Industry figures indicate that sales for a business this size could generate $700,000 in the first year.

The owners already have agreements to plan four premium events in Year 1. They are expecting that the first two events will take place during the first quarter and will generate $135,000 each in revenue and will cost the company $75,000. The third event will take place during the second quarter and will generate $125,000 in revenue and cost $70,000. The last event of the year will take place during the third quarter and will be the largest, generating revenue of $175,000 with an expected cost of $100,000.

Competitors are charging 15 percent more than M&C, because they are established in the industry. M&C thinks it could raise its prices by adding a unique competitive advantage. At this point, its primary selling point is its lower price and flexibility to take on new clients.

Clients are billed after the event and are requested to pay the invoice upon receipt. The business projects monthly operating costs of $5,000, which does not include the two founders' salaries of $75,000 each. The company would like to achieve $10,000 profit for the first year in business.

Activity 8a Pricing Strategies and Sales Projections continued

Step 1 Project sales using the comparative sales approach. Using the information on p. 323, enter the appropriate amounts in the following chart to project sales for your sample company using the comparative sales approach.

Comparative Sales Approach

Industry Research

	High	Low	First-Year Reduction
Range of sales in region			
Range of sales of similar-sized companies			

Competitor Research

	High	Low	First-Year Reduction
Competitor A _____			
Competitor B _____			
Competitor C _____			
Competitor D _____			
Competitor E _____			
Competitor F _____			
Competitor G _____			

Activity 8a **Pricing Strategies and Sales Projections** continued

Step 2 Project sales using the average sale approach. Count the number of sales transactions you expect your sample business to have over each of the first four quarters of its first year. Then calculate the total sales dollars those transactions will generate to project sales using the average sale approach.

Average Sale Approach
Product/Service 1

	Quarter 1	Quarter 2	Quarter 3	Quarter 4
Number of products/services sold:				
Average price per product/service:				
Total sales for product/service 1:				

Assumptions: Note the sales variations that you would expect with this product:

Product/Service 2

	Quarter 1	Quarter 2	Quarter 3	Quarter 4
Number of products/services sold:				
Average price per product/service:				
Total sales for product/service 2:				

Assumptions: Note the sales variations that you would expect with this product:

Product/Service 3

	Quarter 1	Quarter 2	Quarter 3	Quarter 4
Number of products/services sold:				
Average price per product/service:				
Total sales for product/service 3:				

Assumptions: Note the sales variations that you would expect with this product:

Product/Service 4

	Quarter 1	Quarter 2	Quarter 3	Quarter 4
Number of products/services sold:				
Average price per product/service:				
Total sales for product/service 4:				

Assumptions: Note the sales variations that you would expect with this product:

Calculate total yearly sales
Product/Service 1
Product/Service 2
Product/Service 3
Product/Service 4
Total Yearly Sales

Activity 8a **Pricing Strategies and Sales Projections** continued

Step 3 Project sales using the bottom-up approach. Enter the appropriate amounts in the chart below to project sales for your sample company using the bottom-up approach.

Bottom-Up Approach

Question	Formula	Enter amount	Calculation
What are your estimated monthly operating expenses (excluding owner salaries)?	Yearly operating expenses = Monthly operating expenses x 12	$	$
How much salary per year do you (and any other owners) want to make? Your salary will be increased by 10% for employer payroll taxes.		$	$
How much pre-tax profit do you want to make in *dollars*?		$	
What is your sales price per unit? (If multiple products/services are sold, use a weighted average.)		$	
What is your cost of product/ service per unit? (Be sure not to include owner salaries in this cost category if they were already entered above.)		$	
What is your gross margin in dollars per product/service?			$
This is your bottom-up sales projection or the amount of sales needed to cover your cost of sales, operating expenses, and profit expectations.	Number of units/hours sold x selling price		$
This is the number of units/hours you must sell to cover your cost of sales, operating expenses, and profit expectations.	(Yearly operating expenses + salary + pre-tax profit) / gross margin per unit		

Activity 8a **Pricing Strategies and Sales Projections** continued

Step 4 Compare the various approaches and determine sales estimates. Steps 1 through 3 have provided you three estimates for sales for your sample company. Write your conclusions below. Then consider which approach you would base your projected sales on—or develop a compromise among the three approaches.

Comparative Sales Approach
Based on industry and competitors' annual sales $_____

Average Sale Approach
Based on frequency and average price per sale $_____

Bottom-Up Approach
Based on projected expenses and profits desired $_____

Based on the above approaches, my first-year sales estimate for my sample company is $_____*.

* Be prepared to support your estimate with facts from the sample.

Activity 8b **Profit Improvement Practice**

Observe the consequences of making adjustments to revenues and expenses, two factors that affect profitability.

Directions

The primary goal of financial planning is profitability. Entrepreneurs evaluate profitability by looking at revenues and sales, cost of product or service, and operating expenses. Profitability can be improved by appropriately adjusting these amounts. It can be difficult to make adjustments without causing another area of the business to be affected. For example, when prices are raised to increase profitability, the consequences might include losing customers.

Step 1 Make adjustments to increase profitability. Looking at this Income Statement for a full-service car wash, brainstorm a list of items that could be modified to increase profitability for this business, concentrating on areas other than pricing and sales. Write your list on the chart on p. 329.

Full-Service Car Wash
Monthly Income Statement

Gross Revenue (4,200 cars X $10/car)	$42,000
Less: Coupons and discounts (10%)	$4,200
Net Revenue	**$37,800**
Cost of Goods Sold	
Payroll (including taxes and benefits)	$20,000
Cleaning Stock	$2,500
Utilities	$2,500
Total Cost of Goods Sold	**$25,000**
Gross Margin	**$12,800**
Operating Costs (variable)	
Advertising	$1,000
Car damage	$300
Maintenance	$300
Management salary	$2,500
Office expenses	$100
Professional fees	$1,000
Telephone	$200
Uniforms	$350
Total Variable Costs	**$5,750**
Operating Costs (fixed)	
Liability insurance	$500
Property taxes	$1,000
Debt service $500,000 @ 8%	$3,300
Total Fixed Costs	**$4,800**
Net Income	**$2,250**

Activity 8b **Profit Improvement Practice** continued

Step 2 Consider the consequences of making adjustments. Take a good look at your list. For each item, identify the possible consequences of making the adjustment.

Item to be adjusted	Possible consequence of adjustment

Action Step 8.1   Project Sales

Determine a sales projection for your business by using a multi-faceted approach to project an accurate sales figure.

Directions
Use the Sales Projection Tool at www.fasttrac.org/toolkits to make sales projections for your business.

A. **Project sales using the comparative sales approach.** This method is a good place to begin your sales projections because it identifies what the market suggests is realistic. You will uncover this information in research about the industry and competition. When calculating your sales projections, always keep in mind you are projecting your first-year sales. Therefore, when using industry or competitors' sales information, you need to include a first-year reduction to take this into account. Using the information you have uncovered, and making appropriate assumptions, begin to work through the comparative sales approach of projecting sales.

B. **Project sales using the average sale approach.** To project sales using the average sale approach, count the number of sales transactions you expect during each quarter of the year and then estimate the total sales dollars those transactions will generate. You have room to calculate up to four different products or services. This approach will help you consider multiple factors such as variations for different product or service lines, differences in product or service price, or seasonality. For each product or service below, enter amounts in the weekly, monthly, or yearly column. Note the reasons for variations in each quarter sales in the space provided.

C. **Project sales using the bottom-up approach.** Now, take a more focused look at sales starting with the cost of the product or service and the costs to operate the business. The bottom-up method helps to build sales projections that will cover all expenses and provide an appropriate profit. Use the information you have collected and appropriate assumptions. Work through the bottom-up process of projecting sales

D. **Compare the various approaches and determine sales estimates.** Projecting sales in any method is not infallible. The previous approaches have provided three estimates for sales. Record them below. Based on the information you have so far, identify the estimate that most closely resembles your attainable sales. You may need to compromise on an amount that rests in the middle.

Comparative Sales Approach
Based on industry and competitors' annual sales $_____

Average Sale Approach
Based on frequency and average price per sale $_____

Bottom-Up Approach
Based on projected expenses and profits desired $_____

Based on the above approaches, my first-year sales estimate is $_____*.

* Be prepared to support your estimate with researched facts.

Action Step 8.2 **Project My Three-Year Income Statement**

Use the Financial Template to project your Three-Year Income Statement to help you determine overall profitability.

Directions
The Financial Template at www.fasttrac.org/toolkits includes worksheets to help you estimate the potential profitability of your business. The template automatically calculates the Balance Sheet and Income Statement based on the information you enter.

Here are the template worksheets you will use in Modules 8 and 9:

Module 8
❏ Company Information Worksheet
❏ Start-Up Company Set-Up Worksheet (except for Loan Proceeds and Equity Investments)
❏ Sales Worksheet
❏ Inventory Worksheet
❏ Operating Expenses Worksheet

Module 9
❏ Start-Up Company Set-Up Worksheet (only Loan Proceeds and Equity Investments)
❏ Capital Budget Worksheet
  Section A Depreciation (existing capital assets)
  Section B Capital Asset Purchases and Depreciation (post-start-up)
  Section C Other Capital Expenditures
❏ Equity & Debt Worksheet (post-start-up)
  Section A Equity Investment
  Section B Real Estate Loans
  Section C Traditional Business Loan and/or Other Long-Term Loans
  Section D Line of Credit
  Section E Cash Position

The Financial Template worksheets you will complete in Module 8 are centered on the business's profitability. Therefore, the components of profitability will be entered: Sales, Inventory (Cost of Goods Sold), and Operating Expenses. You will also enter the start-up estimates affecting profitability you completed in Module 3.

The worksheets in Module 9 will center on cash: non-revenue cash received and non-expense cash expenditures. Follow the steps below to start using the Financial Template:

Action Step 8.2 **Project My Three-Year Income Statement** continued

A. **Become familiar with the template.** Open the Excel®-based workbook and explore the worksheets. The following answers to frequently asked questions will help guide you.

What do I do first?
When you initially access the file, Excel may prompt you to "Enable Macros." You must enable macros to use the printing options within the workbook. Then, save the template to your own hard drive using another name. This action will allow you keep a fresh version of the template if you want to start over or create another plan.

What's in the template?
The template consists of worksheets (where you enter data) and projected financial statements. The worksheets are presented in a logical sequence for projecting financial information. Your projected financial statements will be automatically assembled as you enter information into these worksheets.

How do I get started?
Step through the worksheets included in the Financial Template. Notice that each worksheet includes instructions on how to enter information that pertains to it. The worksheets you will use for this action step include:
- **Introduction Worksheet** provides valuable information on features of the Financial Template.
- **Company Information Worksheet** asks you to set up your company information and record your company's current financial position.
- **Start-Up Company Set-Up Worksheet** allows you to compile the costs involved in starting your business.
- **Sales, Inventory**, and **Operating Expenses Worksheets** ask you to record budget decisions for the next three years. Changes on these worksheets will automatically be updated on the following financial projections:
  - Monthly Income Statement
  - Monthly Cash Flow Report
  - Year-End Income Statement
  - Year-End Balance Sheet
  - Financial Analysis/Ratios

Two additional functions are provided on worksheets for your convenience:
- **Amortization Schedule** – Figures principal and interest payments on your loans.
- **Print Options** – One click prints out your choice of instructions, worksheets, or financial projections.

Action Step 8.2 **Project My Three-Year Income Statement** continued

B. Gather your financial information and start entering the data. Using the table on p. 315 as a guide, gather the information you have already researched and analyzed related to your Financial Plan. Use the following information to complete the first worksheets of the Financial Template. You will complete the rest of the worksheets after Module 9.

❏ **Introduction Worksheet**
   Read this page first to orient yourself to using the Financial Template.

❏ **Company Information Worksheet**
   The Company Information Worksheet sets up your template by asking five questions about your business. Be sure to answer every question because the answers will help tailor the template to your specific business operations. For example, if you answer *yes* to the question in Step 4, "Is your business solely a service provider? (Yes or No)," the Inventory Worksheet will not become part of your template, since service providers generally do not need to budget for inventory.

   In response to your answer to the question in Step 3, "Is your company a start-up (no historical financial data to enter)? (Yes or No)," the template will prompt you to use one of the following set-up worksheets. If you enter *no* the Existing Company Set-Up Worksheet will be available on the Financial Template. If you enter *yes* the Start-Up Company Set-Up Worksheet will be available. Until you answer this question, neither worksheet is available on the Financial Template.

❏ **Start-Up Company Set-Up Worksheet**
   The Start-Up Company Set-Up Worksheet includes a place to enter Start-Up Funding & Expenditures, those items needed to start your business. Complete this information based on the estimates you prepared for Action Step 3.1 Estimate Start-Up Costs.

   You will be asked how much money you and your investors will initially put into the company as well as the amount you plan to borrow and the expenditures you expect to make before you open your doors. You need not complete this information now. We will be revisiting this worksheet after Module 9 when a complete review of your Financial Plan is possible.

❏ **Existing Company Set-Up Worksheet**
   If you have already started your business, you will enter your historical financial data on the Existing Company Set-Up Worksheet. These figures will be used as a basis to project ongoing financial reports. To build reliable financial projections, start with numbers that are correct.

❏ **Sales Worksheet**
   In the Sales Worksheet, you will enter your estimated monthly sales for three years. To accurately complete this worksheet, you will need to understand the potential demand for your products or services as well as the purchasing habits of your customers, which you have gathered through market research. You will be asked these questions:
   1. What percentage of sales is made to customers paying cash (credit cards included)?
   2. How long on average does it take to collect credit sales?
   3. What percentage of credit sales is considered bad debt (uncollectible invoices)?
   4. What percentage of credit sales is estimated for returns and allowances (products returned for one reason or another)?

Action Step 8.2 **Project My Three-Year Income Statement** continued

You will also be asked to enter your monthly estimated sales for each major product or service category for each year. Start entering sales in the first month you expect to receive sales. Be sure to reflect seasonality, peak sales months, and start-up months in your projections when they apply. You can customize the worksheet by entering the product or service names in the areas provided.

If you sell many products or services, group them into categories for your sales estimates. The worksheet allows up to seven categories. As you detail each projection, consider all the factors that will affect your sales: for example, your capacity, advertising, competitors, seasonality, economic conditions.

Note: The Financial Template is not designed for columns or rows to be added or deleted. By doing so, you run the risk of losing or corrupting the preset calculations, which have been established in other sections of the Financial Template.

An important part of this worksheet is the section for your assumptions. For each sales estimate, briefly explain the basis for the estimate. For example, an assumption for Returns and Allowances might read, "Estimated at .25% based on industry averages for boutique operations." The source of the industry statistic could be included directly after the assumption.

❏ **Inventory Worksheet**
The Inventory Worksheet takes you through the steps to build your inventory projections. All product-based businesses should complete this worksheet since they will have direct costs of goods sold. Service businesses that sell products should also complete it. If you are a service provider and do not sell any products, skip this worksheet.

Businesses that sell only services will not report a direct cost of sales in the Financial Template. All costs of providing the services will be recorded in the Operating Expenses Worksheet.

To accurately project inventory needs, you will be asked these questions:
1. Does your business provide services along with products?
2. What percentage of sales is the average Cost of Goods Sold for your products?
3. How much inventory or raw materials will you be purchasing? Will you be buying some of this on credit? What are the average number of months you are allowed before payment is due?
4. Do you produce inventory in your own plant? What are your production expenses?

For this worksheet, you will think through the various expenses associated with your inventory requirements. The information you gathered on the Financial Facts Worksheets will be helpful in completing this worksheet. The categories on the Inventory Worksheet cover common expenses. Use the "other production expenses" category if your expenses do not fit into those listed.

For each expense, include an assumption, which explains the source of the estimate. Base each assumption on facts researched and be as clear and thorough as possible. This information will help you remember the details supporting the numbers and will help readers of your plan understand the basis for your estimates. The space to enter these assumptions is limited, so be concise. For example, the inventory/raw material purchases of $15,000 for a winery may include the assumption, "15 tons of grapes at $800 per ton and $3,000 inventory to stock gift shop."

Action Step 8.2 **Project My Three-Year Income Statement** continued

A Word about Cost of Goods Sold in the Template

In the Financial Template, your Cost of Goods Sold will automatically be calculated on the Income Statement based on the answers you provide to questions on the Inventory Worksheet. The Inventory Worksheet only captures Cost of Goods Sold for manufacturing and retail businesses. Service businesses will capture their costs for providing services in the Operating Expenses Worksheet.

For example, if a manufacturing or retail business estimates Cost of Goods Sold at a rate of 40 percent, then 40 percent of Sales will be recorded on the Income Statement in the Cost of Goods Sold category each month. This entry generates a Gross Margin of 60 percent, the amount left from Sales after Cost of Goods Sold is deducted.

Cost of Goods Sold represents the amount of inventory sold. As the inventory is sold and amounts are transferred from the Balance Sheet (Inventory account) to the Income Statement (Cost of Goods Sold account), the Inventory balance on the Balance Sheet, will be affected. You will need to consider this change when projecting your inventory purchases and review these amounts on both the Income Statement and Balance Sheet.

You may enter a different Cost of Goods Sold percentage for each of the three years you project in the Financial Template. This adjustment is helpful for start-up businesses as your Cost of Goods Sold percentage is often higher in the beginning until you identify beneficial cost-cutting options or produce larger quantities, which lowers individual costs.

❏ **Operating Expenses Worksheet**

This worksheet will include all the different expenses required to operate the business. The categories on the Operating Expense Projections list common types of operating expenses.

The information you gathered for the Financial Facts Worksheets will be helpful in completing this worksheet. Because it is easy to overlook some expenses, it is a good idea to show other persons your list to see if they can identify anything missing for your business. If you have expenses that do not fit the listed categories, you can rename the "other" categories at the end of the list.

For each expense, include an assumption that explains the basis for the estimate. For example, a company that publishes a small magazine included this assumption for salaries, "Designer @ $1750/ mo beg. in Aug; Editor @ $60K/yr beg. Sept; Promotions Mgr @ $30K, Ad Director @ $1K/mo + 15% comm., Publisher @ $60K/yr."

C. **Review the financial statements completed to this point.** After you have entered all of your financial data into the Financial Template, print off and review the financial statements generated from it. At this time, concentrate on the Balance Sheet and Income Statement. The Cash Flow Report will be explored in greater detail in Module 9.

Review the statements for errors you may have made in entering data. Then, read the statements to understand the profitability potential of the business. Use the Reality Check *Financial Statements Review* on p. 316 to further explore this critical aspect of feasibility.

Monitoring Cash Flow and Seeking Funds

This module will give you the information you need to complete your Financial Plan. You have already evaluated your business's ability to achieve start-up costs and profitability. This module will help you concentrate on the third aspect of financial success—cash flow.

Whether you are looking for start-up money or considering the cash you need for operations, your business may need funding from many different debt and equity sources. This module will help you determine the amount of cash you need to start and sustain your business throughout the first few years. It also offers ideas for locating sources of cash so you can identify the sources appropriate for starting and operating your business and avoid the financial planning failures that many entrepreneurs make. Finally, you will explore the many tools available to monitor your ongoing cash needs.

Key Questions
- How do I project expected cash flows for my business?
- What kind of funding will I need for operations and growth?
- Who are my potential funding sources?
- What are some ways to strengthen the cash flow of my business?

Action Steps   **Due Date**

❏ 9.1 Project My Three-Year Monthly Cash Flow Report   _____

❏ 9.2 Finalize My Financial Plan   _____

❏ Read Module 10 Implementing Next Steps   _____

❏ _____   _____

❏ _____   _____

❏ _____   _____

Cash Is King

You have probably heard the saying that "Cash is King." In business, no other saying could be more true. Without cash it is impossible to pay for the expenses and purchases integral to the success of your business. Cash is the lifeline of any business. It purchases equipment and pays for other aspects of the business that build profit. Without cash the business will ultimately fail.

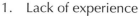

According to the U.S. Census Bureau's Business Information Tracking Series, one third of venture start-ups close before the end of the second year in business. After the sixth year in business, over 60 percent of business start-ups are closed. The reasons for closure are many. Sometimes the entrepreneur shuts down the business by choice. All too often the business fails and the entrepreneur is forced to close the doors.

Thousands of articles, research studies, and books have been written about the reasons for failure and how to avoid them. Whatever source you review, it will probably include most, if not all, of these top ten reasons businesses fail.

1. Lack of experience
2. Insufficient money
3. Ignoring the competition
4. Poor inventory management
5. Uncontrolled or unexpected growth
6. Poor location
7. Over-investment in fixed assets
8. Poor credit arrangements
9. Low sales
10. Lack of proper planning

Of these reasons for business failure, six are directly related to the entrepreneur's financial plans. Some relate to profitability, but most relate to having the right amount of cash when cash is needed.

How can you avoid these fatal errors? Simply by diving into the planning process, just as you are doing in this program. Business planning helps you identify ways to avoid these problems. Another study, at the University of Arizona, found that entrepreneurs who complete an entrepreneurship course:

• Are three times more likely to start new businesses.
• Are three times more likely to be self-employed.
• Have 27 percent higher annual incomes than other jobs they've held and own 62 percent more assets.

Cash management is a critical skill that *all* entrepreneurs must have. When you implement sound financial planning and monitoring, you can build a successful business with healthy cash flow.

The Importance of Cash Planning

A former college professor and educational consultant, Jim Schott is fearless about learning. But acquiring business savvy has been one of his toughest assignments.

Retiring from academia in 1989, Schott subsequently launched a cheesemaking business, Haystack Mountain Goat Dairy. Learning how to manage goats and make cheese has been far easier than mastering the financial aspects of the new venture, admits Schott. "To some extent, the business has grown in spite of me," he says.

Schott initially financed Haystack by cashing in some personal investments, and the Niwot, Colorado company produced its first batch of chevre in 1992. During the next five years, Haystack grew quickly, evidencing annual revenue increases of 30 to 40 percent.

Despite his company's burgeoning sales, Schott was having a hard time paying bills. "I was constantly short on cash, which I couldn't understand," he says. "We were continuing to sell more cheese, and yet we seemed to be getting poorer. It felt like I was carrying around a leaky bucket."

Part of the solution was naming the problem: When Schott took FastTrac® NewVenture™ in 1998, he realized that Haystack's cash-flow problem was directly linked to its growth. "Growth costs money," Schott points out. "You're always ahead of the income curve with your costs. We were profitable on paper, but that didn't mean we had cash on hand when we needed it."

One strategy that improved finances was establishing partnerships with regional dairies, which provided Schott with an additional supply of milk without having to invest in more goats and land. Schott also rolled over his bank credit lines into loans, which helped his cash crunch.

By the late 1990s, Haystack had paid down some of its debt load, but faced another cash-flow challenge: The company had outgrown its production facility and needed new equipment.

In response, Schott searched for investors and found someone who was interested in becoming a partner. The two men negotiated for nearly a year before coming to an agreement. But the day before the prospective partner was to sign the final papers, he got cold feet and called off the deal.

Fortunately, this setback proved serendipitous. Seven of Schott's employees stepped forward and volunteered to invest in Haystack, raising $50,000. "It really turned out to be the best thing," Schott says, noting that the other individual had little business experience and no background in the natural foods industry.

"I wanted investors who really understood our company," he continues. "Besides having a fine product, I also attribute Haystack's growth to the principles we adhere to. We try to bend over backwards to give people the kind of service we feel they deserve, whether it's a local restaurant or a distributor. I was worried that outside investors would only be concerned with the return on their investment—and how quickly they got it."

Haystack made more headway in 2002 when Schott hired an employee with expertise in financial analysis to serve as CFO. "For the first time ever, I feel confident that I know the real costs to produce our product," Schott says, referring to pro forma financial reports his CFO develops, which are based on milk-supply estimates. (Milk supply is determined nearly a year in advance when goats are bred, so those figures are critical to forecasting future cheese production, which, in turn, affects Haystack's revenue and income.)

Formal financial forecasts have made a big difference in managing growth. "Previously, we were tracking cash flow by the seat of our pants," Schott says, explaining that he would look at monthly cash flow from preceding years and try to make some predictions. "Today we have a better fix on finances, which enables us to be much more proactive about solving cash-flow problems. If we fall behind in sales, we change something, such as cutting back on staff or looking for greater efficiencies."

To have successful cash management you will need to follow these steps:

1. **Measure your cash needs.** You need to know how much you need, when you will need it, and what it will be used for.

2. **Seek potential funding sources.** You will want to find sources of cash that offer funding terms that match your own goals for those funds.

3. **Monitor ongoing cash needs.** You must establish goals for cash flow and use these goals to monitor your ongoing cash needs.

First, let's take a look at the nature of cash. What is cash flow and where does it come from?

Cash Flow

Cash flow refers to all the money that comes into your business and goes out of your business. When you think about it, cash in your business will take many forms: loans, revenues, debt payments, payroll, inventory purchases, and expenses. All of these represent elements of the cash flow in your business. When the cash stops flowing in and out of your business, the business dies. You cannot maintain a business without cash.

Cash vs. Profits

Entrepreneurs use cash to start businesses, support continued growth, and purchase assets that generate revenue. Cash, then, is used to build profits. But if cash is used to build profits, then what is the relationship between profits and cash flow? Another way to ask this question is to ask how cash flow is different from Net Income (or profit)? In Module 8 you discovered that Net Income is calculated by subtracting from Sales, the cost to produce those sales (Cost of Goods Sold) and the expenses necessary to operate the business (Operating Expenses).

> **Net Income Equation**
>
>   *Sales*
> − *Cost of Goods Sold (or Cost of Sales)*
> = *Gross Margin*
> − *Operating Expenses*
> = *Net Income*

The Income Statement reports this equation in detail. From the Income Statement you can see whether your business is producing a profit or a loss. If you're producing a profit (showing a positive Net Income), are you also producing a positive cash flow? Not necessarily. Keep in mind two primary questions when analyzing cash flow and Net Income:

1. What financial transactions are included in the Net Income Equation that *do not* affect cash flow?

2. What financial transactions are excluded from the Net Income Equation that *do* affect cash flow?

Let's look at these two types of transactions.

Non-Cash Transactions That Affect Net Income

Two expense accounts in particular can reduce your Net Income during a reporting period, but will not affect the cash balance of your business. These non-cash expenses are *Depreciation* and *Amortization*.

Remember in Module 8 that Betty's Trucking, Inc., depreciated a tractor and trailer over seven years? The depreciation of the assets occurred regularly over the expected useful lives of the assets to match the expense of the equipment with the revenues generated by them. Although depreciation is recorded as an expense on the Income Statement, it does not have an impact on the cash balance of the company. The only impact that these assets will have on cash relates to the actual purchase and sale of the asset itself.

Amortization is similar to Depreciation but relates to the recording of *intangible* assets, or those assets that have no physical existence, such as goodwill. Amortization is treated like Depreciation. It is a non-cash expense to the business. An amount is recorded on the Income Statement, but that amount does not represent a cash transaction during that time period.

TIP An Income Statement may show a lower profit due to depreciation and amortization expenses, but your cash flow is unaffected.

Cash Transactions That Do Not Affect Net Income

The Income Statement excludes several transactions that may affect your cash flow. These transactions include any cash received or paid out for something other than revenue or expenses. Non-revenue transactions include cash received from funding sources such as lenders or investors. Non-expense transactions might include cash paid for the principal portion of debt repayments, purchases of equipment and inventory, and payments to the owners of the business (dividends or draws). All of these transactions can have a significant affect on the cash flow of your business and will be included in the Cash Flow Report but not on the Income Statement.

Cash Transactions That Do Not Affect Net Income

Payments to owners and investors

Purchases of inventory

Purchases of fixed assets

Payment of prepaid expenses and security deposits

Principal payments of loans to lenders

Income Statement and Cash Flow Report

Consider the differences reported on the first month's Income Statement and Cash Flow Report on p. 343 for a consulting firm with three employees and five clients. This business writes checks to purchase office supplies and payroll is paid every two weeks.

On January 31, the consulting firm will prepare and mail invoices to its clients for $39,000 total revenue. This amount is posted on the Income Statement because the money is expected to be received. The $39,000 has not been collected yet, and will not show up on the Cash Flow Report until it is.

Because of this delay in collecting the fees, the owners contributed $36,000, which provided enough cash to get them through the first month. They will still need money to get them through the second month as Net/30 terms were given to clients, which means that their customers do not have to pay for the services for thirty days. As a result, the payments for the invoices may not be received until as late as March.

The only payment that the company has not made immediately is for outside services from financial and computer support consultants. So, you won't see the $1,850 for these services on the Cash Flow Report until February.

You should also learn to recognize cash transactions that do not affect cash flow in your business. Activity 9a will introduce you to the questions you need to ask and answers concerning your own business by looking at a sample business's cash flow situation.

Now let's look at some other issues related to cash flow.

Measuring Cash Flow

The first step to healthy cash flow is to measure your cash needs. If you are starting a business, this calculation includes the cash you need prior to start-up, as well as ongoing needs for operations and growth. Traditionally, entrepreneurs have used several different methods to measure cash flow, some more effective than others.

The Checkbook

One of the most common and least effective ways entrepreneurs attempt to measure their cash flow is to look at the balance in their checkbook. A positive balance is better than a negative one; however, a positive balance in the checkbook can give you false confidence that all is well. A simple look at the checkbook balance ignores the critical steps of cash flow management that include monitoring accounts receivable, paying bills, accounting for cash shortfalls, investing idle cash, and forecasting cash needs.

The Cash Cycle

A more accurate and useful way to measure and plan for cash flow is to analyze your business's cash cycle. The delay between the time you spend cash to generate a sale and the time you receive cash from the customer is called the cash cycle. Just as Jim Schott felt that he was carrying around a leaky bucket in his goat dairy business, many times when planning their cash needs business owners don't consider the drain on cash flow that the cash cycle can have.

As an example, consider when a lawn care service company sends an employee to your house to mow your lawn. The employee mows your lawn and several other lawns during that day and throughout the remainder of the week. At the end of the week the employee receives a paycheck for work completed. You may continue to have your lawn mowed weekly throughout the remainder of the month; however, you might not

Cash Management

1. Measure your cash needs.
2. Seek potential funding sources.
3. Monitor ongoing cash needs.

TiP The shorter the cash cycle, the quicker cash is generated and brought back into the business.

Consulting Company Example Income Statement	
	JAN
Net Sales (less returns & allowances)	$39,000
Cost of Goods Sold	-
Gross Margin	**39,000**
Operating Expenses	
Advertising	750
Bad Debt Expense	-
Bank Charges	-
Depreciation & Amortization	1,450
Dues & Subscriptions	-
Insurance	1,000
Licenses & Fees	-
Marketing & Promotion	1,400
Meals & Entertainment	-
Miscellaneous	-
Office Expense	-
Office Supplies	3,400
Outside Services	1,850
Payroll Expenses	
Salaries & Wages	17,500
Payroll Taxes	3,750
Benefits	1,250
Professional Fees	-
Property Taxes	-
Rent	6,000
Repairs & Maintenance	-
Shipping & Delivery	-
Telephone	450
Training & Development	-
Travel	-
Utilities	-
Vehicle	-
Other	-
Other	-
Other	-
Total Operating Expenses	**38,800**
Operating Income	**200**
Interest Expense	-
Other Income (for example, interest)	-
Income Before Taxes	**200**
Income Taxes (if C Corp)	-
Net Income	**$200**

Consulting Company Example Cash Flow Report	
	JAN
Cash In	
Cash Sale	$ -
Collections from Accounts Receivable	-
Equity Received	36,000
Loans Received	-
Other Cash In (receipts from other assets)	-
Other Cash In (for example, interest, royalties)	-
Total Cash In	**36,000**
Total Cash Available	**36,000**
Cash Out	
Inventory Expenditures	
Inventory/Raw Material (Cash)	-
Inventory/Raw Material (Pd on Account)	-
Production Expenses	-
Operating Expenses	
Advertising	750
Bank Charges	-
Dues & Subscriptions	-
Insurance	1,000
Licenses & Fees	-
Marketing & Promotion	1,400
Meals & Entertainment	-
Miscellaneous	-
Office Expense	-
Office Supplies	3,400
Outside Services	-
Payroll Expenses	
Salaries & Wages	17,500
Payroll Taxes	3,750
Benefits	1,250
Professional Fees	-
Property Taxes	-
Rent	6,000
Repairs & Maintenance	-
Shipping & Delivery	-
Telephone	450
Training & Development	-
Travel	-
Utilities	-
Vehicle	-
Other	-
Other	-
Other	-
Paid on Account	-
Non-Operating Costs	
Capital Purchases	-
Estimated Income Tax Payments	-
Interest Payments	-
Loan Principal Payments	-
Owner's Draw	-
Other Cash Out	-
Total Cash Out	**35,500**
Monthly Cash Flow (Cash In - Cash Out)	**500**
Beginning Cash Balance	**-**
Ending Cash Balance	**$500**

receive a bill from the lawn care company until the end of the month. If you pay your bill immediately, then the company would have completed its cash cycle of the services provided to you within approximately one month.

Only after the cash cycle is completed has cash been generated from a sale. Keep in mind that the business operates and pays employees before cash from sales is received. What would happen if the employees who mowed didn't receive their paychecks when they expected? Would they continue to be motivated to work hard or would they be looking for work elsewhere? Companies with a very long cash cycle, such as pharmaceutical companies and commercial construction firms, usually depend on significant funding sources to provide the funds necessary until cash is collected by selling the products or services. You should quickly recognize the difference between cash flow and profits, so you can prepare alternative cash flow sources to cover costs until the cash cycle is completed.

When measuring the cash cycle, concentrate on four primary components:
- **Accounts Receivable** – The length of time it takes customers to pay for products/services
- **Inventory** – The length of time raw materials and inventory are held before manufacture and sale
- **Accounts Payable** – The length of time it takes you to pay your bills
- **Payroll** – The length of time between paying employees

Later in this module you will learn how to use *ratios*, a standard accounting tool, to monitor the cash cycle by looking closely at these four primary components.

The Cash Flow Report
The most valuable method of measuring, analyzing, and planning cash flow is the Monthly Cash Flow Report. This report can be used to forecast cash sources and uses monthly, seasonally, and annually. In this way, you plan for cash needs on a short-term as well as long-term basis.

This module prepares you to project a Three-Year Monthly Cash Flow Report. Not only will this report help you monitor the cash effects of the cash cycle components—Accounts Receivable, Inventory, Accounts Payable, and Payroll—you will also be planning for cash shortfalls, forecasting additional cash needs, and planning to invest idle cash.

You have already projected a Three-Year Income Statement using the Financial Template in Module 8. You will go through a similar process in Action Step 9.1 to project your Three-Year Monthly Cash Flow Report.

After you have entered all appropriate financial information into the Financial Template in Action Step 9.1, you will be able to identify projected cash shortages within your business. You must plan for these cash shortages, so you can locate adequate funding to cover the shortfalls. In Action Step 9.1, you will enter the cash you receive for items other than revenue and expenditures that are not deducted from revenue.

Non-Revenue Cash Received – Non-revenue cash includes equity investments and loan proceeds. If you expect to receive the money before starting your business, it should be recorded on Start-Up Funding & Expenditures in the Start-Up Company Set-Up Worksheet. All money received after the doors have been opened for business will be recorded on the Equity & Debt Worksheet.

Non-Expense Cash Expenditures – The business will have many cash expenditures that are not considered expenses and are not deducted from revenue to determine profitability. These items do not immediately affect profitability, but their impact on cash significantly affects the financial health of your company.

Non-expense cash expenditures include these purchases:

Capital Expenditures
- Computer Equipment
- Equipment & Machinery
- Furniture & Fixtures
- Leasehold Improvements
- Vehicles
- Building
- Land

Other Expenditures
- Prepaid Expenses
- Security Deposits
- Payouts to Owners and Investors

One non-expense cash expenditure includes equity payments (non-salary) made to owners and investors as compensation for their involvement in the company. Depending on the legal structure, these payments can take many forms. In sole proprietorships, the owner can receive a check at any time for compensation. The owner is not on a regular salary. This payment is called an *owner's draw* because money is drawn out from the company. This amount is not an expense or an asset. It is considered a reduction in equity.

Equity distributions in other legal structures are called by different names. Corporations call it a *dividend*. Limited liability companies call it a *distribution*. It can also be called a *payout* or *draw*. No matter what it is called, it amounts to a reduction in equity.

Seeking Funding Sources

Once you can clearly project and monitor your cash flow situation, you may identify times when you will need to seek outside funding to improve your cash position. If so, you will want to seek the sources of funding that have a real desire to fund your business. The funding criteria offered by these sources, such as amount, cost, and control, need to match your business's financial goals. Hundreds of funding options exist out there. Don't get confused by the number of options. Not all funding sources will be available to you. Take time to identify your own goals for funding to match them with sources that will be more likely to help you.

As you begin to identify the cash needs of your business, you should also keep in mind the different phases of business growth. Each stage has its own funding needs. As your business progresses through different stages, plan and prepare for cash flow shortages and have funding sources ready to provide the cash you need.

Once you have determined your funding goals and the stages in which you will seek funding, you are ready to survey the types of funding sources available to determine which ones may be the best fit.

Cash Management
1. Measure your cash needs.
2. Seek potential funding sources.
3. Monitor ongoing cash needs.

Funding Goals

All money is not the same. When providing money, funders have specific goals they intend to accomplish with the relationship. Through discussions, you can find out fairly easily what the investor or lender wants. The key question is whether you can go along with it. You must consider your personal vision as you learn the intentions of potential money sources. Six major aspects of funding you should consider are *time, amount, use of funds, cost, control*, and *consequences*.

Time – Seeking outside money sources may take months of almost full-time effort. If your enterprise is in its early stages of development, you may have to take that time at the expense of other critical activities. Time may also be an issue for lenders. They may have to wait for your business to reach a certain stage, be acquired by another business, enter another round of funding, or go public before they receive their return on investment. Although you cannot promise equity partners a specified payment at a predetermined time, you can—and must—promise creditors when they will be paid. You both should know exactly when you will make your final payment.

Amount – The amount of money you need to finance the company has a bearing on available sources. You might be able to get immediate capital from equity partners to cover start-up or growth plans. The amount you can acquire through debt financing depends on your business's ability to begin making the payments immediately, which may be difficult to verify in the early stages of your business. Good financial research, planning, and projections can help you pinpoint the amount you need.

Use of Funds – Will the money be used for fixed assets, inventory, accounts receivable, or research and development? Each of these options requires different kinds of money. For example, a coffee shop owner seeking funds to purchase an espresso machine that will be useful for several years in producing revenue would likely seek a loan with a payback schedule of a similar time frame. In this way, the debt repayment is due in the same years that income will be generated with the machine. You need to match the term of the lending with the use of the funds. Using short-term debt to finance long-term fixed assets is a common mistake. Short-term loans usually finance seasonal inventory and accounts receivable. Long-term loans finance equipment and other long-lasting initiatives.

Cost – Money is expensive. Consider these costs: Private investors, investment bankers, or venture capitalists want 25 percent to 100 percent return per year for their funds. One of the reasons for the continued popularity of bank financing is that it is the cheapest source of money.

Control – Many entrepreneurs feel that one of the main reasons they are in business for themselves is to control their own destiny. Keep this in mind when bringing in investors, because new owners will usually want to have a say in how the business in run.

Consequences – Anyone who has ever borrowed money and not been able to repay it knows that lenders are in a position to force borrowers to pay. If they do, the worst consequence might be that you will have to close your business. Careful planning and strong, accurate projections can help you avoid such negative consequences.

Some entrepreneurs prefer to raise capital through investors who take an equity position in their businesses. Others prefer to borrow from a lender. Some do both.

Consider the sources you began exploring in Module 3, Action Step 3.3. For example, you may have found a potential equity source who will give you money immediately but the costs are high. Or, your bank will take eight weeks to put your loan together and the proceeds may not be used for working capital. Use the Reality Check *Establish Funding Goals* to record your goals and establish which sources best match these goals for the type of funding you may need in your business.

Once you have determined your goals for obtaining funds, consider when your business will need additional funds. At what stage of business do you anticipate a difficulty in cash flow?

9

Reality Check ✓   **Establish Funding Goals**

In reviewing internal and external sources of funding, I will pay close attention to the aspects that are most critical to meeting my needs:

❏ **Time** – I need the money by _____.

❏ **Amount** – The amount I will need is _____.

❏ **Use of Funds** – The money will be used for _____.

❏ **Cost** – I am willing to pay _____.

❏ **Control** – I am willing to give up _____.

❏ **Consequences** – I am willing to risk _____.

When reviewing internal and external sources of funding, consider your needs and the potential source's needs.

Stages of Business

Funding sources have different goals when they provide money to businesses. Depending on the stage that the business is in, the funders will expect different returns on the money they have invested. Some funding sources seek an ongoing relationship, others work towards promoting small businesses, and some are simply trying to earn as high a return as possible on their investment. The goals and expectations of funding sources are always important to know as you seek funds in the different stages of your business. In Module 3 you read about start-up, operational, and growth phases of funding your business. Let's consider a more refined look at the stages of business as they relate to funding.

Conception and Start-Up Stages

Most entrepreneurs must rely on their own money sources when first starting a business. Even financial institutions in business to loan money are reluctant to lend to start-ups. This position isn't personal; it is based on the high risk of business start-ups. Generally banks will only lend money to start-ups if the borrower has a good credit history, can provide solid collateral to secure the loan, and will personally guarantee the loan. Be prepared to look at your personal financial situation to identify sources of start-up funding, such as personal savings or a home equity loan. If your own personal financial situation doesn't reveal funding sources, then consider whether you might have any friends or family who would be interested in making an initial investment in your business. Many entrepreneurs start their business on the side while they are still employed. Keep this in mind if you are having difficulty finding other start-up funding.

Funding Stages

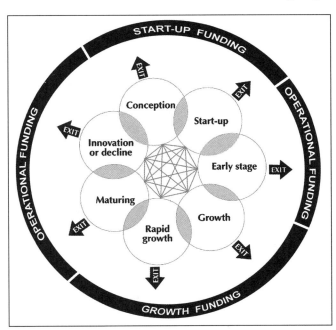

High-growth ventures may seek funding from angel investors during the conception and start-up stages. You'll need to be prepared prior to meeting with these investors; they will be expecting a significant return on their start-up investment. Sometimes you'll hear this type of financing referred to as *seed funding*. Seed funding is provided during the conception stage for developing a concept, creating the initial product, and carrying out the first marketing efforts. The company is usually very young (around one year) and has not produced a product or service for commercial sale.

Early Operating Stage

The early operating stage can put a great deal of stress on a business's daily cash flow balance. Many entrepreneurs will seek lines of credit to give them the flexibility of having the funds available when they need them. Banks are much more interested in lending to businesses with an operational track record, so obtaining loans for purchases of equipment and other large items is generally easier at this stage than at start-up. Keep in mind that in the early operating stage, friends and family might also become more interested in investing.

For those businesses with high-growth opportunities, angel investors might also be interested in getting involved by providing both funding and expertise. Alternative sources also become more available to you as your expertise grows. You may be aware of customers, suppliers, or even competitors who could become a source of cash flow through joint-venture arrangements or other agreements.

Growth and Rapid Growth Stages

Growth may mean expanding the number of locations, adding a new production facility, or just kicking up operations to accommodate new markets. Increasing levels of payroll, purchasing more inventory, and buying new equipment generally takes a lot of cash flow. All of these expenditures are expected of a business in the growth stage. Because they are expected, funding is somewhat easier to obtain. Funding sources for this phase will include banks, angels, venture capital investors, private placements, and even initial public offerings. You will want to find high-quality business advisers to help you through the maze of funding in your growth stage.

Maturing Stage

When the revenues of the business begin to plateau, the business is moving out of the growth stages and into a mature operating stage. At this stage, companies usually remain somewhat stable as long as they continue to respond to market needs.

The funding during this stage is similar to the early operating stage. Since these businesses have already established relationships with lending institutions, lines of credit or short- and long-term notes will typically already be in place. However, lenders will also recognize that the business is moving towards a need to innovate to avoid a decline in future sales, so they will be keeping a close watch on the business.

Cash Flow Sources

Funding sources will be either internal or external to the business. After you have considered the goals and timing of your funding, you should think about whether your best opportunity for funding comes from internal or external sources. Nolan Bushnell, founder of Atari®, Chuck E. Cheese Pizza®, and sixteen other businesses, spent millions of dollars of his own funds to provide seed money for his various ideas. He also raised millions of dollars from the public, which obviously had great faith in his ideas. Internal sources include not only cash flow generated from the profits of the business, but also funds provided by the entrepreneur and those close to the entrepreneur. External sources of cash flow include debt and equity options. Most external funding sources have a preference about getting involved during a certain stage of business growth.

Internal Cash Flow Sources

Internal sources of funding have the advantage of being less expensive and taking less time to secure. The disadvantages of using internal sources of funding may include not having a close relationship with an outside lending source when one is needed, not accumulating a credit history, and inconsistency in the available cash because of fluctuations in the company's cash flow situation.

Current Employment – Probably the most risk-free approach to starting a business is to stay employed either full-time or part-time. This approach allows you to use earnings from your current employer to fund your business during the start-up stage. Generally, this approach will last as long as it takes to get the business up-and-running and able to pay you a salary. Although the benefits of starting your business without having to borrow or bring in investors are many—you're in control at no cost—be sure to understand the limitations this approach will have on your current employment, your ability to get your business started, and your personal life.

Personal Savings and Home Equity Loans – Using personal savings or borrowing money from the equity you have built in your home are by far the most effortless and inexpensive ways to obtain funding for your business. By using your own funds you will also maintain total control of your business.

You will want to take into consideration a few issues, however, before pulling these funds into your business. First, how will using your savings or home equity impact your personal financial security? This issue may be less urgent if you are single without the responsibility of any dependents. Even so, what impact could losing this money have on your future?

One reason not to personally finance your business is that for your business to develop a credit history, it will need to borrow money. As you develop a relationship with a bank or lending company and repay the loan, your business is creating a credit record. This record is tracked by the financial institution that lent the money, as well as other companies that track credit ratings.

Friends and Family – Money borrowed from relatives and friends can sometimes be another easy source of funding. Although this source of funding may be external to the business and its owners, it is an internal source because it is obtained solely through close, personal relationships. Generally these sources will not require completed applications or certain credit scores. The strings attached to these loans or equity investments, however, may be rather tangled. Before receiving these funds, be sure to fully understand all requirements and expectations of the funding source. Take into consideration the potential fallout (loss of friendships or uneasy family gatherings) if something goes wrong. You should establish a clear understanding of the risk associated with the investment, as well as repayment expectations for loans that include interest rate, term life insurance to pay your debt in case something happens to you, and contingencies for not being able to repay the loan.

One recent college graduate wanted to start a tent production business with a friend and needed $20,000 for his share of the venture. The only people he knew he might be able to approach in order to raise this kind of money were his parents. He struck the following deal with his mother and father. First, they would loan him the $20,000 at 8 percent interest. To insure payback of the loan in case something happened to

TiP Using your current job to fund the start-up of your business can find you scrambling to find the time for two full-time jobs.

TiP Establishing a credit rating for your business is important if your business will ever need additional operational or growth funding in the future.

him, he would obtain a $20,000 term life insurance policy, naming his parents as the beneficiaries. He would pay the interest monthly to his parents. If the business declared bankruptcy, he would still be required to pay the 8 percent interest until the loan principal was repaid.

Credit Cards – Many entrepreneurs use credit cards as a means to jump start a business. One reason is that they can get money quickly with little, if any, application process. Credit card debt should only be used for a specific purpose with a plan to approach more traditional, less expensive funding options in the future.

As with any other debt, credit card debt must be repaid. This payment process can often be difficult given the combination of a business's tight cash flow and the credit card company's excessive interest rates. Because credit card debt is unsecured, it is a personal debt. Using credit cards can risk your personal assets.

Here are some tips for using credit card debt safely:

- Treat the debt as a regular loan with a set payback period and affordable monthly payments. In other words, never borrow more than you can pay back.
- Look for low, fixed interest rates. Moving your balance from card to card, for a time, can help you keep these low rates.
- Take advantage of the incentives of the credit card such as cash-back bonuses for purchases you might normally write a check for. To avoid taking on too much debt, never charge more than you have established in your monthly budget.
- Make sure that any cash-advance checks are made out to your company—and make a copy for your records. This way you'll have proof that the cash advances were used to expand your company and not used for personal expenditures.

Current Earnings (Profits) – Existing businesses are expected to generate cash flow from current earnings. At the completion of the cash cycle, your business should have cash left over after all expenses have been paid. This internal cash flow is an integral part of every business because until a business becomes profitable, in most cases it is paying out more in expenses than it is receiving in sales. After it reaches profitability, the cash it generates can be used to pay back loans, finance growth, or to pay dividends to the owners.

In the marketplace today, many ventures have a long lead time before they can reach a cash break-even point and eventually receive profits. Amazon.com® had massive investments in brand development and infrastructure while it still lost money. Biotech firms also endure long lead times for research and development and Food and Drug Administration trial costs before making profits.

> **TIP** Although the flexibility and price of family funding may be favorable, the potential fallout can be detrimental. Many entrepreneurs believe protecting personal relationships is worth the additional cost and added restrictions of using external sources of funding.

Reality Check ✓   Internal Sources

Check the following internal sources of funding you would consider for your business.

- ❏ Current employment
- ❏ Personal savings and home equity loans
- ❏ Friends and family

- ❏ Credit cards
- ❏ Current earnings (profits)

You should consider all the options of internal funding sources and weigh their advantages in speed and cost against the advantages of external sources of funding. External cash sources may help you build a credit history or develop your network of advisers and business associates in ways that internal sources cannot.

External Cash Flow Sources

You may need to acquire funding from external sources that must be repaid according to a specific set of terms and conditions to fund the financial needs of your venture. The money to pay back loans generally comes from sales. So, in effect, you are taking an advance against future earnings to help start and grow the business. Other investments, such as equity investments, may not have a specific payback schedule, but these will typically cost you quite a bit more in the long run.

Creative Funding Sources

Creativity is required in most areas of your business, including finding funding sources. To find these creative sources of financing, look for people who could benefit from what your company offers. These people, often termed *stakeholders*, are ones most interested in seeing your company succeed. They have a stake in your success. In other words, when you win, they win. Stakeholders might include suppliers, the landlord, and customers. They may be able to help by providing favorable terms of payment; if they are in a position to provide financing, all the better.

Customers – In some instances customers want products so badly they will either put a deposit down with their orders or supply the money an entrepreneur needs prior to getting the job done. Customers can be an inexpensive source of money. Even if they must be given a discount for paying COD, you may be ahead financially.

A Doggone Good Idea

An entrepreneur from the Great Plains spotted an opportunity when he recognized a problem affecting home builders. Environmentalists and governmental regulators complained that the increase in home building had a negative effect on wildlife such as the prairie dog. Capturing the animals and moving them to uninhabited areas resulted in higher costs to the developers and presented potential dangers such as bites and the spread of infectious diseases.

The entrepreneur obtained agreements from developers and contractors who desperately needed this service to pay him in advance to remove and relocate the prairie dogs. He reengineered the large compressor on an old wheat truck to pull air in instead of blowing it out and added a hose large enough in diameter to pull a prairie dog through it and into a cage. With the customers in hand, Dog Gone, Inc., removed the prairie dogs effectively and efficiently. The ride made the little animals dizzy, but they quickly recovered unharmed.

Suppliers – If you do not pay for purchased items when they are received, then vendors are helping to finance your operation. The longer you can delay paying vendors, the more your venture is being financed by suppliers' money. This practice is called *extended terms*, and the vendor must agree to them before you can take advantage of them. Thus, suppliers can become a source of money.

The cost of this money may be another matter. If your business must forgo pay-early discounts, the financing may be costly. Choosing to extend terms rather than take a 2/10, Net 30-day discount, costs about 36 percent annually. You can save 2 percent a month by paying the invoice within ten days rather than taking the full thirty days to pay.

Professional Advisers, Business Acquaintances – Lawyers, CPAs, other business professionals, and business acquaintances have been known to invest in an enterprise if the prospects look bright enough. After all, they are often looking for a good investment. These investors may also become part of the management team, bringing with them certain skills and knowledge critical to the future growth of the business.

Sometimes a business acquaintance has other contacts. These contacts may make additional resources available that can nurture your new firm. You never know where these investors may come from, so always be looking for opportunities to expand your network of business contacts.

Leasing Companies – Leasing is becoming a more popular financing strategy. Equipment or asset leasing, including the sale and subsequent lease back of an asset, can be a major source of capital.

Generally, lease payments cost less than loan payments on equipment. To fully understand the long-term ramifications of a lease, however, be sure that a thorough evaluation of the lease arrangement is performed. Your evaluation needs to include an analysis of the tax, financial and cash flow impact that the lease will have on your business.

One of the benefits you might identify in your evaluation is that leasing can free you from purchasing equipment that will be obsolete with changing technology. For example, a computer expected to have a 20 percent residual value in three years could be worthless in one year. The lessor accepts this risk. Many lessors provide takeouts, rollovers, or upgrades for technological changes so your business can have state-of-the-art equipment.

Microloan Programs – Essentially, microloans are small business loans that help you start or expand a business. Some start as low as a few hundred dollars and go up to about $35,000. The Small Business Administration (SBA) is now helping fund microlending programs.

Loans are typically made for purchasing inventory and other working capital needs. You will typically find that these lenders will charge higher interest rates than banks, but in return they will usually provide free technical assistance. These lenders usually require less collateral than conventional business lenders, because they recognize that borrowers are just beginning to establish credit.

Traditional Funding Sources

After exploring the opportunities with creative sources, consider more traditional funding sources such as banks, angel investors, and venture capital investors. These funding sources may be more recognizable within the business community, but keep in mind that these sources have more stringent requirements to be met before they will provide loans or equity investments to start-ups.

Here are some tips for finding the right bank and loan officer:
- Search for banks that target businesses like yours.
- Obtain referrals from entrepreneurs, accountants, lawyers, or consultants.
- Establish a business account where you do your personal banking.
- Look for full service banks that participate in SBA lending programs.
- Ask about the banking services you want for your business.

Bank Loans – Banks are a traditional source of funding to small business owners. Their principal role has been as a lender offering short- and long-term loans and lines of credit. The SBA-guaranteed lending program encourages banks and non-bank lenders to make long-term loans to small businesses because the SBA shares the lenders' risk. This arrangement allows lenders to make loans they usually wouldn't make.

Successful banking relationships are built on the personal relationship you develop with your banker. You should start early, because developing relationships and securing loans takes time. The ability of a bank to lend money to a start-up business varies and depends on the number of current loan requests and the existing loan commitments of the bank.

TIP If you get turned down for a loan from several banks, don't take it personally. Ask the lending officers why they turned you down. If their concerns are legitimate, consider revising your Business Plan.

Bank financing is attractive to business owners because they maintain control at a reasonably low cost. Payback timing and other terms are usually not flexible; however, you can sometimes negotiate these. Finding a lender with expertise in your industry will help ensure that you receive the right type of financing at the right time.

Personal Velocity

Securing a loan is often a matter of whom you know, maintains Judith Griggs, founder of Preferred Machine Tools (PMT) in Fort Worth, Texas. "If you know successful business people who can refer you to a bank, you're going to be taken a lot more seriously," she says.

Networking is especially important for entrepreneurs like Griggs, who operates a large-machinery dealership. "I have everything going against me when it comes to getting a loan," says Griggs, who buys and sells computer controlled metal-cutting equipment to manufacturers. "My business is run on cash. I get paid prior to shipment, so I have no accounts receivable, a lot of inventory, and nothing that banks traditionally look for when making a loan."

When Griggs launched PMT in 1996, she funded the company with credit cards and established a small line of credit with her bank to finance her inventory. Over the next three years, referrals from friends and former colleagues helped Griggs increase that line of credit by 400 percent. Within a few years, Griggs needed to inject a large amount of capital or money to repair her office and showroom, which had been flooded three times due to a nearby construction site that disrupted the drainage system. Griggs applied for a Small Business Administration (SBA) loan, but was turned down.

A few weeks later, Cle Royal, Griggs' FastTrac® facilitator, found out about an SBA luncheon and urged her to attend. The event gave Griggs a chance to meet program executives and loan officers—including the ones who had turned her down. Griggs introduced herself to as many people as possible, asking why her loan had been refused and updating them on PMT's recent milestones. Getting up-close and personal paid off: Bank officials reviewed Griggs' file and asked her to resubmit her application. Within three months, Griggs closed on her loan.

Griggs believes that her activity in business organizations like the Fort Worth Chamber of Commerce and Women's Business Center has also been a plus in winning financing.

Being involved benefits entrepreneurs in a variety of ways, Griggs says: "From a practical standpoint, it puts you in touch with people who know banks and can steer you to the right one when you need a loan. If they know you, they'll have a better feel for which bank will understand your business and be more interested in working with you." There's also a psychological advantage, she adds: "When lenders see that you're out and about, you immediately become more credible in their eyes."

Banks generally offer these types of financing:
• Lines of credit
• Short-term loans
• Long-term loans
• SBA-backed loans

Lines of Credit – When a line of credit is awarded to your business, you can draw upon the funds, to a maximum level, whenever you need them. This type of funding is appropriate to cover seasonal fluctuations in sales or regular cash shortages. You determine the amount and terms of the line of credit in advance based on the needs of your business and the policies of the lending institution.

In most cases, you will pay lines of credit within a year. The bank may impose other policies such as not using the line of credit for two months after you pay the balance. The rate on a line of credit will vary based on the institution and your business. In general, the rate is often 1 – 2 points over the prime interest rate for established companies and slightly higher for new businesses.

"Make sure you get the right type of loan for your business," says Judith Griggs of Preferred Machine Tools in Fort Worth, Texas. Although thrilled to obtain a $250,000 SBA loan, Griggs later discovered that the fixed-term, seven-year note didn't really suit her needs.

"Because my business is buying and selling equipment, I need to replenish inventory often, and I would have been better off getting a larger credit line," she explains.

"Be careful how many banks you approach for a loan," adds Griggs. If too many banks pull your credit records and no action is taken, it can depress your credit scores.

Short-Term Loans – A short-term note is your written promise to pay a stated sum on or by a specific date, usually in one year or less. While your new business may not qualify for a line of credit from a bank, you might have success in obtaining a one-time, short-term loan to finance your temporary working capital needs. If you have established a good banking relationship with a banker, he or she might be willing to provide a short-term note for one order, for seasonal inventory, and/or for accounts receivable buildup.

Depending upon the deal you negotiate, these loans are either *secured* (collateralized) or *unsecured* (signature loan). For a secured loan, you pledge collateral to offset the loss to the lender should you default on the loan. If you fail to meet the terms of a secured note, the lender asks the court to take possession of whatever asset you pledged as collateral and sell it. The proceeds of the sale are then applied to the amount due on the note. The loss of collateral will not release you from all liability on the debt if the collateral sale proceeds are not enough to pay off the loan.

One entrepreneur borrowed $20,000 from the bank, using his company's injection-molding machine for security. After several months, he realized that he could not repay the amount borrowed, so he stopped making payments to the bank.

The bank went to court and received a legal document that allowed the sheriff to take possession of the molding machine. The molding machine was sold for $5,000, which was shared by the lender and the attorney. The entrepreneur still owed the lender $15,000, in addition to interest, legal fees, and court costs.

Long-Term Loans – Depending on the purpose of the loan, a long-term loan will typically have a payback period between two and fifteen years. For loans obtained to purchase equipment and vehicles, the payback period will vary between two and seven years. If the loan is used to purchase real estate, the payback will be longer. Beware balloon payment provisions within your loan agreements and the impact that they have on cash flow. If included, balloon provisions stipulate that the loan be paid off prior to the end of the loan period. For example, a fifteen-year note for the purchase of a building could have a balloon provision in year five. So although the amount of each monthly payment is based on a fifteen-year amortization schedule, which keeps the payments lower, the loan must be refinanced at the end of five years. By requiring the ability to re-assess the business's financial condition and adjust the interest rate accordingly, the bank reduces the amount of risk it incurs during the loan period.

You will find that the interest rates, loan origination fees, and terms on long-term loans vary greatly based on the lending institution's policies and your business's age and financial status. Although the amount or type of collateral may be negotiable, these loans are never unsecured.

SBA-Backed Loans – The Small Business Administration is not a lender, so it does not provide direct loans to businesses. Instead it has several programs that may help you secure loans with reasonable terms. The primary programs are the 7(A) and 504 Loan Guaranty Programs. Through these programs, you can receive small business loans through participating lending institutions, which are then guaranteed by the SBA.

Lending institutions approved to participate in SBA loan programs can help provide information and assistance throughout the SBA loan application process. The main advantages of this program go to the bank. Think of the SBA as a sort of underwriter for the loan. It's like an insurance policy to the bank, and it allows them the opportunity to make loans they otherwise might decide were out of the bank's lending parameters. They have a guarantee from the SBA that if the loan recipient is unable to repay the loan, the SBA will repay a portion of the debt to the bank. The lender incurs very little risk. The main advantage for you is that you may be able to get a loan through this program when you couldn't get a loan traditionally.

Here are some smart tips for obtaining an SBA-backed loan:
- Establish a banking relationship with a full-service bank that participates in SBA lending programs.
- Develop a Business Plan that contains proper financial projections, including a Three-Year Monthly Cash Flow Report, a Three-Year Income Statement, and a Three-Year Balance Sheet.
- Prepare a current, personal financial statement for any principals involved in the venture.
- List the collateral to be offered as security, including an estimate of the present market value of each item.
- Identify the amount of the loan request and the purpose for which the funds will be used.
- Make an appointment with your loan officer and request a loan.
- If the loan is turned down, ask about the possibility of using the SBA Guaranty Loan program.

TIP Reputable lenders are in business to make loans to people who need money and can prove they are able to pay it back.

TIP To request an SBA-backed loan, entrepreneurs with at least 20 percent ownership in a company must submit personal financial statements during the application process and personally guarantee that the funds will be repaid.

All commercial lenders, including the SBA, evaluate loan applications by reviewing the following elements:

- **Cash flow of the business** – A careful cash flow projection should assure the banker that your business can repay the loan. In today's lending environment, most lenders are primarily cash flow lenders, which means that your business has to show it is profitable and self supporting. A good cash flow projection shows the viability of your business from a cash perspective. Remember, to a lender cash is king.

- **Character of the management team** – From a banker's perspective, the character of the management team reflects its willingness to pay. A record of non-payment or a prior personal bankruptcy, for example, might cause a banker to view a borrower's character as too risky. The kind of person you are has a lot to do with the kind of reception you will get at the local bank. If you have a reputation for being honest, straightforward, and responsible, chances are better that you will get your loan application approved. Character is fundamentally a personal factor. It includes many intangibles such as integrity, reputation, and background. A full resume has to be part of your financing proposal to reveal your character. Even if your banker has known you forever, include a resume anyway. Other decision makers at the bank may not know you as well. Your education, experience, and history are important. You'll probably have to sign personally for a loan while your business is small. Remember: when you're starting a business, you are your business. So a loan to your business isn't a transaction with some big faceless corporate entity; it's a loan to you. Self-marketing is an important part of your financing package.

- **Collateral available** – Collateral ties you to the deal. Experience shows that people who have their own assets on the line fight harder to make a deal work than people who are working with little of their own money at risk. Collateral also comforts the banker. Bankers really don't want to seize your collateral because they have no desire to be secondhand equipment dealers or sell out your stocks and bonds. But they like to have some recourse just in case your business fails. Bankers are not in business to take risks or bet on a long shot. For that matter, neither should you. Most studies of successful business owners show a profile of moderate risk-taking: not too conservative, but certainly not too eager to take unjustified risks. By putting up collateral, you show that you are committed to the success of your business.

TiP Even if you establish your company as a corporation, a bank may require your corporate officers to personally guarantee that the loan will be repaid.

- **Owner's equity contribution** – You have to have at least as much at risk as the bank or other investors. This doesn't mean that your borrowing capacity is limited to what you can put in personally, but it does mean that you need to have some of your own cash in the deal (plus, in some cases, the cash investment from other investors). The "creative financing" deal is not generally appropriate for business owners who plan to succeed. Your banker may ask you to secure more capital before granting a loan. Additional equity contributions can provide a cushion for the business and give your banker a sense of security about lending you money.

- **Condition** – The state of the economy and of business generally will be an issue in lending. If the economy in your area is not doing well, the risk of your deal will be magnified. Economic factors may be beyond your control but, once again, will affect your banker's decision. If times are tight, carefully planning a new venture becomes even more essential.

- **Credit** – Your credit history is a key piece of the puzzle for your banker. How have you handled credit in the past? If you have paid your debts more or less on time, you don't have a history of bankruptcy or creditor lawsuits, and you have proven that you can use credit effectively, your banker's concerns will be somewhat eased. A good credit record seldom causes the banker to make a loan, but a bad record will cause him or her to deny credit.

Bank Smart

"You always hear that you should develop a relationship with a bank before you need a loan," says Dixie Junk. "Yet when so many other issues are demanding your attention, it's hard to take that advice – especially if you're not having a cash flow problem."

Dixie and her husband, Robert, launched Jünk Architects, PC, in 1987 while living in New York. Within a few months, the company's revenue was running three times its overhead, a pleasant situation that continued for many years, so the Junks saw no need to spend time with bankers. "In fact, for the first ten years of business, we did everything possible to avoid talking to the bank," Dixie admits.

In 1997, however, the couple realized their mistake when they sought an expansion loan, which took longer than they expected. Dixie explains. "From a business perspective, we would have been better off developing a relationship with a small independent bank, because they tend to be more flexible with loans."

Fortunately, the Junks were strong on strategy. Before they approached any banks, the architects assembled a comprehensive package that included cash flow projections, aging schedules for accounts receivable and payables, equipment and furniture assets, corporate and personal tax returns, and a statement of net worth. The package also contained some of the firm's marketing materials, resumes, references, and articles from newspapers and magazines that mentioned Jünk Architects.

With the help of advisers from the Helzberg Entrepreneurial Mentoring Program, the Junks picked seven or eight banks to approach, ranking the institutions in reverse order of the likelihood they would receive a loan. "That gave us a chance to practice our presentation," Dixie says. "We tweaked it a little each time, and by the time we got to the banks on our short list, we were much more confident."

The Junks secured both a loan and line of credit, and since then, the architects have worked hard to maintain close ties with their bank.

When approaching a bank for financing, you will need to know:
1. How much you want vs. how much you need.
2. How the money will be used.
3. How it will be repaid.
4. When you will need it.

You will need to show:
1. A written business plan with completed financial projections.
2. A specific loan request.
3. What's in it for the lender to provide money to your business.

Angel Investors – Angels are private investors who provide the majority of equity-based funding to start-up stage entrepreneurs. These sources of capital are typically high net worth, former business owners and entrepreneurs who have successfully exited their businesses and seek to invest both time and money in early stage ventures. These investors may participate in multiple funding *rounds*, with each round of investment taking place at a different point in the business's growth and need for additional funds. Funding start-up companies is high risk (with 10 to 15 percent of invested companies providing most of the return on investment to angels); consequently, these investors seek high-growth opportunities to invest both their cash and their time. Angels invest

TIP If you are networking, be alert to the possibility that you may be talking to an angel and not know it.

from their personal accounts. Typically, they seek companies with the potential to grow between 10 to 30 times their value in five years.

Angels typically invest in rounds of $250,000 to $1 million with several angels investing $25,000 to $100,000 each. Frequently angels are drawn to ventures because they have an interest in that particular industry or in the entrepreneur. Since angels are experienced businesspersons, you should also expect to engage two or three of these angels in the business, as mentors, advisers, or directors. Look for angels who can bring substantial value to your business, both specific business segment experience and general management skills. Most angels are willing to spend several hours per month helping invested entrepreneurs grow their business.

Angels engage in a diverse set of activities and are not usually full-time investors in early stage companies. Consequently, they tend to invest in local companies, those within two hours' travel time of their residences. Wise entrepreneurs look for angel investors in their neighborhood.

After investing, angels expect frequent reports on the progress of the company in meeting both financial and non-financial objectives. How much and how often will your angel investors require such information? Ask them!

Angels do not publicize themselves as investors. Therefore, they can be difficult to find. They frequently attend events where entrepreneurs gather to informally nose around to see what might be of interest to them. They usually do not disclose their investor status until they have already become interested in the business.

In the past decade, however, investors have formed and joined over 200 new angel organizations in the United States. Angels join these organizations to see more deals and to take advantage of efficient deal processing that organizations have adopted. Like solo investors, angel organizations tend to invest close to home.

TiP To find the angel organization in your region, look in the public directory published by the Angel Capital Association, www.angelcapitalassociation.org.

In regions with no organization, angel investors can be hard to find. Look for them by contacting:
- Early stage service providers (for example, attorneys, accountants, entrepreneurship centers).
- Local governmental economic development agencies.
- Venture capital clubs and other networking associations for entrepreneurs.

Venture Capital Investors – While angel investors primarily fund start-up and early stage businesses, venture capital investors seek later stage companies with phenomenal growth potential—those who need several million dollars to achieve success. Like all equity investment, venture capital money is an expensive funding option, requiring you to sell equity in the business in return for capital. For a high-technology company with a very aggressive growth strategy and an expectation of extraordinary growth, venture capital may be appropriate. Very few companies, however, (fewer than 2,000 in the United States) are successful in attracting first-time venture investment each year.

Venture capitalists usually specialize by industry and stage but, in general, venture capitalists work in all growth industries. Today's investments are predominantly in high technology and life sciences. Most venture capitalists require a round of seed funding before they invest, but a few work at the earliest stages of a technology with scientists and developers.

Venture capitalists are full-time, professional investors of risk capital. They invest funds solicited from state and corporate pension dollars; trusts and endowments, corporate resources, and wealthy families. A good venture capitalist becomes a part of the venture building team, with the CEO and other executives. Unlike an angel who is investing personal money, though, venture capitalists have a responsibility to their own investors to maximize the return on investment. Because of these expectations, venture capitalists will want to cash out of the business in five to seven years, through the sale or merger of the company or, more rarely, through an Initial Public Offering (IPO).

When thinking about contacting venture capital firms, entrepreneurs should consider the following characteristics:

- **Size of market** – Venture capitalists are looking for high-growth potential, which usually translates into a $1 billion market, and a new company that can capture at least $100 million in revenue over five years.
- **Types of investments** – Venture capitalists are looking for new markets, new technologies or radically different ways to do old things. For the most part, venture capitalists are interested in technology-based, high-growth ventures.
- **Minimum investments** – The average round of venture capital investment is $7 – 8 million, but a few venture capitalists will invest as little as $500,000 in highly promising companies with an overall need for $3 – 5 million in financing. Sometimes early stage businesses will have multiple rounds of venture capital financing. The earlier the stage the riskier the investment—and this risk must be mitigated by a highly attractive business opportunity. If you need less than $2 million in total funds, angels are really your only equity option.
- **Management team**—Venture capitalists look for a management team with experience in the market in which they operate. They also value prior experience in start-up companies. You should be able to clearly show how key positions— chief executive officer, chief operating officer, chief financial officer, vice president of sales, and chief technology officer—will be handled in your venture.
- **Venture capitalist's participation** – Like angels, most venture capitalists play active roles in the firms in which they invest. In a very real sense, when you take equity capital, your investor becomes a partner in the operations of your business. They usually place representatives on the board of directors and will take steps to ensure the CEO has the experience necessary to grow your company as planned.
- **Cost of investment** – Venture capitalists invest with the expectation of *cashing out* the investment within five years for a return of at least five times their investment and often much more. This exit is usually achieved though a sale or merger of the company or through an IPO.

You must carefully plan communication with venture capitalists. Seek venture capitalists who invest in your industry and business stage. Few entrepreneurs find money by blanket e-mailing their business plans to all venture capital firms they can find. The old adage is still true, "It's not what you know, but who you know." The best way to get your Business Plan noticed is through a referral from an attorney, board member, angel investor, entrepreneurship center, trade organization, or other personal contact.

Another opportunity for you to find interested venture capitalists is through venture capital competitions or events. Many entrepreneurial organizations plan venture capital conferences that introduce entrepreneurs to potential investors. At these events, you can receive mentoring and pitch your company to hundreds of potential investors.

Good consultants can also help you raise capital. Angels and venture capitalists, however, are almost never willing to invest in companies who have contracted with consultants who require a success fee. Equity investors seek entrepreneurs who write their own business plans and network extensively to find sources of capital.

The story of Scott Cook's search for venture capital for Intuit® (the maker of QuickBooks®) is fairly typical. He contacted twenty venture capitalists and was turned down by all of them. Only after raising money from friends and family, writing his own ads, and receiving orders was he able to obtain funding.

When you get the opportunity to talk with angels and venture capitalists, be straightforward about your business plans and financing needs. Be prepared to discuss these issues:

- Your plan to meet the growth expectations in the areas of business that most interest the venture capitalist
- Your management team: key positions filled and plans for the future
- Your role in the business, now and in the future
- An appropriate exit strategy, with specifics of which public companies might be interested in acquiring your company in the future, and why

Once you initiate a relationship but before you are funded, maintain open communication to keep venture capitalists updated about your progress and setbacks.

Private Placements – A private placement is the sale of securities not involving a public offering. This type of financing may take the form of debt, equity, or a combination of the two. Private placements are exempt from scrutiny by the Securities and Exchange Commission (SEC) so long as companies meet certain guidelines.

Preparing a private placement memorandum may cost anywhere from $3,000 to $20,000 or more, depending on the complexity of the venture. Wealthy passive investors often are attracted to fund private companies. Neither angel investors nor venture capitalists require private placement memoranda for investment. They prefer to depend instead on extensive study of the entrepreneur, management team, and business plan to validate the investment opportunity.

You can make a private placement directly, but more commonly investment bankers, broker/dealers, and financial consultants handle these matters much as they would handle other types of financing. Consult a knowledgeable investment lawyer or accountant before attempting a private placement offer.

Paying for the preparation of a private placement memorandum does not guarantee your company is fundable or that any investor may be interested in funding the company. Carefully study other possible sources of capital for start-up and ongoing ventures prior to paying for the preparation of a private placement memorandum.

Initial Public Offerings – An initial public offering, also referred to as *going public*, results from a privately held company electing to sell a portion of its common shares of stock through public markets. Going public is very expensive and also involves significant regulations and restrictions. Although this option is very unlikely for successful start-up ventures (fewer than 200 venture companies go public annually in the United States), public markets are excellent sources of large amounts of money to fund company growth. IPOs can provide an opportunity for early angels and venture capitalists to eventually liquidate their investment, as their shares later become eligible for public trading. While IPOs are often described as an exit strategy, they are primarily opportunities for promising companies to raise significant amounts of capital to fuel the continued growth of the business.

External Sources

Check the following external sources of funding you would consider for your business.

❑ Lines of credit
❑ Short-term notes payable
❑ Long-term notes payable
❑ SBA-backed loans

❑ Angel investors
❑ Venture capital investors
❑ Private placements
❑ Initial public offerings

Traditional internal and external funding sources may or may not provide you with the best option for cash flow. You have to evaluate the cost of each of these funding sources in terms of interest charges and expected dividend payments to owners and other non-cash considerations such as loss of control, bringing in business partners, and public scrutiny of business operations. After your evaluation, if you determine that you need additional funding and the traditional funding sources are not going to cover any or all of your cash flow needs, then you might want to consider alternative cash flow sources.

Alternative Funding Sources
Alternative funding sources are primarily available to existing businesses that have created some value they can use to generate cash flow. You can consider some alternative sources now that may be helpful to you in the future. You may want to plan ahead to use them in your financial projections.

Factoring – Factoring applies to companies with Accounts Receivable; therefore, it is not usually an appropriate way to finance the start-up stage. Factoring is a way to short-term finance by selling accounts receivable to a commercial financing company called a *factor*.

Factoring does not use your Accounts Receivable as collateral. Instead, Accounts Receivable are sold directly at a discounted value to a factoring company. Factors do all of the collection work, which includes mailing the invoices and doing the bookkeeping. This process means that customers will be notified that their accounts are owned by and payable to the factor.

Joint Ventures / Strategic Alliances – Sometimes other firms with an interest in your business will form a strategic partnership to help you accomplish tasks. The firm wants to benefit from your work. For example, if you were working on a new toxic waste disposal system, you may find a waste management firm to finance your work. The strategic alliance would probably involve a specific agreement that provides benefits to everyone involved. For example, you would receive the resources of the larger firm and it would receive exclusive licensing rights to the resulting technology.

In other cases, you can use a joint-venture arrangement to help finance your operations. Two or more firms can share the same assets such as the plant, offices, and people, thus lowering their capital needs. New venture incubators are based on the principle that they can help a new firm get started by furnishing some of the fixed assets it needs on a basis it can afford.

Find a Partner

Hair Prosthesis Institute (HPI) of Nashville, Tennessee, which makes custom-hair prosthetics for women and children, was growing faster than owner Sheryl McCaleb had anticipated. She had already increased her physical space to 1,200 square feet from 800 but needed to expand again.

She began to look for property to buy and found a 9,000-square-foot office building a mile from her original office. One problem, however, was that the building needed considerable "TLC." Not only would McCaleb need to raise more than $700,000 to buy the building, but she would also need a sizeable amount for repairs and renovation.

McCaleb didn't have that kind of capital—or enough collateral for a jumbo mortgage. Her solution: Find a partner with financial wherewithal.

She joined forces with a friend in the building-supply business, and the two formed a limited liability company (LLC) to make the purchase. "He asked for controlling interest, but I didn't mind because he brought so much to the table," McCaleb says. Besides financial liquidity, the partner had a long track record of business success and could mentor McCaleb.

What's more, the partner's building-supply connections enabled the duo to get discounts on materials needed for the renovation. McCaleb also bartered as much as possible, exchanging HPI's services for lower rates on everything from cleaning to new carpeting. The lower renovation costs enabled McCaleb to keep rents down, which benefited HPI as one of the building's new tenants. Eventually, McCaleb bought out her partner with a buy-sell agreement set up when the building was purchased. She is now the sole owner.

Buying the building has given HPI tremendous flexibility, McCaleb says: "The way the building is laid out makes it easy for us to expand as we need to."

Sale of Distribution Rights – Often people will pay money for distribution rights to a product. Naturally, to get a lot of money from a distributor, you must be prepared to give a lot in return. The distributor may ask for the rights to a large area, such as everything east of the Mississippi. Before selling these rights, you should require performance guarantees.

Reality Check ✓   Alternative Sources

Check the following alternative sources of funding you would consider for your business.

❏ Factoring   ❏ Joint ventures / Strategic alliances   ❏ Sale of distribution rights

---

As you think about your business's future funding needs and review the information you've just read, you can use the chart on p. 363 to help you remember which types of funding are most commonly used during the different stages of business. This chart should help you put your fund-raising energies where they will be most effective for that time in your business cycle.

Funding sources can be valuable when you choose them for a specific purpose. Consider these reasons for choosing a funding source:
1. The funder's capacity fits the size/needs of your business.
2. The funder understands your industry.
3. The funder will help manage the financial aspects of your company.
4. The funder will take an active role in the management overall.

Most funding sources have a preference about getting involved during a certain stage of business funding. The checks in the following chart indicate the stages when the type of funding is commonly used.

Type of Funding	Conception and Start-Up	Early and Mature Operations	Growth and Rapid Growth
Current Employment	x		
Personal Savings and Home Equity Loans	x	x	
Friends and Family	x	x	
Credit Cards	x		
Current Earnings		x	x
Customers	x		
Suppliers	x		
Professional Advisers or Business Acquaintances	x	x	
Leasing Companies	x	x	
Microloan Program	x	x	
Bank Loans		x	x
Angel Investors	x		
Venture Capital Investors			x
Private Placements			x
Initial Public Offering			x
Factoring		x	
Joint Ventures / Strategic Alliance		x	x
Sale of Distribution Rights		x	x

Projecting cash flow and identifying potential outside funding sources are two of the three primary elements of healthy cash flow. The third element is monitoring your business's ongoing cash needs as the business grows and matures.

Monitoring Ongoing Cash Needs

In Module 2 you encountered the comparison of searching for business opportunities to mining for gold. The analogy also applies to monitoring cash flow. A gold miner does not strike it rich in one panful of gold dust. The miner who accumulates wealth goes out every day, dips pan after pan in the river, swirls their contents, pays close attention to what stays in the pan and what sloshes out, protects the findings, and eventually sees a return on these efforts.

So it is with business. Just because you have enough cash to start the business does not ensure continued success. You must have cash along the way to support operations and business growth. As you have seen, your cash needs change in each stage of business as the operations and profits fluctuate. At times, you will need a great deal of cash to seize opportunities that present themselves. At other times, you will have surplus cash and need to identify successful investing opportunities to make the most of your cash. To be successful, you must monitor ongoing cash needs. This process means establishing goals for cash flow and using these goals to make changes in cash expenditures or funding.

Cash Management

1. Measure your cash needs.

2. Seek potential funding sources.

3. Monitor ongoing cash needs.

You have had many opportunities in this program to establish cash flow goals for your business. In this section, we will concentrate on tools for monitoring cash flow. These tools include ratios and cash cycle components—Accounts Receivable, Inventory, Accounts Payable, and Payroll. You will use your Monthly Cash Flow Report to plan for cash shortfalls, forecast additional cash needs, and determine where to invest idle cash.

Ratios

Financial ratios are an important tool you can use to analyze the activity and results of your business. A major responsibility of a business owner is setting goals and expectations for the company and then monitoring the results. Ratios allow you to perform a high-level review of your business to see if certain areas need a closer look. In Module 8 you learned about ratios that monitor profitability. This module is concerned with ratios that track cash performance.

TiP Only make decisions based on ratios calculated with consistent and realistic numbers.

Measurements are only as good as the numbers that go into them. Be sure that you are using accurate financial information. If you need help, find a financial adviser to help you analyze your financial information and set up a ratio analysis for your business. If you feel you understand the process, then you can replicate this analysis in the future. Otherwise, keep your adviser involved periodically (monthly or quarterly) throughout the year to help you assess your company's successes and needs for improvements.

Ask these questions about your financial ratios:
- **How consistent and realistic are the numbers used to calculate the ratios?** If the numbers have been tallied inconsistently, are not realistic, or are not up-to-date, the ratios will be of no value.
- **How closely do the individual ratios compare with company policies?** Company policies should be established to help the business meet financial goals. For example, most entrepreneurs set a standard for the number of days they will allow credit terms. If they allow customers a Net/30 payment schedule, then their Day Sales Outstanding should be near 30 days. This number would confirm that the company is following the policy to collect on receivables within 30 days.
- **How closely do the individual ratios compare with other companies within the industry?** A very valuable use of a company's ratios is to compare them with other businesses in the same industry. In doing so, you can learn ways to improve overall profitability. For example, you might find that your company is in a very small minority of companies with a slow inventory turnover; you are keeping inventory longer than most other companies within the industry. Since this practice is a poor use of cash, you need to evaluate the reasons and make improvements in your inventory policy.

Liquidity Ratios

Liquidity Ratios measure the amount of cash or investments that can be converted to cash to pay expenses and short-term debts. Liquidity Ratios determine your ability to meet current liabilities. The two most common Liquidity Ratios are the *Current Ratio* and the *Quick Ratio*.

The Current Ratio is calculated using Current Assets and Current Liabilities. A 2:1 Current Ratio is usually considered ideal. In other words, your business has twice as many Current Assets available as it has Current Liabilities.

The Quick Ratio is the ratio of Current Assets (minus inventory) to Current Liabilities. This information determines if you have sufficient cash, receivables, and marketable securities available immediately to pay off current debts. This number should be at least 1.0.

Liquidity Ratios

Current Ratio

How it is calculated	Total Current Assets / Total Current Liabilities
What it measures	Whether your company has enough liquidity to pay its short-term obligations.
What it tells	This ratio tells whether enough cash is available to pay the bills. Theoretically, a current ratio of 2.0 is preferred for most companies. Watch this ratio closely. If it begins to go down, your company's cash position may erode quickly. The quickest way to increase cash is to improve sales.

Quick Ratio

How it is calculated	(Current Assets – Inventory) / Current Liabilities
What it measures	Whether your company's assets minus inventory will provide enough liquidity to cover its short-term obligations.
What it tells	Also referred to as the acid test, the quick ratio shows whether the company has enough cash to meet its short-term obligations. A 1.0 ratio is usually preferred. If this number is going down, then sales are not strong enough to meet daily cash obligations. Quick cash management intervention is required.

Other types of financial ratios include Risk Ratios and Efficiency Ratios.

Risk Ratios

Risk Ratios measure what portion of the company belongs to people outside the company including how much money the owners could lose to creditors. The Debt Ratio compares your Total Liabilities to your Total Assets. If this number is higher than 1, your company owes too much to outsiders and has a negative net worth. The Debt to Equity Ratio compares what you owe (liabilities) to what you or others have invested in the company (equity). You should strive to have more equity than debt so that this number stays at 1 or below.

These ratios can help you understand the level of debt your business should carry. The right amount of debt can be good for your business because it can allow you to finance the growth of your business. But too much debt can drag your business down as you try to keep up with debt and interest payments.

Risk Ratios

Debt Ratio

How it is calculated	Total Liabilities / Total Assets
What it measures	The proportion of assets financed by creditors' funds (debt).
What it tells	A Debt Ratio of more than 1 means negative net worth. In other words, if a company could sell all of the assets for full value, it would still not have enough money to meet all its obligations. This ratio will vary depending on the industry, so you will want to be familiar with the ratio benchmarks within your industry.

Debt to Equity Ratio

How it is calculated	Total Liabilities / Total Equity
What it measures	How much the company relies on debt versus equity financing.
What it tells	The more a company's debt exceeds its net worth, the less likely it is to obtain financing. As this number increases, your company's ability to obtain financing decreases. Additionally, the owner's position is weakened and those that own the debt (banks, large suppliers) can establish control of the company. This ratio will vary depending on the industry, so you will want to be familiar with the ratio benchmarks within your industry.

Now let's look at some ratios that can help run your business more effectively.

Efficiency Ratios

Efficiency Ratios tell how well you are conducting business. These ratios measure how quickly inventory moves (Inventory Turnover Ratio), how well you collect Accounts Receivable (Days Sales Outstanding), and what kind of sales your company's assets generate (Investment Turnover Ratio).

How well you establish business policies and follow them can have a significant impact on sales. For example, you may establish a Net/30 payment term for your customers that allows them thirty days before they must pay the net amount on the invoice. This policy does not mean, however, that you will receive all of your expected invoice amounts in exactly thirty days. Many businesses that owe you money will stretch the terms as far as they can to improve their own cash flow. In this case, you must stick to your policies and enforce your Net/30 terms with an active collection process.

Efficiency Ratios

Inventory Turnover Ratio

How it is calculated	Cost of Goods Sold / Average Inventory
What it measures	Shows how often inventory turns over.
What it tells	High turnover is generally good. It indicates popular merchandise. High turnover may also indicate insufficient merchandise and lost sales. This ratio will vary depending on the industry, so you will want to be familiar with the ratio benchmarks within your industry.

Days Sales Outstanding (DSO)

How it is calculated	Average Accounts Receivable / (Net Sales / 365)
What it measures	Average number of days it takes customers to pay their bills.
What it tells	How effective your company is at collecting money and how much "float" it must finance. DSO shows how effective a company's credit policies are. Remember, the tighter the credit policy, the lower the DSO. That policy, however, may also reduce sales. When evaluating your DSO ratio, keep in mind the cash position of the business, as well as the availability of additional funds to finance your customers' purchases. This ratio will vary depending on the industry, so you will want to be familiar with the ratio benchmarks within your industry.

Investment Turnover Ratio

How it is calculated	Net Sales / Average Total Assets
What it measures	The amount of sales generated by the assets.
What it tells	How efficiently your company uses its assets. This measurement shows how quickly and how often an asset (piece of machinery or investment) pays for itself. If an older piece of equipment works more slowly but pays for itself three times in a year, while a newer model takes two years to pay for itself, the owner must reflect on whether the payoff is worth the greater investment. This ratio will vary depending on the industry, so you will want to be familiar with the ratio benchmarks within your industry.

It is not important that you calculate every ratio each time you analyze your cash flow. You may, however, use several ratios to help guide improvements in specific areas of your business. Reviewing and monitoring the cash cycle may be a way you can zero in on specific ratios that indicate a need to adjust operations to improve cash flow.

Cash Cycle

If you are short of time, like many entrepreneurs, you may feel you have a limited time to spend on ratio analysis. If so, try using the cash cycle to evaluate your cash position. The *cash cycle* measures the time it takes a dollar to flow from Cash through Inventory through Accounts Receivable and back to Cash. The cash cycle is the primary factor in measuring and evaluating a company's cash available to meet current obligations. Combined with profitability analysis (see Module 8), the cash cycle helps indicate a business's long-term ability to meet its obligations.

Because of the four accounts involved—Inventory, Accounts Receivable, Accounts Payable, and Payroll—the cash cycle can look deeper into your financial situation than any one of the above ratios. The cash cycle combines these four ratios.

Days Inventory

Days Inventory measures the number of days that cash resources sit unused in the form of raw materials or unsold inventory. Days Inventory compares your average inventory balance to the total Cost of Goods Sold (for product-based companies) or Cost of Sales (for service-based companies). Then, by multiplying this figure by 365 days, you can determine the average number of days raw materials, finished goods, or merchandise are held before they are sold. Since the fewer days you hold inventory the better, a low Days Inventory will benefit the cash cycle the most. When inventory goes unsold, your cash cycle lengthens because your cash is tied up in raw materials and merchandise. Compare your Days Inventory ratio to that of other businesses in your industry to determine if you are reducing your inventory at an acceptable rate. For service companies without inventory, parts, or other merchandise, Days Inventory will be zero.

$$Days\ Inventory\ =\ \left(\frac{Average\ Inventory}{COGS\ per\ year} \right) x\ 365\ days$$

Days Receivable

Collections on Accounts Receivable are measured by calculating Days Receivable, which is the time it takes customers to pay for products or services. Days Receivable measures how many times your receivables turn over each year by comparing your average Accounts Receivable balance to the total annual credit Sales. Then, by multiplying this figure by 365 days, you can determine the average number of days it takes customers to pay their invoices. An acceptable Days Receivable ratio will reflect your collection policy. For example, if you allow your customers 30 days to pay and your Days Receivable is 32 days, you are doing an acceptable job of collecting cash from your customers. Anytime customers are slow in paying you for products and services already sold, your cash cycle lengthens.

$$Days\ Receivable\ =\ \left(\frac{Average\ Accounts\ Receivable}{Sales\ per\ year} \right) x\ 365\ days$$

Days Payable

Days Payable measures the time it takes for you to pay your bills to suppliers who have allowed you credit terms. Your Accounts Payable balance represents payments still due to vendors who have allowed you credit terms. These vendors are likely supplying materials or services that you use in offering your products or services (Cost of Goods Sold or Cost of Sales). Days Payable compares your average Accounts Payable balance with the annual Cost of Goods Sold or Cost of Sales and then multiplies by 365 days to determine the average number of days it takes for you to pay your bills. An acceptable Days Payable ratio will reflect your payment policy. For example, if your vendors allow you 30 days to pay your invoices and your Days Payable is 28 days, you are doing an acceptable job of paying your bills. For service companies that do not have Cost of Sales calculated and included within their Income Statement, the Days Payable ratio will be zero. Still, if vendors have allowed payment terms, the delay between the time a service business receives services or products and the time that it actually pays for them represents an estimated Days Payable ratio.

$$Days\ Payable\ =\ \left(\frac{Average\ Accounts\ Payable}{COGS\ per\ year} \right) x\ 365\ days$$

Days Payroll Accrual

Days Payroll Accrual measures the time it takes for you to pay your employees. This ratio assumes that your primary costs for payroll relate to offering your product or service (Cost of Goods Sold). Days Payroll Accrual compares your Average Payroll Accrual with the annual Cost of Goods Sold or Cost of Sales then multiplies that number by 365 days to determine the average number of days in your payroll cycle. Your Days Payroll Accrual should reflect your payroll cycle. For example, a bi-weekly payroll should yield a Days Payroll Accrual of around fourteen days, and a Monthly Payroll Accrual should be around thirty days. For service companies that do not have payroll related to Cost of Goods Sold or Cost of Sales, the payroll cycle is measured in days. For example, a business that writes payroll checks every Friday would have a Days Payroll Accrual of seven days. This estimate should give you a fairly accurate number to compare with your Days Payroll Accrual.

$$Days\ Payroll\ Accrual\ =\ \left(\frac{Average\ Payroll\ Accrual}{COGS\ per\ year} \right)\ x\ 365\ days$$

Cash Cycle

To calculate the number of days in the cash cycle for your business, perform the following calculation:

Cash Cycle = Days Inventory + Days Receivable − Days Payable − Days Payroll Accrual

Using the cash cycle to measure and analyze cash can help you establish cash management controls. These controls will help you tighten your cash cycle. The shorter your cash cycle, the more efficient your business. Your industry will have certain standards, such as allowing 30 days for customers to pay, that you must consider. Keep in mind these ideas for shortening your cash cycle:

Inventory – Your goal is to keep inventory moving as fast as possible.
- Make judicious inventory purchases
- Liquidate slow-moving or obsolete inventory
- Seek extended payment terms for your purchases of raw materials and inventory

Accounts Receivable – Your goal is to receive payments as soon as possible.
- Offer incentives for prompt payment.
- Aggressively pursue overdue accounts.
- Put unreliable payers on shorter payment terms or COD (Cash on Demand).
- Bill on a timely basis.

Accounts Payable – Your goal is to hold payments as long as possible without incurring past-due charges.
- Buy from firms offering longer payment terms.
- Don't pre-pay without receiving adequate benefit.

Payroll Accrual – Your goal is to keep payroll cash as long as possible without improving your own cash position on the backs of your employees.
- Make sure your paydays are similar to others in your industry.
- Be careful about changing the paydays just to improve the company's cash position; employees take their paychecks very seriously.

TIP The IRS takes a *very* dim view of businesses that fund their operations with payroll taxes that should have been paid to the government.

Keep in mind that ratios are an important tool for your business, but you should not make decisions based solely on ratios. Use these tools to identify areas of your business where you need to dig into and research unexpected results. By helping you pre-identify those areas where you need early research, ratios can save you a lot of time and energy.

Summary

This module explores financial components that affect the cash flow your business will need to operate and grow. It also helps you analyze and investigate potential funding sources to determine the most realistic opportunities for funds. With this information in hand, you will be able to explore ways to monitor your ongoing cash needs using the Monthly Cash Flow Report, financial ratios, and cash cycle. You will use the Financial Template to project your cash flows from operations and determine funding needs.

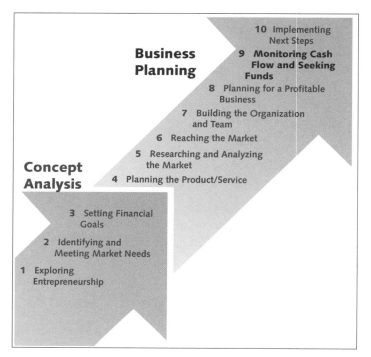

Key Things to Remember

- Businesses can operate without profits for a time, but never without cash. "Cash is King!"

- Cash is needed to support a successful start-up, to create stable operations, and to seize opportunities as they become available.

- Funding sources must be carefully researched, analyzed, and interviewed to establish a relationship in which everyone's needs concerning time, amount, use of funds, cost, control, and consequences can be met.

- Ongoing cash needs must be monitored to identify future cash needs and improved operations to maximize cash flow.

- The Financial Template can be used to project when you will need cash during the first three years of operations.

You are nearly through your initial business planning process. Completing the financial modules will give you the final information you need to make good decisions about starting this business. In Module 10 you will put your plan together, conduct your final tests of feasibility, and determine your next steps.

Activity 9a   Cash Flow Management

Analyze projected cash flow information and provide suggestions for improved cash flow to the company.

Directions
The relationship between cash and profits can be confusing. You need cash to purchase equipment and support operations in order to build profits. You need profits to replenish cash. This activity will help you distinguish between cash and profits. You will also explore the ways accountants report these two financial aspects on the Income Statement and Cash Flow Report. Using an Income Statement and Cash Flow Report for a sample company, you will project the next month's expected cash flow and make recommendations to the company on ways to improve cash flow.

Step 1 Project February profits and cash flow. Using the information concerning this sample company on p. 372 and the following information provided by your facilitator, project February's profit on the Income Statement and cash flow on the Cash Flow Report.

Check the following option chosen by the facilitator:
- ❏ **Option 1** – Project February's information with the expectation that January's amounts continue to be the same throughout February.
- ❏ **Option 2**– Project February's information by making adjustments to January based on the following information:

Step 2 Discuss cash flow management options. After projecting February's Income Statement and Cash Flow Report, analyze your findings and answer the following questions:

1. Is the profit adequate to generate cash flow?

2. Is the cash flow sufficient to fund cash flow needs?

3. What changes, if any, would you make to improve cash flow?

Activity 9a   Cash Flow Management   continued

Consulting Company Example Worksheet

Income Statement	JAN	FEB
Net Sales (less returns & allowances)	$39,000	_____
Cost of Goods Sold	-	_____
Gross Margin	**39,000**	_____
Operating Expenses		
Advertising	750	_____
Bad Debt Expense	-	_____
Bank Charges	-	_____
Depreciation & Amortization	1,450	_____
Dues & Subscriptions	-	_____
Insurance	1,000	_____
Licenses & Fees	-	_____
Marketing & Promotion	1,400	_____
Meals & Entertainment	-	_____
Miscellaneous	-	_____
Office Expense	-	_____
Office Supplies	3,400	_____
Outside Services	1,850	_____
Payroll Expenses		
Salaries & Wages	17,500	_____
Payroll Taxes	3,750	_____
Benefits	1,250	_____
Professional Fees	-	_____
Property Taxes	-	_____
Rent	6,000	_____
Repairs & Maintenance	-	_____
Shipping & Delivery	-	_____
Telephone	450	_____

Cash Flow Report	JAN	FEB
Cash In		
Cash Sales	$ -	_____
Collections from Accounts Receivable	-	_____
Equity Received	36,000	_____
Loans Received	-	_____
Other Cash In (receipts from other assets)	-	_____
Other Cash In (for example, interest, royalties)	-	_____
Total Cash In	**36,000**	_____
Total Cash Available	**36,000**	_____
Cash Out		
Inventory Expenditures		
Inventory/Raw Material (Cash)	-	_____
Inventory/Raw Material (Pd on Account)	-	_____
Production Expenses	-	_____
Operating Expenses		
Advertising	750	_____
Bank Charges	-	_____
Dues & Subscriptions	-	_____
Insurance	1,000	_____
Licenses & Fees	-	_____
Marketing & Promotion	1,400	_____
Meals & Entertainment	-	_____
Miscellaneous	-	_____
Office Expense	-	_____
Office Supplies	3,400	_____
Outside Services	-	_____

Activity 9a **Cash Flow Management** continued

Consulting Company Example Worksheet

Income Statement

	JAN	FEB
Training & Development	-	
Travel	-	
Utilities	-	
Vehicle	-	
Other	-	
Other	-	
Other	-	
Total Operating Expenses	**38,800**	
Operating Income	**200**	
Interest Expense	-	
Other Income (for example, interest, royalties)	-	
Income Before Taxes	**200**	
Income Taxes (if C Corp)	-	
Net Income	**$200**	

Cash Flow Report

	JAN	FEB
Payroll Expenses		
Salaries & Wages	17,500	
Payroll Taxes	3,750	
Benefits	1,250	
Professional Fees	-	
Property Taxes	-	
Rent	6,000	
Repairs & Maintenance	-	
Shipping & Delivery	-	
Telephone	450	
Training & Development	-	
Travel	-	
Utilities	-	
Vehicle	-	
Other	-	
Other	-	
Other	-	
Paid on Account	-	
Non-Operating Costs		
Capital Purchases	-	
Estimated Income Tax Payments	-	
Interest Payments	-	
Loan Principal Payments	-	
Owner's Draw	-	
Other Cash Out	-	
Total Cash Out	**35,500**	
Monthly Cash Flow (Cash In - Cash Out)	**500**	
Beginning Cash Balance	**-**	
Ending Cash Balance	**$500**	

Action Step 9.1   Project My Three-Year Monthly Cash Flow Report

Use the Financial Template to project your Three-Year Monthly Cash Flow Report and determine cash needs for start-up, operations, and growth.

Directions

The action steps in Modules 8 and 9 will help you create a professional looking Financial Plan. Since you have been gathering this information throughout the program, the task of building the Financial Plan will be easier. See the table on p. 315 in Module 8 for a complete list of sources of information for action steps in Modules 8 and 9.

The Financial Template activities in Module 9 center on your business's cash flow. You will enter your expected cash sources and expenditures. These are the template worksheets you will use for this action step:

❏ **Capital Budget Worksheet**

    Section A Depreciation (existing capital assets)

    Section B Capital Asset Purchases and Depreciation (post-start-up)

    Section C Other Capital Expenditures

❏ **Equity & Debt Worksheet (post-start-up)**

    Section A Equity Investment

    Section B Real Estate Loans

    Section C Traditional Business Loan and/or Other Long-Term Loans

    Section D Line of Credit

    Section E Cash Position

❏ **Start-Up Company Set-Up Worksheet** (Start-Up Funding & Expenditures Loan Proceeds and Equity Investments only)

A. **Gather your financial information and start entering the data.** Using the table on p. 315 of Module 8 as a guide, gather the information you have already researched and analyzed related to your Financial Plan.

    1. Load the most up-to-date Financial Template you used for Action Step 8.2.

    2. Save the file using a new name to identify the action step and the date. For example, "MyFinancials_ Projections_0111.xls." This step creates a new version of the Financial Template file that contains all previous work completed.

    3. Use this new template file to begin entering new financial information into the worksheets described on pp. 375 – 376.

Action Step 9.1 **Project My Three-Year Monthly Cash Flow Report** continued

❏ **Capital Budget Worksheet**

You will enter your budget for capital expenditures and other uses of cash on the Capital Budget Worksheet of the Financial Template. The different sections of this worksheet will guide you through the process of recording the cash you expect to spend after start-up for such things as equipment, owner's draws, and dividend payments. You should record start-up purchases on the Start-Up Funding and Expenditures Worksheet.

Capital Budget Worksheet shows you how to record the purchase of capital assets, depreciation, and money paid to the owner and investors. Read each section carefully as some assets such as land require unique methods for recording depreciation. Record information for the categories that apply to your business.

If you will be paying yourself a salary, that figure belongs in the production expenses for the Inventory Projections or in the Operating Expense Projections not in the Capital Budget. If you will be withdrawing funds for yourself that are not a salary, they will be listed as owner's draw in the Capital Budget. You may decide to pay yourself a salary and have an owner's draw, but do not list the same figures in both worksheets.

Include assumptions when appropriate. After you complete the Capital Budget Worksheet, you may want to view other sheets in the Financial Template to see how the data links to the other worksheets and the financial statements. Include your capital budget projections in the Appendix of your Business Plan.

❏ **Equity & Debt Worksheet**

In this step, you will record how and when money will be invested or loaned to the business over a three-year period. The Equity & Debt Worksheet takes you through the steps for equity investment, real estate loans, traditional business loans, and lines of credit. This worksheet will calculate your cash balances to show whether you have adequate financing.

You will enter funds received for business operations *after start-up* on the Equity & Debt Worksheet in the Financial Template. You should enter start-up funding on the Start-Up Funding and Expenditures Worksheet. The Equity & Debt Worksheet is divided into several sections that represent the type of funding you plan to include in your Business Plan. The funding you receive may include both *equity* (money provided by owners of the company) and *debt* (money loaned to the company by outside sources). Questions in the template will prompt you in each section to determine if that form of funding is to be added to the planning period. If they apply, you will record the equity investment, new loans received, and loan payments on existing and new loans. You will be asked these questions:

• How much of your own cash and/or other investors' cash will be sought as equity?
• Do you have an existing loan on real estate (building, land) or are you planning to seek a real estate loan during the planning period?
• Do you have an existing business loan or are you going to acquire a business loan for start-up, operations, or growth of the business?
• Do you have an existing line of credit (a short-term loan used to cover cash shortfalls as they occur) or are you planning to get a line of credit?

The template provides an analysis section that shows cash balances based on all your projections for spending and sales as well as borrowing and equity investments you have made to this point in the process. You will be prompted to evaluate the cash balance to determine if it is sufficient to support the start-up, daily operations, and growth of your company. The template offers several options if you still find yourself needing additional cash to support business operations.

Action Step 9.1 Project My Three-Year Monthly Cash Flow Report continued

❏ **Equity & Debt Worksheet, Section E Cash Position**

This section of the Equity & Debt Worksheet is the reality check for your Financial Plan. Once you have recorded your plans to obtain investments and loans in Sections A through D, review the cash balances for each month in the three-year period. Are any months near or below $0? If so, the worksheet lists four options to consider, then you can make adjustments accordingly.

If you need help in determining how much of the loan repayment is principal and how much is interest, use the Amortization Schedule Worksheet.

❏ **Start-Up Company Set-Up Worksheet**

You have already entered the start-up items needed for your business in the Start-Up Company Set-Up Worksheet. You will add to this information the amount you and your investors will initially put into the company as well as the amount you plan to borrow in the Start-Up Funding & Ependitures Worksheet on this page.

Complete this worksheet after all the other worksheets. Once the Equity & Debt Worksheet is complete, you will have a much better sense of the amount of cash you will need to support the business until the profits begin to generate enough cash to support itself.

B. **Review the Cash Flow Report.** After you have entered all of your financial data into the Financial Template, print off and review the Cash Flow Report. Review the statements for errors you may have made in entering data.

Action Step 9.2 Finalize My Financial Plan

Use the Financial Template to evaluate the profit potential and cash flow strength of your business for feasibility based on your personal financial goals, and use the Business Plan Template to write a narrative summary of your Financial Plan.

Directions
Congratulations! You have completed the financial projection process. This action step will help you prepare the information needed to complete the financial section of the Business Plan. There are three steps involved in completing the Financial Plan. First, print the statements you need for your Business Plan. Second, analyze the results. Third, complete the written portion of your Financial Plan.

A. Print out the financial statements. Use the Print Options Worksheet to print the following financial statements to include in your Business Plan:
- Monthly Income Statement
- Monthly Cash Flow Report
- Year-End Income Statement
- Year-End Balance Sheet
- Financial Analysis/Ratios

The worksheets you used to project the information are also a useful resource for your Business Plan. Use the Print Options Worksheet to print the following worksheets that apply. These documents should be included in the Appendix of your Business Plan:
- Historical Balance Sheet, if you have one
- Start-Up Funding & Expenditures
- Sales Projections
- Inventory Projections
- Operating Expenses Projections
- Capital Budget Projections
- Equity & Debt
- Amortization Schedule

B. Analyze the financial statements. Now that your financial statements are complete, you need to conduct a final review to confirm that the business's profit and cash flow potential match your own personal financial goals.

1. According to your Income Statement, is the business profitable? Is there Net Income?
   - ❏ Yes. Is the level of profit reasonable for a start-up in your industry?
   - ❏ No. If it is not profitable and a Net Loss is reported, then how much is the loss? Is this loss expected?

Annual losses may be expected during the start-up and early stages of your business. Monthly losses may also be expected during the yearly business cycle. For example, your revenue stream may be very seasonal like many retail stores. These businesses may experience losses throughout the year until the holiday shopping begins in the fall. During that time of year, these businesses will need to generate strong revenues to cover the losses experienced earlier in the calendar year.

Action Step 9.2 **Finalize My Financial Plan** continued

2. According to your Income Statement, is your required salary included?
   - ❏ Yes. Can you reduce your salary requirements if the business does not meet projections?
   - ❏ No. What adjustments need to be made to provide you the salary you need?

   A business's financial success is directly tied to the financial goals of the entrepreneur. If the business does not meet your personal financial goals, you should consider making changes to the business concept or explore a different concept that will produce more positive projections.

3. According to your Cash Flow Report, is the ending cash balance positive every month?
   - ❏ Yes. Is there enough cash to support growth opportunities, or unforeseen events such as poor payers, equipment break-down, or additional expenses not estimated?
   - ❏ No. How much additional cash is needed? Will you be able to obtain that much cash?

   When you review for profitability, the primary question is whether the business will eventually generate an adequate amount of cash to support operations, pay back loans, and pay an adequate rate of return to owners. If you are not able to generate enough cash flow to cover these, you should continue your financial statements past the third year to identify whether the business will, at any point in time, generate enough cash flow.

4. According to your Balance Sheet and other financial ratios, are the figures consistent with industry standards?
   - ❏ Yes. Are there any opportunities to make improvements to the financial performance of your business to improve your Balance Sheet and financial ratios?
   - ❏ No. Which ratios are inconsistent with industry standards? For the ratios that show deficiencies, will you be able to make adjustments to your Business Plan to bring your ratios in line with your industry expectations?

   Although some of the Balance Sheet figures will vary somewhat, be prepared to explain why your balances are significantly different from the industry standards. Looking at the liquidity, risk, and efficiency ratios, how do your ratios compare to similar businesses? You will want to identify areas where improvements are needed.

C. **Complete the written portion of the Financial Plan.** A narrative summary of your Financial Plan will appear in front of the financial statements. For this action step, you will describe your start-up costs, sales and income projections, cash requirements, sources of financing, and exit strategy. The template asks these questions to help you focus on the highlights of your Financial Plan. The modules where you have worked on the answers are listed for your convenience.

Action Step 9.2 **Finalize My Financial Plan** continued

Business Plan

Start-Up Costs
What are your estimated costs to start this business? Are these one-time costs (expenditures) or ongoing costs (expenses)?

Module 3

Sales Projections
What are your sales projections for the next three years? Where did you get the information to project financials? Are the projections reasonable?

Module 8

Income Projections
What are your net income projections for the next three years? When will your company be profitable?

Module 8

Cash Requirements
How much cash will be required to cover start-up costs, operations, and/or growth?

Module 9

Sources of Financing
Based on cash requirements to start, maintain operations, and grow, will you seek debt or equity financing? How much is the cost of obtaining these funds?

Modules 3 and 9

Exit Strategy
What is your overall plan for growth? How will this plan enable you to obtain a wealthy harvest upon exit? What are your specific plans for going public, selling the business, merging the business, or other?

Module 2 and www.fasttrac.org/toolkits

Implementing Next Steps

Throughout this FastTrac® NewVenture™ program, you have researched, analyzed, tested, modified, written, and rewritten sections of your Business Plan. By completing the action steps in the previous modules, you have created all the major content for your Business Plan. You not only know more about your business concept, but you know more about yourself than when you started.

The value of the FastTrac® business planning process is in helping you see how all the different aspects of your business fit together. Completing a Business Plan is like fitting all the pieces of a puzzle together. In this final module, you will add those last puzzle pieces and check for missing pieces. For the first time in the program you will complete all the module action steps *before* the next session rather than after. This module guides you through adding the final touches to your plan, evaluating and presenting the plan, and testing for feasibility. Then, you will determine the next steps necessary to turn your dream of starting a business into a reality.

Key Questions
- What are the final steps in the business planning process?
- How can I effectively communicate my Business Plan in an oral presentation?
- What are some pitfalls to avoid as I implement my business?
- What are my next steps?
- What resources are available in my community for ongoing business planning?

Action Steps   Due Date
❏ 10.1 Feasibility Checklist   _____
❏ 10.2 Create My Executive Summary   _____
❏ 10.3 Finish and Assemble My Plan   _____
❏ 10.4 Identify Next Steps   _____
❏ _____ _____
❏ _____ _____
❏ _____ _____

Evaluating the Business Plan

You are nearly finished with your first phase of business planning. As you may have guessed by now, business planning is never fully completed. Every aspect of your business requires monitoring, adjusting, and revisiting throughout its life. But for now, you are nearly ready to celebrate the accomplishments of this first round with your business planning process.

This module includes two important decision points in your business planning process. First, you will encounter the Feasibility Checklist. This checklist will validate the feasibility of the business concept and its match with your personal vision. You will be asking, "Is this business feasible for me as I have conceived and projected it?"

Second, you will make another decision about whether to start this business or pursue another business idea. Whether or not you choose to pursue the business as you have projected it these past few weeks, you will still be asked to present the results of your business planning experience at the final FastTrac® session.

Before you continue with Module 10, you should take a little time to be sure you have finished all the action steps in earlier modules. These actions steps need to be completed before you can finalize your plan and proceed with the feasibility testing and presentation required by this final module.

Test for Feasibility

The first major decision point of Module 10 is to test your overall concept for feasibility. You have been testing and evaluating and reworking it throughout the program. Action Step 10.1 asks you to complete the Feasibility Checklist one last time using all the knowledge and information you have gleaned throughout the program. This checklist helps you identify the major criteria that can make or break your business. By evaluating your planned business against these criteria, you can ensure that your business plan creates the best chances for your venture's success.

For More Information

about testing for feasibility, go to www.fasttrac.org/toolkits.

Before starting any business, think about the strength of your product or service, the potential of the market, and the profitability of the venture. Some weaknesses may be easily overcome, while others may not. If you cannot improve your score on a low-rated criterion on the Feasibility Checklist, verify whether this low-scoring criterion is one that you identified as non-negotiable. If so, you will need to take note of it later when you determine whether or not you will pursue this concept.

The Feasibility Checklist criteria can also be used to develop benchmarks for continued growth in the product or service, market, and financial areas. If you decide to start your business, you can use this checklist to set targets and refer to these benchmarks periodically to assess your progress. This checklist can be used throughout the life of your business.

Remember, the business in this checklist is considered a perfect business, one that does not exist in real life. No one expects your business to be perfect; however, be realistic in terms of its potential. The Feasibility Checklist in Action Step 10.1 provides important information to consider when deciding whether to start your business, modify it, or abandon the concept. Can the current weaknesses be overcome through modifications?

Match with Personal Vision

Many people start businesses without analyzing how well the business will meet their own personal goals. As a result, business owners may find themselves unhappy, unfulfilled, and wanting out of the business they built.

One aspiring entrepreneur dreamed of opening a barbeque restaurant in which she and family members, pulling together and sharing the same vision, would work. Her Business Plan proved her concept was sound, the market was there, the funds were available, and the profitability likely. As she planned the hours of operation and the different roles each family member would fill, she realized that, at least initially, they would all need to be at the restaurant most of their waking hours. While this was her vision, it was not her family's. They had other interests beyond working at a restaurant. She abandoned the barbeque restaurant and continued to search for a venture consistent with her personal vision and her family's happiness.

One way to avoid this situation is to compare your Business Plan to your personal vision before you start the business.

Compare your Business Plan to the personal vision you developed in the first three modules of this program. This comparison provides you the opportunity to make sure the business fits your aspirations. After comparing your Business Plan to your personal vision in Reality Check *Match With Personal Vision*, you may decide to make changes in one or the other. If they are not compatible, you would be wise to pursue something else. Matching your personal vision with the right business is essential for long-term satisfaction.

Whether your business concept perfectly matches your personal vision or needs modifications, you have plenty of material to complete the written portion of your Business Plan and prepare an oral presentation for your fellow participants in the next session.

Remember that business plans are living documents. Even if you choose to radically modify this business concept or apply your newly gained entrepreneurial skills to an entirely different concept, you will want to experience the satisfaction of having completed this planning process. As you finish writing your Business Plan, develop your Executive Summary, and finalize other documents, you will have a stronger grasp on what is good about this concept and what still needs to be adjusted. You can choose from the written plan what to emphasize in your oral presentation during your final program session.

TiP It does not matter if your plan rates high in feasibility if it is not aligned with your personal vision. The ideal business for one person may not be the ideal business for another.

Match Plan and Vision. Testing a business concept against your personal vision provides a safeguard against starting the wrong business.

Match With Personal Vision

Go back and review the goals you stated in Action Step 1.1 Create My Personal Vision on pp. 27 – 31 and Action Step 3.4 on pp. 117 – 127. Then, evaluate your business concept as fully planned with your personal vision and financial goals. If the Business Plan does not allow you to meet the goals most important to you, determine how you can modify your plan to do so. If you cannot reconcile the differences, consider whether to abandon this specific business concept.

❏ Does my Business Plan still match my personal goals?

❏ Does my Business Plan still match my professional goals?

❏ Does my Business Plan still match my financial goals?

List your goals that do not match the proposed business.	Identify changes you could make in the proposed business to increase its match with these goals.

Completing the Business Plan

Your Business Plan is a reflection of your professionalism. While readers evaluate the business concept you present to them in the final document, they will also be evaluating *you* based on how well your plan is put together. They will assess the Business Plan on how easy it is to:

- Find information quickly.
- Determine the strengths of the business concept.
- Understand your overall goals and objectives.
- Read the plan.

Your Business Plan will include the components listed on the Business Plan Components table. You have probably written many drafts throughout the program. With your research complete and the main content written, you are ready to add the final components to your plan—the Cover Page, Executive Summary, Table of Contents, and Appendix.

After the plan is put together, you should review it for completeness and accuracy. You can use the Reality Check *Business Plan Checklist* on pp. 388 – 391 for easy reference. You will remember using this checklist from the Reality Check *Critique a Start-Up Business Plan* in Module 4. Now you can use it to evaluate the completeness and effectiveness of your own plan. Your plan should also be critiqued by a trusted mentor.

Business Plan Components

Business Plan Component	Should be:	Refer to:
Cover Page	Completed with this module	Action Step 10.3
Executive Summary	Completed with this module	Action Step 10.2
Table of Contents	Completed with this module	Action Step 10.3
Management and Organization Plan	In draft format	Action Step 7.1
Product/Service Plan	In draft format	Action Step 4.1
Marketing Plan	In draft format	Action Steps 5.1, 5.2, 5.3, 5.4, and 6.3
Financial Plan	In draft format	Action Step 9.2
Appendix	Completed with this module	Action Step 10.3

Executive Summary

The Executive Summary is a brief overview of the entire Business Plan. It should not be more than two to three pages long. Readers will find the answers to most of their questions in this summary.

As you write the Executive Summary, keep in mind your intended reader and the purpose of presenting the plan. Every time you present your plan to a new audience, you will want to consider writing a new Executive Summary. That way you can highlight the information the new audience is most interested in. Individual attention to readers' needs is more likely to gain their attention to your request.

Action Step 10.2 will help you complete your Executive Summary.

TiP The Executive Summary is the only section of the plan that some evaluators read. If the Executive Summary does not clearly and concisely convey your business concept and its uniqueness, most lenders or investors will read no further.

Reality Check ✔

Executive Summary

What types of persons would have a better understanding of your business if you shared your Executive Summary with them?

❏ Suppliers

❏ Vendors

❏ Potential employees

❏ Potential advisory board or board of directors members

❏ Potential customers

❏ Other _____

Cover Page

An effective Business Plan Cover Page will do two things: create a positive first impression and communicate key information. The Cover Page can be creative, but should be simple, useful, and easy to read. Make it as easy as possible for lenders and investors to contact you. Include phone numbers and e-mail addresses and double-check their accuracy. Question anything that may detract from the credibility of your plan.

If you are going to distribute your Business Plan to several different investors or lenders, assign a different number to each plan on the Cover Page. This system will allow you to track Business Plans out for review. It also may discourage recipients from copying

TiP Consider having recipients of copies of your plan sign a non-disclosure agreement in which they agree to refrain from revealing the contents or ideas of the plan to anyone else.

or widely distributing the plan to others. It is advisable to include a statement, such as, "The contents of this plan are proprietary and confidential. It is not to be duplicated in any way." Remember, if you disclose information without a signed non-disclosure agreement, you may lose your ability to protect the information through trade secrets, patents, or other types of legal protection.

Action Step 10.3 provides questions to answer when compiling your Cover Page.

Table of Contents

TiP Carefully proof the Table of Contents when the Business Plan is complete. Double check all page numbers. You convey a sloppy image if the page numbers are off.

An organized and accurate Table of Contents will help you and the readers of your plan find information quickly. The Table of Contents lists subject headings and subheadings with accompanying page numbers. This list helps you and the readers of your plan find specific information. You can add dividers and tabs to the final Business Plan for easy referral to the different sections.

The following is an example of how the Management and Organization section should appear in the Table of Contents.

TABLE OF CONTENTS

MANAGEMENT AND ORGANIZATION 4
    Legal Form of Business.. 4
    Management Team... 4
    Board of Directors / Advisory Board 4
    Recruitment and Selection of Employees........................ 5
    Compensation and Ownership..................................... 5
    Employee Reward and Incentive Plan 5
    Communication.. 6
    Infrastructure... 6

Create the Table of Contents after the rest of the Business Plan is final, using the instructions in Action Step 10.3. That way, the heading and subheading titles are established and the page numbers should not change.

Appendix

The main sections of your Business Plan should not include excessive detail or technical specifications. An Appendix is the appropriate place to put all supporting information for the details discussed in the Business Plan. These documents lend credibility to your plan. Use Reality Check *Appendix* to determine what types of documents you need to gather to include in your Appendix. Action Step 10.3 gives you further directions for compiling the Appendix.

Appendix

The following documents you have developed or gathered in this program should appear in the Appendix rather than in the text of your Business Plan. Check which of the following documents you will include in your Appendix:

❏ Worksheets from the Financial Template including: Start-Up Company Set-Up Worksheet, Start-Up Funding & Expenditures; Sales Worksheet; Inventory Worksheet; Operating Expenses Worksheet; Capital Budget Worksheet; Equity & Debt Worksheet; and the Amortization Schedule (if applicable)

❏ Detailed resumes of the management team or key personnel who are or will be working in the venture

❏ All employee contracts, stock option plans, and retirement plans

❏ Personal financial statements for each of the principals

❏ Copies of patents, copyrights, and intellectual property registrations

❏ Copies of actual agreements such as legal structure, sales contract, distributor contract, non-compete/non-disclosure, and other legal documents

❏ Samples of product/service brochures or other advertising

❏ Copies of any logos already developed

❏ Copies of reference letters, recommendations, or endorsements less than twelve to sixteen months old

❏ Copies of related market studies or articles from trade journals or other appropriate media, including the source and date

❏ Professional photographs of the product, facilities, or equipment

❏ Customer-signed orders or letters of intent

❏ Related information to support the industry study, such as demographics or magazine articles, including the source and date

❏ Detailed descriptions of products

❏ Map showing the location of business

❏ Copy of any credit reports on the business

Assembly

After writing the Executive Summary, creating a Cover Page and Table of Contents, and collecting Appendix documents, your next step is to assemble your Business Plan. An orderly Business Plan will make it easy for you and your readers to use.

A logical order and complete document are also critical if you are seeking outside funding. When reviewing a Business Plan, lenders and investors learn more than the details about the proposed business venture; they learn about the person or team who prepared the plan. They look for attention to detail, thoroughness, and professionalism in addition to a credible plan. These indicators help them assess if the person or team who put the plan together has the professionalism to manage the money that they will lend or invest. The Business Plan is the lender's first indication of the kind of work the team can do.

A simply bound, well-written, grammatically correct, and properly organized plan is far more likely to be well received than a handsomely bound, well-illustrated plan that contains spelling errors, is poorly organized, or includes unsupported assumptions. Business Plans that include attractive design elements, simple fonts, and lots of white space are easier to read.

For More Information

on evaluating your Business Plan using a comprehensive checklist of style, format, and content go to www.fasttrac.org/toolkits.

Order for Each Section

Each Business Plan section should begin on a new page in the following order:

Cover Page
Table of Contents
Executive Summary
Management and Organization Plan
Product/Service Plan
Marketing Plan
Financial Plan
Appendix

Reality Check

Business Plan Checklist

After your Business Plan is assembled, review it for completeness and accuracy. For each section, this Business Plan Checklist identifies what information should be included in your plan and tips on how it should appear. The Business Plan Checklist helps you evaluate if your plan includes key content and is well written.

By evaluating your plan against this checklist, you will find changes may need to be made. These changes will make your plan more readable, concise, complete, fact-based, and error free.

Overall Readability

Yes	No	
❏	❏	Language is concise (does not read like a novel or term paper).
❏	❏	Each section stands on its own and clearly defines and satisfies its objective.
❏	❏	Facts are supported with sufficient documentation.
❏	❏	Conclusions drawn from facts are reasonable.
❏	❏	Contents are supported with sufficient charts and graphs.

Overall Spelling/Grammar/Math

Yes	No	
❏	❏	Spelling is correct.
❏	❏	Grammar is clean.
❏	❏	Math is error-free.

Overall Formatting

Yes	No	
❏	❏	Font choice is readable.
❏	❏	Spacing between lines is sufficient.
❏	❏	Plan contains headings and subheadings.
❏	❏	Formatting on headings and subheadings is consistent.
❏	❏	Plan includes page numbers.
❏	❏	Formatting on page numbers is consistent.
❏	❏	Plan contains enough white space for readability.

Business Plan Checklist continued

Cover Page / Table of Contents

Yes	No	
❏	❏	Cover Page contains name of business.
❏	❏	Cover Page contains chief executive's name.
❏	❏	Cover Page contains address, telephone, fax numbers, e-mail, and Web address.
❏	❏	Cover Page contains company logo.
❏	❏	Page numbers in Table of Contents correspond correctly.
❏	❏	Appendix includes a Table of Contents.

Executive Summary

Yes	No	
❏	❏	Does not exceed three pages and wholly describes the new venture.
❏	❏	Describes the unique features and benefits of the product/service.
❏	❏	Identifies the management team and supporting infrastructure.
❏	❏	Explains the opportunities found within the industry.
❏	❏	Contains plans for targeting a market segment and penetrating it.
❏	❏	Specifies how much money the company needs and how funds will be obtained.

Management and Organization

Yes	No	
❏	❏	Explains the legal form of business.
❏	❏	Lists key management positions, including primary job responsibilities.
❏	❏	Identifies the board of directors/advisory board members, including primary contributions expected.
❏	❏	Documents the process of recruiting and selecting employees.
❏	❏	Clarifies the compensation and employee reward systems.
❏	❏	Establishes credibility of the management team.

Products/Services

Yes	No	
❏	❏	Describes product/service in plain language (not too technical).
❏	❏	Describes product/service in specific terms (not too broad).
❏	❏	Provides evidence that the product/service is technologically feasible.
❏	❏	Identifies unique features.
❏	❏	Identifies special benefits.
❏	❏	Wholly explains product/service limitations and potential solutions.
❏	❏	Wholly explains product/service liabilities and potential solutions.
❏	❏	If applicable, identifies production process and facility plans.
❏	❏	Provides backup suppliers and subcontractors.
❏	❏	Anticipates future related products/services and spin-offs.
❏	❏	Describes how intellectual property will be created and protected.
❏	❏	Lists requirements from regulatory agencies.

Business Plan Checklist continued

Marketing Plan – Industry Profile

Yes   No

❏   ❏   Focuses on current size and growth potential of the industry.
❏   ❏   Discusses industry trends and opportunities associated with each.
❏   ❏   Addresses geographic locations, seasonality, and industry profit characteristics.
❏   ❏   Identifies existing distribution networks.

Marketing Plan – Competitive Analysis

Yes   No

❏   ❏   Identifies direct, indirect, and future competition.
❏   ❏   Contains matrix to illustrate competitive position in marketplace.
❏   ❏   Describes competitive advantage.

Marketing Plan – Market Analysis and Penetration

Yes   No

❏   ❏   Contains customer profile.
❏   ❏   Contains target markets and size of each.
❏   ❏   Fully illustrates the image of the company.
❏   ❏   Describes plans to reach the market, including customer service, location, sales force, licensing and distributing.
❏   ❏   Addresses plans for advertising and promotion.
❏   ❏   Includes plans for marketing through technology, including the Internet.
❏   ❏   Discusses other penetration strategies, including publicity, telemarketing/direct mail, Web site, and trade shows.
❏   ❏   Describes plans for evaluating market penetration effectiveness.

Marketing Plan – Pricing

Yes   No

❏   ❏   Addresses pricing strategy.
❏   ❏   Contains price sheet.
❏   ❏   Includes volume and special pricing information.
❏   ❏   Contains the company's pricing policies.

Financial Plan

Yes   No

❏   ❏   Sales and profit projections appear to be reasonable.
❏   ❏   Assumptions and projections are wholly supported.
❏   ❏   All operating expenses have been included.
❏   ❏   Hidden costs have been identified.
❏   ❏   Salaries and other benefits are in line with industry standards or entrepreneur's goals.
❏   ❏   Contingency plan seems reasonable if sales forecasts go unmet.
❏   ❏   Figures on various documents are consistent.
❏   ❏   Sources of debt or equity financing are appropriately identified.
❏   ❏   Exit strategy is clearly defined.

Business Plan Checklist continued

Appendix

Yes	No	
❏	❏	Contains resumes of the management team and key personnel.
❏	❏	Contains all employee contracts, stock option plans, retirement plans.
❏	❏	Contains personal financial statements for each of the principals.
❏	❏	Contains patent and copyright approvals.
❏	❏	Contains such agreements as partnerships, sales, distributor contracts, non-compete/non-disclosure, corporate bylaws, and other legal documents.
❏	❏	Contains copies of product/service brochures or other advertising samples.
❏	❏	Contains copies of all logos already developed.
❏	❏	Contains copies of recent reference letters, recommendations, and endorsements.
❏	❏	Contains copies of market studies or articles from trade journals or other media.
❏	❏	Contains professional photographs of the product.
❏	❏	Contains detailed outlines of the operating and control systems.
❏	❏	Contains customer-signed orders or letters of intent.
❏	❏	Contains documents that support the industry study.
❏	❏	Contains detailed description of high-tech products.

Mentor Review

You can ask trusted advisers to review your completed Business Plan. Their feedback can be immensely valuable in determining the strengths and weaknesses of your plan.

Before you send it out for review, however, verify that you have followed the suggestions from Module 4, p. 160 – 161, concerning the use of personal pronouns, undocumented facts, and negative words and phrases. When you are comfortable with the tone and style of your plan, you are ready to send it out for mentor review. If possible, someone familiar with your industry should review the plan. Ask your reviewer to check for these components:

Product/service feasibility – What inherent risks does the mentor see in providing this product/service? What expansion potential is there? Do governmental regulations exist that are not discussed in the plan?

Market feasibility – Does the Marketing Plan accurately describe the potential of the market? Is the market penetration plan reasonable and affordable?

Financial feasibility – Are the revenues and expenses accurately portrayed? Can the necessary start-up funds be obtained? Is an exit strategy identified?

Presenting the Business Plan

Presenting the Business Plan to an audience is not always at the top of the "Things Entrepreneurs Love to Do" list. Yet, the ability to give an effective presentation is an important skill that can contribute to your success as an entrepreneur. If you are passionate about your business concept, you will want to tell people about it. That's why a presentation of your plan is recommended as a part of the FastTrac® program. Here are some suggestions for preparing to present your Business Plan to your fellow participants.

Know Your Audience

You may find that you need to present an oral version of your plan to selected audiences. Your plan may have more than one audience and several different reasons for its presentation.

As you prepare your presentation, consider your audience and the purpose for the presentation. This step will help you to design the presentation to meet the needs of the audience. For example, looking at the investment opportunity your business has to offer a potential investor will help communicate a key message important to that investor. In this way, your needs will be better met, too, because the audience will gain a clearer understanding of your business and the role they could play in it. Use Reality Check *Business Plan Presentation* to clarify your audience and purpose for presenting your plan.

Business Plan Presentation

Place a check mark next to the audience(s) you want to present to, then draw a line to the purpose of the presentation for that audience. You should have no more than 2 or 3 purposes for each presentation. Revisit this Reality Check whenever you consider presenting your Business Plan. Example shown.

Audience	Purpose
☑ FastTrac® facilitators and participants	Planning for success
❑ Advisory board	Solicit feedback
❑ Board of directors	Recruiting
❑ Banker or other potential lenders	Orientation
❑ Entrepreneur club	Communication
❑ Family and friends	Strategic planning
❑ Management team	Funding
❑ Mentors	Professional support
❑ Potential employees	
❑ Potential investors	

Develop a Venture Presentation for Mentors and Peers

Putting together a winning presentation is an art. It takes preparation and lots of practice. Most entrepreneurs can present themselves in a professional and convincing manner if they invest the time and effort required.

Think about the presentation you will make in the next session to your facilitators, mentors, or fellow participants. You should take into consideration the instructions given in the previous session. How much time will you have to present? What does your audience already know about you and your business? What aspects of the business planning process will be of most interest to them? How can you highlight what this program has taught you about starting this business?

Remember, even if the tests for feasibility indicate that you should go a different direction than your original idea, you have learned much about yourself, about your industry, and about your concept that you can present in the next session. Use Reality Check *Oral Presentation* to make some notes about the content for your presentation.

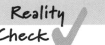

Oral Presentation

An oral presentation should cover the following ten basic areas in an engaging way. Jot down information in each area that may be of particular interest to your audience.

Company history and background

Concise product/service description

Proprietary rights

Unique features and competitive advantage

Management team

Market analysis

Financial picture, cash needs, and purpose of new investments, if any

Growth and spin-off opportunities

Potential risks

Exit strategy for potential investors to capitalize on their investment (if presentation is about securing funding)

Practice Makes Perfect. The more opportunities you take to present your plan, the more comfortable you will be when the stakes are really high.

Develop a Venture Presentation for Investors

Talking to a room full of potential investors is very different from selling a product/service to customers or presenting your business concept to fellow participants. Features and benefits pitches used for customers do not necessarily excite investors. Descriptions of your learning process are irrelevant to them. The subject of your presentation to investors is not *your* product or service but *their* money: **Who** will use it, **why** it's needed, **how** it will be spent, **what** return it will bring, and **when**.

Investors are interested in seeing the big picture at the beginning of the venture presentation. They want an engaging story about the venture's profitability, profit margins, management team, product development, size of market, competitive climate, and market niches.

Some entrepreneurs present their investment opportunities solo, while others include their key management members. Many investors prefer to meet with and hear from the management team. Alone or in a group, you must be convincing and display leadership ability and passion. These characteristics are crucial to success in raising investor money. Remember, investors bet on the person; the product or service is secondary.

When giving your presentation to investors, leave ten minutes for questions and answers, the most important part of the presentation. This time allows you the opportunity to build a rapport with potential investors and establish the credibility of the management team. Anticipate questions and prepare responses. It is better to answer questions when they are asked than to say you will get to that later. The questioner wants an answer now, not later.

One entrepreneur who was extremely successful in raising money in the early stages of his business start-up, took his Business Plan presentation "off Broadway" before meeting with the big money sources. He first gave his presentation to smaller investors in outlying areas as a way to hone his presentation skills and anticipate the questions investors typically ask. He was then well prepared to give his presentation to investors he had identified as potential key players. You might consider what opportunities you have to practice presenting your plan.

Use Visual Aids

Even if you're a charismatic public speaker, include visual aids in your presentations. The visuals should highlight the presentation, stimulate interest, and accentuate key points rather than tell the whole story. Visual information should not be repeated word-for-word in the presentation. The audience is already reading this information and will not be impressed by having it read to them. The information displayed in your visuals should highlight key points concerning the Business Plan.

TiP Regardless of the technology you use, take a set of overhead transparencies or handouts to your presentation as a backup.

Many experts warn against giving a live demonstration during a venture presentation. Technical glitches can ruin your presentation. When Bill Gates held a huge press conference to introduce Windows® 98, the computer presentation did not work. If it can happen to Bill Gates, it can happen to you.

One caution about using audio-visuals: Remember to maintain eye contact with the audience not the screen, computer, or overhead projector. The people you are presenting to should receive your consistent attention. A good presenter does not hide behind audio-visuals, but instead focuses on interacting with the audience.

These audio-visual tips can help your presentation appear professional:
- Make sure visuals can be seen from the back of the room.
- Keep information on visual aids to a minimum.
- Present only one key idea per visual.
- Limit the use of colors to no more than three, not including photographs that might be included.
- Use no more than two different typefaces and a 30-point or larger font size for projected words.

and helpful tips on creating a clear and persuasive Business Plan presentation go to www.fasttrac.org/toolkits.

Implementing Next Steps

After completing the planning process, testing for feasibility, and compiling the Business Plan and presentation, you have reached a decision point: whether to start this business or pursue something else. Complete Reality Check *What Now?* to help you in this process.

Reality Check ✔

What Now?

Ask yourself these questions:

	Yes	No	Not Yet
Did I prove a market will buy my product/service?	❑	❑	❑
Did I prove a reasonable expectation that the business will be profitable?	❑	❑	❑
Did I find solutions to reduce or eliminate the problems identified?	❑	❑	❑
Will this business get me where I want to go?	❑	❑	❑
Am I ready to commit to further planning and hard work?	❑	❑	❑

Now choose one of the options below:

❑ Pursue a modified plan

❑ Reconsider my goals

❑ Abandon concept

❑ Go ahead with concept

Start Smart

While evaluating whether to open a computer repair business that would provide onsite service to consumers and small businesses, Scott Revare pinpointed several weaknesses in his business model. The potential for a large competitor entering the market led him to abandon that concept and instead co-found Smart401k®. Revare and his partner, a financial adviser, developed a computer-based system to provide customized retirement investment recommendations for employees with retirement plans through their workplace. While Smart401k continues to grow and attract customers nationwide, Revare's original decision to abandon the first concept was confirmed when the megastore Best Buy® entered the onsite computer repair market in Revare's community. "I was bothered by the nagging thought that a more established company could easily move into this business. I wanted to find a niche that would stay unique at least until we established ourselves. I'm glad I listened to that small, nagging voice."

Starting the Business

Starting your business will be an incredible journey. The Business Plan will serve as your road map. At times, you will be able to follow the plan exactly. Other times, you will need to adjust the plan to fit the current or anticipated environment.

Once in business, periodically check your progress against your plan. Planning helps you understand details and analyze how they impact the success of the business. Dedicating time to planning lets you work on your business, not just in it.

TiP Throughout this journey, remember to celebrate your successes and learn from your mistakes.

As you begin your business, revisit some of the critical steps outlined in your plan. For example, you will want to know the exact amount of money you need and the most likely source for it. The financial modules have put you further down that road than you were when you started the program. You will also want to uncover answers to the legal issues such as structuring the business, proprietary rights, and contracts you encountered in Modules 4 and 7. The infrastructure you build will also help make your business successful. These people may include attorneys, accountants, consultants, and bankers. Your networking experiences in this program should give you confidence to find them.

Action Step 10.4 Identify Next Steps will help you identify the steps necessary to start your business after completing the plan.

Pursuing Something Else

The business planning process can save you a great deal of time and money. If you decide to pursue something else, after studying a business concept that, upon closer examination, proves not to be a good risk, the business planning process has still been successful. You have learned what you needed to know about your business concept. Rather than pursue a risky concept, you may choose to consider several options including:

TiP Most statistics show that 40 percent of new business start-ups fail within the first year. Most of these businesses should never have been started in the first place. Smart entrepreneurs walk away from business concepts that are not feasible.

- Identifying and researching a new business idea.
- Getting more education and training.
- Improving your own personal financial situation for funding a business.
- Getting a job in the industry to learn more about it before starting a business.

If the business planning process has led you to pursue a different business idea in search of something more feasible, you are fortunate. You have saved valuable resources—the time and money that would otherwise have been invested in the business. Now, you can apply the planning process to another business idea.

TiP It's okay to abandon a business idea in search of something else. Just like Hollywood producer Samuel Goldwyn once said, "I had a monumental idea this morning, but I didn't like it."

Maybe you have decided business ownership is not for you. You can still use your newly developed planning skills to make you a more attractive employee in the workplace. Most organizations need persons with entrepreneurial skills who can analyze and evaluate business opportunities. The planning process you have gained in this program is a valuable skill you will use time and time again.

Thriving in Your Entrepreneurial Role

As you lead your business from conception to start-up to ongoing success, consider your role in it. In addition to operating your business by following your plan, you need to consider ways to avoid pitfalls, stay in touch with key advisers, and evaluate opportunities to give back to the people and communities who have helped you succeed.

Avoiding Pitfalls

If you are starting a business, realize that others have been on the same path and their experiences can help you as you make decisions each day. Remember the top ten reasons businesses fail presented in Module 9 on p. 338? Go back and review them for a moment, and then consider these additional risk factors to help you avoid pitfalls as you implement your plan:

Business Plan – One of the biggest pitfalls is running a business without a plan. Without a plan, the business is run by default—whatever happens each day becomes the plan. Businesses that don't have a sense of direction may coast for a while, but why take the risk? Following a plan helps decision-making, motivation, goal-setting, and hiring. It also provides the basis for mid-course corrections. Not knowing what to expect wastes time, money, and energy—all very scarce resources for a new venture. The point is that you should not put the plan you have just written on the shelf once your business is in motion. Business Plans are living documents that can help you plan your course, but should be revisited, revised, and renewed as your business evolves.

Sharing the Plan – Another pitfall is that you never implement the plan. Whether the plan is on paper or in your mind, sharing it with others in the business is essential. If your personnel are unaware of the plan, they can be working at cross-purposes. The staff knows a lot about your business and can contribute ideas to improve decision-making along the way.

Process Standardization – Another potential pitfall is not developing processes to standardize quality, cost, and customer service. Financials, customer satisfaction, and morale can be the strengths of your business if you take the time to develop and communicate the way these things should be done each time tasks arise.

Documentation – A business can be the most substantial investment you own. But if you never document its functions, processes, and operational procedures, it is as if you own stock you can't prove exists. If a key person leaves or is unavailable for work, that person's duties may not get done, which—in the worst cases—might bring the business to a halt.

Revenue versus Investment – Your mindset and view of your business can make a big impact on how it is built and run. If you view the business as a revenue stream, you may be driven by immediate crises and the next sale. You might overlook planning, delegating, and managing. If you view your business as an investment, however, you will watch, research, and nurture it to achieve the return you expect for the risk you take.

Key Measurements – Another potential pitfall is not monitoring key success measurements. Finding out how the business is doing annually or even monthly is not enough. Key measurements can quickly reveal the financial impact of a variety of business activities. For example, you don't have to wait for the monthly sales figures to come from the accounting department to know how well your sales team is doing. Monitoring the number of sales calls per day, the number of proposals each week, and the close ratios of these proposals can tell you immediately how well it is going. If a salesperson's key measurements are faltering, you can make corrections before the impact on revenue is past recovery. Develop and monitor the key measurements for your business.

TIP *You must learn from the mistakes of others. You can't possibly live long enough to make all of them yourself.* —Sam Levenson

TIP Spend time on your business. Don't compromise your long-term vision for short-term gains by seeing your business as only a revenue generator instead of an investment.

Duties – As a business grows, it requires additional staff. Every day businesses are adding staff without written job descriptions or performance standards. Think about how inefficient that approach is and how much smoother a business operates if everyone knows what is expected of them. You need to feel comfortable that when you are off site your business is behaving as it should—that job descriptions and performance standards are in place to control the flow of work.

Team – A management team works best when it is made up of people with complementary styles and skills. When a team becomes dysfunctional, the business can lose its focus. The value of a complementary team is that business operations will be balanced, but it can also be the source of significant friction from the clash of complementary skills with different approaches. Take time to understand the perspectives of your management team and encourage communication.

The planning time you have invested in this program will help you avoid many of these pitfalls. You can change the top ten reasons businesses fail (See Module 9, p. 338) into positive reasons why your business has a great chance of succeeding. When you complete the planning process, you will be able to say these are the top ten reasons for your success:

1. I have experience in entrepreneurship and business planning and am developing a personal network of peers, mentors, and advisers.
2. I will raise the money I need through debt and equity sources.
3. I know and understand the opportunities and threats that the competition presents and have clearly identified my competitive advantage.
4. I have a plan to control and manage inventory to make the most of my money.
5. I am planning for growth.
6. I will research to seek the best location or distribution channel for my business.
7. I will purchase only the assets needed to produce the revenue projected.
8. I will seek good credit terms with my suppliers and give standard terms to my customers.
9. I will implement my Marketing Plan to achieve the projected level of sales.
10. I will complete and implement my Business Plan for success!

Getting Support

Throughout this program, you have bounced ideas off of others, shared your excitement as your plans progressed, and expressed your disappointment when results did not match your expectations. If you take the initiative, this peer network can continue to help you by providing support and advice throughout your entrepreneurial journey.

What separates new entrepreneurs from success is often access to industry knowledge and insider networks. Developing this knowledge often begins with the guidance of successful, experienced entrepreneurs. They know where the pitfalls are and can help you avoid many rough spots. Using mentors, advisers, and community resources can make the difference between success and failure for your business. They can serve as a sounding board, provide you with information, and help you make contacts at critical points as you start your business.

Mentors

In Homer's *Odyssey*, Mentor is the character who teaches and nurtures Odysseus' son while his father is away. The word *mentor* has evolved to refer to an experienced person who develops a one-on-one relationship offering advice and nurture to a less knowledgeable person. An effective mentor can be an experienced entrepreneur in the same type of business or a professional who works with entrepreneurs and understands what is required for success.

In addition to those relationships you are able to develop on your own and in this program, you may find other programs that pair entrepreneurs with a mentor. It's worthwhile to check if any formal mentoring programs exist in your community or find an online mentoring program.

Formal mentoring programs – Some formal mentoring programs may be available to you through organizations that serve entrepreneurs in your community. The organizations offering formal mentoring typically pair a successful entrepreneur with a less experienced entrepreneur. The match is usually based on type of business, goals, stage of business, personality, and other relevant criteria. Most formal mentoring programs specify the types of businesses they wish to assist.

Internet mentoring programs – A mentor connected to you via the Internet can help you understand your type of business without threatening potential competitors. For example, the Aspen Institute® offers MicroMentor®, an online mentoring program based in San Francisco, for very small business owners, or microentrepreneurs, in underserved communities. This program matches a microentrepreneur with a successful entrepreneur, often in the same industry.

Rani Saijo, owner of a small bookstore in rural Willits, California, used MicroMentor to find business expertise that did not exist in her town. Saijo said, "My mentor has the ability to take little unconnected problems and refocus them. I didn't realize how much I needed that support. I had been thinking about how to develop that [support] locally, but this has been so valuable because my mentor understands my type of business."

Informal mentoring – Informal relationships are set up directly by the mentee and the mentor. The informal relationship may grow out of casual contact, such as membership in the same chamber or industry association, or through community volunteer work, or it may be facilitated by another person, such as a peer or relative. It is appropriate to ask others if they would be interested in helping you as a mentor and explain what you would like in a mentoring relationship. Realize that not everyone has the time or inclination to be a mentor.

To be most effective, the mentoring relationship should have some agreed-upon structure and focus. The mentor and mentee should discuss these parameters:
- What are you going to focus on during the time you spend together?
- How often will you meet?
- How will you meet and communicate—in person, over the phone, online?
- How long will the relationship last?

Advisers and Board Members

Another source of experience and expertise that can benefit your business is an advisory board or a board of directors, as we discussed in Module 7. Board service is a more formal way of enlisting guidance and counsel than mentoring. Boards can strengthen and provide critical support to start-up companies. Members of advisory boards should be chosen for their range of skills and expertise. They can be a tremendous resource to an entrepreneur.

Accepting Advice

After selling his successful Helzberg Diamonds® chain of stores to Warren Buffet, Barnett Helzberg founded HEMP, the Helzberg Entrepreneurial Mentoring Program. He says, "Advice might be easier to accept if you forget the word *advice*. Think of mentoring as a way of making your thought processes clearer, sharper, and more richly seasoned.

"Seek advice from multiple mentors. If you get a good idea from one outsider, namely A, another good idea from B, and a third from C, chances are your solution will be X. That is, the composite of the good ideas from each of the outsiders plus your own good ideas. In all cases, help from at least a couple of mentors outweighs a mantra from a lone guru.

"Peers make terrific mentors. In corporate parlance, mentors are generally older and wiser executives. As an entrepreneur, you needn't be so limited." A peer can bring a set of skills different from your own.

"Finally, and most of all, chemistry counts. At HEMP, we strive to pair people who work well together, humbly acknowledging that we won't always be right about something as elusive as chemistry. What we do know is that simpatico has little to do with superficial factors, such as mentor and protégé being in the same industry. That's one reason why most of our pairings aren't industry-specific.

We also know that we want our pairs to develop associations that continue throughout the years. When we succeed, there are no words to describe the sense of accomplishment; when we fail, we uncouple, re-couple, and move on."

Boards of directors, with a legal role in the company, are a legal part of a business's organization, with by-laws, governance issues, as well as a fiduciary responsibility. An effective board can be invaluable in guiding you and your business to success.

Don't expect your mentor or adviser to provide you with easy answers. Mentors can help you see the pros and cons of a decision, exposing a variety of possible approaches, and then letting you come to your own decision.

Community Resources

TiP The most successful entrepreneurs take advantage of multiple resources.

Make it a priority to use the resources for entrepreneurs that are available to you. Small Business Development Centers, chambers of commerce, entrepreneur groups, colleges and universities, and libraries are some of community resources that may be helpful to you as you launch your business. Counseling, classes, research, referrals, and peer groups are other resources from which you may benefit. As you build your network, be sure to include persons who offer community resources for entrepreneurs.

Many states and communities have agencies and offices to help entrepreneurs start a business. Some have one-stop shops where you can obtain how-to booklets, forms, and guidance. Most states have Web sites designed to assist in starting a business with forms to download, step-by-step guides, and links to appropriate governmental offices and agencies. Browsing the Internet using "business assistance center" or "starting a business" and the name of the state as search terms should help you locate the proper site.

Staying in Touch

Using the list below, write down some names of potential mentors, advisers, or entrepreneurial resources you can benefit from in your entrepreneurial journey. If you are proceeding with your business, these will be people who can help in that process. If you are modifying your concept, starting over, or pursuing another idea, identify people who will be supportive and creative in helping you on your way.

Three people I would feel comfortable asking to engage in a formal mentoring relationship with me:

Three people I especially would like to work with in an advisory capacity (either on a board or informally):

Community resources I have identified as a crucial sounding board for developing myself as an entrepreneur or growing my business:

Other advisory resources I plan to check out (for example, online mentoring groups or formal mentoring programs):

Giving Back

In mentoring and advising relationships, you are the recipient. You get advice, support, and encouragement. As an entrepreneur, you also have the ability to give back. You can shape your community—not only through how you conduct your business and how you treat your customers and employees, but also through supporting the community as a whole. Most entrepreneurs are passionately motivated to share their success by giving back.

Ewing Marion Kauffman believed that giving back was the highest form of citizenship. Kauffman said that his work in philanthropy was the most fun he had ever had. He applied his time, energy, and resources to the things that gave his life meaning. The first lesson of Kauffman's life is that one person can make a difference.

TIP The Kauffman Foundation has developed a Giving Back to Entrepreneurship site at www.kauffman.org/givingback.

TiP The power to make a difference comes when you look inside to find what you have to give.

You don't need a fortune to give back in meaningful ways. Today, emerging philanthropists are discovering the power they have to improve people's lives by giving back to entrepreneurship, from mentoring, teaching, promoting innovation, and serving on boards to contributing financially or through their companies. As one entrepreneur-philanthropist put it, "The joy of giving back is unbelievable. It's like watching your children grow and be successful."

Changing Lives

Nancy Richards knows how difficult it can be for entrepreneurs to get on their feet. When the firm Richards worked for in the mid-1980s wasn't interested in her idea for managing and marketing foreclosed inventory, she launched her own business. First Preston Management of Dallas manages and markets foreclosed property acquired by banks and the government, putting homes back into the hands of families and private owners.

"We started with nothing—knocking on doors, making phone calls to pitch our concept. We know how tough it is when no one wants to help you," she says. "So we looked at all the things we do in these houses—protect, clean, repair, mow, appraise, broker, advertise, sell and close—and primarily picked small businesses owned by women, minorities, and veterans who could do the work and significantly build their businesses."

While Richards' decision to contract with small businesses is admittedly more complicated than hiring one firm to do it all, she's convinced the return far exceeds any costs. "We have some 2,000 ambassadors in every city and town in the United States where we do business: loyal, hardworking people who gave us roots in their communities along with a great reputation," says Richards.

In addition to training brokers across the U.S. to market and oversee properties through the Internet, First Preston also conducts homebuyer seminars and sponsors the building of Habitat for Humanity® homes across the country. Many Preston employees volunteer on builds for Habitat.

Richards' work with Habitat made her realize that home-ownership is only part of a family's journey out of poverty. People in need of homes—many of them single women with children—live with the more urgent need of meaningful employment.

In association with the Grameen Foundation, an international organization that provides small loans to low-income entrepreneurs, First Preston began a microloan program in Dallas which has funded more than 300 new entrepreneurs. First Preston is also the largest fund raiser and contributor to the Dallas Metropolitan YWCA, helping provide women with health services and child care. "The work we do is much larger than mending and selling homes," says Richards. "It's about changing lives." She finds herself blessed but also humbled by her success.

"The truth is, tremendous success is humbling; you understand there is a greater purpose than personal gain. At the end of the day, I'd much rather be recognized for the work I've done in the community than for just running a business."

Summary

With your Business Plan in hand, you are ready to start the business you have envisioned through this planning process. Or maybe the Business Plan writing process is the first step in your journey through many business concepts until you find the one that matches your personal vision. Even if you don't start a business right away, the planning process is a skill you can use time and again throughout your life. In this module, you learned how to complete the final steps in the business planning process.

Throughout this FastTrac® NewVenture™ program, you have learned that:

- A competitive advantage is vital for long term sustainability.
- Your role as entrepreneur must evolve as the business grows.
- Cash flow is paramount. Without it, your business cannot start or continue.
- Your business is a success if it helps you reach your personal, professional, and financial goals.
- The planning process is a proven way to think through all the various aspects of starting a business before you commit financial resources.

You have learned that successful entrepreneurs:

- Seek assistance from trusted advisers, mentors, and outside professionals.
- Communicate their business concept and plans clearly and concisely to their team, their customers, and their funders.
- Consider their exit strategy before they start the business.
- Set profitability goals and regularly measure the business's progress against them.
- Develop products and services that meet the needs of the market.
- Look for new opportunities on a continual basis.
- Involve the right people in their business.
- Help others individually or through the community.

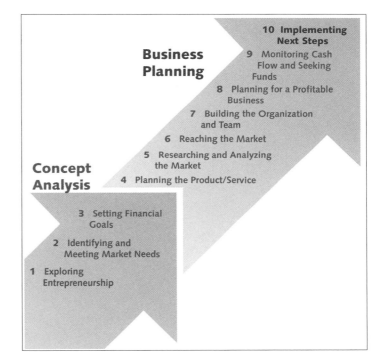

Action Step 10.1 Feasibility Checklist

Identify strengths and weaknesses in my Business Plan and test it for feasibility.

Directions
You can identify strengths and weaknesses in your Business Plan and test it for feasibility by using the Feasibility Checklist on pp. 405 – 411 or by going online to www.fasttrac.org/toolkits.

A. **Review the Business Feasibility Checklist.** Review the criteria in the left-hand column of the checklist. The ideal, or perfect, business has all these things. Then follow the remaining steps to test each area of your business for feasibility against the list of ideal criteria.

B. **Rate your business.** Using a scale from 1 to 5 (1 means your concept absolutely does not meet these criteria and 5 means your concept entirely meets these criteria), rate your business concept against the model business criteria by circling the statement that most closely resembles your business.

Action Step 10.1 **Feasibility Checklist** continued

Product/Service Feasibility

	1.	2.	3.	4.	5.
a. Customers perceive a need for product/ service.	Customers are totally clueless about my products/services.	Customers must be educated about my products/ services before they see a need for it.	Customers must be convinced to buy from me instead of my competitors.	Customers need my products/ services and will often select them over competitors'.	Slam dunk! My customers need my products/ services and want to buy from me.
b. Product/Service is ready to sell.	I have not started developing my product/service.	I could have problems; I'm still developing my products/services.	I have sold some products/ services, but they are not completely tested or trouble free.	I have thoroughly tested my products/services and am fixing the problems.	It's all figured out! My products/ services work well with minimal problems.
c. Product/Service has unlimited life.	Products/services must be sold quickly so they don't perish or become obsolete.	Products/services have a relatively short life cycle which makes profits minimal.	No sweat, I can make a profit before the life cycle ends for my products/ services.	Products/services have a fairly long life cycle which will allow for ample profits.	Products/services can be sold forever! The life cycle is unlimited.
d. Product/Service is unique and protectable.	I just don't have anything proprietary; all I offer is similar to the competition.	Product/service is not proprietary, but it stands out from the competition.	I'm going to do my best to create proprietary rights for my products/ services.	My product is somewhat unique in function or style and can be legally protected.	Got it covered! My products are unique in function and style and can be legally protected.

Action Step 10.1 Feasibility Checklist continued

Product/Service Feasibility

	1.	2.	3.	4.	5.
e. Product/Service is not regulated by the government.	Yikes! Complying with regulations is going to require lots of time and money.	The regulations are undergoing change, possibly requiring more time and expense.	It's okay. The regulations are reasonable, but I'll have to watch them closely.	It's easy to comply with regulations for my specific products/services.	I'm free! Regulations are limited to those imposed on all businesses.
f. Product/Service line has expansion potential.	My product/service has no expansion potential.	Right now, I only have one product/service to sell.	Definite expansion potential. Will require hard work to make it happen.	I have the beginnings of a product/service line with several things to sell.	My products/services complement each other, and I can easily add more to sell.
g. Product/Service has no liability risk.	I'm worried; I may encounter a large legal risk selling my products/services.	I'm not sure what the risks are in selling my products/services.	I can afford to protect myself for the risk involved in selling my products/services.	I will have minimal risk selling my products/services; I can afford to protect myself.	No problem! I'll have no liability risk selling my products/services.

Product/Service Feasibility Score: _____

Action Step 10.1 Feasibility Checklist continued

Market Feasibility

	1	2	3	4	5
a. Market can be recognized and measured.	My customers could be just about anyone, so targeting a certain group may not be easy.	I have many potential customers, so I need to do more research to find my target market.	I have identified my potential customers, but they will be somewhat difficult to reach because of their demographics or buying patterns.	With some effort, I can use my customers' demographics/buying patterns to find them.	My potential customers are easy to find because of their demographics or buying patterns.
b. Existing competition has identifiable weaknesses.	I have lots of competition who have been in this business longer than I.	I have no competition! Hmmm, I wonder why?	I have identified my competition, but I do not know its weaknesses.	I know my competition and its weaknesses, but I need more research.	I have limited competition, and I know its weaknesses.
c. Distribution system is established and receptive.	I must develop a brand new distribution system.	My current distribution system offers only limited options.	I've found a distribution system already established with several options.	Several distributors seem receptive to carrying my products/services.	Unbelievable! Distributors are calling me wanting to carry my products/services.
d. Customers purchase frequently.	Customers will only buy once from me, so I must find new customers all the time.	Most customers will only buy once from me.	Customers will buy more than once, but not frequently.	Some customers will purchase products/services frequently.	Wow! Customers purchase similar products/services very frequently.
e. Business has great news value.	My business has zero news value.	My business just doesn't seem to have great news value.	I think I can come up with an angle to get some publicity.	I know my business has news value, and I can get some good media coverage if I work at it.	My business is so new and interesting that getting in the news is super easy!

Action Step 10.1 Feasibility Checklist continued

Market Feasibility

	1	2	3	4	5
f. There is an identifiable competitive advantage in the marketplace.	A competitive advantage would be hard to find.	There is a small competitive advantage in the marketplace.	I'm not sure a competitive advantage exists.	A small, identifiable competitive advantage exists in the marketplace, and I am in a somewhat unique position to use it.	There is an identifiable competitive advantage in the marketplace, and I am in a unique position to use it.
g. There are few competitors to serve the needs of the market.	There are many competitors to serve the needs of the market.	There are quite a few competitors to serve the needs of the market.	The competition is not clear.	There are a few competitors to serve the needs of the market.	There are almost no competitors to serve the needs of the market.
h. The business concept can be modified to serve the needs of a specific, underserved market niche.	The business concept cannot be modified to serve the needs of a specific, underserved market niche.	The business concept can be modified with some difficulty to serve the needs of a specific, underserved market niche.	The business concept might be modifiable to serve the needs of a specific, underserved market niche.	The business concept can be modified to serve the needs of a specific, underserved market niche.	The business concept can easily be modified to serve the needs of a specific, underserved market niche.
i. The customer profiled would respond favorably to the current business concept.	I don't think the customer profiled would respond at all to the current business concept.	The customer profiled would respond somewhat unfavorably to the current business concept.	How the customer would respond to the current business concept is unclear.	The customer profiled would respond somewhat favorably to the current business concept.	The customer profiled would respond very favorably to the current business concept.
j. There is a sufficient market for the business.	There is an insufficient market for the business.	There is a relatively small market for the business.	The size of the market is not clear.	The size of the market seems sufficient enough.	There is a perfectly sufficient market for the business.

Market Feasibility Score: _____

Action Step 10.1 **Feasibility Checklist** continued

Financial Feasibility

	1.	2.	3.	4.	5.
a. Funding is easily obtained.	I'm going to have to invest a huge amount, maybe more than I am willing to risk.	I'm not really sure how much funding my business will require.	I need to invest quite a bit of money, but I can afford to risk it.	I need to invest a moderate amount of money; I can afford to risk it.	No sweat! I don't have to invest much money at all; I can comfortably risk it.
b. Revenue stream is continuous.	I never know what's going to come in because of seasonality, large contracts, and other factors.	Monthly sales will fluctuate significantly but are somewhat predictable.	Our sales vary somewhat from month to month due to sales cycles and products offered.	Most of the time, sales will be steady from month to month.	We can always count on steady sales from month to month.
c. Money is collected prior to sales.	We send out a bill for products/services and wait over 30 days for customers to pay.	We send out a bill for products/services and the typical customer pays within 30 days.	Customers pay at the time of service or when they receive the product.	Our customers make an upfront deposit that covers the direct costs of the product/service.	Cash is King! The entire price of the product/service is paid prior to delivery.
d. Hiring and retaining employees is easy.	Turnover will be high. The cycle of hiring and training will be continuous.	I will spend lots of time and money hiring and training employees.	For now, I can control labor costs by using sub-contractors as the company grows.	I will have well-qualified employees and expect a low turnover rate.	This is great! I will have top employees and a zero turnover rate!
e. Inventory/Service providers are dependable.	I do not have a clue where to get most of the inventory/supplies I need.	I'm not completely sure where I'm going to get the inventory/supplies I need.	I've found them, but only a few companies can give me what I need.	Many companies can supply what I need.	No problem! Numerous companies with good reputations can supply what I need.

Action Step 10.1   **Feasibility Checklist**   continued

Financial Feasibility

	1	2	3	4	5
f. Gross margin* is 100 percent.	1. My gross margin is low since our costs of direct materials and labor are high.	2. My gross margin is fairly low since our costs of direct materials and labor are relatively high.	3. My gross margin is average with average costs of direct materials and labor.	4. We have some costs of direct materials and labor, but they are lower than average.	5. Nearly 100 percent! No significant direct costs of materials or labor exist.
g. Legal problems do not exist.	1. I've got problems. I am already facing legal action. For example, violation of a non-compete from a former employer.	2. I will have problems. I have multiple business owners, high liability products, leasing issues or products that must be legally protected.	3. I am concerned about protecting my personal assets from legal liability.	4. Legal problems do occur in this industry, but most can be anticipated and managed with proper planning.	5. Few lawsuits or legal harassments occur in this entire industry.
h. Market will allow price adjustments to increase profitability.	1. Prices are set by law.	2. I have very little flexibility in pricing.	3. I cannot tell if sales are affected by price increases, which would improve profitability.	4. Sales to potential customers are somewhat unaffected by price increases.	5. Sales to potential customers are unaffected by price increases.
i. Wealth is generated through exit strategy.	1. I will not be able to sell my business when I am ready to exit.	2. I don't know if I can sell my business without me as the owner.	3. I will be able to sell some of the proprietary assets of the business.	4. I will be able to get a reasonable amount of money since I plan to build proprietary assets.	5. My exit strategy will allow for a profitable way out of the business.

* The gross margin is the amount left over after the business pays direct materials and labor costs of the product/service.

Financial Feasibility Score: _____

Action Step 10.1 **Feasibility Checklist** continued

C. **Evaluate your business.** When you test a Business Plan against the Feasibility Checklist, no particular score guarantees a feasible business. Generally, for a Business Plan to be feasible it must achieve at least half of the possible points overall and at least half of the possible points in any of the three sections. A score less than 3 for any individual criterion indicates a weakness in the Business Plan, which requires further consideration.

D. **Identify one or two criteria you rated low.** Consider ways you can improve these scores as you move through the start-up and operating phases of your business. Do you need more information, a unique marketing strategy, or creative solutions? Most scores can be improved over time. List several options that could raise the scores of the low criteria you identified.

Criteria that rated low	Ways to improve these criteria

Action Step 10.2 **Create My Executive Summary**

Create an Executive Summary that accurately represents my Business Plan.

Business Plan

Directions
If you want readers to spend time reviewing your lengthy Business Plan, you must hook them in the Executive Summary. A good way to do this is to incorporate an edited version of your one-minute marketing speech from Module 1 into your Executive Summary. The Executive Summary should highlight critical information about the venture and draw from these key sections of the Business Plan:

Venture Description
Management and Organization Plan
Marketing Plan
Financial Plan

Avoid these common mistakes when writing the Executive Summary:
• Too much superficial data that fails to inspire the reviewer to read further
• Failure to identify unique features and benefits of the proposed product/service
• Too much technical information
• Long sentences and phrases
• Too much trivial information
• Failure to specify what you hope to accomplish with the business
• Failure to identify how much money the company needs, its uses, sources, and repayment

The Executive Summary is often the most-used section of your Business Plan. When you want to give someone an overview of your business, you may want to use a version of your Executive Summary rather than a full-length Business Plan. You could distribute it to potential infrastructure members or provide copies to people who are interested in your business to build a network of persons who believe in your vision for your business.

Use the questions listed below or in the Business Plan Template to create an Executive Summary for your Business Plan. If you have an existing business, also include the following information:
• When and why the company was formed
• The marketing history of the product/service
• The company's annual sales, profits, and overall performance to date

Executive Summary **Sources**

Venture Description Action Steps 1.2, 2.2, 4.1, Activity 4a, Reality Check *One-Minute Marketing Speech,* Reality Check *Features and Benefits*
What business is your venture in, and what is the current stage of development?
Current stage of development may be start-up, initial operations, expansion, rapid growth, or stable operations.
Briefly describe your business model.
What is unique about the product/service, and what proprietary rights does the business have?

Action Step 10.2 **Create My Executive Summary** continued

Management and Organization Plan   Action Step 7.1

What form of organization does the business operate under, and why?

Who are the key management team members and what skills do they have to help the business?

Who are the key support groups for your management team, including accountants, attorneys, consultants, board of directors, and advisory board members?

Marketing Plan   Action Steps 5.1, 5.2, 5.3, 5.4, and 6.2

What is the market like in terms of the industry, the customer, customer needs, product benefits, the venture's target markets, and the market penetration plan?

Who are the major competitors, and what are their strengths and weaknesses?

What are your market penetration plans? Include specific facts and figures from your market research.

Financial Plan   Action Steps 3.1, 3.3, 8.1, 8.2, 9.1 and 9.2

What will it cost to start this business?

What are the projections for sales and net profit?

How much cash will be needed to start and operate this business?

What sources of financing have been, and will be, sought?

How much money has been contributed by the entrepreneur?

What is your exit strategy?

Action Step 10.3 Finish and Assemble My Plan

Create a Cover Page, Table of Contents, and Appendix for my Business Plan.

Directions
Using the information and questions below and in the Business Plan Template, complete the Cover Page, Table of Contents, and Appendix of your Business Plan.

❏ **Cover Page**
The Cover Page should include basic information the reader needs to locate or contact the company. Lenders and investors may choose to ignore the Business Plan if they cannot easily find contact information. Include the following information on your Cover Page:

Business name
Motto or tag line
Logo
Date the plan was prepared
Entrepreneur's name and title
Company name
Business or home address, including city, state, and zip
Entrepreneur's phone/fax numbers and other contact information
E-mail address and Web sites

If available, your company logo should be displayed on the Cover Page. A picture or sketch of the product/service can also be very valuable. Artwork can be effective when it is relevant to the business concept and professional in appearance.

❏ **Table of Contents**
The Business Plan Template will insert page numbers on the Table of Contents automatically, but they will need to be updated as you add to your plan. Use your mouse to highlight the page number or select the section of the Table of Contents you want to update and then press F9 to update the numbers.

❏ **Appendix**
Your credibility can be made or lost by the contents of the Appendix. If references are accurate and complete, readers will soon stop checking the assertions found in the body of the plan and accept them. If they discover inaccuracies or missing data, however, they will question the accuracy of everything else in the plan.

A separate Table of Contents at the beginning of the Appendix should list all of the documents contained in the Appendix. Any references in the body of the Business Plan to information located in the Appendix should refer to the document title and its page number.

This program does not provide a template for the Appendix. All documents can be included in the Appendix just as they are. You should prepare a Table of Contents at the beginning of your Appendix to identify the location and type of documents included. See the Reality Check *Appendix* on p. 387 of this module for the list of documents you determined should be included in your Appendix. Compile your Appendix when all the other parts of the plan are complete.

Action Step 10.3 **Finish and Assemble My Plan** continued

❏ **Fonts and Format**

An easy-to-read font and a simple design work best. An 11- or 12-point font in a serif style, such as Times, is the easiest for most people to read. Gimmicks such as all caps and excessive use of bold or underlining detract from the importance or significance of the text. If you have already established a brand identity, use your logo, fonts, and color scheme.

Each page should incorporate adequate white space. White space makes the text easier to read and provides a place for taking notes. Using wide margins, between 1 and 1.25 inches, and bulleted lists of information whenever possible can add white space. Titles, graphs, and other appropriate graphics increase the interest and readability of the plan. Finally, each page should be appropriately numbered.

For more information on simple formatting and design for Business Plans see sample plans at www.fasttrac.org/toolkits.

❏ **Printing and Binding**

Print your Business Plan on white or light-colored, standard-sized paper, 8.5 x 11 inches. Color ink can be used effectively for the headings, subheadings, and graphs. Too much color will detract from the content of the Business Plan.

For external readers, the best type of binding secures the pages, makes it easy to flip back and forth, and lies flat on a desk. Most office supply stores and copy centers offer affordable, professional binding services. Avoid flimsy, acetate covers with detachable spines. If the Business Plan is being used internally, three-ring binders work well. This type of binding will allow you to remove or replace pages as you update them. The Business Plan can also be shared electronically by creating a .pdf file or word processing document.

Action Step 10.4   Identify Next Steps

Identify the steps necessary to start your business after writing the plan.

Directions

Your Business Plan is complete. What's next? This activity provides a checklist you can use to determine the next steps to turn your dream of starting a business into a reality. Review the checklist provided. Insert an X next to the items that will be your next steps in starting this business. Be sure you place the X in the column representing the month in which the action should be completed. This checklist provides space for the first four months of start-up. A one-page example of the list appears first for you to see how it works. For a full-year example or a full-year blank copy, go to www.fasttrac.org/toolkits. The Excel®-based chart online will allow you to make changes to fit your business's particular needs.

Action Step 10.4 **Identify Next Steps** continued

Action Steps	Person Responsible	Done ✔	Month 1		Month 2		Month 3		Month 4	
			1st Half	2nd Half	1st Half	2nd Half	1st Half	2nd Half	1st Half	2nd Half
Local and State Regulations										
Apply for licenses										
Business license	Mary						X			
State license	Mary						X	X		
Occupational license	Mary					X				
Professional license	Mary					X	X	X	X	
Apply for permits										
Health department	Bob								X	X
Fire department	Bob								X	
Sign	Bob					X				
County	Bob						X			
Investigate other pertinent licenses, permits										
Fictitious name	Bob							X		
Liquor license	n/a									
Zoning	Bob					X				
Advisory Board										
Identify potential advisory board participants	Mary				X	X	X			
Invite to participate	Mary						X			
Identify location and refreshments to be served	Mary						X			
Notify participants of meeting date, time, and place	Mary							X		
Prepare agenda for first meeting	Mary								X	
Hold meeting	M, B, & J									X

EXAMPLE

Action Step 10.4   **Identify Next Steps** continued

Action Steps	Person Responsible	Done ✔	Month 1		Month 2		Month 3		Month 4	
			1st Half	2nd Half	1st Half	2nd Half	1st Half	2nd Half	1st Half	2nd Half
Local and State Regulations										
Apply for licenses										
Business license										
State license										
Occupational license										
Professional license										
Apply for permits										
Health department										
Fire department										
Sign										
County										
Investigate other pertinent licenses, permits										
Fictitious name										
Liquor license										
Zoning										
Advisory Board										
Identify potential advisory board participants										
Invite to participate										
Identify location and refreshments to be served										
Notify participants of meeting date, time, and place										
Prepare agenda for first meeting										
Hold meeting										

Action Step 10.4 **Identify Next Steps** continued

Action Steps	Person Responsible	Done ✔	Month 1		Month 2		Month 3		Month 4	
			1st Half	2nd Half	1st Half	2nd Half	1st Half	2nd Half	1st Half	2nd Half
Legal Structure for Business										
Review characteristics of various legal forms										
Interview three attorneys										
Choose attorney										
Meet with attorney to discuss all legal issues										
Create appropriate legal form										
Determine if EIN is needed; if so, apply										
Intellectual Property Protection										
Develop non-disclosure document										
Register trademarks										
Investigate potential intellectual property rights										
Insurance Protection										
Obtain bids for general liability, product liability, errors & omissions										
Obtain bids for group, medical										
Obtain bids for fire, theft, business interruption										
Obtain bids for life, key person										
Obtain bids for Workers' Comp and other necessary policies										
Evaluate costs associated with all insurance bids										
Purchase all necessary insurance coverages										

Action Step 10.4 **Identify Next Steps** continued

Action Steps	Person Responsible	Done ✔	Month 1		Month 2		Month 3		Month 4	
			1st Half	2nd Half	1st Half	2nd Half	1st Half	2nd Half	1st Half	2nd Half
Location Considerations										
Identify location needs (office, retail, production, home office)										
Make rent vs. buy decision										
Contract for each location										
Design floor plan for each facility										
Take possession of location										
Obtain bids for build out and/or leasehold improvements										
Contact utility company for service										
Contact telephone company for service										
Identify and secure appropriate Internet service										
Identify and secure security service or system										
Furniture and Equipment										
Determine required furniture										
Make rent vs. buy decision										
Research sources of furniture and costs										
Place order for furniture										
Create list of start-up office supplies										
Purchase start-up supplies										

Action Step 10.4 **Identify Next Steps** continued

Action Steps	Person Responsible	Done ✔	Month 1		Month 2		Month 3		Month 4	
			1st Half	2nd Half	1st Half	2nd Half	1st Half	2nd Half	1st Half	2nd Half
Technology										
Develop a technology plan (communication, info dissemination)										
Research costs and characteristics of:										
Telephone system										
Computers										
Facsimile (stand-alone vs. computer based)										
Mobile communication systems										
Personal Digital Assistants (PDAs)										
Internet service provider										
Shredder										
Create Internet presence										

421

Action Step 10.4   Identify Next Steps continued

Action Steps	Person Responsible	Done ✔	Month 1		Month 2		Month 3		Month 4	
			1st Half	2nd Half	1st Half	2nd Half	1st Half	2nd Half	1st Half	2nd Half
Accounting and Recordkeeping										
Develop accounting system (forms, flow, checks & balances)										
Decide if bookkeeping will be internal or external										
Determine and calendar appropriate tax payment deadlines										
Order checks, forms (invoices, work orders)										
Determine method of payroll (internal/external processing)										
Investigate advantages/ disadvantages of employee leasing										
Interview accountants										
Choose accountant										
Determine frequency of meetings with accountant										
Financial Institution (Banking)										
Investigate characteristics and reputations of several banks										
Open appropriate accounts										
Negotiate line of credit										
Schedule meeting with lending officer to develop relationship										

Action Step 10.4 **Identify Next Steps** continued

Action Steps	Person Responsible	Done ✔	Month 1		Month 2		Month 3		Month 4	
			1st Half	2nd Half	1st Half	2nd Half	1st Half	2nd Half	1st Half	2nd Half
Human Resources										
Identify positions to be filled										
Write job specifications										
Write job descriptions										
Determine strategy for finding people										
Implement strategy for identifying candidates										
Confirm understanding of legal issues of interviewing										
Determine legal issues of personnel files (I-9; health records)										
Create personnel record keeping system										
Design employee training program										
Identify sources of continuing education for management										
Consultants										
Complete analysis of human resource capabilities										
Determine need for professional consultants										
Identify professional consultants to use										

Action Step 10.4 **Identify Next Steps** continued

Action Steps	Person Responsible	Done ✔	Month 1		Month 2		Month 3		Month 4	
			1st Half	2nd Half	1st Half	2nd Half	1st Half	2nd Half	1st Half	2nd Half
Marketing										
Review marketing strategy										
Develop Marketing Activities Schedule for plan implementation										
Confirm marketing plan contains networking strategy										
Begin networking										
Financial Management										
Develop cash flow monitoring system										
Develop key financial data monitoring system										